I, Digital

Personal Collections in the Digital Era

Edited by Christopher A. Lee

**SOCIETY OF
American
Archivists**

CHICAGO

Society of American Archivists
www.archivists.org

Printed in the United States of America

Graphic Design by Sweeney Design, kasween@sbcglobal.net.

Library of Congress Cataloging-in-Publication Data

I, digital : personal collections in the digital era / edited by Christopher A. Lee.
   p. cm.
 Includes bibliographical references and index.
 ISBN 1-931666-38-5
1. Personal archives—Digitization. 2. Family archives—Digitization. 3. Archival materials—
Digitization. 4. Digital preservation. I. Lee, Christopher A.
 CD977.I22 2011
 929'.10285—dc23
              2011027010

Table of Contents

Part 3—Implications for Memory Institutions

Introduction

Christopher A. Lee

...only if we better understand personal recordkeeping practices can we hope to do a better job at capturing and preserving those records for posterity.

—Adrian Cunningham, 1996

Many archivists and archival institutions have a collecting mission that includes personal papers, manuscripts, and other noninstitutional materials. Despite a massive increase in the volume and complexity of personal digital collections, the literature designed specifically to guide archivists' thinking about personal digital materials has long been limited to a few scattered journal articles and research project websites. *I, Digital* aims to fill this gap. It explores issues, challenges and opportunities in the management of personal digital collections, focusing primarily on born-digital materials generated and kept by individuals, as opposed to electronic records that are generated within and managed by formal organizational recordkeeping systems. It represents a convergence and synthesis of literature and thinking about how cultural institutions can grapple with new forms of documentation and how individuals manage (and could potentially better manage) the digital information that is part of their contemporary lives. One of the book's main objectives is to expose the archival profession to an active body of highly relevant research that has traditionally been published outside of the archives literature and not typically represented at archives conferences. It also seeks to expose other audiences (e.g., those with an interest in personal information management) to the principles, insights, and activities of the archival profession.

An Obligatory Note on Terminology

I, Digital bridges discussions from a diverse set of cultures and disciplines. An endemic characteristic of such efforts is "creative tension" in the use of various terms. In cases when it is considered particularly important to do so, authors of the chapters often provide working definitions of specific terms. The most obvious divide is between the language of Personal Information Management (PIM) and Archives and Records Management (ARM); even these very labels are subject to dispute.

There is also a diversity of terms used within the literatures of the collecting professions (librarians, archivists, museum curators) over what to call the *set of traces* that are left behind by individuals as they engage in the activities of their lives. One distinction that has received considerable attention—particularly in the U.S. literature—is between institutional records (records whose primary use is related to documenting and supporting the activities of an organization) and "manuscripts" (materials whose primary use is related to the activities of an individual in his or her personal life). The British Library, for example, favors the term *eManuscripts* for digital materials created by individuals. The term *manuscript* carries specific mechanical connotations (being written by hand) that are often not strictly accurate. An alternative term, *personal papers,* is often used instead. However, a great deal of personal material is not actually captured or retained on paper, so this is also not ideal.

A phrase that one will frequently encounter in this volume is *personal archives.* It is important to note that Australian authors tend to use the term *archives* much more holistically than U.S. authors. In the Australian archival literature, archives are all records of "continuing value," regardless of where they reside or who is currently caring for them.[1] By contrast, the North American archival literature tends to consider archives to be the places, collections or set of associated activities that reside on the receiving end of the "archival threshold." From this perspective, many types of documentation can serve as "personal records," but they are only personal archives when they have been transferred to the care of professional archivists within a formally recognized repository.

Another commonly used phrase is *personal recordkeeping*. The term *recordkeeping* is usually used to include both activities that are often labeled *records management* and activities that are often labeled *archival administration*; recordkeeping encompasses care for records both within their creation environment and in any environments that are used to care for them thereafter. The scope of personal recordkeeping is very close to the stated scope of much writing about PIM, with the primary difference being the strong emphasis of the former on the *record* as the primary unit of analysis. A record is a subset of all information created by an entity (individual or organization) that has been designated as requiring a certain degree of coherence and integrity over time, in order to serve as evidence or documentation of something.

I have chosen to use the term *personal collection* within the title of this book in an attempt to find the closest thing to neutral ground that might exist within this complex ecosystem of rich, sometimes complementary, but sometimes conflicting, terminology. Roughly speaking, a personal collection is a sizable aggregate of an individual's personal traces that the individual or someone else has identified and attempts to manage over time as a relatively coherent unit in order to reflect something important about that individual. This is certainly not a formal definition, nor is it even a working definition that is applied consistently throughout the book. Instead, it is simply a working notion of a common area of interest that has served as a point of intersection for writings by a very thoughtful set of authors who have contributed to this volume.

Trends Related to Personal Digital Collections

Historically, individuals and families have accumulated and managed personal collections. Most of these collections have been relatively small and have not left the homes of the collectors. Many of the materials have been lost due to the "hazards of time."[2] However, collections of a few prominent individuals and families made the transition into collecting institutions. Many cultural institutions were initially seeded by personal collections of influential people.

Over the past half century, five trends have dramatically changed the nature and status of personal collections: professionalization; professional convergence around digital preservation; increased storage capacity available to individuals; distribution of collections; and research focusing on individual stories.

First, work within collecting institutions has become increasingly professionalized. This has included specialization, professional education, professional associations, conferences, journals, specialized language, and social norms. As work becomes more professionalized, there is more consensus about what types of activities fall within the scope of the profession and which do not. This is what Andrew Abbott has called the "jurisdiction" of a profession.[3] Professionalization has dramatically raised the expectations for how institutions must care for and provide access to collections in order to be considered "professional" in their activities. For example, the archival literature reflects numerous widely held expectations about engagement with records creators, formal transfer agreements, standardized description, environmental controls, storage materials, access controls, reference services, and outreach; there is a diversity of views about appropriate approaches to implementation and degree of emphasis on the various expectations, but it would be very unusual for anyone in a professional forum to flatly dismiss their relevance to archivists.

Similarly, museum curators and librarians operate within their own sets of expectations about the scope and nature of their work. Setting a clear boundary around a set of professional activities is a powerful way to focus attention, mobilize resources, and establish sufficient coherence across the activities to get good things done. However, the boundary also increases the "transaction costs" for interacting with people and groups who are not part of the profession. The fragmentation of libraries, archives, and museums, for example, can inhibit those institutions from collectively responding to the challenges and opportunities of personal digital collections. A strong focus within the professional archival literature on methods and procedures within the context of formal repositories can also inhibit archivists from working with everyday citizens, genealogists, and various other types of amateur enthusiasts to collectively ensure that personal digital archives can be meaningfully and appropriately used in the future. In short, long-term care for personal digital collections faces the two sides of the professionalization coin: focused development and progress within associated professions has spawned many valuable resources, concepts, and methods that could be mobilized to address personal digital collections; while these same developments make it difficult to mobilize across the professions. Collective efforts will require concerted boundary spanning, and *I, Digital* is one step (hopefully, among many) in that direction.

A second trend is that previously distinct communities have come to recognize that they share challenges associated with long-term care of digital resources. Digital objects are different from purely spatio-temporal objects in that they are recreated each time they are used, based on interactions of numerous technological components. In order to ensure meaningful access and use of digital objects over time, one must plan for and respond to changes to the technological components, the ways the components interact, user needs, and mechanisms for use. Digital preservation is a multilayered, complex endeavor. There has been increasing recognition—particularly since the mid-1990s—across both collecting institutions and other types of organizations responsible for stewardship of data over long periods, that many of the fundamental issues of digital preservation are shared across contexts and could be better served through communication across institutional and professional boundaries.[4] In many ways, this trend has the potential to counterbalance the issues of professional fragmentation discussed above.

A third important trend is that individuals have gained more ability to create and store materials that they find meaningful, useful, or simply more convenient to keep than to discard. In the developed world, a typical consumer can conveniently create a vast array of information artifacts that were previously much more difficult and expensive to produce, including text, images, moving images, audio, structured data, microcontent (e.g., tags, bookmarks), and many combinations thereof. Although computers regularly overwrite many types of data, the default computer behavior related to user-created files usually is to retain them until the user makes a conscious act to delete them. Various factors make it increasingly less likely for individuals to delete files that they have created, resulting in a proliferation of data in personal digital archives:

- Deleting takes time, attention, and a conscious commitment to the idea that something will definitely no longer be needed.

- The cost and size of the storage medium required to store a given number of bits has decreased dramatically every year and is likely to continue decreasing for the foreseeable future, which means that many individuals do not have to worry about running out of space.

- The number and types of storage media that an individual may have at his/her disposal (e.g., thumb drives, telephones, cameras, mobile phones, desktop computers, laptop computers, external drives, and disks) also continues to grow.

- Increasingly sophisticated technologies for both searching over and reusing digital data provide a strong case for keeping things "just in case" one might find them to be useful in the future.

A fourth, very closely related, trend is that personal collections have become more widely distributed than in the past. The issue of personal *fonds* being spread across multiple locations is certainly not new, but the magnitude of this phenomenon is. In addition to the various types of storage media discussed above, there has been a significant movement of many types of personal information into "cloud computing" environments.[5] Whereas many organizations are entering formal arrangements in which they pay "cloud providers" to host their content, the services upon which individuals rely are often provided for "free." Rather than providing direct financial payment, individuals usually pay by allowing the company access to their personal data, willingness to view advertisements, or both. Such arrangements rarely provide the individuals with much control over how their information will be managed or retained over time. Individuals often use different computing environments to carry out different tasks; this can be because of limitations of the technology (interoperability issues) or based on deliberate decisions of individuals (e.g., switching to email when a blog exchange has become too personal, maintaining different social media profiles for different social contexts, keeping some family photos in a shared online space while keeping others on a hard drive).

Finally, researchers have placed considerably more emphasis than they did several decades ago on the importance of personal stories, voices, and perspectives. Many fields of study in the social sciences and humanities now use personal accounts as sources of data and recognize aspects of personal subjectivity to be legitimate topics of research. Numerous schools of thought in social theory, literary criticism, and historiography have also questioned positivist or "grand narrative" approaches, advocating instead for a focus on individual interpretations and perceptions. Social historians, feminist scholars, family historians, and genealogists all rely heavily on personal information traces (within archives or elsewhere) to answer their questions. This trend foregrounds the importance of personal digital collections and suggests many communities of interest that have a strong stake in appropriate treatment of personal digital information.

These five trends have a significant impact on the system of professions and professional activities related to personal digital collections.[6] The trends greatly enable many new activities, but they can also impose serious constraints on collaboration and innovation. The chapters of *I, Digital* were written within this context.

Building on a Diffuse Literature

The chapters of *I, Digital* build on—and will hopefully contribute to—several different bodies of literature. Although it is impossible to completely disentangle them, I have found it useful to consider five associated areas of literature: the administration of personal papers and manuscript collections; electronic recordkeeping; digital data recovery and forensics; personal information management; and the design of tools for user-generated collections.

Administration of Personal Papers and Manuscript Collections

Libraries and archives have a long history of collecting personal papers and manuscripts. In the United States, there were numerous organizations (particularly historical societies) that focused on the care of both organizational records and manuscript materials long before the archival profession was formally professionalized. Ever since the formation of the National Archives and the Society of American Archivists in the 1930s, personal papers and manuscripts have been part of the archival profession's charge, but their status has often been ambiguous. Several prominent authors have argued that the primary focus of the profession should be on official government records. Some have gone so far as to dismiss personal papers and manuscripts as not being true archival records and thus not worthy of professional archival attention. Much ink has been spilled onto the pages of North American archival journals over the status of both non-institutional records and the "manuscripts tradition" more generally.[7] The Australian archival literature has been characterized by a similar tension, addressed most explicitly in a special issue of *Archives and Manuscripts* in 1996 on "Personal Recordkeeping: Issues and Perspectives."[8]

One consequence of the profession's ambivalence is that practical guidance and empirical findings about the archival treatment of personal papers and manuscripts has tended to be underrepresented in the published professional literature. This has been particularly true in the last several decades, as notions of evidential value, recordkeeping systems, and institutional accountability have driven much of the research. Ironically, this has occurred at the same time that the boundary between personal and official recordkeeping systems has continued to blur. Given how much of records management is carried out by individuals "at the desktop," and the extent to which personal and organizational materials are intermingled on those same desktops, all records professionals can benefit from a more informed view of personal information practices and principles. In 2006, Toby Burrows lamented, "Though the range of issues relating to personal electronic archives has been relatively well-documented, there is as yet little in the way of systematic investigation of solutions and approaches."[9] However, there are positive signs that this is changing.

A growing number of librarians and archivists have been gaining hands-on experience with personal digital collections. Several informative conference papers and publications have come out of this stream of activity, often in the form of case studies.[10] Two important, very relevant projects have been Digital Lives and Personal Archives Accessible in Digital Media (Paradigm). The Digital Lives project aimed "to explore how individuals use, organise and manage their digital collections."[11] The Paradigm project investigated "issues involved in preserving digital private papers through gaining practical experience in accessioning and ingesting digital private papers into digital repositories, and processing these in line with archival and digital preservation requirements." The Paradigm project's most visible product has been a "Workbook on Digital Private Papers."[12] Another recent project generated a white paper based on a series of site visits and meetings of those working with the born-digital components of three significant literary collections.[13] In her book *Electronic Records in the Manuscript Repository*, Elizabeth Dow summarizes important considerations and discusses strategies for approaching collecting scenarios in which "the materials are in fact the donor's so the curator works with them only as a consultant, armed with knowledge, but no actual power."[14] And in "Managing Electronic Records in Manuscript Collections," Michael Forstram articulates the Beinecke Library's approach to describing electronic records.[15]

Electronic Recordkeeping

The archival literature has given at least some attention to issues of computerization since the 1940s, and by the late 1970s and early 1980s the archival literature included many reports on the actual and potential use of computers to support the internal operations of archives. Numerous articles and reports have also called for members of the archival profession to revise their theories and practices, and take a more active role in addressing the management and preservation of digital objects. Despite these calls for action, active discussion of electronic records in the archives literature is still surprisingly young and underdeveloped.

The Society of American Archivists (SAA) made important, early contributions with the publication of proceedings of a 1979 conference about machine-readable records[16] and *Archives and Manuscripts: Machine-Readable Records.*[17] The Records and Archives Management Programme (RAMP) of the United Nations Educational, Scientific and Cultural Organization (UNESCO) also issued publications that advanced early thinking on electronic records.[18] Several other important books about electronic records were introduced into the archives and records management literature in the 1990s,[19] and SAA published a set of eight electronic records case studies in that decade.[20]

The electronic records literature has grown considerably since the 1990s. There have been many books,[21] as well as significant treatment in the serial publications of records management professional associations, including *Information Management* published by ARMA International. Professional archival journals have also included a substantial number of pieces that address electronic records,[22] but the attention to personal digital collections in archival journals has been relatively limited.[23] Much of the recent attention to electronic records management has been driven by concerns about legal compliance, with the enactment of policies and mandates including the U.S.

Health Insurance Portability and Accountability Act (HIPAA) (1996), European Data Protection Directive (1998), Information Security Management, Code of Practice for Information Security Management (2000), U.S. Sarbanes-Oxley Act (2002), Basel II (2004), revised U.S. Federal Rules of Civil Procedure (2006), many prominent court cases, and the growth of a massive electronic evidence discovery industry.[24] Legal compliance has become a driving factor for electronic records management in many organizations, leading one author to conclude that all other organizational "considerations must yield to information's role in litigation processes."[25] Several initiatives have created guidance for record creators (within organizational contexts), including Managing the Digital University Desktop (MDUD)[26] and the Preservation of Electronic Mail Collaboration Initiative (EMCAP).[27]

When the archival literature on electronic recordkeeping has directly addressed personal records, the discussion has usually focused on issues of professional jurisdiction[28] rather than elaborating specific principles or methods for dealing with personal electronic records. Frequent topics of discussion have been whether manuscript curators have been marginalized by the major electronic records projects of the 1990s, whether a definition of archival records as conveyors of evidence is inconsistent with the goals of manuscript curators, and whether an excessive focus on accountability diminishes the larger societal mission of archives as conveyors of social memory. As with so many professional issues, competing interpretations of fundamental terms are major sources of tension and confusion. It should be no surprise that an archivist responsible for manuscript collections would take issue with the statement that "archivists are in the evidence business" if she interprets "evidence" to mean solely "that which is admissible in a court of law." Likewise, "archives are instruments of accountability" would also not sit well with her, if accountability is taken to mean only "ensuring that public officials appropriately discharge their legal duties." The working reality of many archivists—who are often responsible for both institutional and non-institutional records—requires working definitions of core terms that are quite broad and multifaceted. Recordkeeping practices serve multiple interests, objectives, and "accountabilities"[29] along many dimensions at various levels simultaneously: legal, institutional, professional, ethical, cultural, social, historical, and personal.

Contemporary scholarship about electronic records has been strongly influenced by the continuum model of recordkeeping.[30] The archival literature on electronic records over the past several decades has placed a strong emphasis on understanding and engaging records creating environments, rather than waiting passively for records to eventually cross the archival threshold. One of the fundamental questions for the profession—and one that has received very little attention—is how to successfully apply continuum thinking to electronic records that are created outside of formal organizational recordkeeping structures.

Archivists and librarians have recently begun to focus considerable energy and resources on web archiving (i.e., identifying, harvesting, and preserving materials available from the Web).[31] As with materials residing on personal computers, the boundaries between personal materials and official records are often very unclear. Professionals engaged in web archiving must often consider annual reports, organizational publications, blogs, wikis, and YouTube videos all in the same set of selection activities, rather than insisting on a stark line between the official and unofficial. Several recent initiatives have focused on appraisal of "social web" materials, which are often characterized as forms of personal expression but also document much of the "business" of contemporary society.[32]

Digital Data Recovery and Forensics

The literature on digital archives tends to place a great emphasis on the "virtual" (i.e., intangible) nature of electronic resources. Computer systems have "an illusion of immateriality by detecting error and correcting it,"[33] but it is essential to recognize that digital objects are created and perpetuated through physical things or phenomena (e.g., charged magnetic particles, pulses of light, holes in disks). This materiality brings challenges, because data must be read from specific artifacts, which can become damaged or obsolete. However, the materiality of digital objects also brings unprecedented opportunities for archival description, interpretation, and use. Digital resources are composed of interacting components that can be considered and accessed at different levels of representation (bitstream; file as accessed through a filesystem; files as rendered through specific applications; records composed of multiple files; larger aggregations such as websites). Some of the "types of historical indications that an electronic text may contain" include program of origin, system of origin, traces of transmission, and typists and their interaction with programs.[34] To ensure integrity and future use, archivists must make decisions regarding treatment at multiple levels of representation.

There is a substantial body of information within the underlying data structures of computer systems that can often be discovered or recovered. Recovery of data from physical media has been a topic of discussion in the professional library and archives literature for several years.[35] There is also a large and quickly expanding industry associated with digital forensics, which focuses on the discovery, recovery, and validation of information from computer systems that is often not immediately visible to common users. Several authors have recently investigated the use of forensic tools and techniques for acquiring digital collections in libraries and archives.[36] The Prometheus[37] and Presidential Electronic Records Pilot System (PERPOS)[38] projects have developed software for data extraction, focusing on needs of specific collecting contexts. Born Digital Collections: An Inter-Institutional Model for Stewardship (AIMS) and futureArch are exploring workflows that include forensic copies from digital media. Another project, Computer Forensics and Born-Digital Content in Cultural Heritage Collections, has also provided a significant contribution to this discussion.

Personal Information Management (PIM)

Personal Information Management refers to "both the practice and the study of the activities people perform in order to acquire, organize, maintain, retrieve, use, and control the distribution of information items such as documents (paper-based and digital), Web pages, and email messages for everyday use to complete tasks (work-related and not) and to fulfill a person's various roles (as parent, employee, friend, member of community, etc.)."[39] It "places special emphasis on the organization and maintenance of personal information collections (PICs) in which information items, such as paper documents, electronic documents, email messages, web references, and handwritten notes, are stored for later use and repeated reuse."[40] After emerging as a distinct area of study in the 1980s,[41] PIM has become a very active area of research in recent years. Several professional associations have been involved in hosting a regular PIM workshop series since 2005. PIM was the topic of a special issue of *Communications of the ACM* in January 2006, and a piece in the *Annual Review of Information Science and Technology* in 2007.

Despite all of the recent energy and attention to PIM, the literature has been relatively constrained in its focus. Although PIM is intended to be inclusive of all aspects of personal information management, the primary focus of the literature has traditionally been the retrieval of personal information. However, several authors have broken that mold in recent years by examining issues of selection, management, and sharing of information over time. Several of the *I, Digital* authors are contributing to this new stream of research within PIM.

The archival literature about personal papers often emphasizes the relatively unruly ways in which the materials tend to be organized and acquired. However, the story does not end there. The study of personal recordkeeping should not be "a study about chaos but one about the impulses driving individuals and families to create, maintain, and use their own records."[42] PIM represents a significant body of research that suggests definite patterns of behavior in the personal creation, management, and use of information.

Tools and Support for User-Generated Collections

When discussing software to support electronic recordkeeping, the archives and records management literature has often emphasized large, enterprise-wide systems. Two very visible sources of industry guidance for such systems are DOD 5015.02[43] and the Model Requirements for Management of Electronic Records (MoReq).[44] Such guidance documents—and tools designed to fulfill their requirements—can be valuable for electronic recordkeeping in large institutional environments. However, it is unclear how they could support the management and preservation of and access to materials created by individuals outside such formal structures.

One potential response is to provide tools to individuals that will allow them to engage in better recordkeeping (creation, capture, management and preservation) practices themselves. Richard Cox has argued that "archivists might have a better chance of being successful in the preservation of private, non-organisational records if they worked with software manufacturers to create commercial products that individuals could acquire that enable the long-term maintenance of their electronic files and the more easy transfer of these personal papers to real or virtual repositories."[45] Archivists can also contribute to, support, and take advantage of efforts to develop open-source applications and services for use by individuals.

There have been several recent initiatives to develop tools to allow individuals to better manage their personal digital collections.[46] Major software vendors have also entered this arena with products such as Apple's Time Machine, Norton 360, and Windows Live OneCare, which help individuals to keep their bits safe. A particularly active area of development has been tools and services for personal web "archiving."[47] ContextMiner[48] and ArchivePress[49] are designed for building collections from the social web, such as YouTube and blogs.

Finally, there are various targeted documents designed to provide guidance for individuals to manage their own digital materials as cultural resources. The Image Permanence Institute has created several such documents.[50] In relation to online personal content, the Electronic Frontier Foundation provides a service called TOSBack to inform consumers of the terms of service related to systems that they use,[51] and Google maintains a site called the Data Liberation Front that provides instructions for getting information into and out of Google services.[52]

What This Volume Is *Not* About

> We have become a nation of snoopers.
>
>   —U.S. Representative Cornelius Gallagher, 1966 [53]

This volume does not place much emphasis on the vast databases of relatively discrete and structured data about individuals that are being collected, managed, and mined by the private or public sector—that is, "the systematic capture of everyday events"[54] that is generating "a vast network of stored information about the populace that must rival the infinite account books of Heaven."[55]

Now that so many human behaviors and interactions are carried out through the generation and exchange of symbolical representations in digital form, individuals leave behind a vast number of micro-traces. According to one estimate, less than half of the "portion of the digital universe created by individuals . . . can be accounted for by user activities—pictures taken, phone calls made, emails sent—while the rest constitutes a digital 'shadow'—

surveillance photos, web search histories, financial transaction journals, mailing lists, and so on."[56] In other words, "data is the perspiration of the Information Age,"[57] and plenty of organizations are standing by to soak up the sweat. Private sector examples include credit card companies, credit agencies, marketing companies, voter data aggregators, search providers, and online retailers. Public sector examples include data warehouses of tax collecting agencies and intelligence agencies. The massive amount of data related to individuals and their transactions is evidenced by numerous companies that report or are believed to be running web server farms that number in the tens of thousands.[58] The aggregation of the various "shards of data" held by public and private entities about a person can be considered to be his or her "digital dossier."[59]

While such data have both contemporary importance and significant potential future research value,[60] the data are often outside of the control of either individuals or records professionals, and are generally managed as diffuse units of data, rather than as "personal collections." Even more importantly, the diffuse digital dossier about a person "fails to capture the texture" of her life.[61] The digital dossier does not usually serve one of the most important purposes of personal archives: giving voice to the individual. Contributions to *I, Digital* focus on materials that are directly *of* (and often purposely shared *by* or *with*) individuals, rather than all digital information that is *about* individuals. For example, rather than investigating the various forms of surveillance of individuals by corporate or government actors, this volume places considerable emphasis on "participatory surveillance."[62]

Another noteworthy set of activities that are not a direct focus of this volume are those that allow individuals to submit their own stories and items to larger, shared repositories. Prominent examples include the BBC's WW2 People's War project and Virginia Tech's April 16 Memorial Website.[63] Such projects hold great promise for representing and preserving individual voices that would be missed by collecting driven exclusively by institutional recordkeeping requirements, much as oral history efforts have done for many years. However, they do not directly address the much wider universe of digital materials being created and collected by individuals, which is the focus of *I, Digital*.

Summary of Contributions to this Volume

I, Digital brings together insights, findings, and perspectives of authors with expertise in various aspects of the management of digital information. This introduction explains the scope and motivation for *I, Digital*, as well as setting it within the context of related literature. The remainder of the volume is sectioned into three parts, with the first part devoted to conceptual foundations and motivations.

Robert Capra and I have jointly authored "And Now the Twain Shall Meet: Exploring the Connections between PIM and Archives." Capra is a Post-Doctoral Fellow, and I am an Associate Professor at the School of Information and Library Science, University of North Carolina, Chapel Hill. In this chapter, we describe how, over the past two decades, two complementary, but relatively unconnected, streams of literature have emerged: electronic recordkeeping (ERK) and personal information management (PIM). The former builds upon long-standing principles and practices in archives and records management (ARM), while the latter has its strongest roots in human-computer interaction and information science. A fundamental issue that cuts across both areas of literature is how to make meaningful use of information artifacts when one is no longer embedded in the original context of creation, capture, or use. The ARM literature formulates this as secondary use, while the PIM literature focuses on refinding and reuse. In this chapter, we identify and elaborate on areas of commonality and difference in these two areas of study. We conclude with several open research questions and argue that there is great potential for research that is attentive to the complex set of factors that PIM and ARM can collectively bring to these questions.

In "Ghosts in the Machine: Towards a Principles-Based Approach to Making and Keeping Digital Records," Adrian Cunningham, Director of Strategic Relations at the National Archives of Australia, argues that "it is time to take a step back from discussing time-bound, technology-specific practical strategies and technical solutions and to focus instead on a more enduring, principles-based approach to dealing with the complex realities of digital recordkeeping." He proposes twelve principles, which are adapted from a set of principles developed by the International Council on Archives for institutional recordkeeping. In the process of articulating and justifying the relevance of the twelve principles, Cunningham makes a strong case for collaboration and mutual learning among those responsible for personal records and organizational records.

Cathy Marshall, who is a Senior Researcher at Microsoft Corporation and an Affiliated Researcher at Texas A&M University, explores "Challenges and Opportunities for Personal Digital Archiving." She begins with a discussion of two 1995 quotations, one from John Seabrook and the other from Jeff Rothenberg. She contrasts the visions from those authors with the state of contemporary personal collections, which are likely to be composed of "thousands and thousands of pictures, hours and hours of undifferentiated digital video footage, music both purchased and shared, personal finances, the beginnings of what will one day be extensive medical records, email messages important and trivial, and countless other files representing day-to-day interactions with the computer and with other people by means of the computer." Personal digital collections are not only diverse but also "apt to span many repositories, storage media, and file systems." Management of personal digital archives over time "is a problem that extends far beyond accurately rendering obsolete formats." The rest of Marshall's discussion is organized around three questions: What's in a personal digital collection (as a matter of selection and appraisal)? What is the "technological basis" for individuals' storage, maintenance, and preservation of their personal digital collections? What are individuals' stewardship practices and what practices should they be taught? The result is a sober assessment of strategies and options for stewardship of personal materials.

Sue McKemmish is a Professor at Monash University's Faculty of Information Technology. In 1996, she published a very reflective and influential piece called "Evidence of Me . . . " in which she explored the nature of personal record-keeping and social mandates for "witnessing to individual lives." In her chapter for this volume, entitled "Evidence of Me . . . in a Digital World" McKemmish revisits her earlier piece within the context of new technologies, record forms, and practices. Building on Derrida's claim that "mutation in technology changes . . . the possibility of archiving," she explores the relationship between personal and public recordkeeping, as well as the place of records within a wide array of potential "memory stores" about individuals. Along the way, McKemmish investigates and challenges many conventional archival assumptions about personal archives.

The second part of *I, Digital* is devoted to particular types, genres, and forms of personal traces; areas of further study; and new opportunities for appraisal and collection. "'Three Backups Is a Minimum': A First Look at Norms and Practices in the Digital Photo Collections of Serious Photographers" was authored by Kristina Spurgin, who is a Doctoral Candidate at the School of Information and Library Science, University of North Carolina, Chapel Hill. Spurgin argues that amateur photographers fall at the boundary between three different arenas that have been represented in previous literature: "institutions and organizations, casual snapshooters collecting mainly family photos, and unknown individuals sharing, tagging, and annotating photo collections on the Web." Spurgin investigates the "norms and expectations of the social world of photography" and implications for the practices of amateur photographers. She reports on preliminary analysis of a year of discussion threads from an online forum devoted to discussing collection management and digital photography workflow. She asks whether "there is anything new and important to learn from studying the personal collection management of amateur photographers," and the answers are very compelling. She places this investigation within a larger context of personal collections related to activities pursued as "serious leisure," and argues that "photographs alone do not comprise the photography-related collections of amateur photographers."

In "Collecting the Externalized Me: Appraisal of Materials in the Social Web" I argue that, with the adoption of highly interactive web technologies (frequently labeled "Web 2.0"), forms of individual documentation and expression are often inherently social and public. Such online environments do allow for personal documentation, but they also engage external audiences in ways not previously possible. This opens up new opportunities and challenges for collecting personal materials, particularly within the context of archival appraisal. The chapter explores the nature and characteristics of user-generated content on the Web and various ways in which principles of archival appraisal can be operationalized in an environment in which collecting takes the form of submitting queries and following links. As with any other case of archival appraisal, the fundamental questions relate to what one is attempting to document and why.

The final section of *I, Digital* addresses the practical implications of the issues raised in the previous chapters for the strategies and practices of professionals who work in memory institutions. Tom Hyry and Rachel Onuf published a piece in 1997 called "The Personality of Electronic Records," in which they made a strong case for widening the professional discourse on electronic records to be more inclusive of concerns related to personal materials. In this volume, Hyry, who is Director of Special Collections at the University of California, Los Angeles (UCLA), and Onuf, who is Archives Analyst for the Archivists' Toolkit project, have again joined forces in "Take It Personally: The Implications of Personal Records in Electronic Form." They explore the major opportunity of digital recordkeeping to reflect "digital contexts" and for "future social historians and others invested in documenting regular folk." They argue that the archival profession "has come full circle, back to the idea that the records we need to preserve are rooted in larger systems—but now in online networks, rather than organizational recordkeeping systems—and archivists need to focus on holistic capture of this data in order to meaningfully document the individual." They conclude by elaborating several recommendations: explicitly collect the digital; develop enhanced access systems; and embrace and acquire new skills.

In the chapter by Leslie Johnston, Digital Media Projects Coordinator at the U.S. Library of Congress, titled "Making It Usable: Developing Personal Collection Tools for Digital Collections," she reports on her earlier work at the University of Virginia (UVa) Library. Johnston explains that a major assumption of the UVa Library "while developing its Digital Collections Repository was that the library was responsible not only for collection and repository building, but also for the creation of tools for collection use." She reports on the development of a User Collection Tool to organize personal digital media collections, a PageComber tool to gather images from the open web, and the Collectus digital object collector tool to develop portfolios of all object types and create presentations. This work, and Johnston's articulation of the development process, provides many lessons for other memory institutions that hope to actively engage with record creators, and better integrate digital library systems with the environments being used by individuals in support of their scholarly activities.

In "Curating the I, Digital," Susan Thomas, Digital Archivist at Oxford University's Bodleian Library, examines how the Bodleian Library has been adapting and evolving to address contemporary personal archives. She offers an overview of the Bodleian's activities, both in terms of everyday practices and two very influential projects that I discussed earlier: Paradigm and futureArch. The efforts of Thomas and her colleagues serve as a compelling and informative model for memory institutions across the globe that are undergoing the transition toward incorporating born-digital materials into their regular operations and practices.

When it comes to personal collections, we live in exciting times. Individuals are living their lives in ways that are increasingly mediated by digital technologies. While this mediation presents many technical challenges for long-term preservation, it also provides unprecedented opportunities for documenting the lives of individuals. There is a growing community of practice related to the acquisition and management of personal digital collections, with many of the participants being archivists, special collections librarians and manuscript curators. The PIM research community also continues to engage in valuable research, with many signs that they can serve as valuable collaborators with archival researchers. I believe that *I, Digital* can serve as a catalyst in a process of growing attention to and progress with personal digital collections, which is already underway. I look forward to great things ahead.

Notes

1. Sue McKemmish, "Introducing Archives and Archival Programs," in *Keeping Archives*, ed. Judith Ellis (Port Melbourne, Australia: Thorpe, 1993), 1–24.

2. W. Peter Ward, "Family Papers and the New Social History," *Archivaria* 14 (1982): 63.

3. Andrew Delano Abbott, *The System of Professions: An Essay on the Division of Expert Labor* (Chicago: University of Chicago Press, 1988).

4. Christopher A. Lee, "Defining Digital Preservation Work: A Case Study of the Development of the Reference Model for an Open Archival Information System" (PhD dissertation, University of Michigan, 2005).

5. John B. Horrigan, "Use of Cloud Computing Applications and Services" (Washington, DC: Pew Internet and American Life Project, 2008).

6. Abbott, *System of Professions.*

7. Curtis W. Garrison, "The Relation of Historical Manuscripts to Archival Materials," *American Archivist* 2, no. 2 (1939): 97–105; Richard C. Berner, "Manuscript Collections, Archives, and Special Collections: Their Relationships," *Archivaria* 18 (1984): 248–54; Luke J. Gilliland-Swetland, "The Provenance of a Profession: The Permanence of the Public Archives and Historical Manuscripts Traditions in American History," *American Archivist* 54 (1991): 160–75.

8. Adrian Cunningham, "Editorial: Beyond Corporate Accountability," *Archives and Manuscripts* 24, no. 1 (1996): 6–11.

9. Toby Burrows, "Personal Electronic Archives: Collecting the Digital Me," *OCLC Systems and Services* 22, no. 2 (2006): 87.

10. Jeremy Leighton John, "Digital Manuscripts: Capture and Context" (paper presented at the E-mail Curation: Practical Approaches for Long-term Preservation and Access workshop, Newcastle, UK, April 24–25, 2006); Catherine Stollar and Thomas Kiehne, "Guarding the Guards: Archiving the Electronic Records of Hypertext Author Michael Joyce" (paper presented at the New Skills for a Digital Era colloquium, Washington, DC, May 31–June 2, 2006); Anne Summers and Jeremy Leighton John, "The W.D. Hamilton Archive at the British Library," *Ethology, Ecology and Evolution* 13, no. 4 (2001): 373–84.

11. Peter Williams, Jeremy Leighton John, and Ian Rowland, "The Personal Curation of Digital Objects: A Lifecycle Approach," *Aslib Proceedings* 61, no. 4 (2009): 340–63.

12. Susan Thomas and Janette Martin, "Using the Papers of Contemporary British Politicians as a Testbed for the Preservation of Digital Personal Archives," *Journal of the Society of Archivists* 27, no. 1 (2006): 29–56; Paradigm project, *Workbook on Digital Private Papers*, 2007, http://www.paradigm.ac.uk/workbook/ (principle authors were Susan Thomas, Renhart Gittens, Janette Martin, and Fran Baker).

13. Matthew G. Kirschenbaum, Erika Farr, Kari M. Kraus, Naomi L. Nelson, Catherine Stollar Peters, Gabriela Redwine, and Doug Reside, "Approaches to Managing and Collecting Born-Digital Literary Materials for Scholarly Use" (College Park, MD: University of Maryland, 2009).

14. Elizabeth H. Dow, *Electronic Records in the Manuscript Repository* (Lanham, MD: Scarecrow Press, 2009), xii.

15. Michael Forstram, "Managing Electronic Records in Manuscript Collections: A Case Study from the Beinecke Rare Book and Manuscript Library," *American Archivist* 72, no. 2 (2009): 460–77.

16. Carolyn L. Geda, Erik W. Austin, and Francis X. Blouin, eds., *Archivists and Machine-Readable Records: Proceedings of the Conference on Archival Management of Machine-Readable Records, February 7–10, 1979, Ann Arbor, Michigan* (Chicago: Society of American Archivists, 1980).

17. Margaret Hedstrom, *Archives and Manuscripts: Machine-Readable Records*, Basic Manual Series (Chicago: Society of American Archivists, 1984).

18 Harold Naugler, *The Archival Appraisal of Machine-Readable Records: A RAMP Study with Guidelines* (Paris: General Information Programme and UNISIST United Nations Educational Scientific and Cultural Organization, 1984); Charles M. Dollar, *Electronic Records Management and Archives in International Organizations: A RAMP Study with Guidelines* (Paris: General Information Programme and UNISIST United Nations Education Scientific and Cultural Organization, 1986); Katharine Gavrel, *Conceptual Problems Posed by Electronic Records: A RAMP Study* (Paris: United Nations Educational, Scientific and Cultural Organization, 1990).

19 David Bearman, ed., *Archival Management of Electronic Records*, Archives and Museum Informatics Technical Report No. 13 (Pittsburgh, PA: Archives and Museum Informatics, 1991); David Bearman, *Electronic Evidence: Strategies for Managing Records in Contemporary Organizations* (Pittsburgh, PA: Archives and Museum Informatics, 1994); Barbara Reed and David Roberts, eds., *Keeping Data: Papers from a Workshop on Appraising Computer-Based Records* (Dickson, ACT, Australia: Australian Council of Archives and the Australian Society of Archivists Incorporated, 1991); Charles M. Dollar, *Archival Theory and Information Technologies: The Impact of Information Technologies on Archival Principles and Methods*, Vol. 1, Informatics and Documentation Series, ed. Oddo Bucci (Macerata, Italy: Università degli studi di Macerata, 1992); William Saffady, *Managing Electronic Records* (Prairie Village, KS: ARMA International, 1992, 2nd ed. 1998, 3rd ed. 2002); Margaret Hedstrom, ed., *Electronic Records Management Program Strategies*, Archives and Museum Informatics Technical Report No. 18 (Pittsburgh, PA: Archives and Museum Informatics, 1993); Tora K. Bikson and Erik. J. Frinking, *Preserving the Present: Toward Viable Electronic Records* (The Hague: Sdu Publishers, 1993); Richard J. Cox, *The First Generation of Electronic Records Archivists in the United States: A Study in Professionalization*, Vol. 3, Primary Sources and Original Works, ed. Lawrence J. McCrank (New York: Haworth Press, 1994); Stephen Yorke, ed., *Playing for Keeps: The Proceedings of an Electronic Records Management Conference Hosted by the Australian Archives* (Canberra, Australia: Australian Archives, 1994); David O. Stephens and Roderick C. Wallace, *Electronic Records Retention: An Introduction* (Prairie Village, KS: ARMA International, 1997); and Edward Higgs, ed., *History and Electronic Artefacts* (Oxford, England: Clarendon Press, 1998).

20 Charles M. Dollar and Deborah S. Skaggs, *Using Information Technology to Build Strategic Collaborations: The State of Alabama as a Test Case—A Case Study in Archives Management* (Chicago: Society of American Archivists, 1996); Jean E. Dryden, *Implementing Descriptive Standards at the United Church Central Archives: A Case Study in Automated Techniques for Archives* (Chicago: Society of American Archivists, 1997); Elaine D. Engst and H. Thomas Hickerson, *Developing Collaborative Structures for Expanding the Use of University Collections in Teaching and Research* (Chicago: Society of American Archivists, 1998); Thomas J. Galvin and Russell L. Kahn, *Electronic Records Management as Strategic Opportunity: A Case Study of the State University of New York, Office of Archives and Records Management* (Chicago: Society of American Archivists, 1996); Anne Gilliland-Swetland, *Policy and Politics: The Archival Implications of Digital Communications and Culture at the University of Michigan* (Chicago: Society of American Archivists, 1996); Grant Alan Mitchell, *Approaching Electronic Records Management in the Insurance Corporation of British Columbia: A Case Study in Organizational Dynamics and Archival Initiative* (Chicago: Society of American Archivists, 1997); Thomas D. Norris, *Prison Inmate Records in New York State: The Challenge of Modern Government Case Records* (Chicago: Society of American Archivists, 1996); Barbara Reed and Frank Upward, *The APB Bank: Managing Electronic Records as an Authoritative Resource* (Chicago: Society of American Archivists, 1997).

21 Judith A. Ellis, ed., *Selected Essays in Electronic Recordkeeping in Australia* (O'Connor, ACT, Australia: Australian Society of Archivists, 2000); Bruce W. Dearstyne, ed., *Effective Approaches for Managing Electronic Records and Archives* (Lanham, MD: Scarecrow Press, 2002); Luciana Duranti, Terence M. Eastwood, and Heather MacNeil, *Preservation of the Integrity of Electronic Records* (Dordrecht: Kluwer Academic, 2002); Saffady, *Managing Electronic Records*; David O. Stephens and Roderick C. Wallace, *Electronic Records Retention: New Strategies for Data Life Cycle Management* (Prairie Village, KS: ARMA International, 2003); Luciana Duranti, ed., *Long-Term Preservation of Authentic Electronic Records: Findings of the InterPARES Project* (San Miniato, Italy: Archilab, 2005); Julie

McLeod and Catherine Hare, eds., *Managing Electronic Records* (London: Facet Publishing, 2005); Alistair G. Tough and Michael Moss, eds., *Record Keeping in a Hybrid Environment: Managing the Creation, Use, Preservation and Disposal of Unique Information Objects in Context*, Chandos Information Professional Series (Oxford: Chandos, 2006); and Philip C. Bantin, *Understanding Data and Information Systems for Recordkeeping* (New York: Neal-Schuman, 2008).

[22] For analysis of electronic records publications in the 1990s in the major North American archival journals, see Richard J. Cox, "Searching for Authority: Archivists and Electronic Records in the New World at the Fin-De-Siécle," *First Monday* 5, no. 1 (2000), http://firstmonday.org/article/view/721/630.

[23] Adrian Cunningham, "The Archival Management of Personal Records in Electronic Form: Some Suggestions," *Archives and Manuscripts* 22, no. 1 (1994): 94–105; Adrian Cunningham, "Waiting for the Ghost Train: Strategies for Managing Personal Electronic Records before It Is Too Late," *Archival Issues* 24, no. 1 (1999): 55–64; Sue McKemmish, "Evidence of Me . . . " *Archives and Manuscripts* 24, no. 1 (1996): 28–45; Verne Harris, "On the Back of a Tiger: Deconstructive Possibilities in 'Evidence of Me . . . '" *Archives and Manuscripts* 29, no. 1 (2001): 8–21; Tom Hyry and Rachel Onuf, "The Personality of Electronic Records: The Impact of New Information Technology on Personal Papers," *Archival Issues* 22, no. 1 (1997): 37–44; Lucie Paquet, "Appraisal, Acquisition and Control of Personal Electronic Records: From Myth to Reality," *Archives and Manuscripts* 28, no. 2 (2000): 71–91; Frank Upward and Sue McKemmish, "In Search of the Lost Tiger, by Way of Sainte-Beuve: Re-Constructing the Possibilities in 'Evidence of Me . . . '" *Archives and Manuscripts* 29, no. 1 (2001): 22–42; Susan E. Davis, "Electronic Records Planning in 'Collecting' Repositories," *American Archivist* 71, no. 1 (2008): 167–89; and Michael Forstram, "Managing Electronic Records in Manuscript Collections: A Case Study from the Beinecke Rare Book and Manuscript Library," *American Archivist* 72, no. 2 (2009): 460–77.

[24] Michele C. S. Lange and Kristin M. Nimsger, *Electronic Evidence and Discovery: What Every Lawyer Should Know Now*, 2nd ed. (Chicago: Section of Science and Technology Law, American Bar Association, 2009); *Electronic Records Management and E-Discovery: Leading Lawyers on Navigating Recent Trends, Understanding Rules and Regulations, and Implementing an E-Discovery Strategy* (Boston: Aspatore, 2010); Jeffrey J. Fowler and William H. Dance, *Preserving Electronically Stored Information: A Practical Approach*, E-Discovery Portfolio Series. (Arlington, VA: BNA Books, 2009).

[25] Thomas Y. Allman, "Fostering a Compliance Culture: The Role of the Sedona Guidelines," *Information Management Journal* 39, no. 2 (2005): 55.

[26] See http://www.ils.unc.edu/digitaldesktop/.

[27] See http://www.records.ncdcr.gov/emailpreservation/.

[28] Abbott, *System of Professions.*

[29] Elizabeth Yakel, "The Social Construction of Accountability: Radiologists and Their Record-Keeping Practices," *Information Society* 17, no. 4 (2001): 233–45.

[30] Jay Atherton, "From Life Cycle to Continuum: Some Thoughts on the Records Management-Archives Relationship," *Archivaria* 21 (1985–86): 43–51; Sue McKemmish, "Placing Records Continuum Theory and Practice," *Archival Science* 1, no. 4 (2001): 333–59.

[31] Adrian Brown, *Archiving Websites: A Practical Guide for Information Management Professionals* (London: Facet, 2006).

[32] Richard Entlich, "Blog Today, Gone Tomorrow? Preservation of Weblogs," *RLG DigiNews* 8, no. 4 (2004); Catherine O'Sullivan, "Diaries, Online Diaries and the Future Loss to Archives; or, Blogs and the Blogging Bloggers Who Blog Them," *American Archivist* 68, no. 1 (2005): 53–73; Helen R. Tibbo, Christopher A. Lee, Gary Marchionini, and Dawne Howard, "VidArch: Preserving Meaning of Digital Video over Time through Creating and Capture of Contextual Documentation," in *Archiving 2006: Final Program and Proceedings, May 23–26, 2006, Ottawa, Canada*, ed. Stephen Chapman and Scott A. Stovall (Springfield, VA: Society for Imaging Science and Technology,

2006), 210–15; Carolyn Hank, Songphan Choemprayong, and Laura Sheble, "Blogger Perceptions on Digital Preservation," in *Proceedings of the 7th ACM/IEEE Joint Conference on Digital Libraries: Vancouver, British Columbia, Canada, June 18–23, 2007: Building and Sustaining the Digital Environment: JCDL 2007* (New York: ACM Press, 2007), 477.

33 Matthew G. Kirschenbaum, *Mechanisms: New Media and the Forensic Imagination* (Cambridge, MA: MIT Press, 2008), 12.

34 John Lavagnino, "The Analytical Bibliography of Electronic Texts" (paper presented at the Joint Annual Conference of the Association for Literary and Linguistic Computing and the Association for Computers and the Humanities, Bergen, Norway, 1996), 181.

35 Seamus Ross and Ann Gow, *Digital Archaeology: Rescuing Neglected and Damaged Data Resources* (London: British Library, 1999); Deborah Woodyard, "Data Recovery and Providing Access to Digital Manuscripts" (paper presented at the Information Online 2001 Conference, Sydney, Australia, January 16–18, 2001).

36 Jeremy Leighton John, "Adapting Existing Technologies for Digitally Archiving Personal Lives: Digital Forensics, Ancestral Computing, and Evolutionary Perspectives and Tools" (paper presented at iPRES 2008: The Fifth International Conference on Preservation of Digital Objects, London, UK, September 29–30, 2008); William Bradley Glisson, "Use of Computer Forensics in the Digital Curation of Removable Media," in *Proceedings of DigCCurr2009: Digital Curation: Practice, Promise, and Prospects*, ed. Helen R. Tibbo, Carolyn Hank, Christopher A. Lee, and Rachael Clemens (Chapel Hill, NC: University of North Carolina, School of Information and Library Science, 2009), 110–11; Simson Garfinkel and David Cox, "Finding and Archiving the Internet Footprint" (paper presented at the First Digital Lives Research Conference: Personal Digital Archives for the 21st Century, London, UK, February 9–11, 2009).

37 Douglas Elford, Nicholas Del Pozo, Snezana Mihajlovic, David Pearson, Gerard Clifton, and Colin Webb, "Media Matters: Developing Processes for Preserving Digital Objects on Physical Carriers at the National Library of Australia" (paper presented at the 74th IFLA General Conference and Council, Québec, Canada, August 10–14, 2008).

38 William E. Underwood and Sandra L. Laib, "PERPOS: An Electronic Records Repository and Archival Processing System" (paper presented at DigCCurr 2007, the International Symposium on Digital Curation, Chapel Hill, NC, April 18–20, 2007); William Underwood, Marlit Hayslett, Sheila Isbell, Sandra Laib, Scott Sherrill, and Matthew Underwood, "Advanced Decision Support for Archival Processing of Presidential Electronic Records: Final Scientific and Technical Report," Technical Report ITTL/CSITD 09-05 (Atlanta: Georgia Tech Research Institute, October 2009).

39 William Jones and Jaime Teevan, "Introduction," in *Personal Information Management*, ed. William P. Jones and Jaime Teevan (Seattle: University of Washington Press, 2007), 3.

40 William Jones, "Personal Information Management," in *Annual Review of Information Science and Technology*, ed. Blaise Cronin (Medford, NJ: Information Today, 2007), 453.

41 Thomas W. Malone, "How Do People Organize Their Desks? Implications for the Design of Office Information Systems," *ACM Transactions on Information Systems* 1, no. 1 (1983): 99–112; M. Lansdale, "The Psychology of Personal Information Management," *Applied Ergonomics* 19, no. 1 (1988): 55–66.

42 Richard J. Cox, "The Record in the Manuscript Collection," *Archives and Manuscripts* 24, no. 1 (1996): 51.

43 Assistant Secretary of Defense for Networks and Information Integration, "Electronic Records Management Software Applications Design Criteria Standard," DoD 5015.02-STD (Arlington, VA: U.S. Department of Defense, 2007).

44 "Model Requirements for the Management of Electronic Records: Update and Extension," MoReq2 Specification (Hampshire, UK: Serco Consulting, 2008).

45 Richard J. Cox, "The Record in the Manuscript Collection," 54.

[46] Prominent examples include: Collectus and Digital Object Collector Tool (see Leslie Johnston, "Development and Assessment of a Public Discovery and Delivery Interface for a Fedora Repository," *D-Lib Magazine* 11, no. 10 (2005), http:// dx.doi.org/10.1045/october2005-johnston); eSciDoc (see Matthias Razum, Frank Schwichtenberg, Steffen Wagner, and Michael Hoppe, "eSciDoc Infrastructure: A Fedora-Based E-Research Framework," in *Research and Advanced Technology for Digital Libraries: 13th European Conference. ECDL 2009, Corfu, Greece, September 27–October 2, 2009, Proceedings*, ed. Maristella Agosti, José Borbinha, Sarantos Kapidakis, Christos Papatheodorou, and Giannis Tsakonas (Berlin: Springer, 2009), 227–38); Gnowsis (see Leo Sauermann, Gunnar Aastrand Grimnes, Malte Kiesel, Christiaan Fluit, Heiko Maus, Dominik Heim, Danish Nadeem, Benjamin Horak, and Andreas Dengel, "Semantic Desktop 2.0: The Gnowsis Experience," in *The Semantic Web: ISWC 2006: 5th International Semantic Web Conference, ISWC 2006, Athens, GA, USA, November 5–9, 2006: Proceedings*, ed. Isabel F. Cruz, Stefan Decker, Dean Allemang, Chris Preist, Daniel Schwabe, Peter Mika, Michael Uschold, and Lora Aroyo (Berlin: Springer, 2006), 887–900); Haystack (see David Karger, Karun Bakshi, David Huynh, Dennis Quan, and Vineet Sinha, "Haystack: A General Purpose Information Management Tool for End Users of Semistructured Data," in *Proceedings of the Second Biennial Conference on Innovative Data Systems Research*, Asilomar, CA, USA, January 4–7, 2005 (Asilomar, CA: CIDR, 2005), 13–26); HOPPLA (see Stephan Strodl, Florian Motlik, Kevin Stadler, and Andreas Rauber, "Personal & SOHO Archiving," in *Proceedings of the 8th ACM/IEEE-CS Joint Conference on Digital Libraries* (New York: ACM Press, 2008), 115–23); IRIS/OpenIRIS (see Adam Cheyer, Jack Park, and Richard Giuli, "IRIS: Integrate. Relate. Infer. Share" (paper presented at the Workshop on the Semantic Desktop: Next Generation Personal Information Management and Collaboration Infrastructure, ICSC 2005, Galway, Ireland, November 6, 2005)); Pliny (see John Bradley, "Pliny: A Model for Digital Support of Scholarship," *Journal of Digital Information* 9, no. 26 (2008), http://journals.tdl.org/jodi/article/view/209/198); Presto (see Paul Dourish, W. Keith Edwards, Anthony LaMarca, and Michael Salisbury, "Presto: An Experimental Architecture for Fluid Interactive Document Spaces," *Transactions on Computer-Human Interaction* 6, no. 2 (1999): 133–61); RepoMMan (see Richard Green and Chris Awre, "RepoMMan: Delivering Private Repository Space for Day-to-Day Use," *Ariadne* 54 (2008), http://www.ariadne.ac.uk/issue54/green-awre/); Hydra (see Richard Green and Chris Awre, "Towards a Repository-enabled Scholar's Workbench: RepoMMan, REMAP and Hydra," *D-Lib Magazine* 15, no.5/6 (2009), http://dx.doi.org/10.1045/may2009-green); UpLib (see William C. Janssen, Jeff Breidenbach, Lance Good, and Ashok Popat, "Making UpLib Useful: Personal Document Engineering" (Palo Alto, CA: Palo Alto Research Center, 2005)); and Zotero (see Daniel J. Cohen, "Zotero: Social and Semantic Computing for Historical Scholarship," *Perspectives* 45, no. 5 (2007)).

[47] For example, see Diigo (http://www.diigo.com), Find it! Keep it! (http://www.ansemond.com), and Spurl (http://www.spurl.net), as well as several Firefox add-ons and archiving features built into many of the major blog hosting services.

[48] See http://www.contextminer.org. See also Gary Marchionini, Chirag Shah, Christopher A. Lee, and Robert Capra, "Query Parameters for Harvesting Digital Video and Associated Contextual Information," in *Proceedings of the 9th ACM/IEEE-CS Joint Conference on Digital Libraries* (New York: ACM Press, 2009), 77–86.

[49] See http://archivepress.ulcc.ac.uk.

[50] Jannette Hanna and Daniel Burge, "Preserving Digital Memory Files," http://www.archivaladvisor.org/shtml/art_presdigmem.shtml; "Saving Digital Prints," http://www.archivaladvisor.org/shtml/art_savdigprint.shtml; "Saving Digital Storage Media," http://www.archivaladvisor.org/shtml/art_savdigmedia.shtml.

[51] See http://www.tosback.org.

[52] See http://www.dataliberation.org.

[53] Robert Ellis Smith, *Ben Franklin's Web Site: Privacy and Curiosity from Plymouth Rock to the Internet* (Providence, RI: Privacy Journal, 2000), 311.

54 Simson Garfinkel, *Database Nation: The Death of Privacy in the 21st Century* (Beijing: O'Reilly, 2000), 11.

55 Mark Poster, *The Mode of Information: Poststructuralism and Social Context* (Chicago: University of Chicago Press, 1990), 71.

56 John F. Gantz, Christopher Chute, Alex Manfrediz, Stephen Minton, David Reinsel, Wolfgang Schlichting, and Anna Toncheva, "The Diverse and Exploding Digital Universe: An Updated Forecast of Worldwide Information Growth through 2011" (Framingham, MA: IDC, 2008), 2.

57 Daniel J. Solove, *The Digital Person: Technology and Privacy in the Information Age*, Ex Machina: Law, Technology and Society (New York: New York University Press, 2004), 19.

58 Rich Miller, "Who Has the Most Web Servers?" *Data Center Knowledge*, May 14, 2009, http://www.datacenterknowledge.com/archives/2009/05/14/whos-got-the-most-web-servers/.

59 Solove, *Digital Person*.

60 Seamus Ross, "The Expanding World of Electronic Information and the Past's Future," in *History and Electronic Artefacts*, ed. Edward Higgs (Oxford, England: Clarendon Press, 1998), 5–27.

61 Solove, *Digital Person*, 49.

62 Anders Albrechtslund, "Online Social Networking as Participatory Surveillance," *First Monday* 13, no. 3 (2008), http://firstmonday.org/article/view/2142/1949.

63 See http://www.bbc.co.uk/ww2peopleswar and http://www.vt.edu/remember/memorial. For other examples, see the BBC's Capture Wales (http://www.bbc.co.uk/wales/audiovideo/sites/galleries/pages/capturewales.shtml); City Stories Project (http://www.citystories.com); COINE—Cultural Objects in Networked Environments (Geoff Butters, Amanda Hulme, and Peter Brophy, "Supporting Creativity in Networked Environments: The COINE Project," *Ariadne* 51 (2007), http://informationr.net/ir/10-3/paper232.html, and http://www.uoc.edu/in3/coine); Forever LifeStories (http://www.forevernetwork.com/lifestories); Living Cultural Storybases (http://www.storybases.org); Montana Heritage Project (http://www.montanaheritageproject.org); Moving Here: 200 Years of Migration to England (http://www.movinghere.org.uk); Myfamily.com (http://www.myfamily.com); National September 11 Memorial and Museum at the World Trade Center (http://www.national911memorial.org); and Statue of Liberty—Ellis Island Foundation (http://www.ellisisland.org).

Part 1

Conceptual Foundations and Motivations

And Now the Twain Shall Meet: Exploring the Connections between PIM and Archives

Christopher A. Lee and Robert Capra

Determining the appropriate practices for capturing, selecting, managing, and disseminating personal digital traces is a complex challenge that requires numerous forms of expertise. Successful research related to the curation of personal digital collections is likely to be both highly collaborative and interdisciplinary. This chapter focuses on two specific areas of research in which there are numerous opportunities for mutual learning and collaboration. Over the past two decades, two complementary, but relatively unconnected, streams of literature have emerged: electronic recordkeeping (ERK) and personal information management (PIM). The former builds upon long-standing principles and practices in archives and records management (ARM), while the latter has its strongest roots in human-computer interaction and information science. We identify and elaborate on commonalities and differences in these two areas of study.

Many human practices will be most effective if they are informed by solid research. Few readers are likely to challenge this statement in the abstract. However, the statement does not address the much more challenging questions of which human practices to inform through research and what types of research to conduct. A set of human practices is a particularly good candidate for research attention if it:

1. Is rapidly evolving;

2. Is complex (both internally and in its relationships with other phenomena and practices); and

3. Has increasing impact on the lives of individuals.

The curation of personal digital information is a set of human activities that scores very highly on all three of the above criteria.

In much of the world, individuals' activities generate a diverse array of digital traces, including digital artifacts that they create intentionally and other traces that are unconscious byproducts of actions that they take through the use of computers. Determining the appropriate practices for capturing, selecting, managing, and disseminating personal digital traces is a complex challenge that requires numerous forms of expertise. Successful research related to the curation of personal digital collections is likely to be both highly collaborative and interdisciplinary. The introduction to this volume describes a number of "streams of activities" within the research and professional literature that are relevant to personal digital collections. In this chapter, we focus more specifically on two areas of research in which we believe there are numerous opportunities for mutual learning and collaboration.

Over the past two decades, two complementary, but relatively unconnected, streams of literature have emerged: electronic recordkeeping (ERK) literature and personal information management (PIM) literature. The former builds upon long-standing principles and practices in archives and records management (ARM), while the latter has its strongest roots in human-computer interaction (HCI) and information science. A fundamental issue that cuts across both areas of literature is how to make meaningful use of information artifacts when one is no longer embedded in the original context of creation, capture, or use. The ARM literature formulates this as secondary use, while the PIM literature focuses on refinding and reuse. In this chapter, we identify and elaborate on areas of commonality and difference in these two areas of study.

Core Archival Concepts Relevant to Personal Information Management

Archivists and records managers are in the business of managing and providing perpetual access (and helping others to manage and provide perpetual access) to relatively fixed traces of human activity. The core unit of analysis for these traces in ARM is the record, which is a bounded information artifact "in a fixed form that is created or received in the course of individual or institutional activity and set aside (preserved) as evidence of that activity for future reference."[1] ARM theory and practice place great emphasis on:

- Integrity of records over time.
- Creation and perpetuation of metadata that reflects the relationships between different records and between records and the people or human activities that are documented by the records.

Four fundamental concepts that support ARM goals are provenance, fonds, original order, and chain of custody. The *provenance* of a record is its "life history." Although the concept had precedents in the archival writing and practices of several countries of the seventeenth, eighteenth, and early nineteenth centuries,[2] the first widely recognized articulation of the principle of provenance—called *respect des fonds*—was in France in 1841.[3] For purposes of describing archival collections, one of the most important aspects of provenance is the identification of one or more origins or sources of a record (for example, the person who wrote a diary entry or the specific business transaction that generated a receipt). However, provenance more broadly "consists of the social and technical processes of the records' inscription, transmission, contextualization, and interpretation which account for its existence, characteristics, and continuing history."[4] According to the principle of provenance, records from a common origin or source should be managed together as an aggregate unit and should not be arbitrarily intermingled with records from other origins or sources.

The etymology of the term *provenance* is from the Old French, meaning *origin* or *cause*.[5] If one were only interested in simple, discrete artifacts created by individuals acting in isolation, the concept of provenance would be relatively easy to apply. In practice, there are several major complicating factors associated with the concept of provenance.

First, records are treated in the aggregate, often making it difficult or impossible to definitively identify specific sources for all of the records that constitute the aggregations. One way to address this is to identify record "creators" in the abstract, in the sense of legal "persons" rather than specific individuals. For example, one could consider all of the records from a given small organization or unit within a larger organization to have the same provenance, even though the roles, job titles, and specific individuals working for that organization changed over time. Such a high-level application of the concept of provenance has been common in archival practice, largely for reasons of "administrative convenience."[6] Even this abstraction approach can lead to serious challenges, given the complex and evolving structures of contemporary organizations, which often do not lend themselves to one-to-one mappings between bodies of records and organizational entities.[7]

Second, there are many different interactions with records that are important to document in order to understand the records' origins and "life history" (e.g., those who influenced the creation of the records, those who received them, custodians who transformed them over time), not simply one isolated moment of creation. These considerations illustrate the importance of provenance not only as the source of a record but also as a "history of the ownership . . . used as a guide to authenticity or quality" and "a documented record of this" history.[8]

Finally, many important aspects of the "origin" of records are not individuals or groups of individuals, but are instead functions, activities, and transactions.[9] Descriptions of provenance that are based solely on named individuals or units within an organizational chart can fail to reflect important aspects of records' place within a workflow or social process.

Given the complex and evolving relationships between entities (e.g., people, agencies) and records, provenance is not simply a matter of identifying the one person who created a record at a point in time but instead "relate[s] a multitude of contextual entities to a multitude of recordkeeping entities in a multitude of ways."[10]

None of the above challenges are specific to electronic records. However, the distributed and interactive nature of digital objects does often heighten the importance of the factors. For example, early guidance on the appraisal of electronic records points out that "there are many joint federal-provincial or federal-state programmes which result in the creation and even 'sharing' of records," a situation complicated further by "conflicting records schedules and archival limitations."[11] In digital environments, it also can be important to consider provenance at levels of granularity finer than an entire record, such as why a specific data element appears within a dataset and where specifically the data element was generated;[12] and to include additional technical components in one's notion of provenance, such as system configuration information.[13]

A core abstraction associated with provenance is the *fonds*, which is "the entire body of records of an organization, family, or individual that have been created and accumulated as the result of an organic process reflecting the functions of the creator."[14] In the case of personal archives, "the *fonds* of an individual is a site where personality and the events of life interact in documentary form."[15] The fonds is an "intellectual construct" rather than a "physical entity."[16] The materials that constitute an individual's fonds are often not co-located and are often distributed across various systems. "One body of records can derive from many creators, and one creator can leave records in many physical locations."[17] Experience in attempting to apply the concept of fonds to archival description shows that, due to organizational and functional changes within the entities creating records, the fonds cannot be treated as a clearly bounded category of records.[18] Fonds should often be treated as a "living creation,"[19] rather than a fixed, discrete set of materials.

According to the principle of *original order*, archivists should organize and manage records in ways that reflect their arrangement within the creation environment. The concept of original order had some precedent in archival writings of late-nineteenth-century Italy,[20] but it was most strongly influenced by Prussian archival practice in the late nineteenth century.[21] Its most widely recognized articulation within the context of archival description was the *Manual for the Arrangement and Description of Archives*—known as the "Dutch Manual"—which was originally published in 1898 and first published in English translation in 1940.[22] For personal records, the principle of original order implies that archivists should carry forward (either by perpetuating or attempting to reconstruct) the peculiar ways in which individuals label and organize their own records.

There are two primary motivations for retaining original order:

- It "preserves existing relationships and evidential significance that can be inferred from the context of the records."[23] This supports what Hugh Taylor calls "authentic pattern recognition."[24]

- It "exploits the record creator's mechanisms to access the records, saving the archives the work of creating new access tools."[25]

Traditionally, original order has taken the form of relatively simple box and folder structures. Applying the concept of original order to electronic records is not straightforward.[26] When characterized as a hierarchical folder structure, the concept of original order can map very easily to the folder structure of an individual's computer workspace. One compelling argument for retaining original order in a digital environment is that—even if that order is messy and idiosyncratic—it conveys meaningful information about the recordkeeping context, and additional layers of description can be laid on top of that order to facilitate various forms of navigation and access.[27] However, electronic records often cannot be so easily characterized, and attempting to reduce them to a simple hierarchy can rob electronic records of much of their evidential and informational value.[28] Rather than simply "freezing or restoring one particular past arrangement as 'the' original order,"[29] original order is most usefully understood within the context of a larger, ongoing chain of custody.

The *chain of custody* is the "succession of offices or persons who have held materials from the moment they were created."[30] For purposes of legal compliance, authenticity, evidential integrity, and legal admissibility, the ideal recordkeeping system would provide "an unblemished line of responsible custody"[31] through control, documentation, and accounting for all states of a record and changes of state (e.g., movement from one storage environment to another, transformation from one file format to another) throughout its existence—from the point of creation to each instance of use and (when appropriate) destruction.

The reality of contemporary information management is rarely consistent with the recordkeeping ideal. In most cases, the best that an information professional can do is to capture or create limited documentation of the portion of the chain of custody that occurred before the records were first encountered, and then attempt to provide much more detailed chain of custody control and documentation from that point forward. For example, an archivist acquiring a floppy disk containing records from a donor often will not know with certainty what the states and transitions of the records were before they were last saved onto that disk, but she can use various forms of information (e.g., other records, discussions with the donor) to make inferences about earlier points in the "life" of the records. Tom Nesmith points out that archivists' knowledge about various aspects of the "origins of a record" are "bathed in hypothesis."[32] Likewise, a forensic investigator can take great care to ensure that the bits stored on a computer that was seized at a crime scene have not changed since the time that the computer was seized, but anything that happened on the computer before that point is a matter of informed speculation.[33]

Core PIM Concepts Relevant to Archives

Personal information management (PIM) has been defined as "both the practice and the study of the activities people perform to acquire, organize, maintain, retrieve, use, and control the distribution of information items such as documents (paper-based and digital), Web pages, and email messages for everyday use to complete tasks (work-related and not) and to fulfill a person's various roles."[34] One source of complexity—and potential confusion—is that the PIM literature addresses both *personal information* management (i.e., management of information that is from or about individuals), and personal *information management* (i.e., the management by individuals, of information, whether or not the information itself is considered "personal"). PIM often considers not just information that is created or received by an individual (e.g., authored documents or correspondence), but also information that is experienced by or otherwise directed toward an individual (e.g., articles one has read). PIM draws on research in human-computer interaction and information science, but it also includes aspects of knowledge management, cognitive science, and classification theory.

Early PIM research identified the cognitive complexities involved with recall, recognition, and categorization of personal information; the importance of "filing" and "piling" strategies; the reminding function that artifacts perform; and the distinguished and "overloaded" role of email in personal information management.[35] Recent PIM research has been influenced by the Keeping Found Things Found project,[36] a series of workshops on PIM,[37] and an increased interest in addressing information overload. Work has focused on topics such as cross-tool PIM,[38] the problem of refinding information,[39] managing personal health information,[40] dealing with information "scraps,"[41] and issues people face when keeping digital and nondigital information.[42]

William Jones defines the notion of a *personal space of information* (PSI), which includes both information under a person's control and information about her that is stored by others.[43] Like the archival fonds, a PSI is an abstract aggregation of one's personal information which is often distributed across various systems rather than being completely co-located. A *personal information collection* (PIC) is a subset of a person's overall PSI,[44] which often shares a common storage format or access method.[45] Some examples of PICs include a physical pile of papers, an iTunes playlist, and a digital photograph collection stored on a hard drive.

William Jones and Jaime Teevan describe three broad categories of PIM activities:

- *Finding and refinding:* These are typically considered as separate tasks in PIM. The strategies and approaches for finding an item for the first time may differ from the approaches used to refind the item at a later date.[46]

- *Keeping:* Jones defines keeping as "decision-making and actions relating to the information item currently under consideration that *impact* the likelihood that the item *will be found* again later."[47] Jones's definition allows for both a positive impact (e.g., filing) or a negative impact (e.g., deleting) on the likelihood of refinding the item. Individuals may choose keeping actions not only for the purpose of refinding, but also to support their ongoing access to the information (e.g., preservation). William Jones, Harry Bruce, and Susan Dumais identify techniques commonly used for keeping (e.g., email to self, print-outs, saving URLs) and factors that may affect keeping methods (e.g., portability, persistence, preservation, context, reminding).[48] Jones also describes "the keeping decision" that individuals face with the information they encounter, emphasizing cases in which keeping is carried out in order to promote "personal re-use."[49]

- *Meta-level activities:* These include maintaining, organizing, and managing aspects of a personal space of information.[50] Organization and management of personal information can be especially difficult because of the evolving and overlapping nature of personal information needs.[51] Organization is often motivated by a goal of future reuse. Managing privacy and ownership of personal information are also important PIM concerns.[52]

Although each of the above categories actually includes a complex spectrum of activities, it can be informative to consider them as dichotomous variables, forming a 2-by-2-by-2 cube (see figure 1):

- Finding/Refinding: (1) search, (2) browse/navigate
- Keeping: (1) save everything, (2) selectively save
- Organizing/Managing: (1) file/organize, (2) heap storage (unorganized piles)

Although PIM behavior can fall anywhere within the cube, two particular combinations are of interest and exemplify divergent approaches:

- Save everything; keep everything in one big pile; refind by keyword search.
- Selectively save; organize by filing; refind by browsing folders.

Individual users may adopt different aspects of these approaches for different collections within their personal spaces of information. For example, one study found that individuals retrieved files by browsing then sorting; retrieved email by sorting/scanning; and retrieved bookmarks by scanning recently added or frequently accessed items.[53]

Intersections and Differences between PIM and ARM

This chapter is based on a fundamental belief that the ARM and PIM research communities have a great deal to learn from each other. The ARM literature and PIM literature explore many common issues but address them quite differently. Some of the differences simply involve using different words for similar concepts; in other cases, there are fundamental differences on focus, orientation, and background assumptions. Table 1 summarizes several

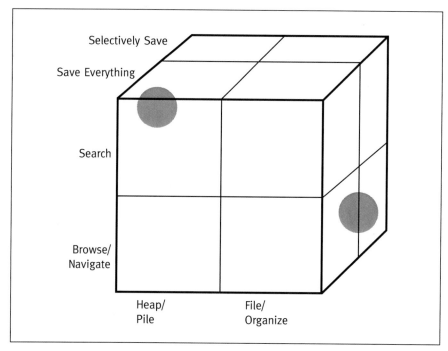

Figure 1. PIM activities viewed as dichotomous variables in a cube.

major areas of intersection and difference. In the following subsections, we elaborate on each.

Time Scale

This dimension deals with the relative amount of time for which the stored information is preserved, or the time frame that is of concern when considering a piece of information. A large part of PIM research focuses on information in current use. Ian Cole identifies "three levels of filed information":

- *Action information:* "that being dealt with or to be dealt with in the near future."

- *Personal work files:* "filed, according to some strategy, in the immediate office environment."

- *Long-term, archive storage:* "structured storage systems, away from offices, where people send information of no direct relevance to their predicted work schedule."[54]

Cole's orientation toward these categories is quite different from that of an archivist. Whereas the archival literature emphasizes the importance of provenance and original order for future use, Cole states:

> For "action information," items relating to a particular function have to be kept together and easily accessible; without this facility information access will be less efficient because of fragmentation of relevant information in the system. This is not so important for "personal work file" storage, and less so for "archive" storage.[55]

Table 1. PIM and ARM areas of intersection and difference.

Issue	PIM literature focus and orientation	ARM literature focus and orientation
Time scale	Relatively short term	Relatively long term
Main user tasks to support	Refinding, reminding, reuse, and sharing	Discovery, understanding, sense-making, storytelling, investigation, proof
Ownership of materials and recordkeeping goals	Belong to the individual	Belong to the employer and professional records manager/archivist
Role and importance of contextual information	Recalled contextual cues help individuals refind and reuse materials more efficiently	Helps someone from a completely different context to make meaningful use of the materials
Predominant attitudes toward selection	Keeping a preponderance of information and traces of user activity can be useful to the individual (but acknowledgment of potential costs and privacy concerns)	Removal of materials that do not have continuing value is desirable and appropriate
Purposeful organization of information	Depends on the type/role of individuals and their organizational behaviors (filers/pilers, spring-cleaners, occasional filers)	Professional arrangement and description based on formal recordkeeping conventions, provenance, original order, aggregate-level descriptions, and addition of contextual information
System requirements emphasized	Unobtrusive features, because PIM tasks are often secondary to some other primary tasks	Persistence, sustainability, trustworthiness, and authenticity

Cole's categories are similar to three types of information described by Deborah Barreau and Bonnie Nardi:

- *Ephemeral:* information with a "short shelf life"; things like grocery lists and some email.
- *Working:* "frequently used information that is relevant to the user's current work needs and that has a shelf life of weeks or months."

- *Archived:* information that "has a shelf life of months or years, but is only indirectly relevant to the user's current work."[56]

PIM has often focused on how people manage ephemeral and working information. However, there is also interest in longer-term information storage, especially in understanding and helping people to manage information across time, which can involve numerous factors associated with migration across computer systems. Preservation of personal collections has also been explored in the PIM literature.[57]

Applying Barreau and Nardi's terms, records professionals are responsible for helping record creators to identify the *ephemeral* materials that can be discarded, gain control over the *working* materials for purposes of short-term use, and apply appropriate disposition to the *archived* materials by either: managing them in place; transferring them into a local record center, document management system, or preservation environment; or transferring custody to a more long-term home (usually an archival repository).

In comparison to the PIM literature, the archival literature tends to focus on relatively long time scales. "For archivists, access is not the issue—access over time is."[58] Traditional archival language has been to speak of records with "permanent" value, though there has been a recognition over the past several decades that "continuing value" or "enduring value" can be more appropriate labels, because appraisal and preservation decisions occur at various points throughout the existence of records and often must be revisited over time.[59] The concept of continuing value becomes particularly important with electronic records, because digital curation requires frequent investments of resources over time.[60] Within the context of digital collections, the definition of *long term* from the Reference Model for an Open Archival Information System (OAIS) has been very influential:

> A period of time long enough for there to be concern about the impacts of changing technologies, including support for new media and data formats, and of a changing user community, on the information being held in a repository. This period extends into the indefinite future.[61]

Main User Tasks Supported

A common scenario in PIM is one in which a person is looking for information that she personally experienced in an earlier, direct interaction with the information as creator, recipient, or user. In contrast, ARM principles and practices are primarily concerned with supporting the use of records by individuals who were not part of the context in which the records were originally created, received, or used. In other words, PIM focuses strongly on support for individual memory, while ARM focuses strongly on support for organizational and social memory. This difference in orientation between PIM and ARM is reflected in the main user tasks emphasized in their respective literatures.

Refinding is a central PIM activity that, for many people, occurs multiple times a day: relocating an email message about an appointment, reaccessing a file in a directory structure, revisiting a web page to get details about an event. People may organize and store information so that they themselves can reaccess and make use of it at some future point in time. Often refinding is accomplished using one of two broad methods, identified by Jaime Teevan, Christine Alvarado, Mark Ackerman, and David Karger as *orienteering* and *teleporting*.[62] In the orienteering approach, the user takes a series of small steps to move toward the information being sought. The orienteering process often involves partial re-creation of previous "situated actions"[63] by recovering aspects of the context in which those actions took place. For example, a user rebrowsing through a series of web pages to get to the desired information is likely to be using this approach. A characteristic of the orienteering approach is that, at each point in the process, the local context is evaluated to make a determination of what step to take next—there is relatively little preplanning. By contrast, in a teleporting approach, the user attempts to go directly to the information using a predetermined plan. This could be through the use of a keyword search, typing in a URL, or clicking a shortcut to get to a desired document.

Different types of refinding tasks are supported by different approaches. Tasks in which the user is looking for a particular item and may recall textual or metadata cues may be well-suited to keyword searching and filtering. Tasks that involve refinding several items may be well supported by a mixture of searching and browsing strategies to allow the user to exploit both recalled details and the ability to recognize the sought-after information. Robert Capra and Manuel Pérez-Quiñones outline and investigate different types of refinding tasks: refinding the exact same information as was originally found; refinding fungible information or using a fungible source; refinding a subset of the original information; and refinding information that has moved from its original location.[64]

For many PIM tasks, there is also an important *reminding* goal. Research has found that the location of documents in the office often plays not only a finding function, but also an important reminding function.[65] Participants in these studies describe *not* filing a document because of (among other factors) a fear that they would forget it, or forget that they needed to do something with it. Thomas Malone distinguishes finding and reminding in terms of intentionality. If a person sets out to find something and does, then she has *found* the thing. However, if a person sets out to find one thing and happens across something else, then she has been *reminded*. This distinction can be extended to include situations in which the person's goal is to be reminded (e.g., scanning through the items on her desk). The reminding function is central to many PIM tools and is an active area of PIM research.

Another important PIM task is *keeping,* which usually implies "keeping for one's self." In contrast, *recordkeeping* in the ARM literature tends to concern itself with a wider set of stakeholders, including those engaged in the activity that generated records, but also those with an interest in ensuring that the records are authentic and accessible outside their original context, including (but not limited to) citizens, genealogists, journalists, historians, attorneys, and auditors.

Two further sets of tasks addressed by both the PIM and ARM literature are the reuse of items and the sharing of items with others. Many studies related to PIM have placed considerable emphasis on the socially embedded aspects of information management practices; examples include earlier investigations of the elusive "paperless office"[66] and more recent research related to the use of technology (e.g., mobile phones, online photo sites, social bookmarking) that facilitates more sharing than in the past.[67] No field of study can take on all problems, but instead carves off its own portion of a larger ecology of research. PIM, as its name implies, has placed most of its emphasis on the creation and use of information by individuals. Other sister fields—computer-supported cooperative work (CSCW), computer-mediated communication (CMC), management of information systems (MIS)—have focused much more directly on issues of information sharing and use among groups. In addition, recent work on collaborative search has overlaps with PIM research, but focuses more on the activities among a group of individuals collaborating to find information.[68]

The archival literature, on the other hand, has tended to emphasize the principles and practices of those working within archival repositories, with relatively little investigation of how individuals generate, manage, or use the materials that are within their care. Archival description is very labor-intensive and involves addition of considerable information to help the user know the place of a given item within its original context. In comparison to the PIM community, the archival profession has provided relatively little support for discovery of individual items, particularly due to the practical limits of description with analog materials, which must be applied to aggregates, such as folders and series, rather than individual items.

Within the U.S. archival profession, there is a very influential distinction, introduced by T.R. Schellenberg in the 1950s, between the primary and secondary value of records.[69] The primary value of records is derived from using the records for reasons that are identical or very similar to the reasons that the records were created. The beneficiary of the primary value of records—often called a primary user—is someone associated with the activity that generated the records (e.g., an employee of a government agency who consults information on a form that was submitted to the agency, an individual who examines the picture on a postcard that she received). It is in relation to understanding and supporting primary value and primary users that ARM professionals can potentially learn the most from the PIM community.

The secondary value of records is derived from using the records for reasons different from those for which the records were created. The beneficiary of the secondary value of records—often called a secondary user—is "everyone else," that is, anyone who makes meaningful (direct or indirect) use of the records but was not associated with the activity that generated the records. Examples of secondary users include a genealogist looking for names in Civil War records, an epidemiologist identifying traces of illness diffusion by perusing diaries, and a citizen collecting evidence of housing discrimination by analyzing Sanborn fire insurance maps. It is in relation to understanding and supporting secondary value that the PIM community can potentially learn the most from ARM professionals.

Within the ARM literature, particularly in the U.S., the records housed in archival repositories have traditionally been seen as providing secondary value. Under this view, "primary values usually are of secondary importance" to an archivist,[70] based on the assumption that "records are preserved in an archival institution because they have value that will exist long after they cease to be of current use, and because their values will be for others than the current users."[71]

The distinction between primary and secondary use is a very helpful way to differentiate between certain broad categories of activity. However, it is important to note that primary vs. secondary use is a matter of numerous subtle differences in degree, rather than a rigid and absolute difference in kind. Information behaviors and the roles of individuals are complex, overlapping, and evolve over time. See table 2 for a representation of the relative emphases and contributions of related fields of research.

Ownership of Materials and Recordkeeping Goals

The boundary between home and work—and the associated boundaries between personal and work-related information spaces—has undergone dramatic transformations in much of the Western world over the past two

Table 2. Primary emphasis of disciplines related to handling of information artifacts.[72]

Value category	Type of engagement	Unit of analysis considered when defining stakeholder needs	
	Direct = Direct encounters or interactions (e.g., seeing, handling, saving) with information artifacts **Indirect =** Indirect relationships (e.g., responsible for, party to) with information artifacts	**Individual**	**Group**
Primary Value to those directly associated with activity documented by the material	Direct	• Personal information management	• Group information management • Computer-supported cooperative work
	Indirect	• Knowledge management	• Records management • Management of information systems
Secondary Value to those not directly associated with activity documented by the material	Direct	• Human-computer interaction • Information retrieval	• Archival administration • Group information retrieval
	Indirect	• Electronic discovery • Digital forensics	• Information policy

centuries.[73] At the beginning of the nineteenth century in the United States, for example, work and home life were usually closely connected. Farmers and business proprietors usually made their living very close to, or directly out of, their homes. The pace and schedules of family life and work life were also closely connected.

Around the middle of the nineteenth century, society became much more urbanized and industrialized, resulting in the widespread creation of "special-purpose organizations"[74] and much more of a distinction between home (the place of family and privacy) and work (the place where one "clocked in" for distinct periods of productive activity). The structures of large hierarchical organizations began to take on a power and life of their own.[75] In both the private and public sectors, the associated trends of bureaucratic growth, managerial professionalization, and systematization of operations continued throughout the late nineteenth century and into the twentieth century. After the First World War and Russian Revolution, many state structures became "involved in regulating affairs of human beings which at one time were considered matters of entirely personal concern," which resulted in "more records to administer, preserve, and prepare."[76] Although a substantial portion of the population continued to work for small organizations,[77] the modern notions of work as a place unto itself influenced everyone.

At the same time that the bureaucracies associated with work were thriving, home life began to change, due in part to the diffusion of numerous information and communications technologies into the home.[78] Early adoption of computers in the home tended to be for a combination of "education, play, work, and basic word processing."[79] Studies of home computing in the 1990s found that computers were usually located in communal spaces rather than private spaces, reinforcing their presence within home and family life.[80] Although definitions and reported statistics vary, it is clear that many people now engage in various forms of "telework," which pushes work out of the office and into other places.[81] Conversely, "workplaces have become more 'porous' and permeable—integrating more influences from the outside world—as individuals engage in such online diversions as trading stocks or viewing images of their children in day-care centers."[82]

In addition to literally "bringing work home" to be completed outside the office, research on the relationships between work and home life has identified two phenomena: "*spillover*, whereby a stress in either the work or home domain results in stress in the other domain for the same individual," and "*crossover*, whereby a stress experienced by an individual's spouse in the workplace leads to stress being experienced by the individual at home."[83] The availability of networked information technology provides many new avenues for both spillover and crossover (e.g., using a work email account to tell a colleague about concerns related to a sick family member, expressing job frustrations through a personal social networking account, sending a text message to a spouse to convey frustration from a meeting while at work). Of course, not all boundary crossing is about stress or concerns; spillover and crossover can also transfer positive emotions and dispositions.[84] In terms of information practices, the current technological landscape also allows one to transfer messages of celebration, fulfillment, and levity across work-home boundaries (e.g., using a work email account to send out a birth announcement, bragging about a successful job interview through a personal social networking account, sending a text message to a spouse to celebrate an impending promotion).

More than fifty years ago, Lester Cappon observed:

> . . . often the line between institutional archives and personal papers cannot be easily or sensibly drawn. The problem would not arise if officials of both governmental and private agencies, in their original filing procedure, segregated their business and personal correspondence... But the daily effort to maintain such segregation entails discipline rarely self-imposed and hardly enforceable by administrative order; in fact, few officials are even aware of the problem.[85]

Frank Burke also points out various cases in which records have characteristics of both personal and organizational records, concluding that "the line between official records and personal papers is sometimes very thin, and open to interpretation." He describes manuscript curators' collecting of records from prominent individuals, which are "personal only in that they have been segregated from the corporate mass and portray only (or mainly) the role of the individual" but primarily document "activities of an individual within that office."[86]

The current interpenetration between work time/space and personal time/space has created a great deal of anxiety for many professionals who are responsible for the management of organizational records, as illustrated in the following passage from a leading records management publication:

> The intersection of an employee's personal and work life and responsibilities has long been a difficult subject area for both employee and employer. This tension has increased over time as longer work hours and greater demands on employees make for an ever-longer workday. Often, it also means that employees work at home in the evening and on weekends. In many cases, this work is done on a computer provided by the employer for the purposes of facilitating the employee's at-home work. In many other cases, however, the work is performed on a computer owned by the employee or by someone else living in the employee's residence. If the employee is doing substantive work on the employer's behalf from such a computer, employee and employer may at some point find themselves in an adversarial position. The employer may expect or assume that it has some property right to at least some of the computer's contents, while the employee may assume that contents on a personally owned computer is [sic] his or hers in its entirety and that the employer has no right of access to it.[87]

Those with a strong interest in formal records management regimes and strict regulatory compliance are faced with information practices that are not easily controlled or compartmentalized. According to Jo Ann Oravec, "Managers who expect employees not to use the Internet for some amount of off-task activity severely misjudge the nature of workplace life—which is solidly infused in online interaction."[88]

To complicate the data ownership and management picture even further, many individuals make use of commercial services that host their personal information online. While "69 percent of online Americans use webmail services, store data online, or use software programs such as word processing applications whose functionality is located on the Web," they "show high levels of concern when presented with scenarios in which companies might use their data for purposes users may or may not fully understand ahead of time."[89] This is further evidence of the discontinuity between (1) many individuals' apparent presumption that the management of the information they create is completely a matter of their own discretion, and (2) a complex information landscape in which the information is often concurrently subject to numerous competing interests and mandates.

The orientation of the PIM and ARM literature in response to the current, messy information landscape is quite different, but also potentially complementary. In general, the PIM literature treats both the information being managed and information management goals as belonging to the individual. The primary focus of PIM is making life easier for the user, following the user's lead on what is important to retain, and how it can most easily be navigated. While others have a say in one's information practices during childhood, possibly under care in old age and after death, "one's adult life will involve personal control and use."[90] Recent research related to information needs that transcend the individual include collaborative information retrieval,[91] group information management (GIM),[92] and family information practices.[93]

By contrast, ARM is chiefly concerned with contributing to the stewardship and shaping of collective memory, which is an inherently shared endeavor.[94] Angelika Menne-Haritz argues that archivists are in the business of social "amnesia prevention" and "common remembrance," which requires not only storage but also "access to the raw material for memory."[95]

One major focus of ARM is organizational or corporate memory, which is advanced through the care of records as organizational assets. An associated assumption in the literature and practices associated with institutional archives is that records and their management belong to the organization that employs the individual and the information professionals (records managers and archivists) who are ultimately responsible for their care. By law and policy, most of the materials one creates at work belong to the organization. As a result, the professional literature of ARM has focused heavily on formal recordkeeping mandates and efforts to reflect institutional structures or functions, often failing to address the messy reality and incentive structures in which record creators actually operate.

Beyond the context of institutional records, ARM professionals are often concerned and charged with the stewardship of materials to support and participate in processes of societal or cultural memory formation.[96] Although the specific requirements for cultural memory are often not articulated in formal recordkeeping policies, the curation of society's documentary traces does aim to fulfill various "social mandates"[97] associated with widely held values, including "socio-cultural accountability."[98] Within the context of individual recordkeeping, Margaret Hedstrom points out: "People do not use photographs exclusively—or perhaps even primarily—as a way to capture or view the evidence of the past. Rather these visual images serve as triggers that evoke memories and challenge or reinforce assumptions about how things really were or really looked."[99]

A persistent issue in the PIM literature is *information fragmentation*[100] —the "stovepiping" of personal information into different systems. This fragmentation often leads to situations in which the information needed for a task is spread across many different systems using many different interfaces. Complete integration of one's personal information sources is an ongoing and elusive goal. However, efforts such as the Semantic Web,[101] the Semantic Desktop,[102] and the MIT Haystack project[103] are developing tools, infrastructure, ontologies, and metadata standards for integration and sharing of information across systems.

While many of the causes of information fragmentation are based on technological limitations and business models, often people purposely keep information separate, in order to create boundaries between different aspects of their lives. And a very common assumption in the ARM literature is that materials with continuing record value should be purposely segregated from other materials, in order to ensure evidential integrity and perpetual access. Rather than insisting on consistency across all data sources, often "heterogeneity needs to be resolved at the step where the data provider exposes its data to its counterparts."[104] Completely seamless access and management of all one's personal information is neither probable nor desirable.

Role and Importance of Contextual Information

Both the PIM and ARM literature emphasize the importance of contextual information. Within information systems, contextual information associated with a given "target digital object" is conveyed through metadata or other objects that are associated with that object.[105]

Much of the early PIM interest in contextual information was based on the desire to better support finding (primarily refinding) documents through "cue enrichment,"[106] based on the insight that "we remember far more about documents than can be used in [traditional] retrieval procedures"[107] so it can be beneficial to cultivate and exploit "contextual cues" as additional access points.[108] Because so many of the PIM scenarios focus on information that an individual has personally encountered before, context is often "remembered context."[109]

The PIM literature has further elaborated and investigated several ways in which contextual information can help users refind and make sense of information. First, context is essential to a wayfinding or orienteering process of refinding. As users navigate through an information space, they look for contextual cues to guide them toward the information they seek. Barreau and Nardi describe an approach they observed called *location-based finding* in which users go to the location (e.g., folder) where they think the target information is located and then scan the items. If the item is not there, they then go to another location and repeat this process.[110] Contextual information such as other files and timestamps can play a large role in this process to help users recognize whether they are in the "right" location.

Contextual information can also help users with making sense of the information they find. For example, people often turn to other sources for contextual information about their PIM if one source is insufficient. Consider a scenario in which someone is trying to determine the most up-to-date version of a document he is working on with a coauthor. In addition to looking at timestamps in the file system, he may use additional contextual information stored in email exchanged with the coauthor.

Although the term *provenance* does not appear frequently in the PIM literature, there is a widespread recognition that traces of user activity are essential to PIM. For example, the date, time, user account, and application used to create or view a file can often be just as important (or more important) than the contents of the file itself. If objects can be supplemented with documentation of the "events that comprise their use," those traces can be re-presented to users as part of their future use of the objects.[111]

Contextual information has also been used by PIM systems such as Margin Notes,[112] the Remembrance Agent,[113] CyberDesk,[114] and Haystack[115] to help make connections between documents, email messages, web pages and other artifacts on which a user is working. These systems use information about the current state of the user's workspace such as open documents, applications, and web pages to make inferences and suggestions that may aid the user in her current or future tasks.

In archives, contextual information often helps someone from a completely different context (called a *secondary user* in the archives literature) to make meaningful use of the materials. "In order to understand any object and its significance, the person experiencing it must have a context to set it in."[116] Contextual information can help to reflect "the organizational, functional, and operational circumstances surrounding materials' creation, receipt, storage, or use," as well as "relationship to other materials."[117] Common tools for providing contextual information in ARM are file plans, accession records, and finding aids. Michelle Light and Tom Hyry argue for the incorporation of further contextual information throughout the lifecycle of the finding aid.[118] There has also been important work over the past several years toward formalizing the structures used to encode contextual information associated with archival collections.[119] As in PIM, a major question in ARM is how much and what types of contextual information to capture and retain. Wendy Duff and Verne Harris point out: "Context, in principle, is infinite. The describer selects certain layers for inclusion, and decides which of those to foreground."[120]

Predominant Attitudes toward Selection

Within the context of selection and appraisal, there are two factors that make digital objects very different from analog artifacts. First, every instantiation (i.e., access or use) of a digital object is based on the generation of one or more copies of its content. Copies are loaded into the computer's working memory in order to be processed; written to caches and numerous other "temporary" storage locations; transferred over networks; and, sometimes, consciously saved as files by users. The second factor is that digital storage is relatively cheap, and its price per byte continues to fall.

Added to the above factors is the difficulty of predicting the need or desire to use any given information artifact (analog or digital) in the future. One can never know with certainty whether, when, or how someone might benefit from using a particular item. Precise determination of primary use value is notoriously difficult, and precise determination of secondary use value is simply impossible. After all, "who can project himself into the future and foresee its requirements?"[121] Archivists have long recognized that "practically any paper may conceivably be of some use, to somebody, at some time."[122] Efforts to determine all possible future use scenarios can easily lead into the "realm of the imponderable," because "any scholar with a little intellectual ingenuity can find plausible justification for keeping almost every record that was ever produced."[123] Stated more bluntly, "if we are to let our visions of possible use prevail, we may as well give up the idea of selection entirely. Anything is possible."[124]

This all leads to a natural question: Why not keep everything? Given the characteristics of digital information, it is at least technically feasible to capture and store copies of almost everything that a user has created, received or otherwise encountered through her use of computers.[125] Taken even further, one could potentially even capture and store various traces left behind by "everyday objects [that] have been computationally enhanced and networked" (e.g., thermometers, navigational devices, heart rate monitors).[126]

The biggest differences between the PIM and ARM literature may be related to how they answer the "why not keep everything?" question. The PIM literature aims to better understand and support individual behavior; while the ARM literature aims to inform the practices of professionals who have been charged with determining how to appropriately allocate institutional resources—often in the form of taxpayer money—over time. PIM primarily addresses selection as a matter of individual behavior, while ARM primarily addresses selection as a matter of responsible, institutional investment of limited resources. One of the reasons that PIM and ARM provide different answers is that they are actually responding to a different question. For PIM, the practical elaboration of the question is: "Why should I not keep everything that I encounter?" For ARM, the practical elaboration of the question is: "Why should our archives not collect everything that we possibly can from the personal holdings of every individual whose life might fit within our institution's collecting mission?" For an individual to keep everything, she needs software and storage to capture the bits that pass through her own personal space or computer environment. For an archives to keep everything, it first has to get copies of everything (logistically impossible) and then commit to providing meaningful and appropriately controlled access to it over time (professionally unrealistic and an irresponsible allocation of scarce resources).

The PIM research community has investigated both how people address selection criteria and how technology can support different selection strategies for saving personal information. Keeping activities can be broadly considered in terms of either saving as much as possible or selectively saving items that are perceived to be of value or importance in the future. Jones characterizes selection in terms of "the keeping decision" and describes it as central to PIM and a "fundamentally difficult thing to do." Jones also describes the tradeoffs that must be weighed when deciding to keep something: the storage space, having too much information, and not having the right information.[127] Options may include not saving the information because it is not deemed to be relevant enough or because it can be easily re-obtained, or saving the information because it is something that is personally important.[128]

Proponents of "keep everything" approaches point out that disk storage is cheap and argue that users should keep as many traces of activity as possible because it is difficult to predict what will be useful later—either in terms of the value of the items themselves, or in terms of the context that may help a user refind a related item. In order for "keeping everything" to be a reasonable approach for individuals, they must have and be able to use tools that can search and filter the information for refinding and reuse. Proponents of more selective saving strategies argue that saving too much information adds too much "noise" that makes it more difficult to relocate and be reminded of things that are of interest. In practice, people are likely to choose a point along a continuum of these strategies that fits their individual needs. Combining aspects of both, they may save many items related to certain topics or activities, and few related to others. They may also choose to manually organize some types of information but leave other information less structured, depending on the perceived value of the information and their anticipated needs to reaccess or reuse it.

Recall that reuse is one of the main PIM tasks. For this reason, the ability of the individual to reproduce and reuse the material tends to be a major selection criterion assumed (implicitly or explicitly) by the PIM literature. Note that refinding is not a sufficient condition for reuse. The individual must also have the technical components (hardware and software) and appropriate "knowledge base"[129] to make meaningful use of the item. For example, if an individual refinds a file on his computer, but it is encoded in a format that he cannot open or render with any of the software at his disposal, he will not be able to reuse the contents of the file. Supporting this bridge between refinding and reuse—usually called digital preservation—is an essential area of ARM.

In contrast to the PIM literature, the ARM literature frequently identifies retention scheduling and appraisal as being among the most important functions of recordkeeping. Authors frequently cite appraisal as the archivist's most important responsibility.[130] Terry Cook goes so far as to claim that "appraisal is the *only* archival function."[131] The selection and appraisal of archival materials has a long tradition. It has received the most emphasis during periods of information explosion related to the dramatic growth of social structures. Many European countries had established practices for reducing record volume as early as the eighteenth century,[132] and England had legal provisions for "sortation and destruction" by the middle of the nineteenth century.[133] By the early twentieth century, the very influential British archivist Hilary Jenkinson stated that "the question of the bulk of present day Archives is a new and serious matter."[134]

Within the U.S. context, ARM became professionalized at the same time that the country was undergoing a massive increase in document production that strongly influenced the orientation and priorities of the professional literature. The 1930s–1950s saw dramatic growth in both the size and complexity of the public sector. The U.S. National Archives and the Society of American Archivists were both established in the 1930s. Consistent with earlier advances in Europe,[135] both the SAA and the U.S. archival literature were strongly influenced by government archivists—who were facing this information explosion—for the next several decades.[136] In 1938, Charles M. Gates argued that "our efforts to discover more [records to collect and preserve] must now be reconciled with the patent impossibility of preserving for future generations the staggering mass of routine records produced each year,"[137] and in 1940, Helen Chatfield declared that "the ever present space problem which is such a bugbear to administrative offices will always be with us."[138] It is worth noting that the archival profession in Australia emerged under many similar pressures during the middle of the twentieth century.[139]

The response of archivists was to begin taking selection decisions more seriously, and also to more actively intervene into the operations of government agencies' recordkeeping practices. The latter included the formation of a distinct area of professional activity in the U.S. called *records management,*[140] which provides guidance and systems for users to identify:

- The majority of materials that can be destroyed after a given period.

- A smaller set of materials that warrant transfer to a temporary (but longer term) records center.

- An even smaller set of materials that should be transferred to an archives for long-term preservation.

According to an early discussion of the new field of records management:

> From the remote centuries, historians have been wont to treasure every scrap of written record, on wood, stone, silk, papyrus, or skin. In the proliferous present, all this is changed. It is like the shift from an economics of scarcity to an economics of plenty. New conditions prevail and new principles come into play. More records are now created, both in government and elsewhere, than can imaginably be saved or than would ever be used if they were saved. Many must be plowed under, and the problem becomes one of intelligent selection.[141]

At the same time, G. Philip Bauer of the U.S. National Archives was arguing that there were limits to the public's ability to fund preservation of records, and government archivists should engage in cost-benefit determinations of record value.[142] Several decades of experience with the records of organizations have reinforced the early statement, "Masses of usable data should not be retained for indefinite periods of time on the mere chance that they may some day be employed."[143] The most influential voice in the U.S. appraisal literature was Theodore R. Schellenberg, who also worked in this period of public records explosion, and concluded, "The costs of maintaining them are beyond the means of the most opulent nation. Nor are scholars served by maintaining all of them." He argued that public "funds must be applied judiciously for the preservation of the most important of these resources."[144]

According to ARM criteria, most materials do not have long-term value, and eliminating records without long-term value is a positive contribution to social and organizational memory. There are also numerous legal and ethical issues associated with confidentiality, intellectual property, and respecting the interests of individuals represented by the records, which become increasingly complex with the volume and diversity of materials. In its discussions of potentially saving everything, the PIM literature has also raised issues of privacy, legal accountability, and information overload.[145] However, the PIM literature has generally not associated these issues with formal electronic records retention; it has not addressed the institutional desirability and value of disposing of information that is no longer needed.

In additional to the above logistical reasons to select materials for retention, there is also a reason that is associated with interpretation and sensemaking. If the creator has disposed of materials, that also provides important information about the materials that were retained: they were presumably important enough to retain for some reason. By analogy, a visitor to an art museum would probably not be very happy with the curatorial decision to glue all of the artists' discarded materials back onto the sculptures. Those who encounter the sculptures do not want to see an aggregation of all the raw material that the artist happened to encounter or touch in the course of creating the piece; they want to see what the artist decided to keep, because this is what conveys the meaning of the piece and the expression of the artist.

Another difference between the PIM and ARM literature is the criteria for identifying materials that have continuing value. Within PIM, much of the focus is on personal use patterns that play an essential role in keeping criteria. Within the ARM literature, on the other hand, authors present a much more diverse set of criteria for the appraisal of records. Evidence of use is only one—and often a quite controversial—proposed factor.[146] Other factors include holding public officials accountable; ensuring compliance with law and policy; fulfilling business objectives; advancing efficiency of operations; promoting the rights of citizens; managing organizational risks; contributing to identity formation; documenting important societal functions; protecting unique or at-risk materials; giving voice to disempowered populations; and capturing a "mirror of society." More than twenty-five years ago, Gerald Ham warned that focusing solely on known use patterns—at the exclusion of other factors—places the archivist in the role of simply being a "weathervane" rather than a responsible trustee of social memory.[147]

Purposeful Organization of Information

Meta-level organizational tasks include activities such as filing items into folders with titles (thus adding metadata), piling items into a related group but not giving it a title, piling unrelated items into a group, and tagging items with some pieces of metadata. Many of these activities require cognitive effort and time on the part of users,[148] and it may not always be clear if the effort will be helpful. In the context of paper documents in an office environment, Malone observed:

> (T)hese results...give some support to the claim that people with messy offices do, indeed, have more problems finding information. . . . There is no indication in these results, however, that effort spent keeping an office neat is always worth it.[149]

Studies of PIM organizational behaviors often include participant responses indicating feelings that they could be better organized.[150] Significant "maintenance" activities such as purging may be undertaken only periodically, at critical events such as upgrading to a new computer or email system,[151] or at the end of a project.[152]

In a study of email use, Steve Whittaker and Candace Sidner observed strategies for organization. "No filers" typically had large inboxes and used full-text search to help them locate information. "Frequent filers" studiously filed messages into folders and had relatively small inboxes. "Spring cleaners" used "intermittent clean-ups" every few months in which they made use of folders.[153] Richard Boardman and M. Angela Sasse modified these classifications based on their data and also looked at organizational practices across email, web bookmarks, and file system folder structures. They observed that users often have different organizational strategies for different types of materials (e.g., email, web, files) and that the organizational behaviors of an individual are often difficult to characterize using broad categories such as "messy or tidy, filer or no-filer." They concluded that the perceived value of the information and the style of retrieval are factors that influence how people choose to organize information. For example, users were more likely to organize files when they could see the benefits of the organization in retrieving a file.[154]

PIM and electronic recordkeeping activities both occur on a daily basis, often as secondary tasks to some primary goal. For example, a person looking for information about houses to rent for a summer vacation has a primary goal—to find a good house—but as the person finds promising options, she must engage in some PIM activities. Likewise, someone filing tax returns is likely driven by the goals of complying with the law, fulfilling his responsibilities as a citizen, and possibly getting money back from the government. Along the way, he must create, compile, manage, and retain many records. Often this means that the level of effort that users are willing to invest in PIM and recordkeeping activities may be low.

Hilary Jenkinson—who had a significant impact on both British and American ARM thinking—argued for the importance of the "organic" nature of archives. One of the values of archival records, according to Jenkinson, is that they "were not drawn up in the interest or for the information of Posterity."[155] In other words, one could infer from Jenkinson that it is good that individuals do not focus too heavily on their meta-level PIM activities; such a fixation could result in overly reflexive practices, such as purposely shaping one's personal information collections in order to convey a certain story about one's self to future users. Jenkinson's confidence in the veracity of records was probably overstated at the time, and it certainly does not fully reflect the contemporary environment, in which individuals are often aware that they are creating items "for the record." However, the fact that records were created to serve a particular purpose does increase the likelihood that they will accurately reflect the activities that they document. In most cases, individuals do not have an incentive to falsify records upon which they themselves rely for getting by in their lives.

Classifying information is a cognitively difficult task for most people and presents challenges for information management.[156] Geoffrey Bowker and Susan Leigh Star elaborate the characteristics of an ideal classification system and then explain how and why the lived practice of classification rarely conforms to the ideal.[157] Mark Lansdale describes two problems that can occur with category names. The first is that "it is impossible to generate category names which will be used unambiguously," so "there is an inherent likelihood that the categories used to retrieve information will not correspond to those actually used in filing."[158] ARM has developed and adapted various tools for addressing this problem, including file plans, controlled vocabularies, and naming conventions. In PIM, users may create their own names, but this does not guarantee that they will remember their own classification schemes. The second problem described by Lansdale is that "information in the real world falls into several overlapping and fuzzy categories, which means that any categorisation of an item of information can only be relevant to certain aspects of it, even if it can be used accurately."[159] This complexity of information categorization, in which items often "belong" in multiple categories, makes it difficult to decide how the items should be filed or organized. Lansdale suggests that this may be a motivation for piling—by not filing the item, the person avoids miscategorizing it.

Users' folder hierarchies are typically slow to change,[160] implying that users may have formed habits and familiarity with their own folder structures. Studies have found that users often prefer location-based finding over keyword search, and familiarity with their folder structure may be a contributing factor.[161]

Classification is especially difficult in situations in which the information is new or unfamiliar and the information space is not well-understood. This may lead to incorrect or changing classification schemes, overly broad or overly specific categories, or users simply putting everything into one basket. Experience with the Coordinator,[162] a system based on speech act theory, demonstrated that users often do not want to explicitly label the nature or purpose of their various information artifacts. This could be at least partially attributable to the time and cognitive load involved in classification, but it could also be based on the desirability of fuzziness and ambiguity. Labeling each information object as a specific type of speech act (or from an ARM perspective, as belonging to a specific record series) can fix its meaning in ways that individuals do not find useful and may even find detrimental to their purposes.

A project at the National Archives of Canada developed and tested a prototype system to support electronic recordkeeping within one of the divisions of the archives through "automated workflow technology which permits the automation of the key business processes of the Division." One of the conclusions of the project reflects the challenges of building systems based on fixed categories:

> In an office where people are carrying out multiple tasks at the same time, where the tasks are often ad hoc rather than structured and where the absence of rules can often facilitate rather than hinder the work getting done, the introduction of workflow technologies and associated record keeping needs to be addressed very carefully.[163]

Filing a single item in multiple locations can help alleviate some of the cognitive difficulties of categorization. Some systems allow items to be filed or indexed in multiple ways. For example, several popular email applications allow an email message to be labeled with multiple tags, rather than being placed in one (and only one) folder. Queries can be issued to show all messages with a particular tag, allowing tags to be used in a manner similar to folder names, except that a single message can have multiple tags (i.e., be in more than one group). The use of tagging in popular online environments promotes emergent, rather than preconceived, categories. Many computer operating systems also allow for multiple placement of files through the use of aliases, links, and shortcuts, but the creation of these additional file associations is fairly burdensome for most users to adopt, except for particular cases such as creating shortcuts to applications on the desktop. Current consumer operating systems attempt to facilitate PIM activities by creating file associations that provide multiple navigational paths to a given file (e.g., Favorites, Libraries, desktop shortcuts, and taskbar shortcuts in Windows 7).

Messiness of foldering and variability of an individual's classifications over time can be a barrier to PIM efficiency, but it can also provide a rich source of contextual information to be captured and exploited. Idiosyncratic and even inconsistent organizational practices can provide evidence for the archival value of retaining original order. A snapshot of a user's folders related to planning a wedding, for example, can reveal a great deal about how that person understood and approached the event at a given point in time.[164] Catherine Hobbs argues, "The wealth in the personal record has much to do with the ambiguity of its purpose and intention." An original order that changes over time provides a peek into "the essential moving target of human life being enacted."[165]

System Requirements Emphasized

In many cases, PIM tools are specifically designed to be "lightweight" and "out of the way," because PIM often is a secondary task to some other primary task (such as editing a document). However, in some cases, PIM is the primary task (for example, when collecting information about what new car to buy). Archivists and records managers have also recognized for a long time that recordkeeping tasks are usually not the primary focus of individuals, but are instead an "organic" and "natural byproduct" of the activities in which they engage. The design of a recordkeeping system should be unobtrusive, both to provide a low barrier to entry and to avoid unnecessary interference in the work being documented. However, most of the research and development related to archival information systems has focused on issues of interoperability, scalability, sustainability, and data integrity, rather than ease of use or usability. One difference between short-term and long-term design situations is that computer performance issues can be paramount in the former but tend to be less important in the latter. For example, a desktop search utility that takes forty-five minutes to find a known item is not likely to be adopted. However, search speed is less of a concern for long-term digital curation for several reasons. First, the power and speed of computer systems is projected to increase over time. A task that is slow now because of limits to memory, processing power, or bandwidth could be much faster in the future. Second, long-term preservation often necessitates forgoing current optimization in order to better promote robustness and sustainability.[166] Finally, given their research goals, it is likely that the users of archival materials have more motivation to take on burdensome and time-consuming tasks than individuals who are managing their own materials. Of course, these are all relative differences, rather than absolute system goals. PIM is also concerned with issues of long-term access, and ARM must meet the needs of a demanding user base. However, relative differences are important to consider when designing systems to support personal archives, and they warrant further empirical testing.

Potential for Future Research

The PIM and ARM communities have a great deal to learn from each other. There is much to gain from further collaborative research on issues of common concern. What are some potential directions for future research?

Incentives for PIM and ARM

An issue that both PIM and ARM share, and one which holds great potential for future research collaboration, is the identification, crafting, and advocacy of appropriate incentives for good personal digital curation. For institutional records, formal mandates have often been seen as a major driver and rationale for electronic recordkeeping, but experiences from numerous contexts suggest that attending to the incentives of both individuals and policy makers is essential to effectively implementing changes in information behavior.[167] The need to align systems and requirements with individual norms and incentives is even more important when information is created and managed outside the bounds of formal organizations.

In PIM, there are a number of motivators for people saving and organizing information. Jones, Bruce, and Dumais identify several key functions that motivate and influence the methods that people use:

- The need for portability
- Having multiple ways to access the information
- Persistence (e.g., printing a web page in case it disappears)
- Preservation of the current state of the information (e.g., printing a web page in case it changes)
- Having up-to-date information
- Keeping context about the item (why is it important?)
- Reminding
- Ease of integration with existing systems
- Ability to easily share the information
- Ease of maintenance

It would be very useful to investigate which of the above (or other) motivators are most salient in particular personal recordkeeping situations. If we have a better understanding of the incentives for potential practices, then there is a much better chance of supporting those practices or potentially steering them in more useful directions.

Designing Systems that Are Attentive to Individual Needs and Behaviors

Although maintaining the "organic" quality of record creation has been one of the consistent mantras of archival literature, the research and development surrounding electronic records has often focused on relatively system-centered requirements and models (e.g., MoReq2, OAIS).[168] The requirements and models provide valuable foundations for developing the technical and organizational "back end" for recordkeeping, but they do not, in themselves, address the implementation of "front ends" for individuals that will be useful or used. Two aspects of electronic records management software that could be repurposed for personal recordkeeping are:

- Declaration of certain information items as being worthy of retention as records (i.e., flagging them as being different from other, possibly more ephemeral, information within one's PSI).

- Associating a designated retention period and disposition action with an item or set of items (i.e., background processes that determine how long something will be kept based on metadata assigned by the user or the system).

GrayArea is a prototype tool that contains notions of both these concepts. It allows users to "demote unimportant files" in a folder to distinguish them as being different from other, more important items.[169]

The PIM research community has designed a variety of tools and features that are designed to support the everyday practices of individuals. For example, Stuff I've Seen[170] and Phlat[171] support organization, querying, and exploration of PIM across a variety of information types (e.g., email, web, office documents). The goals of personal recordkeeping over time could benefit from tools with similar interfaces and capabilities. Similarly, there may be tools in use in PERK settings that have features that would benefit PIM. One of the fundamental design challenges of both PIM and personal electronic recordkeeping is to support both curation and use of digital materials in ways that do not become heavy-handed or overly burdensome to users.

Potential PIM Value of Archival Description Structures

Recall that we have characterized the PIM literature in terms of two general approaches: teleporting and orienteering. One potentially fruitful area of future inquiry is the extent to which tools, principles, and practices from archival description can help to address the orienteering approach to PIM. Promising areas of future research include:

- Applying the concept from the International Standard for Archival Description ISAD(G) of describing materials at the level of aggregation that is deemed most important in the particular case.

- Creation of administrative or biographical histories.
- Describing functions differently from how one describes records.[172]

Individual-Scale Digital Preservation

As we discussed earlier, refinding an item is not a sufficient condition for reusing it. Various forms of software, hardware, and metadata must also be in place in order to access, render, and meaningfully use an item's content. The literature on digital preservation is now several decades old and provides numerous models and lessons. However, most of the digital preservation literature focuses on repositories of collections, which are managed by institutions that are professionally committed to long-term care of the materials. Current digital preservation research tends to focus on workflows, procedures, and tools to be applied within repositories. Which of the technical strategies and tools from the digital preservation research community could be used effectively by individuals to provide long-term care for their own materials? The HOPPLA project is attempting to address this question,[173] and there is great potential for further investigation of individual-scale digital preservation.

Meta-Level Research Questions

An important question to raise in both PIM and ARM is whether and to what extent previous research findings still hold now and are likely to hold true in the future. For example, many studies examined email behavior patterns. Are findings from the 1990s or early 2000s still relevant today? Much of the electronic records literature assumes a fairly distinct separation between institutional recordkeeping systems and what the PIM literature calls one's *PSI*. Given changes to technology and personal behaviors over the past decade, do we need to fundamentally reconceive that boundary? Another important meta-level question is where to focus research and development efforts along the spectrum between localized considerations of individuals and shared considerations of larger social units (e.g., organization, enterprise, nation).

Fonds and personal information collections are both very useful abstract entities precisely because they help information professionals and researchers to apply a layer of conceptual order to a messy and distributed body of materials that can be very difficult to unify or centrally control. Michael Franklin, Alon Halevy, and David Maier introduced the concept of a "dataspace" for a collection of information that is related to someone but for which it is not possible to assure the degree of "administrative proximity" (common and coordinated control) or semantic interoperability (sharing the same schema) that one could have with a single, centralized database.[174] iMeMex is an experimental "personal dataspace management system," which uses layers of abstraction to reduce dependence on specific physical storage, network location, data model, and format.[175]

The dataspace concept has important implications for personal electronic recordkeeping. Regardless of whether the primary custodian of the records is an individual or an archival repository, it will be important to design and accept systems that can provide partial integration of diverse information sources and varying degrees of administrative and intellectual control. Archivists have learned that a single, union catalog of all archival materials that fully complies with strict standards for data syntax, structure, content, and data values is not feasible. Instead, archivists have adopted a diversity of descriptive tools—specialized databases, finding aids, catalog records, indexes, name lists—that have never been fully integrated and probably never will be. The developers of the Open Archives Initiative Protocol for Metadata Harvesting (OAI-PMH) recognized that, even among repositories of very well-described collections, it is necessary to "dumb down" their metadata in order to share it across institutional boundaries, because of the diversity of ways in which different collections and types of materials are described.[176]

The role of information artifacts within the lives of individuals usually falls somewhere in between the prototypical scenarios that define the PIM and ARM literatures. Human behavior involves a complex and ever-changing set of overlapping and semipermeable boundaries. If I take a picture at a party, and you appear in that picture, you are likely to feel that you have some stake in how that picture is shared, used, and interpreted. If you send an email message to a loved one from work, you are likely to feel that you have some stake in how that message is managed, even if it is officially an asset of the organization that employs you, which is formally allowed to determine what will happen to the message. Individuals should and do have a strong say in the management of their personal information, but the scope of *personal* is neither rigid nor absolute. Because they are social beings interacting in a social world, humans are impacted by—and have a legitimate interest in— information that other humans create, receive, manage, retain, and delete. There is great potential for research that is attentive to the complex set of factors that PIM and ARM can collectively bring to these questions.

Notes

1 Richard Pearce-Moses, *A Glossary of Archival and Records Terminology,* Archival Fundamentals Series II (Chicago: Society of American Archivists, 2005), 326–27.

2 Maynard Brichford, "The Provenance of Provenance in Germanic Areas," *Provenance* 7, no. 2 (1989): 54–70; Shelley Sweeney, "The Ambiguous Origins of the Archival Principle of 'Provenance,'" *Libraries and the Cultural Record* 43, no. 2 (2008): 193–213.

3 Nancy Bartlett, "Respect Des Fonds: The Origins of the Modern Archival Principle of Provenance," *Primary Sources and Original Works* 1, no. 1/2 (1991): 107–15.

4 Tom Nesmith, "Still Fuzzy, but More Accurate: Some Thoughts on the 'Ghosts' of Archival Theory," *Archivaria* 47 (1999): 146.

5 *Oxford English Dictionary,* Draft Revision (June 2008), s.v. "provenance."

6 Oliver W. Holmes, "Archival Arrangement—Five Different Operations at Five Different Levels," *American Archivist* 27, no. 1 (1964): 26.

7 Peter J. Scott, "The Record Group Concept: A Case for Abandonment," *American Archivist* 29, no. 4 (1966): 493–504; David Bearman and Richard H. Lytle, "The Power of the Principle of Provenance," *Archivaria* 21 (1985): 14–27; Helen Willa Samuels, "Who Controls the Past: Documentation Strategies Used to Select What Is Preserved," *American Archivist* 49 (1986): 109–24.

8 *Oxford English Dictionary*, s.v. "provenance."

9 Bearman and Lytle, "Power of the Principle of Provenance"; Catherine Robinson, "Records Control and Disposal Using Functional Analysis," *Archives and Manuscripts* 25, no. 2 (1997): 288–303.

10 Chris Hurley, "Problems with Provenance," *Archives and Manuscripts* 23, no. 2 (1995): 256–57.

11 Harold Naugler, *The Archival Appraisal of Machine-Readable Records: A RAMP Study with Guidelines* (Paris: General Information Programme and UNISIST United Nations Educational Scientific and Cultural Organization, 1984), 21.

12 Peter Buneman, Sanjeev Khanna, and Wang-Chiew Tan, "Why and Where: A Characterization of Data Provenance," in *Database Theory - ICDT 2001: 8th International Conference, London, UK, January 2001, Proceedings*, ed. Jan van den Bussche and Victor Vianu (Berlin: Springer, 2001), 316–30.

13 Maria Guercio, "Archival Theory and the Principle of Provenance for Current Records: Their Impact on Arranging and Inventorying Electronic Records," in *The Principle of Provenance: Report from the First Stockholm Conference on Archival Theory and the Principle of Provenance, 2-3 September 1993*, ed. Kerstin Abukhanfusa and Jan Sydbeck (Stockholm: Swedish National Archives, 1994), 82.

14 Pearce-Moses, *Glossary of Archival and Records Terminology,* 173.

15 Catherine Hobbs, "The Character of Personal Archives: Reflections on the Value of Records of Individuals," *Archivaria* 52 (2001): 127.

16 Terry Cook, "The Concept of Archival Fonds and the Post-Custodial Era: Theory, Problems and Solutions," *Archivaria* 35 (1993): 33.

17 Laura Millar, "The Death of the Fonds and the Resurrection of Provenance: Archival Context in Space and Time," *Archivaria* 53 (2002): 5.

18 Peter J. Scott and Gail Finlay, "Archives and Administrative Change: Some Methods and Approaches (Part I)," *Archives and Manuscripts* 7, no. 3 (1978): 115–27; Bob Krawcyzk, "Cross Reference Heaven: The Abandonment of the Fonds as the Primary Level of Arrangement for Ontario Government Records," *Archivaria* 48 (1999): 131–53.

19 Michel Duchein, "Theoretical Principles and Practical Problems of *Respect Des Fonds* in Archival Science," *Archivaria* 16 (1983): 81.

[20] Michel Duchein, "The History of European Archives and the Development of the Archival Profession in Europe," *American Archivist* 55, no. 1 (1992): 20.

[21] Ernst Posner, "Max Lehmann and the Genesis of the Principle of Provenance," in *Archives and the Public Interest: Selected Essays by Ernst Posner,* ed. Ken Munden (Chicago: Society of American Archivists, 2006), 36–44.

[22] Samuel Muller, Johan Adriaan Feith, and R. Fruin, *Manual for the Arrangement and Description of Archives: Drawn up by Direction of the Netherlands Association of Archivists,* trans. Arthur H. Leavitt (Chicago: Society of American Archivists, 2003).

[23] Pearce-Moses, *Glossary of Archival and Records Terminology,* 280–81.

[24] Hugh A. Taylor, "The Collective Memory: Archives and Libraries as Heritage," *Archivaria* 15 (1982–83): 122.

[25] Pearce-Moses, *Glossary of Archival and Records Terminology,* 281.

[26] Katharine Gavrel, "Conceptual Problems Posed by Electronic Records: A RAMP Study" (Paris: United Nations Educational, Scientific and Cultural Organization, 1990); Margaret Hedstrom, "Understanding Electronic Incunabula: A Framework for Research on Electronic Records," *American Archivist* 54 (1991): 334–54.

[27] Peter Horsman, "Dirty Hands: A New Perspective on the Original Order," *Archives and Manuscripts* 27, no. 1 (1999): 42–53.

[28] Jim Suderman, "Defining Electronic Series: A Study," *Archivaria* 53 (2002): 31–46; Victor Kaptelinin and Mary Czerwinski, "Introduction: The Desktop Metaphor and New Uses of Technology," in *Beyond the Desktop Metaphor: Designing Integrated Digital Work Environments,* ed. Victor Kaptelinin and Mary P. Czerwinski (Cambridge, MA: MIT Press, 2007), 1–12; Philip C. Bantin, *Understanding Data and Information Systems for Recordkeeping* (New York: Neal-Schuman, 2008); Indratmo and Julita Vassileva, "A Review of Organizational Structures of Personal Information Management," *Journal of Digital Information* 9, no. 26 (2008), http://journals.tdl.org/jodi/article/view/251/200.

[29] Peter Horsman, "The Last Dance of the Phoenix, or the De-Discovery of the Archival Fonds," *Archivaria* 54 (2002): 19.

[30] Pearce-Moses, *Glossary of Archival and Records Terminology,* 67.

[31] Hilary Jenkinson, *A Manual of Archive Administration: Including the Problems of War Archives and Archive Making* (Oxford: Clarendon Press, 1922), 11.

[32] Nesmith, "Still Fuzzy, but More Accurate," 141.

[33] Michael A. Caloyannides, "Digital 'Evidence' Is Often Evidence of Nothing," in *Digital Crime and Forensic Science in Cyberspace,* ed. Panagiotis Kanellis (Hershey, PA: Idea Group, 2006), 334–39; Brian D. Carrier, "A Hypothesis-Based Approach to Digital Forensic Investigations" (PhD dissertation, Purdue University, 2006).

[34] William Jones and Jaime Teevan, "Introduction," in *Personal Information Management,* ed. William P. Jones and Jaime Teevan (Seattle: University of Washington Press, 2007), 3.

[35] Thomas W. Malone, "How Do People Organize Their Desks? Implications for the Design of Office Information Systems," *ACM Transactions on Information Systems* 1, no. 1 (1983): 99–112; M. Lansdale, "The Psychology of Personal Information Management," *Applied Ergonomics* 19, no. 1 (1988): 55–66; Deborah Barreau and Bonnie A. Nardi, "Finding and Reminding: File Organization from the Desktop," *SIGCHI Bulletin* 27, no. 3 (1995): 39–43; and Steve Whittaker and Candace Sidner, "Email Overload: Exploring Personal Information Management of Email," in *Human Factors in Computing Systems: Common Ground: CHI 96 Conference Proceedings,* ed. Michael J. Tauber (New York: Association for Computing Machinery, 1996), 276–83.

[36] http://kftf.ischool.washington.edu; and see William Jones, Harry Bruce, and Susan Dumais, "Keeping Found Things Found on the Web," in *Proceedings of the 2001 ACM CIKM: Tenth International Conference on Information and Knowledge Management: November 5-10, 2001,*

Atlanta, Georgia, USA, ed. Henrique Paques, Ling Liu, and David A. Grossman (New York: Association for Computing Machinery, 2001), 119–26.

37 http://www.pimworkshop.org.

38 Richard Boardman and M. Angela Sasse, "'Stuff Goes into the Computer and Doesn't Come out': A Cross-Tool Study of Personal Information Management," in *CHI 2004: Connect: Conference Proceedings: April 24-29, Vienna, Austria: Conference on Human Factors in Computing Systems,* ed. Elizabeth Dykstra-Erickson and Manfred Tscheligi (New York: Association for Computing Machinery, 2004), 583–90.

39 Jaime Teevan, Christine Alvarado, Mark S. Ackerman, and David R. Karger, "The Perfect Search Engine Is Not Enough: A Study of Orienteering Behavior in Directed Search," in *CHI 2004: Connect: Conference Proceedings,* 415–22; Robert G. Capra, III and Manuel Pérez-Quiñones, "Using Web Search Engines to Find and Refind Information," *IEEE Computer* 38, no. 10 (2005): 36–42.

40 Wanda Pratt, Kenton Unruh, Andrea Civan, and Meredith M. Skeels, "Personal Health Information Management," *Communications of the ACM* 49, no. 1 (2006): 51–55.

41 Michael Bernstein, Max Van Kleek, David Karger, and M. C. Schraefel, "Information Scraps: How and Why Information Eludes Our Personal Information Management Tools," *ACM Transactions on Information Systems* 26, no. 4 (2008): Article 24, 1–46.

42 Mary Czerwinski, Douglas W. Gage, Jim Gemmell, Catherine C. Marshall, Manuel A. Pérez-Quiñones, Meredith M. Skeels, and Tiziana Catarci, "Digital Memories in an Era of Ubiquitous Computing and Abundant Storage," *Communications of the ACM* 49, no. 1 (2006): 44–50; Kerry Rodden and Kenneth R. Wood, "How Do People Manage Their Digital Photographs?" in *CHI 2003: New Horizons: Conference Proceedings, Conference on Human Factors in Computing Systems,* ed. Panu Korhonen, Gilbert Cockton, Thomas Erickson, and Victoria Bellotti (New York: Association for Computing Machinery, 2003), 409–16; and Catherine C. Marshall and Sara Bly, "Saving and Using Encountered Information: Implications for Electronic Periodicals," in *CHI 2005: Technology, Safety, Community: Conference Proceedings: Conference on Human Factors in Computing Systems: Portland, Oregon, USA, April 2-7,* ed. Wendy Anne Kellogg, Shumin Zhai, Carolyn Gale and G.C. van der Veer (New York: Association for Computing Machinery, 2005), 111–20.

43 William Jones, "How People Keep and Organize Personal Information," in Jones and Teevan, *Personal Information Management,* 35–56.

44 Jones and Teevan, "Introduction," in *Personal Information Management.*

45 Richard Boardman, "Improving Tool Support for Personal Information Management" (PhD dissertation, Imperial College, London, 2004), 15–16.

46 Teevan et al., "Perfect Search Engine Is Not Enough"; Capra and Pérez-Quiñones, "Using Web Search Engines."

47 Jones, "How People Keep and Organize Personal Information," 39 (emphasis added).

48 Jones, Bruce, and Dumais, "Keeping Found Things Found on the Web."

49 William Jones, "Finders, Keepers? The Present and Future Perfect in Support of Personal Information Management," *First Monday* 9, no. 3 (2004), http://firstmonday.org/article/view/1123/1043.

50 Jones and Teevan, "Introduction," in *Personal Information Management.*

51 Lansdale, "The Psychology of Personal Information Management."

52 Jones and Teevan, "Introduction," in *Personal Information Management*; Clare-Marie Karat, John Karat, and Carolyn Brodie, "Management of Personal Information Disclosure: The Interdependence of Privacy, Security, and Trust," in Jones and Teevan, *Personal Information Management.*

53 Boardman and Sasse, "A Cross-Tool Study of Personal Information Management."

54 I. Cole, "Human Aspects of Office Filing: Implications for the Electronic Office," in *Proceedings of the Human Factors Society 26th Annual Meeting, Seattle, Washington, October 25-29, 1982,* ed. Richard E. Edwards and Philip Tolin (Santa Monica, CA: Human Factors Society, 1982), 60.

55 Ibid.

56 Barreau and Nardi, "Finding and Reminding"; Deborah Barreau, "The Persistence of Behavior and Form in the Organization of Personal Information," *Journal of the American Society for Information Science and Technology* 59, no. 2 (2007): 307-17; Bonnie Nardi and Deborah Barreau, "'Finding and Reminding' Revisited: Appropriate Metaphors for File Organization at the Desktop," *SIGCHI Bulletin* 29, no. 1 (1997): 76-78.

57 Catherine C. Marshall, Sara Bly, and Francoise Brun-Cottan, "The Long Term Fate of Our Digital Belongings: Toward a Service Model for Personal Archives," in *Archiving 2006: Final Program and Proceedings, May 23-26, 2006, Ottawa, Canada,* ed. Stephen Chapman and Scott A. Stovall (Springfield, VA: Society for Imaging Science and Technology, 2006), 25-30; Catherine C. Marshall, Frank McCown, and Michael L. Nelson, "Evaluating Personal Archiving Strategies for Internet-Based Information," in *Archiving 2007: Final Program and Proceedings, May 21-24, 2007, Arlington, Virginia* (Springfield, VA: Society for Imaging Science and Technology, 2007), 151-56; Catherine C. Marshall, "From Writing and Analysis to the Repository: Taking the Scholars' Perspective on Scholarly Archiving," in *JCDL 2008: Proceedings of the 8th ACM/IEEE Joint Conference on Digital Libraries: Pittsburgh, Pennsylvania, June 15-20, 2008* (New York: ACM Press, 2008), 251-60; Catherine C. Marshall, "Rethinking Personal Digital Archiving, Part 1: Four Challenges from the Field," *D-Lib Magazine* 14, no. 3/4 (2008), http://dx.doi.org/10.1045/march2008-marshall-pt1; Catherine C. Marshall, "Rethinking Personal Digital Archiving, Part 2: Implications for Services, Applications, and Institutions," *D-Lib Magazine* 14, no. 3/4 (2008), http://dx.doi.org/10.1045/march2008-marshall-pt2.

58 Brien Brothman, "The Past That Archives Keep: Memory, History, and the Preservation of Archival Records," *Archivaria* 51 (2001): 79.

59 See use of the term *continuing value* in the definition of *archives* in Frank Evans, Donald Harrison, and Edwin Thompson, "A Basic Glossary for Archivists, Manuscript Curators, and Records Managers," *American Archivist* 37 (1974): 415-33; Leonard Rapport's advocacy for the idea of continuing value, pointing out that this was the term used in the Federal Records Act of 1950, in "No Grandfather Clause: Reappraising Accessioned Records," *American Archivist* 44 (1981): 143-50; and Glenda Acland's claim that "continuing value replaces permanent value in the modern record environment" in "Archivist: Keeper, Undertaker or Auditor," *Archives and Manuscripts* 19 (1991): 9-15.

60 Naugler, *Archival Appraisal of Machine-Readable Records*; Charles M. Dollar, *Archival Theory and Information Technologies: The Impact of Information Technologies on Archival Principles and Methods,* vol. 1, Informatics and Documentation Series, ed. Oddo Bucci (Macerata, Italy: Università degli studi di Macerata, 1992).

61 Reference Model for an Open Archival Information System (OAIS), ISO 14721 (Washington, DC: Consultative Committee for Space Data Systems, 2002), 1-11.

62 Teevan et al., "Perfect Search Engine Is Not Enough."

63 Lucille Alice Suchman, *Plans and Situated Actions: The Problem of Human-Machine Communication* (Cambridge: Cambridge University Press, 1987).

64 Capra and Pérez-Quiñones, "Using Web Search Engines."

65 Malone, "How Do People Organize Their Desks?"; Barreau and Nardi, "Finding and Reminding."

66 Abigail J. Sellen and Richard Harper, *The Myth of the Paperless Office* (Cambridge, MA: MIT Press, 2002).

[67] Moira C. Norrie, "PIM Meets Web 2.0," in *Conceptual Modeling: ER 2008: 27th International Conference on Conceptual Modeling, Barcelona, Spain, October 20-24, 2008: Proceedings,* ed. Qing Li, Stefano Spaccapietra, Eric Yu, and Antoni Olivé (Berlin: Springer, 2008), 15–25.

[68] Raya Fidel, Harry Bruce, Annelise Mark Pejtersen, Susan Dumais, Jonathan Grudin, and Steven Poltrock, "Collaborative Information Retrieval (CIR)," in *The New Review of Information Behaviour Research: Studies of Information Seeking in Context* (Cambridge, UK: Taylor Graham, 2000), 235–47; Meredith Ringel Morris, "A Survey of Collaborative Web Search Practices," in *The 26th Annual CHI Conference on Human Factors in Computing Systems: Conference Proceedings,* ed. Margaret Burnett, Maria Francesca Costabile, Tiziana Catarci, Boris de Ruyter, Desney Tan, Mary Czerwinski, and Arnie Lund (New York: Association for Computing Machinery, 2008), 1657–60.

[69] Schellenberg's distinctions were specifically related to public records in government archives, but we are using the terms here in a more general sense that applies to all archival records, including those in personal collections. See T.R. Schellenberg, "The Appraisal of Modern Public Records," in *A Modern Archives Reader: Basic Readings on Archival Theory and Practice,* ed. Maygene F. Daniels and Timothy Walch (Washington, DC: National Archives and Records Service, 1984), 57–70; originally published in *Bulletins of the National Archives,* October, 1956.

[70] F. Gerald Ham, *Selecting and Appraising Archives and Manuscripts,* Archival Fundamentals Series (Chicago: Society of American Archivists, 1993).

[71] Schellenberg, "Appraisal of Modern Public Records," 58.

[72] For purposes of comparing primary emphasis, each discipline is placed in only one cell. This is not intended to define necessary and sufficient conditions for an issue falling into any given discipline, but is instead intended to reflect the predominant prototypes that define these strongly related areas of inquiry. For a discussion of categories based on prototypes, see George Lakoff, *Women, Fire, and Dangerous Things: What Categories Reveal About the Mind* (Chicago: University of Chicago Press, 1987).

[73] JoAnne Yates, *Control through Communication* (Baltimore: Johns Hopkins University Press, 1989); Alfred Dupont Chandler and Takashi Hikino, *Scale and Scope: The Dynamics of Industrial Capitalism* (Cambridge, MA: Belknap Press, 1990); Nicholas Carr, *The Big Switch: Rewiring the World, from Edison to Google* (New York: W.W. Norton, 2008); Antoine Prost and Gerard Vincent, eds., *A History of Private Life. Volume V. Riddles of Identity in Modern Times* (Cambridge, MA: Belknap Press of Harvard University Press, 1991).

[74] Howard Aldrich, *Organizations Evolving* (London: Sage, 1999), 6.

[75] Alfred D. Chandler, *The Visible Hand: The Managerial Revolution in American Business* (Cambridge, MA: Belknap Press, 1977).

[76] Olga P. Palmer, "The History of European Archival Literature," *American Archivist* 2, no. 2 (1939): 76.

[77] Aldrich, *Organizations Evolving.*

[78] Lee S. Sproull, "Computers in U.S. Households since 1977," in *A Nation Transformed by Information: How Information Has Shaped the United States from Colonial Times to the Present,* ed. Alfred D. Chandler and James W. Cortada (New York: Oxford University Press, 2000), 257–80.

[79] Maria C. Papadakis, "The Application and Implications of Information Technologies in the Home: Where Are the Data and What Do They Say?" (Arlington, VA: National Science Foundation, Division of Science Resources Studies, 2001).

[80] David Frohlich and Robert Kraut, "The Social Context of Home Computing," in *Inside the Smart Home,* ed. Richard Harper (London: Springer, 2003), 127–62.

[81] R. Kelly Garrett and James N. Danziger, "Which Telework? Defining and Testing a Taxonomy of Technology-Mediated Work at a Distance," *Social Science Computer Review* 25, no. 1 (2007): 27–47.

82 Jo Ann Oravec, "Constructive Approaches to Internet Recreation in the Workplace," *Communications of the ACM* 45, no. 1 (2002): 60–63.

83 Niall Bolger, Anita DeLongis, Ronald C. Kessler, and Elaine Wethington, "The Contagion of Stress across Multiple Roles," *Journal of Marriage and the Family* 51 (1989): 175.

84 Evangelia Demerouti, Arnold B. Bakker, and Wilmar B. Schaufeli, "Spillover and Crossover of Exhaustion and Life Satisfaction among Dual-Earner Parents," *Journal of Vocational Behavior* 67 (2005): 266–89.

85 Lester J. Cappon, "Historical Manuscripts as Archives: Some Definitions and Their Application," *American Archivist* 19 (1956): 105.

86 Frank G. Burke, *Research and the Manuscript Tradition* (Lanham, MD: Scarecrow Press, 1997), 11, 275.

87 John C. Montaña, "Who Owns Business Data on Personally Owned Computers?" *Information Management Journal* 39, no. 3 (2005): 37.

88 Oravec, "Constructive Approaches to Internet Recreation in the Workplace," 60.

89 John B. Horrigan, "Use of Cloud Computing Applications and Services," (Washington, DC: Pew Internet and American Life Project, 2008).

90 Czerwinski et al., "Digital Memories," 47.

91 Fidel et al., "Collaborative Information Retrieval (CIR)"; Morris, "Survey of Collaborative Web Search Practices."

92 Wayne G. Lutters, Mark S. Ackerman, and Xiaomu Zhou, "Group Information Management," in Jones and Teevan, *Personal Information Management*; Tara Whalen, Elaine Toms, and James Blustein, "File Sharing and Group Information Management" (paper presented at Personal Information Management: PIM 2008, Florence, Italy, April 5-6, 2008).

93 Laurel Swan, Alex S. Taylor, Shahram Izadi, and Richard Harper, "Containing Family Clutter," in *Home Informatics and Telematics: ICT for the Next Billion*, ed. A. Venkatesh, T. Gonsalves, A. Monk, and K. Buckner (Boston: Springer, 2007), 171–84.

94 Maurice Halbwachs, *The Collective Memory*, 1st ed. (New York: Harper and Row, 1980). For discussions of the active role that archivists play in shaping (rather than simply preserving) memory, see Terry Cook, "What Is Past Is Prologue: A History of Archival Ideas since 1898, and the Future Paradigm Shift," *Archivaria* 43 (1997): 17–63; Verne Harris, "Claiming Less, Delivering More: A Critique of Positivist Formulations on Archives in South Africa," *Archivaria* 44 (1997): 132–41; Robert McIntosh, "The Great War, Archives, and Modern Memory," *Archivaria* 46 (1998): 1–31; and Joan M. Schwartz and Terry Cook, "Archives, Records, and Power: The Making of Modern Memory," *Archival Science* 2, no. 1-2 (2002): 1–19.

95 Angelika Menne-Haritz, "Access—the Reformulation of an Archival Paradigm," *Archival Science* 1, no. 1 (2001): 57–82.

96 Schwartz and Cook, "Archives, Records, and Power"; Kenneth Foote, "To Remember and Forget: Archives, Memory, and Culture," *American Archivist* 53 (1990): 378–93; Mark A. Greene, "The Power of Meaning: The Archival Mission in the Postmodern Age," *American Archivist* 65, no. 1 (2002): 42–55; Carolyn Hamilton, Verne Harris, Jane Taylor, Michele Pickover, Graeme Reid, and Razia Saleh, eds., *Refiguring the Archive* (Dordrecht, Netherlands: Kluwer Academic Publishers, 2002); Randall C. Jimerson, "Archives and Memory," *OCLC Systems and Services* 19, no. 3 (2003): 89–95.

97 Sue McKemmish, "Evidence of Me . . . " *Archives and Manuscripts* 24, no. 1 (1996): 28–45.

98 Joan M. Schwartz, "'We Make Our Tools and Our Tools Make Us': Lessons from Photographs for the Practice, Politics, and Poetics of Diplomatics," *Archivaria* 40 (1995): 40–74.

99 Margaret Hedstrom, "Archives, Memory, and Interfaces with the Past," *Archival Science* 2, no. 1-2 (2002): 30.

[100] Jones and Teevan, "Conclusion," in *Personal Information Management;* Ofer Bergman, Simon Tucker, Ruth Beyth-Marom, Edward Cutrell, and Steve Whittaker, "It's Not That Important: Demoting Personal Information of Low Subjective Importance using GrayArea," in *CHI 2009: Conference on Human Factors in Computing Systems* (New York: Association for Computing Machinery, 2009), 269–78.

[101] Tim Berners-Lee, James Hendler, and Ora Lassila, "The Semantic Web," *Scientific American* 284, no. 5 (2001): 35–43.

[102] Leo Sauermann, Gunnar Aastrand Grimnes, Malte Kiesel, Christiaan Fluit, Heiko Maus, Dominik Heim, Danish Nadeem, Benjamin Horak, and Andreas Dengel, "Semantic Desktop 2.0: The Gnowsis Experience," in *The Semantic Web: ISWC 2006: 5th International Semantic Web Conference, ISWC 2006, Athens, GA, USA, November 5-9, 2006: Proceedings*, ed. Isabel F. Cruz, Stefan Decker, Dean Allemang, Chris Preist, Daniel Schwabe, Peter Mika, Michael Uschold, and Lora Aroyo (Berlin: Springer, 2006), 887–900.

[103] Eytan Adar, David Karger, and Lynn Andrea Stein, "Haystack: Per-User Information Environments," in *Proceedings of the Eighth International Conference on Information Knowledge Management: CIKM '99, November 2-6, 1999, Kansas City, Missouri*, ed. Susan Gauch (New York: ACM Press, 1999), 413–22.

[104] Alon Halevy, "Why Your Data Won't Mix," *Queue* 3, no. 8 (2005): 50–58.

[105] Christopher A. Lee, "A Framework for Contextual Information in Digital Collections," *Journal of Documentation* 67, no. 1 (2011): 95–143.

[106] Cole, "Human Aspects of Office Filing," 18.

[107] Lansdale, "Psychology of Personal Information Management," 55.

[108] Susan Dumais, Edward Cutrell, J.J. Cadiz, Gavin Jancke, Raman Sarin, and Daniel C. Robbins, "Stuff I've Seen: A System for Personal Information Retrieval and Reuse," in *SIGIR 2003: Proceedings of the Twenty-Sixth Annual International ACM SIGIR Conference on Research and Development in Information Retrieval, Toronto, Canada, July 28 to August 1, 2003*, ed. Jamie Callan (New York: Association for Computing Machinery, 2003), 72–79.

[109] Liadh Kelly, Yi Chen, Marguerite Fuller, and Gareth J. F. Jones, "A Study of Remembered Context for Information Access from Personal Digital Archives," in *Proceedings of the Second International Conference on Interaction Context: October 14-17, 2008, London, United Kingdom*, ed. Mounia Lalmas and Anastasios Tombros (New York: ACM Press, 2008), 44–50.

[110] Barreau and Nardi, "Finding and Reminding."

[111] William C. Hill, James D. Hollan, Dave Wroblewski, and Tim McCandless, "Edit Wear and Read Wear," in *CHI '92 Conference Proceedings: ACM Conference on Human Factors in Computing Systems: Striking a Balance, May 3-7, 1992, Monterey, California*, ed. John Bennett, Penny Bauersfeld, and Gene Lynch (New York: Association for Computing Machinery, 1992), 3.

[112] Bradley J. Rhodes, "Margin Notes: Building a Contextually Aware Associative Memory," in *IUI 2000: 2000 International Conference on Intelligent User Interfaces, New Orleans, Louisiana, January 9-12, 2000*, ed. Henry Lieberman (New York: Association for Computing Machinery, 2000), 219–24.

[113] Bradley Rhodes and Thad Starner, "The Remembrance Agent: A Continuously Running Automated Information Retrieval System," in *PAAM 96: Proceedings of the First International Conference on the Practical Application of Intelligent Agents and Multi-Agent Technology, 22nd-24th April 1996, Westminster Central Hall, London, UK* (Blackpool, UK: Practical Application Company, 1996), 487–95.

[114] Anind K. Dey, Gregory D. Abowd, and Andrew Wood, "CyberDesk: A Framework for Providing Self-Integrating Context-Aware Services," in *IUI '98: 1998 International Conference on Intelligent User Interfaces, San Francisco, California, January 6-9, 1998*, ed. Peter Johnson (New York: Association for Computing Machinery, 1998), 47–54.

[115] Adar, Karger, and Stein, "Haystack: Per-User Information Environments."

[116] Arthur Allison, James Currall, Michael Moss, and Susan Stuart, "Digital Identity Matters," *Journal of the American Society for Information Science and Technology* 56, no. 4 (2004): 371.

[117] Pearce-Moses, *Glossary of Archival and Records Terminology,* 90.

[118] Michelle Light and Tom Hyry, "Colophons and Annotations: New Directions for the Finding Aid," *American Archivist* 65, no. 2 (2002): 216–30.

[119] Richard V. Szary, "Encoded Archival Context (EAC) and Archival Description: Rationale and Background," *Journal of Archival Organization* 3, no. 2/3 (2006): 217–27.

[120] Wendy Duff and Verne Harris, "Stories and Names: Archival Description as Narrating Records and Constructing Meanings," *Archival Science* 2, no. 3-4 (2002): 276.

[121] Jenkinson, *Manual of Archive Administration,* 123.

[122] "Report of Ad Hoc Committee on Manuscripts Set Up by the American Historical Association in December 1948," *American Archivist* 14 (1951): 229–40.

[123] Schellenberg, "Appraisal of Modern Public Records," 69–70.

[124] G. Philip Bauer, "The Appraisal of Current and Recent Records" (Washington, DC: National Archives and Records Service, 1946), 6.

[125] Desney Tan, Emma Berry, Mary Czerwinski, Gordon Bell, Jim Gemmell, Steve Hodges, Narinder Kapur, Brian Meyers, Nuria Oliver, George Robertson, and Ken Wood, "Save Everything: Supporting Human Memory with a Personal Digital Lifetime Store," in *Personal Information Management;* Gordon Bell and Jim Gemmell, *Total Recall: How the E-Memory Revolution Will Change Everything* (New York: Dutton, 2009). Note that various encryption and digital rights management (DRM) technologies are designed to prevent uncontrolled copying and reuse of the content of digital objects. However, adoption of encryption and DRM is not widespread in the consumer market, and it is often possible for creative individuals to work around the technology (e.g., by copying directly from the computer's memory, capturing screenshots).

[126] Czerwinski et al., "Digital Memories."

[127] Jones, "Finders, Keepers?"

[128] Jones, "How People Keep and Organize Personal Information."

[129] Reference Model for an Open Archival Information System (OAIS).

[130] Acland, "Archivist: Keeper, Undertaker or Auditor"; F. Gerald Ham, "The Archival Edge," *American Archivist* 38 (1975): 5–13; Frederic Miller, "Use, Appraisal and Research: A Case Study of Social History," *American Archivist* 49, no. 4 (1986): 371–92; Roy C. Schaeffer, "Transcendent Concepts: Power, Appraisal, and the Archivist as 'Social Outcast,'" *Archivaria* 55, no. 4 (1992): 608–19; Barbara C. Craig, "Serving the Truth: The Importance of Fostering Archives Research in Education Programmes, Including a Modest Proposal for Partnerships with the Workplace," *Archivaria* 42 (1996): 105–17; Catherine Bailey, "From the Top Down: The Practice of Macro-Appraisal," *Archivaria* 43 (1997): 89–128; Richard J. Cox and Helen W. Samuels, "The Archivist's First Responsibility: A Research Agenda for the Identification and Retention of Records of Enduring Value," *American Archivist* 51 (1988): 28–42; Helen R. Tibbo, "Archival Perspectives on the Emerging Digital Library," *Communications of the ACM* 44, no. 5 (2001): 69–70; Richard J. Cox, "The End of Collecting: Towards a New Purpose for Archival Appraisal," *Archival Science* 2, no. 3-4 (2002): 287–309.

[131] Terry Cook, "Documenting Society and Institutions: The Influence of Helen Willa Samuels," in *Controlling the Past: Documenting Society and Institutions - Essays in Honor of Hellen Willa Samuels,* ed. Terry Cook (Chicago: Society of American Archivists, 2011), 3 (emphasis in original).

[132] Emmett J. Leahy "Reduction of Public Records," *American Archivist* 3, no. 1 (1940): 13-38; Duchein, "History of European Archives."

[133] Jenkinson, *Manual of Archive Administration,* 115.

[134] Ibid., 116.

[135] During the nineteenth and early twentieth centuries, many European countries established journals related to archives. These were predominantly government publications or publications with "governmental overtones." See Palmer, "History of European Archival Literature," 73.

[136] Cook, "Concept of Archival Fonds."

[137] Charles M. Gates, "The Administration of State Archives," *American Archivist* 1, no. 3 (1938): 138.

[138] Helen L. Chatfield, "The Problem of Records from the Standpoint of Management," *American Archivist* 3, no. 3 (1940): 100.

[139] Hilary Golder, *Documenting a Nation: Australian Archives, the First Fifty Years* (Canberra: Australian Government Publishing Service, 1994).

[140] One of the reasons for the U.S. National Archives' promotion of records management as a distinct occupation was the lack of a formal registry system, which was in place in some European countries. See Richard C. Berner, *Archival Theory and Practice in the United States: A Historical Analysis* (Seattle, WA: University of Washington Press, 1983), 3.

[141] William Jerome Wilson, "Analysis of Government Records an Emerging Profession," *Library Quarterly* 16, no. 1 (1946): 3–4.

[142] Bauer, "Appraisal of Current and Recent Records."

[143] Wilson, "Analysis of Government Records," 14.

[144] Schellenberg, "Appraisal of Modern Public Records," 57, 70.

[145] See, e.g., Czerwinski et al., "Digital Memories"; Karat, Karat, and Brodie, "Management of Personal Information Disclosure"; and Michael Shamos, "Privacy and Public Records," in *Personal Information Management.*

[146] Wendy Duff, "Steadying the Weathervane: Use as a Factor in Appraisal Criteria," *Provenance* 12, no. 1-2 (1994): 83–129; Mark Greene, "'The Surest Proof': A Utilitarian Approach to Appraisal," *Archivaria* 45 (1998): 127–69.

[147] Ham, "The Archival Edge," 8.

[148] Malone, "How Do People Organize Their Desks?"; Lansdale, "Psychology of Personal Information Management."

[149] Lansdale, "Psychology of Personal Information Management," 105.

[150] See, e.g., Malone, "How Do People Organize Their Desks?" and Boardman and Sasse, "Cross-Tool Study of Personal Information Management."

[151] Boardman and Sasse, "Cross-Tool Study of Personal Information Management."

[152] Pamela Ravasio, Sissel Guttormsen Schär, and Helmut Krueger, "In Pursuit of Desktop Evolution: User Problems and Practices with Modern Desktop Systems," *ACM Transactions on Computer Human Interaction* 11 (2004): 156–80.

[153] Whittaker and Sidner, "Email Overload."

[154] Boardman and Sasse, "Cross-Tool Study of Personal Information Management."

[155] Jenkinson, *Manual of Archive Administration,* 11.

[156] Malone, "How Do People Organize Their Desks?"; Lansdale, "Psychology of Personal Information Management."

[157] Geoffrey C. Bowker and Susan Leigh Star, *Sorting Things Out: Classification and Its Consequences* (Cambridge, MA: MIT Press, 1999).

[158] Lansdale, "Psychology of Personal Information Management," 57.

[159] Ibid.

[160] Boardman, "Improving Tool Support for Personal Information Management."

[161] Boardman, "Improving Tool Support for Personal Information Management"; Barreau and Nardi, "Finding and Reminding."

[162] Terry Winograd and Fernando Flores, *Understanding Computers and Cognition: A New Foundation for Design* (Norwood, NJ: Ablex, 1986).

[163] John McDonald, "Towards Automated Record Keeping, Interfaces for the Capture of Records of Business Processes," *Archives and Museum Informatics* 11 (1997): 280, 284.

[164] William Jones, Ammy Jiranida Phuwanartnurak, Rajdeep Gill, and Harry Bruce, "Don't Take My Folders Away! Organizing Personal Information to Get Things Done," in *CHI 2005: Technology, Safety, Community: Conference Proceedings: Conference on Human Factors in Computing Systems: Portland, Oregon, USA, April 2–7*, ed. Wendy Anne Kellogg, Shumin Zhai, Carolyn Gale, and G.C. van der Veer (New York: Association for Computing Machinery, 2005), 1505–08.

[165] Hobbs, "Character of Personal Archives," 132.

[166] Cal Lee, "Never Optimize: Building and Managing a Robust Cyberinfrastructure" (paper presented at History and Theory of Infrastructure: Distilling Lessons for New Scientific Cyberinfrastructures, Ann Arbor, MI, September 28–October 1, 2006).

[167] Wanda J. Orlikowski, "Learning from Notes: Organizational Issues in Groupware Implementation," in *CSCW '92: Sharing Perspectives: Proceedings of the Conference on Computer-Supported Cooperative Work, October 31 to November 4, 1992, Toronto, Canada*, ed. Jon Turner and Robert Kraut (New York: Association for Computing Machinery, 1992), 362–69; Jonathan Grudin, "Groupware and Social Dynamics: Eight Challenges for Developers," *Communications of the ACM* 37, no. 1 (1994): 92–105; "Building Partnerships: Developing New Approaches to Electronic Records Management and Preservation" (Albany: New York State Archives and Records Administration, 1995); Wendy Duff, "Increasing the Acceptance of the Functional Requirements for Electronic Evidence," *Archives and Museum Informatics* 10, no. 4 (1996): 326–51; Brian F. Lavoie, "The Incentives to Preserve Digital Materials: Roles, Scenarios, and Economic Decision-Making" (Dublin, OH: OCLC Research, 2003); J. Timothy Sprehe and Charles R McClure, "Lifting the Burden," *Information Management Journal* 39, no. 4 (2005): 47–52; Anthony M. Cresswell and G. Brian Burke, "The Washington State Digital Archives (Case Study)" (Albany, NY: Center for Technology in Government, 2006).

[168] "Model Requirements for the Management of Electronic Records: Update and Extension (MoReq2 Specification)" (Hampshire, UK: Serco Consulting, 2008); Reference Model for an Open Archival Information System (OAIS); Assistant Secretary of Defense for Networks and Information Integration, "Electronic Records Management Software Applications Design Criteria Standard," DoD 5015.02-STD (Arlington, VA: U.S. Department of Defense, 2007); "Information and Documentation—Records Management," ISO 15489 (International Organization for Standardization, 2001).

[169] Bergman et al., "It's Not That Important."

[170] Dumais et al., "Stuff I've Seen."

[171] Edward Cutrell, Daniel Robbins, Susan Dumais, and Raman Sarin, "Fast, Flexible Filtering with Phlat," in *CHI 2006: Interact, Inform, Inspire: Conference Proceedings: Conference on Human Factors in Computing Systems: Montreal, Quebec, Canada, April 22–27*, ed. Rebecca E. Grinter (New York: Association for Computing Machinery, 2006), 261–70.

[172] Bearman and Lytle, "Power of the Principle of Provenance."

[173] Michael Greifeneder, Stephan Strodl, Petar Petrov, and Andreas Rauber, "HOPPLA—Archiving System for Small Institutions," *ERCIM News* 80 (2010): 18–19.

[174] Michael Franklin, Alon Halevy, and David Maier, "From Databases to Dataspaces: A New Abstraction for Information Management," *ACM SIGMOD Record* 34, no. 4 (2005): 27–33.

[175] Jens-Peter Dittrich, Lukas Blunschi, Markus Färber, Olivier René Girard, Shant Kirakos Karakashian, and Marcos Antonio Vaz Salles, "From Personal Desktops to Personal Dataspaces: A Report on Building the iMeMex Personal Dataspace Management System," in *Datenbanksysteme in Business, Technologie Und Web (BTW 2007), 12. Fachtagung Des Gi-Fachbereichs "Datenbanken Und Informationssysteme" (DBIS), Proceedings, 7–9. März 2007, Aachen, Germany*, ed. Alfons Kemper, Harald Schöning, Thomas Rose, Matthias Jarke, Thomas Seidl, Christoph Quix, and Christoph Brochhaus (Bonn: Ges. für Informatik, 2007), 292–308.

[176] Carl Lagoze, "Keeping Dublin Core Simple: Cross-Domain Discovery or Resource Description?" *D-Lib Magazine* 7, no. 1 (2001), http://dx.doi.org/10.1045/january2001-lagoze.

GHOSTS IN THE MACHINE: TOWARDS A PRINCIPLES-BASED APPROACH TO MAKING AND KEEPING DIGITAL PERSONAL RECORDS

Adrian Cunningham

The digital personal information management environment is both rapidly evolving and becoming increasingly complex and heterogeneous. It is time to take a step back from discussing time-bound, technology-specific practical strategies and technical solutions and to focus instead on a more enduring, principles-based approach to dealing with the complex realities of digital recordkeeping. This chapter proposes a set of twelve guiding principles that will help archivists in planning and delivering programs of advice and assistance to the creators of digital personal records. These principles are an adaptation of a set of principles developed by the International Council on Archives in the field of government/organisational digital recordkeeping, thus illustrating how the two branches of the profession can learn from each other when dealing with digital recordkeeping issues.

During the 1990s I wrote two articles that made some suggestions and proposed some strategies for archivists on the issue of managing born-digital personal records.[1] At the time there was very little discussion of the issue in the archives and records literature and even less evidence of serious engagement with the challenge by practitioners. This lack of attention to what was clearly a critical professional issue, especially when contrasted to the exhaustive attention that had been devoted to the issue of electronic recordkeeping in government and corporate settings, was a point I bemoaned in my 1999 article. The words "head" and "sand" sprang inevitably to mind.

Moving Targets and Continuous Transformation

It is pleasing, therefore, to note the mini-explosion of literature on the topic that has emerged over the past decade, not just in the archives and records field but also more generally in the new field of "personal information management."[2] The publication of this book by the Society of American Archivists provides further evidence of this encouraging trend. Some serious research funding has been invested into exploring various aspects of the issue, particularly in the United Kingdom,[3] and there is growing evidence of archival programs testing out some of the strategies that have been proposed over the years.[4] At the same time, it has become clear that personal digital recordkeeping behaviour is a moving target. Not only is technology in a constant state of evolution, so too is human behaviour in the ways in which it adopts new technologies to support personal interests, activities, and pursuits. It is no longer a matter of negotiating the transition from paper-based personal records to digital personal records. Rather, it is a matter of negotiating the ongoing evolution of digital lives and the opportunities/challenges for capturing and managing the digital evidence of those lives in all their manifestations.

Mobile computing, handheld digital devices, online social networking, Web 2.0, podcasts, and blogs are becoming almost as ubiquitous as email and the more traditional World Wide Web pages. The records of my daughter's gap year travels do not exist in the form of travel diaries, postcards, aerograms, and photograph albums. Instead, the records are on Facebook, Flickr, her mobile phone, the hard drive of her laptop computer, and in a few emails home. A recent Australian survey found that most people aged eighteen to twenty-four regarded their laptop computer as their most valuable asset, while one-quarter of people of all ages said they would save their laptop before all other items in the event of a household emergency.[5] Moreover, for many young people, even the loss of their laptop is unlikely to be the cause of too much grief, as most of their valuable digital information is stored on and/or recoverable from other portable devices or elsewhere on servers provided by third parties such as Flickr and Gmail. In short, individuals are increasingly relying solely on diverse and distributed digital forms of technology to make and keep their vital records and other personal property.

Older individuals, who are more likely to be targeted by archival collecting programs, are usually much more cautious in their adoption of technology, thus making the task of capturing and preserving their born-digital records that much less complex.[6] This is just as well for archival programs that are only now starting to grapple with the challenges associated with digital personal records. The technological generation gap, however, means that strategies devised for the first generation of born-digital personal records will inevitably be inadequate for subsequent generations. Investigations into the digital recordmaking behaviours of personal records creators by the UK Digital Lives research project reveals a curious range of hybrid and unsophisticated digital records behaviours by the ageing cohort of donors who have cooperated with the research.[7] The practical lessons learnt from such research might be useful in the short term, but are unlikely to be generally applicable in ten or twenty years' time.

In an ever-evolving, heterogeneous, and unpredictable personal digital environment, exploring and proposing particular strategies for making and keeping personal digital records is likely to only have limited utility. It is time to identify some core principles that can inform the development of particular strategies and procedures for whatever strange and unforeseen digital personal recordkeeping scenarios and challenges we might encounter in the future.

Learning from Each Other

Identifying core principles might also help personal digital archivists to make better use of some of the experiences learnt in the domain of government and corporate digital recordkeeping—and perhaps even vice versa! When I first argued that personal records archivists had to get over any lingering Jenkinsonian concerns they might have about becoming more involved in the processes of recordmaking by private individuals (because it is usually going to be too late to do anything with digital records after the creator has died), many found my suggestions to be disconcerting, if not totally abhorrent. More recent literature on the issue suggests a growing acceptance of the necessity for getting involved in the records creation process, even though it is acknowledged that this can be challenging to implement because of the difficulties associated with securing the timely cooperation of records creators.[8] Unlike governments and corporations, personal records creators pursue their activities in largely private and unregulated circumstances.

Interestingly, government and corporate recordkeeping professionals experience similar practical difficulties in influencing the behaviour of records creators.[9] Just as private lives are being revolutionised by technology, so too are the ways in which organisations behave in relation to the making and keeping of their digital information assets and evidence. These changes have removed many of the certainties that recordkeeping professionals once relied upon to help ensure good recordkeeping. They have learnt that ensuring good recordkeeping in today's organisations is not simply a matter of designing and implementing a recordkeeping system that meets some predetermined functional requirements (commonly just a digital re-creation of a paper registry system) and then telling people to use that system. They have learnt that the way individuals do their work in today's organisations is fundamentally different to the way it used to be done and that monolithic recordkeeping systems simply do not fit into today's ways of thinking and working.[10] They are learning that the only way to enable good recordkeeping outcomes in today's organisations is to embed clever, unobtrusive recordkeeping solutions into the systems and processes that people actually use, not to impose some additional system and process that will only be ignored as being of nuisance value at best.

Indeed, with the breakdown of corporate/organisational controls on the information flows and information management patterns of individual staff members, the making and keeping of government and corporate information assets is increasingly coming to resemble the anarchic, heterogeneous, and idiosyncratic recordkeeping behaviours of private individuals. The boundaries between work and private life and between work and private information spaces are becoming increasingly blurred.[11] In the future perhaps all recordkeeping, both organisational and personal, will be personal recordkeeping. In other words, organisational recordkeeping systems may become nothing more than the totality of the collected personal recordkeeping systems of its various staff members, past and present. If so, then principles and strategies devised for one should be applicable for the other. All archivists, not just personal records archivists, should have an interest in helping individuals to become digital auto-archivists. All archivists should be interested in devising strategies for managing such records long term—not just in the "personal" space of the first and second dimensions of the records continuum,[12] but in the broader corporate and societal spaces of the third and fourth dimensions of the continuum.

Both individuals and organisations are suffering digital amnesia. Neither really knows how to capture, manage and retain the essential evidence of their activities, decisions, and interests. Technological change allied with related changes in personal and organisational behaviour is the root cause of this amnesia[13]—an amnesia that presents the single greatest challenge facing the recordkeeping profession. This is not a challenge that should be tackled in isolation by the two subtribes of recordkeeping professionals—personal records archivists and government/corporate recordkeepers—because the nature of the challenge and the principles that should inform our professional response to that challenge are remarkably similar for both groups.

Custody also has to be revisited in this context. If today's digital personal records are distributed (rather than centralised) across multiple platforms, servers, domains, and peer-to-peer networking sites, how feasible is it to assume that tomorrow's digital personal archives can be centralised in the custody of a single institutional collection? The challenge may not be what to collect and how to collect and preserve it, but rather what to identify and document and how to ensure its future survival, meaning, and utility in a distributed custody context. Technology offers us the possibility of continuous real-time capture or synchronisation of personal collections that are maintained in distributed repositories or service providers. The commercial sector has not ignored the business opportunities presented by these developments. British Telecom offers a Digital Vault service.[14] The Internet Archive offers to store personal digital content for free in perpetuity, providing the owner is willing to share that content with the world. EMC Corporation is offering its Lifeline software to help individuals manage their digital lives,[15] while Microsoft has an entire research and development taskforce working on a project called MyLifeBits.[16]

In short, the ongoing technological transformation of personal information creation and management creates opportunities for ongoing reconceptualisations of notions of "the archive" and archival endeavour. These reconceptualisations include, but are not limited to, notions of whose lives might be documented in archival programs, how, when, using what records, and within which combination of regimes of custody and access.

Guiding Principles

The suggestion that recordkeeping professionals step back from discussing particular tactics, strategies, and functional requirements to identify and articulate some guiding principles has recently been adopted by the International Council on Archives in its project called Principles and Functional Requirements for Records in Electronic Office Environments. Module 1 of the published output of this project presents four records-related principles and eight systems-related principles that should guide the development and implementation of information systems in organisations wishing to make, keep, and use authentic evidence of business activity.[17] These principles were developed for government and organisational recordkeeping contexts, but with some tweaking can easily be made relevant to the personal recordkeeping context. The following presents and discusses reworded versions of the twelve principles with the aim of commencing a broader pursuit of a principles-based approach to the issue of digital personal recordkeeping.

> 1. *Electronic personal records need to be actively and continuously managed and reliably maintained as authentic evidence of personal activity.*

As human beings increasingly rely on digital technologies to pursue their interests and activities, the electronic information generated by such activities may serve as the only evidence of particular activities or interactions. Maintenance of this evidence in the form of fixed records is necessary for the individuals themselves to keep track of their personal interests and history, while long-term maintenance of this evidence can often provide valuable sources for the purposes of broader societal history and memory. Because of its inherent fragility and rates of software and hardware obsolescence, and because it is often stored across multiple distributed systems and servers, electronic information is highly vulnerable to loss through neglect or mismanagement. Unlike paper records, which can survive in an environment of benign neglect, electronic records have to be actively managed across their entire lifespan (e.g., by making regular backup copies of records on portable media for offsite storage, and by migrating records to new software platforms, service providers, and/or storage media as required).

> 2. *Electronic personal records have to be linked to their context through the use of quality metadata.*

In order for information to have the capability of functioning as records and for those records to be known, manageable, and findable, it is necessary to augment that information with additional data (that is, metadata). Metadata places information in the context of the human activities and computing environment in which it was created and used. It documents relationships between different records both within and beyond a single recordkeeping system; relationships between records and their creators; relationships between individuals and their wider social acquaintances and communities and their business/professional contacts and colleagues; and relationships between individuals/groups and the activities in which they engage (and which are documented in the records). Such contextual information, which may reference other widely distributed sources of information, must be attached to a record as it is necessary to provide the record with sufficient longevity for interpretation and to maximise its value and utility as evidence and as a source of information. Metadata of this kind might, for example, take the form of file/folder titles, and file structures/classification trees used for storing and managing records.

> 3. *Electronic personal records should be kept in ways that do not impede their accessibility to current and future authorised users.*

Electronic records need to be rendered in accessible formats and media to enable searching and retrieval for as long as access to those records is required, including in many cases beyond the lifetime of the creator of those records. Great care should be taken with the use of digital rights management technology. While records may need to be encrypted for secure transmission purposes, they should not be encrypted for long-term storage purposes, as the longer term access to and/or use of decryption keys may not be possible.

4. *Electronic personal records should be disposed of in managed,
    planned, and systematic ways.*

Increasingly, human beings are creating and acquiring enormous quantities of digital information. Only some of this proliferation of information warrants the time and effort that is required to keep and manage it over the medium to long term. Personal recordkeepers should consider their needs for records—what records need to be made and retained to support their individual legal and personal requirements;[18] the forms in which those records should be created and kept; and how long those records need to be retained for evidential and informational purposes. Included in these deliberations should be up-front (rather than after the fact) considerations of which records might be usefully retained following the death of the records creator and appropriate access regimes for those records. Disposal and destruction of records should be planned and systematic, not accidental, ad hoc, post hoc, or the result of neglect or mismanagement. Archival programs can be well placed to provide advice and assistance to personal records creators on these records appraisal and disposal decisions and implementation strategies (including metadata strategies that can help inform and document disposal decisions).

5. *Good personal information management should be a natural part of
    human activity and the conduct of personal affairs.*

Good information management and recordkeeping practices should be integral to the conduct of one's personal activities. When activities are facilitated by or involve the use of digital technologies, the ways in which these technologies are used should support rather than hinder good information management and recordkeeping. If good information management is seen as being onerous and unnatural in such contexts, it will not occur. In the words of Catherine Marshall, "Personal archiving technology should fit organically into everyday practice."[19]

6. *Systems for capturing and managing electronic personal records
    should rely on metadata as an active, dynamic, and integral part of
    the recordkeeping process.*

The existence of good quality metadata is essential if records are going to be meaningful and accessible for future use. This includes the development and implementation of records titling conventions, classification taxonomies, and the mapping of relationships between related records and groups of records. Records should continue to accrue new metadata for as long as they continue to be used and of value.

> 7. *Systems for capturing and managing electronic personal records should ensure interoperability across platforms and domains and over time.*

Electronic personal records often need to be retained for periods of time that exceed the lifespan of the hardware, software, or service provider in which they are created or stored. As such, these records must be able to be shared with and/or migrated to other technology platforms.

> 8. *Systems for capturing and managing electronic personal records should rely as far as possible on open standards and technological neutrality.*

Many software products are developed with built-in proprietary dependencies. That is, the information can only be viewed or used using particular proprietary software applications and/or hardware. Such dependencies can have adverse effects on access and preservation of digital information over the medium to long term. Use of open standards can help to ameliorate some of these technological dependencies.

> 9. *Systems should have the capacity for bulk import and export using open formats.*

Electronic personal records may contain hardware or software dependencies. Software and services used to make and keep these records should ideally incorporate capabilities to remove these dependencies via support for bulk reformatting as part of ingest or export capability or, at a minimum, via non-proprietary encoding of metadata.

> 10. *Electronic personal records must be maintained in a secure environment.*

Personal information management systems must not allow unauthorised access to or modifications of records (including metadata). Where authorised modifications to records are performed, they should be documented.

11. *Wherever possible, metadata should be generated and captured
automatically.*

Human beings are typically unwilling to interrupt their workflow to perform
tasks that are ancillary to executing the primary activity. As such, records
creators are usually unreliable as creators of metadata for individual
information objects, documents, and records. Systems should be adopted
or designed and implemented in a manner that allows automatic population
of required metadata fields, such as author, sender, recipient, and date.
Recordkeeping systems should be designed to be as self-documenting as
possible.

12. *It should be as easy as possible for individuals to create/capture
records of their various activities.*

Recordkeeping should be largely invisible to end-users and incidental to the
conduct of the primary activities in which they participate.

Operationalising the Principles

The principles proposed here are intended to inform practitioners who are
charged with developing and implementing programs for documenting,
collecting, or preserving digital personal records. It would not be helpful to
simply hand the principles to personal records creators with the advice that
they should abide by those principles. Rather, the principles should guide
the development of more practical (and, where necessary, technical) advice
and strategies devised by personal records practitioners and collecting
institutions.

The principles are meant to guide actions and the development of
programs and strategies. They are aspirational statements rather than an
assertion of minimum standards and expectations. In practice it will be
difficult to fully comply with every principle. Indeed, there will be times when
striving to comply with one principle might impede one's ability to comply
with one of the other principles. For example, complying with principle 12
might require some compromises in relation to one or more of the other
principles, and vice versa.

It is acknowledged that there are very real practical constraints on archival
programs—as well as countervailing human preferences and behaviours—that

limit their ability to exert influence on personal recordkeeping behaviours. Nevertheless, if we agree that personal records archivists need to become more involved in records creation processes, then it is useful to have an agreed framework of principles that can inform the drive toward better practice.

Notes

The author would like to thank Cal Lee for his very helpful comments and suggestions. The shortcomings that remain are solely the responsibility of the author.

[1] Adrian Cunningham, "The Archival Management of Personal Records in Electronic Form: Some Suggestions," *Archives and Manuscripts* 22, no. 1 (May 1994): 94–105; and Adrian Cunningham, "Waiting for the Ghost Train: Strategies for Managing Electronic Personal records Before It Is Too Late," *Archival Issues* 24, no. 1 (1999): 55–64.

[2] William Jones, "Finders, Keepers? The Present and Future Perfect in Support of Personal Information Management," *First Monday* 9, no. 3 (March 1, 2004), http://firstmonday.org/article/view/1123/1043.

[3] For example, the Paradigm Project, http://www.paradigm.ac.uk/about/index.html; and the Digital Lives Project, http://www.bl.uk/digital-lives/about.html. See also Susan Thomas and Janette Martin, "Using the Papers of Contemporary British Politicians as a Testbed for the Preservation of Digital Personal Archives," *Journal of the Society of Archivists* 27, no. 1 (April 2006): 29–56.

[4] Susan E. Davis, "Electronic Records Planning in 'Collecting' Repositories," *American Archivist* 71 (Spring/Summer 2008): 167–89.

[5] "Gen Y Puts Laptops First: Survey," http://au.news.yahoo.com/a/-/latest/5249772/gen-y-laptops-survey (accessed January 8, 2009).

[6] See, for example, Genevieve Zook, "Technology and the Generation Gap," *Law and Technology Resources for Legal Professionals* (August 2007), http://www.llrx.com/features/generationgap.htm.

[7] Pete Williams, Katrina Dean, Ian Rowlands, and Jeremy Leighton John, "Digital Lives: Report of Interviews with the Creators of Personal Digital Collections," *Ariadne* 55 (April 2008), http://www.ariadne.ac.uk/issue55/williams-et-al.

[8] See, for example, Davis, "Electronic Records Planning."

[9] This is a common theme in much of the electronic records literature; see, for example, *Assurance and Control Assessment Audit: Recordkeeping* (Canberra: Australian National Audit Office, 2002); K. Schurer, "Survey on the Relationship between Public Administration and Archive Services Concerning Electronic Records Management in the EU Member States" (paper presented at the DLM-Forum on Electronic Records of the European Communities, October 18–19, 1999, Brussels); Linda D. Koontz, *Electronic Records Management and Preservation Pose Challenges* (Washington, DC: U.S. General Accounting Office, 2003); John McDonald, *Information Management in the Government of Canada: A Situation Analysis* (Ottawa: National Archives of Canada, 2000); SRA International, *Report on Current Recordkeeping Practices within the Federal Government* (Arlington, VA: National Archives and Records Administration, 2001); David A. Wallace, "Custodial Theory and Practice in the Electronic Environment," *SASA Newsletter* (January–March 2002): 1, 2, 5, 10, 11; and Robert F. Williams and Lori J. Ashley, *Electronic Records Management Survey: A Renewed Call for Action* (Chicago: Cohasset Associates, 2007).

10 John McDonald, "The Wild Frontier Ten Years On," in *Managing Electronic Records*, ed. Julie McLeod and Catherine Hare (London: Facet Publishing, 2005), 1–17.

11 These trends have been noted repeatedly in the University of Northumbria's research project "Accelerating Positive Change in Electronic Records Management"; see the project website at http://www.northumbria.ac.uk/sd/academic/ceis/re/isrc/themes/rmarea/erm.

12 The records continuum model, as developed by Australia's Frank Upward, consists of four dimensions. The first dimension is document creation; the second is adding information (metadata) for evidential purposes (i.e., creating a record); the third is organizing the records for individual or organizational use; and the fourth dimension is pluralizing the records for wider societal use. In Upward's model it is possible—indeed, desirable—for all four dimensions to coexist simultaneously. See Frank Upward, "Structuring the Records Continuum Part One: Post-Custodial Principles and Properties," *Archives and Manuscripts* 24, no. 2 (November 1996): 268–85.

13 For instance, in 1998 the Australian Law Reform Commission characterized the state of recordkeeping in the Australian Government as "parlous," and concluded that the reasons for its deterioration were a combination of technological change and changes in the processes and culture of public administration, including "multi-skilling," outsourcing, the cutting of "red tape," and the disappearance of filing clerks. Australian Law Reform Commission, *Australia's Federal Record: A Review of the Archives Act 1983* (Canberra: AGPS, 1998).

14 https://digitalvault.bt.com/base/login.jsp.

15 "EMC Helps Consumers Manage Their Digital Lives" (January 2008 press release), http://www.reuters.com.article/pressRelease/idUS133127+07-Jan-2008+PRN20080107.

16 See https://research.microsoft.com/en-us/projects/mylifebits; see also Catherine C. Marshall, "Rethinking Personal Digital Archiving, Parts 1 and 2," *D-Lib Magazine* 14, no. 3–4 (March/April 2008), http://dx.doi.org/10.1045/march2008-marshall-pt1.

17 International Council on Archives, *Principles and Functional Requirements for Records in Electronic Office Environments, Module 1: Overview and Statement of Principles* (ICA, 2008), http://www.ica.org/en/resource-centre (accessed January 12, 2009).

18 By this I mean the medium- to long-term recordkeeping needs of the records creators themselves as determined (with or without outside assistance) by the records creator—requirements that may well differ from the preferences of any archival program that might have a relationship with the individual records creator.

19 Marshall, "Rethinking Personal Digital Archiving," part 2.

Challenges and Opportunities for Personal Digital Archiving

Catherine C. Marshall

Until recently, the question of what people saved and valued centered on physical artifacts (e.g., print photographs, correspondence, and family records). It is only in the last decade or so, with the rise of inexpensive digital recording equipment (e.g., cameras), and equally inexpensive storage, that people began to accumulate significant collections of digital belongings. Using qualitative data gathered across a range of different personal digital archiving studies, this chapter examines the kinds of digital belongings people keep; how they think about deletion and loss; and how these notions translate into strategies and tactics for keeping digital material safe, both at home and in the cloud. The chapter also explores elements of digital stewardship and personal collection building practiced by everyday people with an eye toward guiding them to a set of best practices to supplement what they already do.

It is sometimes difficult to recall that, as recently as the mid-1990s, personal digital media was still an exotic concept. In an article that appeared in the *New Yorker* in the fall of 1995, journalist John Seabrook took pains to explain to the magazine's well-educated readership what was implied by the alien concept of a home page. He wrote:

> In the simplest terms, [a home page] is . . . a place on the Net *where people can find you.* . . . Although building home pages or Web sites . . . is *mainly a commercial enterprise*, it doesn't have to be. It's also a way

> to meet people. . . . You can link your home page to the home pages
> of friends or family, or to your employer's Web site, or to any other site
> you like, creating a kind of neighborhood for yourself. And you can
> furnish it with *anything that can be digitized*—your ideas, your voice,
> your causes, pictures of your scars or your pets or your ancestors.[1]

From today's perspective, this explanation seems self-evident, almost quaint. Yet it is important to reflect on why it seems so, what dates this explanation. That people would amass such enormous quantities of valuable personal digital information was at that time inconceivable; computers and the data they were used to create, process, and consume were mainly the province of the business world.

Furthermore, there were few online venues for storing and sharing personal material—you either had a home page or you didn't. The countless social media services we have grown to rely on—for example, photo-sharing services such as Flickr, video-sharing services such as YouTube, or blogging services such as WordPress—were yet to be offered. Person-to-person sharing was possible via email; but formatted email and email with attachments were still rarities in the consumer world. People were neither accustomed to having a persistent presence and online identity, nor were they used to storing their digital belongings anywhere online except for occasional accounts they purchased from providers such as AOL or Compuserve.

It is interesting to probe Seabrook's assumption about the origins of the material that people were sharing on their home pages. In the past ten or so years, many consumers have quietly migrated from using print and analog media to creating and viewing their own digital content; it is easy to forget that when John Seabrook wrote this article, digital materials were produced by a time-consuming and not wholly satisfying process of digitizing physical artifacts. There were few means of readily producing common kinds of emotionally enduring artifacts like digital photos or movies, and those that were available were still relatively primitive and difficult to work with. Formats had not stabilized; digital image resolution was low; and personal digital media could consume a substantial proportion of a normal person's storage resources. Consider, for example, that in 1995, an inexpensive digital camera cost eight hundred dollars or so, produced grainy 640 by 480 pixel photos, and reproduced colors with unsatisfying fidelity. Furthermore, early digital cameras were bulky and impractical. Laptops were not ubiquitous, so there was often no easy way to upload photos when the photographer was traveling. To make matters worse, a 3.5-inch floppy disk, the most common removable storage medium, held only five or six photos in Tagged Image File Format (TIFF).[2] Post-processing capabilities were similarly primitive: image correction algorithms were still in their infancy.[3] Thus, a state-of-the-art digital camera circa 1995 gave the buyer little to recommend it over a ten-dollar single-use film camera.

But perhaps the most profound shift is social rather than technical: even this recently, people primarily shared and treasured print photographs; archival "originals" used to save the photos and to produce additional print copies were stored as negatives. We have only had a decade to become accustomed to photographs that are born digital, stored as files, and shared and managed electronically. It is vital to remind ourselves of the magnitude of these changes as we go on to consider the state of digital archiving around that time.

In January 1995, Jeff Rothenberg published a groundbreaking article about digital archiving in the widely read magazine *Scientific American*. The article not only described the digital preservation problem and proposed an early technical solution; it was also regarded as a prescient call to arms to the computer science community. We should start thinking about digital archiving now, the article seemed to say, before we begin a fall down the slippery slope into a digital dark ages.

A scenario describing a hypothetical situation circa 2045 formed the linchpin of Rothenberg's article. The concrete problem of digital archiving was framed like this:

> The year is 2045 and my grandchildren (as yet unborn) are exploring the attic of my house (as yet unbought). They find a letter dated 1995 and a CD-ROM. The letter claims that the disk contains a document that provides the key to obtaining my fortune (as yet unearned). My grandchildren are understandably excited, but they have never seen a CD before—except in old movies—and even if they can somehow find a suitable disk drive, how will they run the software necessary to interpret the information on the disk? How can they read my obsolete digital document?[4]

One document. Stored in an unreadable format on an obsolete storage medium evoked by old movies. And a contrived story about how it got there and why we would want to see the document again.

On one hand, this situation is breathtakingly dramatic (the author's legacy is all there, indecipherable, in a single document!); on the other hand, it is more pedestrian than what is true a little more than a decade into this imagined future. Instead, the average consumer is already overwhelmed by the sheer volume of his or her digital belongings. It is not just one document; it is thousands and thousands of pictures, hours and hours of undifferentiated digital video footage, music both purchased and shared, personal finances, the beginnings of what will one day be extensive medical records, email messages important and trivial, and countless other files representing day-to-day interactions with the computer and with other people by means of the computer.

Nor is it accurate to assume one central nexus of storage: today's computer user is unlikely to store his or her files in one place or on one medium; a personal collection is more apt to span many repositories, storage media, and file systems. Even now, most of us have lost track of online accounts and removable media. If a terabyte disk can fit into the palm of one's hand and costs less than a week's worth of groceries, it is easy to see how such a device can be readily misplaced or forgotten. Furthermore, because we have so many portable devices (music players, phones, Universal Serial Bus [USB] keys, digital photo frames) and so many different audiences (our friends, our families, our coworkers and colleagues, our accountants and doctors, strangers with similar interests) it is easy to see how it is in our interest to distribute our personal collections far and wide.

Nor does the scenario represent the complexities of our informal personal information technology (IT) arrangements. Notice that the document's author is both its owner and the person who wrote it onto the compact disc (CD) in question. Access is unquestioned—the document is neither encrypted, nor password-protected, nor stored in an external account—and the CD has apparently either been stored in felicitous circumstances or has been refreshed in the intervening years. In any case, access to it is unimpeded either by intent or by the ravages of time.

In short, to represent the problem as embodied in a single document in a central store, curated invisibly (if minimally) over time, misses many of the most important aspects of personal digital archiving.

Because the article emphasizes access to a single file, already to hand, Rothenberg's solution takes a principled computer science approach: to render a stored digital file at the highest possible fidelity, in a form true to how it was created, complete emulation of the document's original computational environment—the hardware platform, the operating system, and the application used to create the document, at the very least—is necessary.

Emulation is a sophisticated solution for keeping digital objects alive. Through emulation, current hardware and software may exactly imitate the behavior of legacy hardware and software; full emulation of the architectural layers beneath the application allows the application software (or an emulated version of the software) to run just as it did originally, and allows this software to interpret and render the digital file exactly as intended.

Emulation is a complicated archiving strategy because it requires so much information about the original hardware and software environment. Not only must hardware emulation duplicate the processor's behavior (for example, its speed and the operations it supports), which must be fully specified; it must also duplicate the behavior of any necessary peripheral devices and the drivers that access them. An operating system and other platform-level components such as compression/decompression software, fonts, and applications libraries must run on top of the emulated platform. Although emulation may seem straightforward, it is important to remember that computational environments are complex for many reasons and it is difficult to fully specify them; for example, a bug in the original operating system may be paradoxically essential for producing a desired behavior, yet it seems unlikely that the bug would be included in the formal specification. Although they seem straightforward, environmental elements such as fonts may include bits of code to specify, for example, how adjacent characters are kerned.

Given a desire to fully preserve the digital object, it is easy to see why emulation was such an appealing building block for digital preservation. And while emulation is clearly possible—the very nature of computation makes it so—it consumes resources, and may not be necessary. As David Levy pointed out several years after the Rothenberg article appeared, ultimately preservation methods should be dictated by expected use.[5] Will the digital object be edited and continue to evolve? Does it have properties that mitigate against keeping it in a living format? Who will access it and what will they do with it?

So let's step back and look at Rothenberg's scenario from a modern perspective. Consider that as of May 2010, the photo-sharing service Flickr hosted more than 4.6 billion photos; as of April 2009, the photo-sharing service Photobucket hosted more than 7.2 billion photos; and the social networking site Facebook hosted more than 15 billion unique photos.[6] Shifting the focus from Web 2.0 services to people, by 2008, estimates place digital camera adoption in the U.S. at 67 percent of all households; individual households (those who have adopted broadband) store about 14 gigabytes of photos, a figure which is almost doubling yearly.[7] These photos may be centralized on a disk drive (apart from the rest of the user's digital belongings), or they may be scattered far and wide on web services such as Facebook, Flickr, or ImageShack. They may be backed up or otherwise duplicated, or they may be unique; they may have descriptive metadata (tags, titles, or meaningful file names), or they may be only accessible via the files' timestamps.

Multiply this problem by other common media types and digital artifacts, and by burgeoning web storage services and cheap removable personal storage devices like USB drives, and you can begin to see the scope of the problem. Issues such as copyright enforcement and technologies such as digital rights management software bring legal considerations to the table. Because some of the digital material represents what is most private to an individual (be it financial or medical records or emotionally charged love letters), it is reasonable to expect any discussion of digital archiving to take up matters of protecting archival stores against intrusion and to consider subtle issues of privacy, especially where families and friends come into the picture. It might be just as traumatic if *everything* survives the passage of time intact as it would be if *nothing* does.

In short, personal digital archiving is a complex problem that raises social, technical, and legal issues; it is unlikely that this problem will be solved by a single application, web service, service provider, institution, or policy, and certainly it is a problem that extends far beyond accurately rendering obsolete formats. There is a broad frontier of questions and approaches to explore. While it would be most satisfying to offer a system architecture, a mechanism, a representation, or even a coherent story that addresses digital archiving with a holistic solution, it would be misleading to do so. So instead, I will frame the problem by introducing three overarching questions that have arisen from the changes that have occurred since we have grown into digital beings with significant things to archive:

- What does a typical personal digital collection contain?
- What is the technological basis for storing, maintaining, and preserving this collection?
- Which stewardship practices do people bring to bear on the problem and which best practices should they be taught to supplement existing practices?

With each of these questions, I will discuss particular elements of an adaptive solution—one that does not commit to a specific path of technology adoption, one that does not assume the growth of a specific media type (e.g., digital video), or presuppose drastic changes in human behavior.

Figure 1 adapts the digital library framework presented in *Going Digital: A Look at Assumptions Underlying Digital Libraries* to structure these three fundamental questions as arising from the interactions between digital stuff, technology, and human activity.[8] Given this framework, any personal digital archiving effort will necessarily involve a digital collection (or more accurately, an accumulation of digital belongings that neither has the distinct boundaries, nor the acquisition policies of a more formal collection); technology for storing and sustaining digital belongings; and digital stewardship practices.

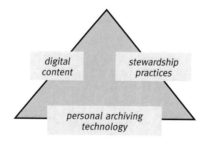

Figure 1. A personal digital archiving framework.

In other words, personal digital archiving will boil down to nothing more profound than deciding what we should keep, how and where we should store it, and what sorts of work people will have to do to keep their digital collections alive. At first blush, the answers seem as simple as the questions. As a strawman collection policy, we will keep everything. A secure central repository containing self-describing digital objects protected by sophisticated access policies will provide people with a facility very close to a digital safety deposit box that uses the emulative principles that Rothenberg—and later Henry Gladney and Raymond Lorie—had in mind.[9] Finally, personal digital stewardship can be modeled after the best practices we have developed to keep important individual collections alive when they are donated to archives, museums, and libraries.[10]

We can dust our hands off and go home, having assigned the question of best practices to professional archivists, the storage question to computer scientists, and having punted on the collection question entirely. Or can we? Let's look at each question in turn; then let's ask ourselves, "Is that all there is?"

What Is in a Personal Digital Collection?

Certainly the most basic question about personal collections centers on what we should keep.

It is very tempting to throw up our hands and say, "Storage *is* cheap. Is there any reason not to keep it all?" Even if our personal digital belongings are accumulating at a truly breathtaking rate, sharp reductions in storage cost make it unlikely that we can break the storage bank. Although we have all had the experience of filling up our hard drives, we usually regard that occurrence as a signal of obsolescence, as a warning sign that it is time to buy a new computer, or at least install a new, more capacious, disk drive.

And why not keep everything? There are plenty of reasons to do so. First—and most importantly—it is very difficult to assess an item's or media type's future worth many years before the value is proven. Although we are confident that some digital assets are indeed worth keeping—the great American novel we have begun writing (and perhaps have returned to at different times through our adult years); our wedding photos; our children's graduation videos—in short, the documentation of life's milestones and evidence of the sweat off our creative brows, there are others of more ambiguous worth. Yet often the candid snapshot turns out to be our favorite photo twenty years down the road. Journals from our high school years that are embarrassing when we are young adults may be rediscovered and valued when we are older. They may even have larger cultural value, or at least emotional significance, to future generations. Conversely, the insurance policy we put in a safe place to grab in case of fire is fodder for the shredder once the policy has expired. Bank records that were a necessity during an IRS audit might be a liability in another situation. Mindful of their value, we often carefully store such records, and do not rediscover them until they are worthless. Even items of great emotional worth may degrade: wedding photos may not be treasured forever if a marriage ends.

Although individual items are of varying value, keeping everything is more or less in line with how many people implicitly manage their personal computers. Rather than deliberately deleting files, they may either leave files behind when they transition to a new computer with the assumption that they can revive the old computer if they discover they need something, or they move the files wholesale to the new machine without examining them.

Three participants in an interview study who were all experienced computer users described this transition process in very similar language:

1. "Whenever I get a new machine, I just transfer everything over. And I just dump the old box."

2. "[When I buy a new computer] I transfer everything. . . . [The computer] is the same [except] it's faster. I should take the time to clean it up at that point, but [I don't]."

3. "I usually transfer stuff from PC to PC when I buy a new one . . . [I] transfer [files] directly by ftp [and put them] usually in my own folder structure." [11]

Let's think about this strategy: what it means is that in the abstract, your computer is a living archive; at any given moment, the computer that you are currently using could possibly store every digital item that has ever crossed your path. Of course, this is seldom true. External storage, web services, old hardware, computers used on the job rather than at home, and any number of forgotten elements of one's personal digital environment may hold a portion of one's personal digital belongings. But for the time being, let's not be so literal. Let's say that a "keep everything" strategy is logistically possible and results in an indefinitely large store of all of your digital stuff for all time. If people are left to their own devices, this mode of accumulation seems to reflect the natural order of things.

It is also important to realize that deletion comes with an associated cost. Why fight against intellectual gravity? After all, deletion is difficult, thankless work; it is cognitively taxing to decide whether to keep something or toss it and the immediate return is minimal. And as yet, there is no Nobel Prize or Oscar awarded for maintaining a neat, well-pruned file system.

Again, in practice, deletion is a far less systematic process than one would hope for or even imagine. It is far more likely that when they are doing something else, people will notice an unfamiliar file name, or encounter an item that seems to be of no persistent value, or assess a piece of email as spam, irrelevant, or no longer interesting, and delete it on the spot (often without even looking at it). Symptomatic of this behavior, during interviews, participants will spontaneously delete a few files as a symbolic act, declaring their distaste for clutter. However, this unpremeditated act does not mean that a participant is committed to spending the next week sorting through her files. For example, in a 2005 study, as we watched a couple going through their hard drive, one of them said to the other: "I don't know what that is. You might as well delete it as far as I'm concerned." In other words, there is no need to look; the file name is unfamiliar, so it is unlikely to be valuable. In spite of the fact that there are probably many such low-value files stored on the computer, the participant somewhat arbitrarily deletes the one that is currently in view, frequently vowing to go after more such files soon.

During the same study, we were observing a participant go through a folder during an exercise in which we asked people to look for the oldest personal file stored on their hard drives. The participant in question encountered a candidate file, did not immediately recognize what it was, opened it, and remembered, thereby setting off a longer reflection about deletion and decision:

> This could've been a seminar or something. Now I remember—[the file's contents describe] what was going to be in the seminar and I didn't go to it. Wow. Yeah. I haven't looked at this stuff in a long time. I mean, it would be sort of interesting to get the pop-up, make a decision on it, and then let it go . . . [in the future] I will become a lean, mean organizing machine.

Yet he did not delete this particular file once he remembered what it was, nor did he delete any of the others he assessed as clutter.

In another study—this time focused on researchers and their personal scholarly materials—one participant was going through his files as I watched. He found a directory on the server replete with files he decided were no longer valuable. As I continued to observe him, the researcher began to delete files without even looking at their contents, only the file names and dates. Sometimes he did not remember their purpose, and sometimes he did:

> The server also stores tons of stuff from when I was working on [project x]. We stored all kinds of shared stuff out there so we could access it. And I need to go through and clean that up because there's gobs of junk out there that should just get deleted . . .
>
> [I ask what a particular file contains.]
>
> I don't remember. That's why it should probably all be deleted. . . . These I think are datasets from various runs. Yeah. This is—no, this is installation files. For various versions of [the software developed for project x]. All this should go. Yeah. These are installation files. They should all go away. They're useless.
>
> [He begins deleting files.]
>
> None of these things mean anything. Except for this. But the line analyzer stuff. I'll never use it. So let's just get rid of that. This stuff should go away. This looks like an archive of the [final version of a conference paper].[12]

Most experienced computer users realize that they delete files in a somewhat arbitrary manner. What varies is whether they plan to someday become more methodical in their curatorial efforts, or whether they accept the vagaries of their own stewardship practices—whether they plan to become lean, clean, organizing machines, or whether they see the endeavor as more or less hopeless.

During another study, a participant acknowledged that his digital stewardship practices were more or less arbitrary. When I asked him whether he ever got rid of digital stuff, he said:

> Yes, but not in any systematic manner. . . . It's more like, I have things littering the desktop and at some point it becomes unnavigable . . . . A bunch of [the files] would get tossed out. A bunch of them would get put in some semblance of order on the hard drive. And some of

them would go to various miscellaneous nooks and corners, never to be seen again.[13]

Another participant, when asked how his files were organized, confessed:

> I keep telling myself that maybe one day I'll basically do the computer equivalent of spring cleaning. I'll just find all these scattered directories and files and sort of clean them, create a fresh hierarchy of 'here are my pictures,' 'here are my movies,' 'here are my documents,' 'here is my music' and get them all cleanly laid out along those lines. And I just never seem to find the time.[14]

There is another, more principled, reason to keep everything. This perspective stems from the idea that the computer will eventually serve as the ultimate memory prosthesis.[15] In other words, the computer's storage is equated with the capacity of human memory, and by extension, deleting corresponds to forgetting.[16] Thus, if we adopt the memory prosthesis perspective, deleting files means that useful context is eliminated, and we lose the ability for every digital item to act as an index to the other digital items that occurred around that time, in that place, or with those people. Deleting files is tantamount to deliberately making a hole in one's memories, inducing amnesia, and potentially reducing the prosthetic power of the computer. But the advantage of keeping everything comes at a price.

Recall the reasons we would keep everything:

- It is difficult to assess value in advance.
- Keeping everything aligns well with current practice.
- Deletion is itself a cognitively demanding exercise.
- People are seldom methodical about culling their files, so why even try?
- A full chronological and contextual record is essential for using one's archives as a memory prosthesis.

Just because it is easier to keep everything than to cull it, does this mean that there is no virtue in the natural falling away of digital belongings through time's gradual erosion? As we examine what people do, a puzzling pattern emerges: people seem to be relying on disk crashes, technology failure, and periodic obsolescence as a way of pruning their collections. It is not that loss does not bother them; it is rather that loss makes their collections more tractable. The accumulated weight of these digital belongings is swept away, so that they can focus their attention on the present. Three quotes from separate interviews conducted in the course of the study cited above confirm that this is a common perspective:

> You want to know the truth? If I blasted my 11,230 emails away, I wouldn't be that bad off probably. Because I'd be able to work on new ones coming in.

> If my hard drive was gone, it really wouldn't bother me all that much, because it's not something I need, need. I just thought it would be nice to keep in around in case I have another [school] assignment just like it.

> I mean, there's plenty of stuff that I've lost that I thought used to matter to me, but not so much. I used to be a real America Online chat guy back in high school. And I'd chat with people from all over the world and one of the cool things is that your logs would get saved and I actually met one of my girlfriends online . . . I could literally go back a year and just look at old chats that we would have. . . . I switched PCs and I just kind of forgot to transfer those files over. Or maybe I wasn't able to. Maybe the formats were incompatible with the new version. I don't remember what happened, but at this point, I've clearly learned not to care. I mean, I thought I would've cared. It might've been nice if I still had them.[17]

This cycle of accumulation and accidental lose may underlie the thousand logistical explanations that consumers offer for failing to back up their computers. In the end, people may be unhappy about data loss, but they shrug it off, all too frequently saying roughly the same thing: "I mean, if we would've had a fire, you just move on." Of course, if you had as many fires as computer crashes, you would look for the arsonist among your friends and family members; you would not simply move on. But we can readily identify some countervailing reasons why we would not keep everything. First and foremost is that although storage is cheap, human attention is far less so. Furthermore, as we will see later in this chapter (and in other chapters of this book), stewardship is more than simply storing digital belongings once on reliable storage; stewardship requires continual attention to the items and media in a collection: Are the formats still active? Is the storage medium still good and still up-to-date? Has virus protection successfully eliminated all threats? Keeping everything places an enormous tax on our stewardship resources. Finally, even if we are careful not to equate computer storage with human memory, keeping everything is impractical from the perspective of the current legal system; we are often instructed to discard certain items.

Thus, from the collection standpoint, what we are looking for varies with value, and that value is not a guaranteed attribute of an item. Most certainly— at the ends of the spectrum—we are looking for the ability to safeguard the things we really care about (even if we are sometimes wrong) and we are looking for the ability to permanently expunge the things we know we never want to see again (which, again, is different from the items of ambiguous worth). But even then, we are left with the vast bulk of the items in the center—those of uncertain value, those that may form the linchpin of our memories or may be not worth looking at in ten years. In other words, most challengingly, for those items in the middle, we are looking for the digital equivalent to benign neglect.

This stratified view of value suggests that a single personal collection may merit several different value-related strategies for keeping digital materials safe. There are at least four categories of value:

- *Known high value items.* There are certainly items in every personal collection that are regarded as of high value (whether value is assessed correctly or not) and thus warrant full archival treatment. These are the things we know we want to keep, and although they vary from person to person, in practical terms, these are usually small in number and identifiable. Most digital archiving strategies to date have been oriented to these items.

- *Medium value subcollections.* Most people can express the value of types of things: I wouldn't want to lose my photos or I'd feel bad if I lost the videos of the kids. Yet examination of these subcollections reveals that they are large and not of uniform value. Some loss would be tolerated, and, over time, some of these items will turn out to be of high value. Certainly people will maintain these things in the present—that is, these items are used in everyday practice and people will copy them from computer to computer. Safety will generally be ensured by making ad hoc copies of the items.

- *Lower value subcollections or media types.* These are subcollections, media types, and items that are of more ambiguous worth. For example, we have seen in the quotes included earlier in the chapter that for many people, overstuffed inboxes or shared music falls into this category. The bulk of the items are a burden rather than a clear benefit, yet there may be items of real value hidden among the detritus. People often express their ambivalence to these items by not backing them up nor copying them to removable media; instead they tempt fate. These are the items left behind when a new computer is purchased. Yet, it seems not worth the effort to delete individual items, and there is enough of worth that one certainly would be reluctant to simply expunge the entire subcollection. Along with items of medium value described above, these subcollections may be preserved through use. The more the items are used, the more valuable they are likely to be, and the better their chance of survival. These items are good candidates for the heuristic approaches that I have sketched out elsewhere.[18]

- *Items of known liability.* As many researchers have asserted, there are items that people would like to "forget"—that is, they would like to delete them from their digital holdings and be certain they will never reencounter them, regardless of the circumstances. Unlike archival deaccession, this deletion is not related to value, but rather is tied up in emotional or legal liability. Hence, deletion must ensure the item is not forensically recoverable.[19]

Storing Personal Digital Archives

At first blush, it is tempting to specify a single central repository for storing our personal digital archives. Then we have control over formats of individual items and can either migrate them or store them in a self-describing way, or provide emulation capabilities to decode them well into the future. Furthermore, sophisticated access policies would enable us to crisply say who has access to what. Our accountant can get at our financial records; our doctor can get at all of our medical records, and our insurance company can get at some of them; our families can look at most of our photos, but perhaps not forward them to people outside of the family. It is easy to come up with a repository that in principle satisfies all of our archival needs.

In practice, however, there are other forces at work. People have their own rationale for putting portions of their overall digital assets in different places. Data safety is an essential side-effect of this de facto distributed storage, but it is unlikely to work the other way around. That is, a centralized archive is unlikely to offer all of the advantages people are already realizing from storing their data in specialized repositories. They won't have the audience they command with Flickr, YouTube, or a blog server; they won't have the functionality offered by various email providers. They won't have local control, as they would by putting the assets on a home server. And although they may have the same level of security they have for financial records stored at their brokerage, they will not be able to conduct transactions.

The follow excerpt from an interview (conducted via Skype's IM functionality) is telling:

> [11:09:24 PM] g says: [There are] 6 [online places where I store things] in all. 1.) school website, 2.) blogspot, 3.) wordpress.com (free blog host, different from wordpress.org), 4.) flickr, 5.) zooomr (for pictures, they offer free "pro" accounts for bloggers, but even for non-pros, they don't limit you to showing your most recent 200 pics only unlike flickr), 6.) archive.org
>
> [11:10:42 PM] cm says: I ask just because you seem to have stuff in a lot of different places (so far two different blog sites, flickr, youtube, msnspaces, . . . maybe yahoo?) . . .
>
> [11:11:07 PM] g says: oh right . . . youtube because people always tell me that they don't feel like downloading my quicktime files from archive.org.

This type of strategy is typical: the participant has stored items in multiple places (sometimes the same items; sometimes different ones) with a plan in mind. She has well-articulated reasons for her choices (Zooomr offers her a free "pro" account, which does not limit her to displaying her two hundred most recent pictures like Flickr does; yet this does not keep her from storing photos on Flickr as well). She is conscious of the fact that different stores reach different audiences (elsewhere in the interview, she states that MSNSpaces reaches a Taiwanese audience that her other blogging accounts don't); this diversity is reflected in her choice of language on the different sites (English or Chinese or a mix of the two). Interestingly, she has already begun losing track of what is where. This confusion is important insofar as a personal archiving strategy that revolves around de facto distributed storage also demands that the user somehow keep track of the far-flung digital assets. Indeed, this challenge is underscored by the fact that data loss is more commonly tied now to losing track of where things are stored and the policies and practices of various storage providers rather than to local crashes and catastrophes under one's own control.[20]

It is tempting to ignore these trends and offer a centralized service to implement the functionality and services we associate with a capable digital repository that takes a long view of storage. But a centralized service will solve only part of the problem at best: it may well be an attractive place to store high-value items of a certain sort—photos, for example, or other types of personal media. But as I have pointed out, other high-value items will be stored in other types of repositories—repositories with capabilities well suited to the type of items stored there.

Hence, what is called for is federation at the metadata level, via a catalog or some other repository that records not only metadata, but also the health and characteristics of other repositories. A catalog can variably store a variety of types of surrogates for individual items, varying from the items themselves (in the event primary storage goes belly-up) to metadata that represents salient features of the remote items. This enables authoritative versions to be stored in the most appropriate place, while the archive keeps track of where the asset is, and any information needed to access it and ensure its ultimate health. This way, our actual distributed store can involve everything from items that are stored as attachments to free email (such as Hotmail, Gmail, or Yahoo mail) to medical records stored in specialized for-pay vault software. Implementing an archive this way allows policies and agreements to be tracked centrally without requiring sensitive information—or media directed at a particular audience—to be similarly centralized.

Network bandwidth use is minimized; security problems are reduced; access is parceled out very naturally; and the sort of loss that we are already observing is minimized. This approach begs the question of format, deferring decoding to access time. This is perhaps a dangerous strategy, and there is no in-principle reason that a user could not be warned of potential obsolescence, since metadata can be used to track storage format and any fonts and codecs necessary to render the item.

This method also acknowledges the need to care for items representing a range of values differently. Perhaps we would want a more fail-safe method of caring for high-value items and to merely ensure that several copies of lower-valued items exist. It also seems that this type of approach can implicitly acknowledge the human tendency toward benign neglect, by gently allowing gradual loss of items of ambivalent value.

Archival Best Practices and Personal Stewardship

As well-known people begin to donate born-digital materials, the engines of their creation (e.g., laptops and desktop computers), and common storage media to libraries, museums, and archives, professional archivists are developing best practices for the stewardship of these personal collections.[21] But the question is, how relevant are these best practices to the consumer at home who has neither the resources, inclinations, skills, nor time to apply them? Can they be scaled back to fit the home user, or are they irrelevant and arcane?[22] Or, even if they are easily understood, are they pragmatically possible from a resource perspective (that is, does anyone have the time to put them into practice)?

What we see when we visit people's homes and workplaces confirms any suspicions we might have about this diverse group of users: they have the best of intentions—they don't actually want to lose data in an uncontrolled way—but they also have other things on their minds. For example, one study participant showed us a yellowed newspaper clipping on a stand near her computer. The year-old technology tips column, "Saving Files with a CD-RW Drive," gave the home user detailed instructions about how to write files to a CD. When asked if she had used the instructions, the woman allowed that no, she hadn't. But she intended to, when she had time. I feel fairly certain that she hasn't followed the instructions, unless a family member has taken over and done it for her.[23]

Because among the digitally prolific there is an implicit tendency to rely on periodic loss to keep uncontrolled growth in check, study participants are beginning to own up that they aren't even sure they believe in digital stewardship. One technologically sophisticated study participant who had lost his personal and business websites because he had not run a recent backup admitted that he wasn't sure he wanted to take responsibility for the loss; furthermore, from his musings, it did not seem as though he intended to implement a backup procedure in the near future:

> It's funny though. If you look at technology, it's just one of those things. I mean, whose fault is it? Is it the user's fault for not backing up? Or is it technology's fault for not being more tolerant and failsafe? In ten years, maybe hard drives and PCs will be so invincible and the Internet will be so pervasive that the concept of backing up will be quaint.[24]

When we talk about teaching archival best practices, it is not only important to identify the best practices or the mode of instruction; it is also vital to specify who will be learning them and who will be implementing them. There are several important things to remember. First, the home archivist is often not the same person as the home IT provider (although home archivist and home IT provider are both ad hoc, fluid roles). The woman with the "Saving Files" clipping next to her monitor is most certainly her family's archivist—at other points, she talks about saving photos, family recipes, and so on—but she is indisputably not her family's informal IT support. That role belongs to her ex-husband:

> I tried to install it [Firefox] and then John [her ex-husband] said, 'Don't install anything on your computer.' . . . I usually defer to John. Because he's the one that's got to come over and maintain it. So I have to make sure that it's okay with him. But Jack [her 18 year old son] . . . will just do whatever he wants.

From the opposite perspective, the capable IT person may have little interest in curating a family artifact. In other words, the person who is capable of creating the CD described in the previous example may not see the need to label it (as would be the impulse of the family archivist). In another interview during the same study, a college student held up an unlabeled CD at an angle so that she could see the contrasting textures that indicate what part of the CD has been written and told us, "It's kind of weird, but with some of these CDs, you can tell how much is written on it by looking."

It becomes apparent that in many home situations, archiving is a cooperative activity, one in which people take different roles with respect to the technology. People tend to rely on each other for informal backups of their own archival efforts. Can't identify someone in a photo? Maybe a friend or family member will be able to tell you.[25] Didn't get a particular shot? Maybe someone else thought to bring a camera. Experience a technology failure? Perhaps the person you sent an attachment to still has it and can recover it for you. The digital stewardship we associate with personal archives is inherently social.

Again referring to the same set of interviews, a student who had lost an autobiographical assignment to a computer virus was able to recover her document from a relative:

> Even my personal statement was saved onto that computer [the virus-infected laptop]. Then luckily, I also emailed it to my cousin, Camilla, at her house. . . . So I said, 'Camilla, do you still have my UCLA personal statement?' She's like, 'Yeah.' So I said, 'Okay, can you please email it.' So then that's how I actually got it back to this computer.[26]

It is not unusual for people to recover lost media socially, for example, from a recipient of an email attachment, or from a collaborator.

At this point, we must return to matters of scale. At the scale of the single digital artifact, individuals are rapidly improving at creating, recording, shaping, mashing up, sharing, and even saving one item at a time. But they are no better at keeping these things around as we scale up along various dimensions (as the individual items grow larger and more numerous; as the number of people we share with grows larger; as the number of devices we use increases; as the time of retaining items approaches decades). In other words, the same practices that allow us to handle one media file often cannot be applied to handle an entire collection.

As one frightening illustration, we posed the following scenario to some interview participants: suppose you had one hour before you knew your local hard drive was going to fail. What would you do? A surprising number started their panic reaction by saving one file at a time—for example, a participant might describe attaching an item that mattered to an email message (we were presuming mail services were still available). In practice, we know this one-at-a-time approach is not feasible.

Matters do not really improve as users become more sophisticated and are able to handle more files at once and move to the cloud. A participant in another study indignantly described losing her collection of personal journal podcasts after a service went under:

> I hosted my podcasts early on on a free service called Rizzn.net . . .
> he then changed rizzn.net to something called blipmedia.com and
> then . . . he decided to sell blipmedia . . . and he never emailed people
> about it . . . suddenly the files were gone and the only news I heard
> about it was when I had to hunt online for what happened.

Thus, if we return to our earlier realization—it is easier to *keep* than to *cull*—we can further muse that it is easier to *lose* than to *maintain*. And that, in a nutshell, encapsulates benign neglect as a personal digital archiving strategy.

Of course, automating whatever practices we can routinize is the best way of taking advantage of the computational platform. There are already personal archiving services that have made substantial headway on providing individuals and small businesses with curation services and mechanisms.[27] It does not seem necessary to spell them out here, except to say that there is plenty of room to investigate services that take advantage of the so-called wisdom of crowds, since that is one point of leverage that is far more available in today's world. In essence, just as there are orders of magnitude increases in the number and genres of things we can create in a digital networked world, there are similar increases in our access to the fruits of other people's labor; if we are clever, we can harness the power of social networks to perform various communal organizing and labeling activities.[28]

Does a Collections-Storage-Practices Framework Cover the Territory?

Obviously, reducing the challenges of personal digital archiving to an interaction among collections, storage, and archival practices is too simplistic. Much falls outside of this framework, especially the question of use as time passes. How will people recover items from a large distributed personal store, especially after they forget what they have and what they don't have?[29] It is important to note that recovery of digital assets from long-term storage is different from implementing a generalized search mechanism.[30] This is the point at which we will pay the price for our storage strategies.

The other notable gaps in this discussion stem from the rapid shifts underway in underlying technologies, shifts that may give us new points of leverage. For example, the replication mechanisms that are already the backbone of institutional stores may be brought to bear on the problem of how we synchronize content among our many personal devices.[31] Once this type of mechanism is in place, we may have a straightforward way of scooping up copies of valuable digital assets as they are replicated and storing them in a repository that lies somewhere between a backup and an archive.[32]

But the main lesson we should take away from this discussion is not that a 'silver bullet' technology will come along and render the problem solved, or that a method of creating self-describing objects will allow our digital assets to be perpetuated into the indefinite future, or even that the first born-digital generation—today's kids—will have a much better understanding of appropriate stewardship practices, and hence will just know what to do. Instead, we should realize that there are many equally valid approaches to creating and maintaining personal digital archives and that all of our digital belongings do not require the same level of attention and protection.

An archive that is in essence a catalog will allow us to federate our digital belongings on the metadata level and will help us resolve issues associated with provenance. This kind of approach will allow different stores to evolve to meet different needs. After all, it is likely we will want to archive our medical records differently from how we archive our financial records. Furthermore, we may even want to devote different resources to our formal portraiture than we do to our cell phone snapshots (recognizing that we may be wrong about their relative value). Different methods thus may be brought to bear on preserving our medium- and low-value items.

Above all, any personal digital archiving solutions should acknowledge the human tendency toward benign neglect. For example, we might want to know that we are about to lose access to our financial records because we have changed banks; we may want our social networking profiles to be safely stored when a start-up's business model proves to be unworkable; we may want to be reminded of our encryption keys and of our many temporary stores.

It is perhaps disappointing that we are not tilting full speed at a digital memory box, a digital safety deposit box, or an infinite digital U-Store-It. The desire to centralize, to fully federate, to unify and standardize is understandable, but it also seems out-of-step with human nature. Although the world offers us plenty of scrapbookers and intergenerational storytellers, we have to remember that these phenomena are exceptional and exclusive: they lose the incidental, the candid, and the accidental—a significant portion of the stuff of history that has to-date been preserved through benign neglect.

Benign neglect is thus a means of transcending the vagaries of accumulation and incorrect assessments of value. Distributed storage reduces the vulnerabilities of centralization, and allows functionality and design to more fully reflect the genres of the stored media. Acknowledging that people will not at once become capable stewards of their own digital belongings gives us a realistic idea of what to expect. Benign neglect and intrinsic distribution can become instrumental in securing a digital future in which we neither keep everything, nor lose everything, nor become shackled by the need to sustain our growing accumulations of digital belongings.

Notes

[1] John Seabrook, "Home on the Net," *New Yorker*, October 16, 1995, 70 (italics mine).

[2] For example, the author still has twenty-nine photos she took on an Apple Quicktake digital camera on a 1995 trip to Graceland, Elvis Presley's home in Memphis. Most of these photos were stored as 225-kilobyte TIFF-format files, except for a few 900-kilobyte high resolution shots.

[3] Without post-processing, it is hard to discern the subject of many of the Graceland photographs; modern correction algorithms are capable of improving the photos to the point where they are viewable. This noticeable improvement in correction capabilities makes a compelling argument for keeping the original rather than a corrected version.

[4] Jeff Rothenberg, "Ensuring the Longevity of Digital Documents," *Scientific American* 272, no. 1 1995: 42.

[5] David M. Levy, "Heroic Measures: Reflections on the Possibility and Purpose of Digital Preservation," in *Proceedings of the Third ACM Conference on Digital Libraries*, ed. Ian Witten, Rob Akscyn, and Frank M. Shipman III (New York: ACM Press, 1998), 152–61.

[6] http://techcrunch.com/2009/04/07/who-has-the-most-photos-of-them-all-hint-it-is-not-facebook/ (accessed May 29, 2010).

[7] From the report *Home Servers and Consumer Storage*, prepared by Parks Associates, a market research firm (Dallas, Texas: July 2008).

[8] David M. Levy and Catherine C. Marshall, "Going Digital: A Look at Assumptions Underlying Digital Libraries," *Communications of the ACM* 38, no. 4 (1995): 77–84.

[9] Henry M. Gladney, "Principles for Digital Preservation," *Communications of the ACM* 49, no. 2, (2006) 111–16; Raymond A. Lorie, "A Methodology and System for Preserving Digital Data," in *Proceedings of the 2nd ACM/IEEE-CS Joint Conference on Digital Libraries* (JCDL '02), Portland, Oregon, July 14–18, 2002 (New York: ACM Press, 2002), 312–19.

[10] Emory Libraries, *Preserving Salman Rushdie's Digital Life* (2008), http://www.youtube.com/user/emorylibraries#grid/user/8A1D63F362925EA9 (accessed August 26, 2010).

[11] The participants were part of the study described in Catherine C. Marshall, Frank McCown, and Michael L. Nelson, "Evaluating Personal Archiving Strategies for Internet-based Information," in *Proceedings of Archiving 2007*, Arlington, Virginia, May 21-24, 2007 (Springfield, VA: Society for Imaging Science and Technology, 2007), 151-56.

[12] This study is reported in Catherine C. Marshall, "From Writing and Analysis to the Repository: Taking the Scholars' Perspective on Scholarly Archiving," in *Proceedings of the 8th ACM/IEEE-CS Joint Conference on Digital Libraries (JCDL '08), Pittsburgh, Pennsylvania, June 16-20, 2008* (New York: ACM Press, 2008), 251-60.

[13] Catherine C. Marshall, Sara Bly, and Francoise Brun-Cottan, "The Long Term Fate of Our Personal Digital Belongings: Toward a Service Model for Personal Archives," in *Proceedings of Archiving 2006*, Ottawa, Canada, May 23-26, 2006 (Springfield, VA: Society for Imaging Science and Technology, 2006), 28.

[14] This quotation is from a field study to understand how consumers acquire, keep, and access their digital belongings. For further information about the study, see Marshall et al., "The Long Term Fate of Our Personal Digital Belongings: Toward a Service Model for Personal Archives."

[15] Gordon Bell and Jim Gemmell, *Total Recall: How the E-Memory Revolution Will Change Everything* (New York: Dutton, 2009).

[16] Evgeny Morozov, "Speak, Memory: Can Digital Storage Remember for You?" *Boston Review* (May/June 2010), available at http://bostonreview.net/BR35.3/morozov.php.

[17] Marshall et al., "The Long Term Fate of Our Personal Digital Belongings."

[18] Catherine C. Marshall, "Rethinking Personal Digital Archiving, Part 2: Implications for Services, Applications, and Institutions," *D-Lib Magazine* 14, no. 3/4 (2008), http://dx.doi.org/10.1045/march2008-marshall-pt2.

[19] Simson Garfinkel and David Cox, "Finding and Archiving the Internet Footprint" (paper presented at the First Digital Lives Research Conference, London, England, February 9-11, 2009).

[20] Marshall et al., "Evaluating Personal Archiving Strategies"; Jeremy Leighton John, Ian Rowlands, Peter Williams, and Katrina Dean, "Digital Lives. Personal Digital Archives for the 21st Century >> An Initial Synthesis" (Digital Lives research paper, March 3, 2010, Beta Version 0.2).

[21] Patricia Cohen, "Fending Off Digital Decay, Bit by Bit," *New York Times*, March 15, 2010.

[22] Certainly many people in this field have made sincere efforts to make archival best practices accessible and have thought about how individuals might implement them at home. See, for example, the Library of Congress's suggestions at http://www.digitalpreservation.gov/you/index.html (accessed May 29, 2010).

[23] Marshall et al., "Long Term Fate of Our Personal Digital Belongings."

[24] The participant was part of the study described in Marshall et al., "Evaluating Personal Archiving Strategies."

[25] Indeed, more recent social media services such as Facebook rely on just this sort of collaborative photo-labeling activity.

[26] Marshall et al., "Long Term Fate of Our Personal Digital Belongings."

[27] Stephan Strodl, Florian Motlik, Kevin Stadler, and Andreas Rauber, "Personal & SOHO Archiving," in *Proceedings of the 8th ACM/IEEE-CS Joint Conference on Digital Libraries* (New York: ACM Press, 2008), 115-23.

[28] I feel compelled to emphasize the "if we are clever" portion of this assertion; it's easy to fall into the trap of thinking that crowdsourcing will solve everything. Obviously, it won't, and there are both good and bad examples of how it works (or to point out resources such as *Wikipedia* that are examples of failings as well as strengths of this approach). See Shilad Sen, Shyong K. Lam, Al Mamunur Rashid, Dan Cosley, Dan Frankowski, Jeremy Osterhouse, F. Maxwell Harper, and John Riedl, "tagging, communities, vocabulary, evolution," in *Proceedings of the 2006 20th Anniversary*

Conference on Computer Supported Cooperative Work (CSCW '06) (New York: ACM Press, 2006), 181–90.

[29] And this does not even consider the question of the digital belongings that are passed from generation to generation, creating a gulf of meaning that becomes even more difficult to surmount. It is hard enough to curate a personal collection for one's own use and the use of one's immediate family and close friends, let alone for use by different generations who are unlikely to share enough context to reconstruct the meaning of particular artifacts.

[30] For a discussion of the challenges of such recovery, see Catherine C. Marshall, "Rethinking Personal Digital Archiving, Part 1: Four Challenges from the Field," *D-Lib Magazine* 14, no. 3–4 (2008), http://dx.doi.org/10.1045/march2008-marshall-pt1. See also Edward Cutrell, Susan T. Dumais, and Jaime Teevan, "Searching to Eliminate Personal Information Management," *Communications of the ACM* 49, no. 1 (2006): 58–64.

[31] Venugopalan Ramasubramanian, Thomas L. Rodeheffer, Douglas B. Terry, Meg Walraed-Sullivan, Ted Wobber, Catherine C. Marshall, and Amih Vahdat, "Cimbiosys: A Platform for Content-based Partial Replication," In *Proceedings of the 6th USENIX Symposium on Networked Systems Design and Implementation* (NSDI '09) (Berkeley, CA: USENIX Association, 2009).

[32] See, for example, offerings such as Sharpcast (http://www.sharpcast.com) or Microsoft's LiveMesh (http://www.microsoft.com/livemesh).

Evidence of Me . . . in a Digital World

Sue McKemmish

The 1996 paper "Evidence of Me . . ." asked wide-ranging and funda-mental questions about how our lives are individually and collectively witnessed and memorialized.[1] The term "evidence of me" was used as a synonym for the personal archive in the broadest sense—encompassing all forms that storytelling takes in human society. Recordkeeping, as a kind of witnessing, was placed within this broader context; but at the same time the 1996 paper explored what is different or distinctive about recordkeeping as a particular kind of witnessing. This chapter revisits "Evidence of Me . . ." in the context of new technologies—exploring personal recordkeeping in the digital world (including the forms that personal records take), the relationship between personal and public recordkeeping, and the relationship between records and other forms of recorded information, other memory stores. In so doing, it challenges conventional configurations of the personal archive, the boundaries we have drawn around the forms that archives take, and between personal and public recordkeeping, and the role of the recordkeeping profession and archival institutions in a digital world. Taking up Jacques Derrida's theme that "mutation in technology changes not simply the archiving process, but what is archivable . . . the possibility of archiving," it looks at how new technologies are having an impact on the fundamental nature of archives as we know them and what it means to be an archivist.[2]

Revisiting "Evidence of Me . . ."

Keep them, burn them, they are evidence of me.[3]

"Evidence of Me . . ." broke new ground by exploring the nature of personal recordkeeping and broad social mandates for its role in witnessing to and memorializing individual lives, and forming part of society's collective memory. It looked for the social mandates for personal recordkeeping in sociology and in creative and reflective writing. Thus it referenced novelist Graham Swift on man as quintessentially the "story-telling animal," needing to leave behind "the comforting marker-buoys and trail-signs of stories,"[4] and Edmund White, writing about the acquired immune deficiency syndrome (AIDS) epidemic, on that very human instinct in the face of death to "record one's own past" and "bear witness to the cultural moment,"[5] to strive for the kind of immortality sought by the ancient Egyptians—to remain present in the memory of men: Graham Swift's "life, after all, beyond a life."[6]

It reflected on sociologist Anthony Giddens' views that: "The existential question of self-identity is bound up with the fragile nature of the biography which the individual 'supplies' about herself; that a person's identity, her ability to sustain 'an integrated sense of self,' is to be found in 'the capacity *to keep a particular narrative going*'"; and how a "process of mutual disclosure" is associated with intimate relationships in the modern age, and that "one dimension of this process can be the writing and keeping of letters."[7]

It cited biographer Janet Malcolm on love letters as "fossils of feeling" and "proof that once we cared,"[8] and Swift in the passage that provided the title of the paper: "keep them, burn them, they are evidence of *me*."[9] Along the "keep them, burn them" spectrum, "Evidence of Me . . ." explored personal recordkeeping behaviours ranging from the obsessive recordkeeping of *The Grass Sister's* eponymous character Ann-Clare[10] to those very personal acts of destruction epitomised by Australian Nobel prize writer Patrick White: "It is dreadful to think . . . that one's letters still exist. I am always burning and burning, and must go out tomorrow to the incinerator with a wartime diary I discovered at the back of the wardrobe."[11] And it pointed to the darker destructive counterparts of the urge to witness and memorialize, in the targeting of archives that accompanies acts of war, genocide, and ethnic cleansing, citing the testimony of Andras Riedlmayer in relation to the Bosnian conflict.[12] Anticipating philosopher Jacques Derrida on the death drive in archiving, and its engendering of archive fever, it pointed to examples of the passion to witness, to record the testimony, to set aside and safeguard the archive in face of the determination to destroy memory utterly so that no trace of the murder and violence is left:

> If there is a passion, it is because we know that not only the traces can be lost by accident or because the space is finite or the time is finite, but because we know that something in us, so to speak, something in the psychic apparatus, is driven to destroy the trace without any reminder. And that's where the archive fever comes from.[13]

In its focus on recordkeeping as "a kind of witnessing," the paper challenged conventional boundaries between archival and other forms of recorded information, while proposing a distinctive role for recordkeeping based on the nature of records as evidence of social and organisational activity. It expanded upon existing definitions of the archival document[14] and extended the role of recordkeeping:

> We are concerned with the nature, purposes and functionalities of a particular form of recorded information, documentary traces of social and organisational activity, that are accumulated and managed by recordkeeping and archiving processes. . . . Recordkeeping is *a kind of witnessing and memory making*, a particular way of evidencing and memorialising our individual and collective lives—"our existence, our activities and experiences, our relationships with others, our identity, our 'place' in the world."[15]

In bringing together stories that tell about witnessing in the broad sense with stories about the particular role of recordkeeping as a form of witnessing, "Evidence of Me . . ." asked fundamental questions about the nature of records as "evidence of me" and "evidence of us," about how our lives are individually and collectively witnessed and memorialized. Here, *witnessing* is used in the Oxford English Dictionary sense of "bearing oral or written evidence," or "furnishing oral or written evidence," but the concepts of oral and written evidence are interpreted broadly to encompass any of the many different forms that recorded information and oral transmission take, including the spoken word, song, music, dance, and ritual. Thus the term "evidence of me" was used in the article as a synonym for the personal archive in the very broadest sense. "Evidence of Me . . ." places recordkeeping, as a kind of witnessing, within this broad context that encompasses all forms

---

The Archival Document

For anyone not familiar with the term, the archival document can best be conceptualised as recorded information arising out of transactions—it is created naturally in the course of transacting business of any kind, whether by governments, businesses, community organisations or private individuals. Recording of transactions may be in any storage media and is increasingly becoming an electronic process. The concept of the archival document is commonplace within European thought, but in English-speaking countries it is often confused with documents that have been selected for retention within an archival institution. The lack of an adequate construct to explain the processes of creating and maintaining recorded information arising out of transactions within English-speaking countries creates a distracting division within the recordkeeping profession between records managers, who look after current archival documents, and archivists, who look after our archival heritage which includes archival documents which have been selected for permanent retention. An understanding of the archival document which encompasses both current and historical documents directs attention to the continuum of processes involved in managing the record of a transaction from systems design to destruction or select preservation . . . . Within this approach, documentation of a transaction is archival from the time the record is created and the archival document retains evidential value for as long as it is in existence . . . .

The archival document also represents the experience of the parties to the transaction which it records. It is more than recorded information. Those archival documents which are selected for permanent preservation become part of the archival heritage of a society, transmitting the accumulated experience of the transactions they document to future generations.

Effective creation and management of the archival document to ensure its integrity and validity is a precondition of an information-rich society and underpins public accountability on the part of both government and non-government organisations, FOI [freedom of information] and privacy legislation, protection of people's rights and entitlements, and the quality of the archival heritage.[16]

---

that storytelling takes, but at the same time explores what is different or distinctive about recordkeeping as a particular kind of witnessing.

In constructing an identity, people seek both to differentiate themselves from others and to identify with others. We assert our own individuality, our uniqueness, with reference to our distinguishing attributes. Yet one way of defining our attributes is by identifying ourselves with others in terms of gender, sexuality, family, age, education, occupation, class, religion, place, ethnicity, nationality, race, and so on. The public and private roles and relationships associated with these attributes are both socially constructed and shaped by the interaction of an individual personality with the social construct of identity. Thus "Evidence of Me . . ." was also concerned with "the collective archives as an aspect of 'evidence of us' in the extensive sense, and the way in which they constitute a form of collective memory."[17]

Recordkeeping in the Continuum

The record is always in a process of becoming.[18]

Like "Evidence of Me . . ." this chapter resonates with understandings of personal recordkeeping from a continuum perspective, providing a reading of personal recordkeeping with reference to the records continuum model.[19]

The writings of Frank Upward on the records continuum model constitute one of the most systematic studies of recordkeeping, evidence, and memory in archival literature. A reading of personal recordkeeping from the first,

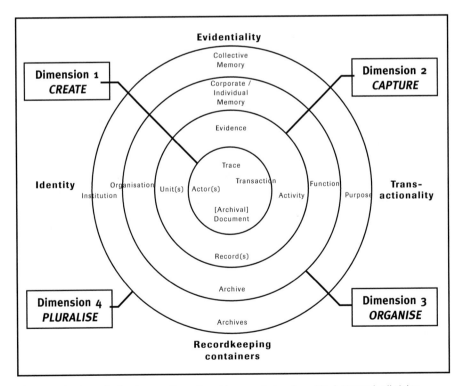

Figure 1. The Records Continuum. Reproduced by permission from Frank Upward, all rights reserved.

second, third, and fourth dimensions of the continuum model highlights the *creation* of records as traces of an event, interaction, experience, or reflection; their *capture* into personal recordkeeping systems or stores that link them to related records and contextualize them in the context of an individual life; their *organisation* as a personal archive to function as long-term memory of our significant functions and interrelationships; and their transformation

---

The Distinguishing Characteristics of Records

Records [can be distinguished from] other forms of recorded information by their ongoing participation in social, business and other processes, broadly defined, i.e., by their transactional and contextual nature. Their evidential qualities are seen as integral to their 'recordness,' and to their intents, multiple purposes, and functionality in terms of governance and accountability, their role in the formation of individual, group, corporate, and collective memory and the shaping of identity, and their value as authoritative sources of information. The concepts of *transactionality* and *contextuality*, as further developed in the records continuum, are complex and multi-layered. Transactionality is defined in terms of the many forms of human interaction and relationships that are documented in records of all kinds at all levels of aggregation. The concept of contextuality is concerned with the record's rich, complex, and dynamic social, functional, provenancial, and documentary contexts of creation, management, and use through spacetime. In the records continuum model framework these concepts find expression in a range of continua:

- The evidential continuum: trace, evidence, corporate and individual [whole of person] memory, collective memory.

- The continuum of recordkeeping objects: [archival] documents, records, the corporate and individual archive, and the collective archives.

- The continuum of identity: actor, work group/unit, organisation/corporate body, and institution.

- The continuum of transactionality: act, activity, function, purpose.

The records continuum model's approach to the roles individuals may play along the identity axis of the model encompasses their roles as actors in social and business acts, units in social and business activities, legal entities with social and business functions, and social entities with institutionalised social purposes. The continuum concept of transactionality encompasses individual acts of communication, and social and business transactions of all kinds, the social and business activities or processes of which they are a part, the social and business functions they fulfil, and the social purposes they serve.[20]

into "evidence of us," enabling records that memorialize individuals to be carried beyond the boundaries of an individual life, *pluralising* them through incorporation into the collective archives so that they can become accessible parts of society's memory.

Records continuum theory posits multiple contexts for recordkeeping and enables multiple points of view. In order to use the records continuum model as an analytical tool to explore features of virtual and physical recordkeeping landscapes, it is necessary to adopt a single point of view, for example, the broader context or ambience of one of the parties to the activities and transactions documented in the records. Adopting the point of view of another party to the transaction gives a different reading as that party's purposes and functions differ from those of other participants. Pursuing this approach teases out what Chris Hurley has termed the *simultaneous multiple provenances of records*—including the ambient context of the individual or organisation that set the records aside, as well as the ambient contexts of other participants in the processes of records creation, accumulation, management, and use.[21]

The records continuum model provides a way of exploring the relationship between personal and public recordkeeping as an interface between two recordkeeping spacetimes: the spacetime of the personal archive and the spacetime of the collective archives.[22] Here, "evidence of me," which functions as personal memory, moves beyond the boundaries of individual spacetime and is transformed into "evidence of us" in collective spacetime. In "Evidence

---

1D Create
The first dimension encompasses the actors who carry out the act (decisions, communications, acts), the acts themselves, the documents which record the acts, and the trace, the representation of the acts.

2D Capture
The second dimension encompasses the personal and corporate records systems which capture documents in context in ways which support their capacity to act as evidence of the social and business activities of the units responsible for the activities.

3D Organise
The third dimension encompasses the organisation of recordkeeping processes. It is concerned with the manner in which a corporate body or individual defines its/his/her recordkeeping regime, and in so doing constitutes/forms the archive as memory of its/his/her business or social functions.

4D Pluralise
The fourth dimension concerns the manner in which the archives are brought into an encompassing (ambient) framework in order to provide a collective social, historical and cultural memory of the institutionalised social purposes and roles of individuals and corporate bodies.

Figure 2. The Dimensions of the Records Continuum Model. Adapted from Frank Upward, 1996.

of Me . . ." this interface was in part explored through the story of how Patrick White, the archetypical destroyer of records, acted to ensure that many of his personal records would never move beyond his own individual spacetime, relying for his own purposes on a form of remembrancing which drew on his prodigious memory. For most of his life he had insisted on the burning of his manuscripts and letters, feeling that looking back was morbid, and that only his novels should survive. Toward the end of his life, he changed his mind, engaging in processes that enabled the movement of "evidence of me" through spacetime, ensuring the *pluralisation* of the "other voices" in his letters.

In the records continuum, records are "always in a process of becoming"[23] –definable only in terms of their multiple and dynamic documentary and contextual relationships, configured and reconfigured by their use in and through space and time. Thus records are depicted as dynamic objects, fixed insofar as their original content and structure can be re-presented, but "constantly evolving, ever mutating"[24] as they are linked to other records and ever-broadening layers of contextual metadata that manage their meanings, and enable their accessibility and useability as they move through spacetime, and are presented or rendered in different formats, using different software and hardware, with different system configuration settings. In a similar way, the personal archive and collective archives, and the relationships between them, are constantly evolving and changing shape. Extending Richard Holmes' wave motion analogy of biographical subjects as subatomic particles—"never existing in all their complexity in any one place or time"[25]– an archival document exists as an act of witnessing in a particular spacetime, but can never be experienced in all its complexity by a witness in any given space and time.

"Refiguring the Archive"

> The archive—all archive—every archive—is figured. Acceptance of this in South Africa has shaped fundamentally the argument—and the processes built upon it—that the country's archives require transformation, or refiguring. The figuring by our apartheid and longer pasts must be challenged, and spaces must be opened up in the archives by a transforming society.[26]

Archival science and practice have traditionally worked with a narrower view of what forms archives and records take than that embraced by "Evidence of Me . . . " continuum thinking, and postmodern and postcolonial archival writers. By and large, oral forms of records, literature, art, artefacts, the built environment, landscape, dance, ceremonies, and rituals have been excluded from the professional meanings given to *record, archive*, and *archives*. These forms of recorded information have been seen as "other," and their potential archival or evidentiary nature rarely figures in modern archival evidentiary paradigms.[27] Hard boundaries have been drawn between personal and public recordkeeping, between the private and the public. And a singular and therefore partial view is embodied in most archival practice, particularly appraisal and description. This view privileges the context in which a single "records creator" operates and is blind to the contexts of others who participated in the activities or events documented in the record as parties to the transactions. The single records creator is privileged in terms of the rights of the various parties or participants in the records captured in the records systems of the creator. Australian practice has introduced the notion of *multiple provenance* to refer to successive creators over time, but mostly still privileges one creator at any given time.

Chris Hurley challenges these approaches with reference to the concepts of simultaneous multiple provenance and parallel provenance. In a two-part article on archival description, Hurley addresses the challenges to traditional practice posed by the postmodernists and understandings drawn from Indigenous perspectives with reference to an emergent concept of simultaneous multiple provenance in which two or more creators, who are part of a singular broader context or ambience, can be identified at the same time.[28] The concept of simultaneous multiple provenance can only be implemented in archival practice within a meta-system which recognises the existence of simultaneous multiple provenances and contested views, does not subsume one to the other, and supports the description of records from the multiple perspectives of the "co-creators" of the records with reference to their different purposes and functions. Hurley also proposes the concept of parallel provenance to provide for situations in which simultaneous multiple provenances are described in parallel systems and there is no meta-system in place in which they can coexist:

> Archival description must necessarily be grounded in a point of view (an ambience). Often, the ambience is unstated—implicit rather than explicit. Different points of view establish an alternative context. Archival theory can be developed to allow the simultaneous documentation of these alternative (parallel) points of view in a single descriptive system or statement. A [meta-] system is to be preferred because it allows for on-going management of collective knowledge. Post-modernist critics have challenged archival theory to provide for an articulation of different voices in the way records are preserved and described. Parallel provenance provides an acceptable method for meeting this challenge without disturbing the traditional respect for provenance.[29]

He illustrates this concept with reference to the parallel provenances of the records of Australia's Stolen Generation of Indigenous children, held by government archives.[30] The descriptive practices of these government archives privilege the role and viewpoint of the official agencies involved—the agencies that set the records aside—over that of the churches and welfare agencies which were also parties to the transactions, and the Indigenous participants in the events, albeit unwilling ones. Hurley argues that the government files simultaneously exist in the context of Indigenous Australians' individual and collective experience as participants in the process: "Those records belong to the narrative of the people upon whom the policies were applied as well as the narrative of those who wrote them and set them aside."[31] The fact that their participation was unwilling, that they were the victims of a government process that, from the perspective of the government of the day, might be labelled child removal, but was experienced by Indigenous Australians as child stealing—a process which abused their human rights, removing children for the stated purpose of assimilating them into white society—gives additional impetus to the postcolonial argument that traditional archival theories and practice, in privileging the singular records creator and treating other parties or participants as subjects of the records, perpetuate their victimisation and play a role in continuing to silence their voices.[32]

This particular example is best defined by Hurley's concept of parallel provenance because it involves what Lynette Russell has termed *incommensurate ontologies,* referring to the possibility that Indigenous and Western knowledge systems or worldviews may be incompatible or irreconcilable.[33] As long as the concept of the singular record creator is the guiding principle in defining provenance, the view of colonial and postcolonial governments of Australia of their child removal policies and related processes—as currently represented in the archival systems of Australia's national and state archives—cannot be reconciled with the view of Indigenous communities: that the children and their families were unwilling participants in acts of child stealing and human rights violation.

Postmodernist and postcolonial ideas, coupled with new social technologies, and Indigenous ways of knowing, are opening up exciting possibilities for "refiguring the archive"; acknowledging parallel record-keeping universes, or even realising an archival multiverse or meta-verse;[34] building shared archival spaces that enable the coexistence of simultaneous multiple provenances; recognising the spiritual and emotional, as well as the intellectual and physical, dimensions of the archive;[35] and transforming the relationships between personal and public recordkeeping. In the postmodern and postcolonial archival discourse, traditional Western archival science ideas about the nature of the record have been challenged by explorations of processes of remembering and forgetting, inclusion and exclusion, and the power relationships they embody.[36] Writing about the renegotiation of the past and transformation of archives in post-apartheid South Africa, Verne Harris has urged archivists not to cling to positivist views of the archival endeavour that focus on custodianship, the physicality of records and archival places, and the record as merely a carrier of memory, but instead to engage in "processes of memory formation," embracing new technologies and postmodernity as well as Indigenous meanings and conceptual frameworks.[37]

A potentially rich stream in the memory metatext addresses the relationship between memory and archives. In "What Is Past Is Prologue," Terry Cook refers to a selection of such texts, including Jacques Le Goff's exploration of the "politics of archival memory,"[38] Patrick Geary's study of medieval archives,[39] and Michael Clanchy's classic work on the transition from oral to written records.[40] Cook points to the need for archivists to explore the field of "memory scholarship" as "it puts into context many unquestioned assumptions underpinning archival theory and conceptualisation."[41]

There is also a growing body of relevant writings by the postmoderns, including Foucault on the "archaeology of knowledge," Derrida on the "archive," and Giddens on "the constitution of society."[42] The influence of their ideas is apparent in the archival literature of recent years, including the philosophical essays of Brien Brothman,[43] much of Terry Cook's and Tom Nesmith's work, which involves reconceptualisations of the nature of records and provenance,[44] the writings on the philosophical and theoretical basis of functional appraisal by Hans Booms,[45] and Verne Harris's explorations of the relevance of Derrida's thinking to archival endeavour, including appraisal and description.[46]

More recently, archival literature written with reference to postcolonial, community, and Indigenous frames of reference has explored the role of archives and records as instruments of colonization and decolonization, linked to social justice and accountability agendas,[47] initiatives relating to pluralising the archival paradigm through education,[48] and explorations of nontraditional forms of the archive, including oral and performative records. For example, Kelvin White has explored the recordness of the mestizaje (songs performed in Afro-Mexican communities of the Costa Chica),[49] and Diana Taylor has conceptualised the performative record as embodied memory in terms of performance as an act of cultural transmission.[50] There is also a growing body of literature that reports on research relating to Indigenous forms of records and oral memory.[51]

In the postmodern and postcolonial archival literature, evidentiary and memory paradigms are shifting, the archive is being refigured, and boundaries are becoming permeable, are redrawn, or even obliterated. As we move further into the virtual world of digital technologies, new ways of negotiating the relationships between records and other forms of recorded information are emerging. It is possible now to envisage a diary, a letter, a poem, a painting, an artefact, an oral memory, an autobiography, a performance, a building, or a landscape:

- Taking multiple forms.
- Being linked to other forms of recorded information in multiple ways.
- Performing multiple functions (as record, publication, museum object, piece of art, part of a historic site).
- Having simultaneous multiple or parallel provenances (as part of a personal or public archive or archives, library, museum, gallery or historic site).

Their capacity to function in multiple or parallel roles depends on how we define and manage them; the social, functional, provenancial, and documentary contexts in which we place them (as public or private record, or museum object, or work of art); and the enabling technologies of our spacetime. Extending the discussion of multiple or parallel provenance, in a digital world we can place records simultaneously in multiple or parallel contexts and thus enable them to perform multiple roles—the song as performance and oral record; the diary as record and publication; a building as part of a historic site and part of an archive; government records as part of personal, community, and public archives; a cave painting as art and archive.

In this virtual world of shifting paradigms and boundaries, is it still possible to define what is distinctive about records and archives? In the Australian records continuum discourse, the differences between records and archives on the one hand, and other forms of recorded information on the other, rest on the transactional and contextual nature of records—their evidential qualities—specifically on:

- Their capacity to function as evidence of our actions and interactions, and

- The *evidence-related* nature of:

  o Their content (capturing transactions that occur in social and business processes).

  o The specific documentary forms (structures) which they take.

  o Their multiple or parallel contexts of creation, management, and use through spacetime—their social, political, legal, functional, and documentary contexts.

The continuum view of the evidentiary nature of records as integral to their role in governance and accountability; the formation of individual, group, corporate, and collective memory and the shaping of identity; and the records' value as authoritative sources of information enables us to distinguish the evidential role that any form of recorded information can play and specify their evidence-related management requirements in a digital world.[52]

Moving Beyond "Evidence of Me . . ."

> Somewhere beyond custody recordkeeping professionals are
> reinventing their mission.[53]

"Evidence of Me . . ." was written for the May 1996 special issue of *Archives and Manuscripts* that focused on personal recordkeeping and consciously rejected the dualism encapsulated in the title of the Australian journal, taking a holistic and integrated approach to corporate and personal recordkeeping. Following "Evidence of Me . . . " this chapter challenges a binary view of digital "materials generated and kept by individuals, as opposed to electronic records that are generated within and managed by formal and organizational recordkeeping systems."[54]

As referenced above, "Evidence of Me . . ." took its title from the novel *Ever After.* Set in the present and the past, *Ever After* tells two parallel stories, one an account of a contemporary life, the other a story pieced together from the notebooks of Matthew Pearce that document his life as a surveyor and amateur archaeologist/geologist, born into a pre-Darwinian world, and his struggles with religious doubt and eventual loss of faith following the publication of *Origin of the Species.* Preserved for posterity, the notebooks become testimony to how "ideas that shook the world" were played out in the microcosm of a private life—"as evidence of me" and eventually also "evidence of us." How would Pearce's notebooks manifest themselves in our twenty-first century world of social technologies? Would his "jotting urge" have led to his participation in an informal network of colleagues and friends, communicating, co-creating, storing, and recording personal public information in a distributed network of blogs and Facebook sites, texting, twittering, and talking via Skype—creating "evidence of me . . . and of us" in a nanosecond? And how might the increasingly obsessive recordkeeping behavior of Ann-Clare in *The Grass Sister,* and her meticulous documentation in letters, photographs, and slides of the details of her intimate, masochistic life, have played itself out online in the networked world of taboo sites explored by Katherine Gallen in a paper which investigates the relationship between the taboo and the archive?[55]

"Evidence of Me . . ." asked some key questions about the nature of records as "evidence of me"—and, by extension, as "evidence of us." Translated into our spacetime, they query:

- The forms storytelling and witnessing take in a digital world.

- The specific role personal recordkeeping plays in witnessing our lives individually and collectively, and forming personal and collective memory in this world, with reference to the way in which Derrida's "mutation in technology" enables new forms of public and personal recordkeeping behaviour and interaction.

- The multiple forms that personal records can take in our spacetime and the relationships enabled between them.

- The relationship between personal and public recordkeeping, the personal and the public archive, and the coexistence of "evidence of me . . . and us" in shared digital spaces.

- The relationship of the record to other forms of recorded information—other memory stores—for example, living memory, learned behaviour, gender and other roles, social and organisational structures, rituals, ceremonies, oral tradition, memoirs, autobiographies, biographies, genealogies, histories, scholarly writings, mass communications, music, paintings, sculpture, literature, dance, film, artefacts, landscapes, and the built environment.

Such questions are made more urgent by the possibilities of archiving that the new technologies of the digital world bring when combined with maturing records continuum, archival postmodern and postcolonial thinking, and understandings drawn from Indigenous ways of knowing. The answers to these questions have profound implications for personal and public recordkeeping, for the shape and nature of the personal archive and the collective archives, and for the profession and practice of recordkeeping and archiving.

Digital Technologies and the "Possibility of Archiving"

The mutation in technology changes not simply the archiving process, but what is archivable . . . the way we experience what we want to keep in memory, or in archive—and the two things are different—is conditioned by a certain state, or a certain structure, of the possibility of archiving. So the archive, the technological power of the archive, determines the nature of what has to be archived. . . . Then, of course for that reason . . . the structure and meaning of the archive is of course dependent on the future, on what is coming, on what will have come.[56]

Digital technologies open up new possibilities of personal recordkeeping behaviours in the continuum in relation to the *creation* of records-as-trace, their *capture* into a personal recordkeeping system or store, their *organisation* as a personal archive, or their *pluralisation* as part of the collective archives.

In a recent article, Eric Ketelaar discusses the nature of personal recordkeeping in our networked, digital world of ubiquitous computing and permanent connectivity through mobile devices.[57] Consider the use of the mobile phone as a communication and networking device, a tool enabling the *creation, capture* and sharing of narratives, visual images, and sound; and the *organisation* and *pluralisation* possibilities of online photo albums, digital scrapbooking, blogging, and *Wikipedia*-like tools and sites. Or the spontaneous recordmaking potential of wearable digital cameras, as a pictorial diary or aide-memoire, equipped with electronic movement, heat, and light sensors, like Microsoft's SenseCam,[58] continuously taking photographs in response to changes in the wearer's environment.

Tim O'Reilly has characterized Web 2.0 technologies as "tools that harness collective net-enabled intelligence." In open source environments, software becomes a service, with users as codevelopers; social technologies and *Wikipedia*-like tools can profoundly change the dynamics of recordkeeping behaviour, records creation and capture; and collaborative categorisation of sites or development of metadata schemas from the ground up—folksonomy—becomes possible.[59] The number of blogs and bloggers has grown exponentially in the last ten years, from the early weblogs of the late 1990s to the myriad blogs today. Blogs and more recent applications like Facebook, YouTube, and Twitter can function or potentially function as an online personal public archive—evidence of *me, my* voice, *my* identity on the Web. Everyman or everywoman can become his or her own archivist.[60] At the same time, the new technologies enable social interaction and activity to be recorded in vast networks of interconnected social networking sites. In these virtual spaces, an individual's blog, Facebook, or YouTube channel simultaneously functions as "evidence of me . . . and of us." And from a records continuum perspective, each posting potentially involves simultaneous acts of *creation, capture, organisation,* and *pluralisation.*

Digital technologies enable the formation and re-formation of virtual personal and community archive(s)—storing and linking to records in all forms and in all places that witness to and memorialize an individual life and her place in the collective life of a community—from the perspective of the life of that individual in a continuing "process of becoming." Increasingly the personal public archive will take the form of linked social technology sites, linked into personal data files via government agency and private company sites. In some cases—but this is unlikely to be the norm—a personal public archive will be coordinated and institutionalised. An example of an institutionalised personal public archive of this kind is the Mandela Archive discussed in the next section. In Australia and the United States we might expect the Prime Ministerial and Presidential libraries and archives to increasingly take on this form.

Web technologies also enable new networked, interactive forms of recordkeeping behaviour, of witnessing both our personal and collective lives, and of integrated personal and public recordkeeping. Eric Ketelaar characterises personal public records that are born digital in web environments, particularly using Web 2.0 applications, as involving a new "social and cultural phenomenon of co-creatorship" between individuals and organisations. He states that "social navigation and community-based adaptation techniques can transform archives into social spaces by empowering records to be open social entities."[61] As Chris Hurley elaborates in his discussion of parallel provenance:

> Parallel provenance also operates at the granular level. All description is scalable. The provenance of a single document or (trans)action can be dealt with using the same methods applicable to a whole series or *fonds*. In the world of cyberspace, networked activity opens up business processes so that shared workspace increases participation by numerous actors in a single workflow regardless of organisational structures (which have traditionally provided the source of ideas about creation and provenance) and decreases communication as a step dissociating one phase of a workflow from another. Electronic records have less well defined boundaries establishing "creation," "control," "maintenance," etc. Ideas about parallel contextual worlds that establish the evidential meaning of such records regardless of organisational boundaries can help illuminate how current recordkeeping can be developed to meet new challenges.[62]

Familiar examples in the government and corporate world include Internet banking, online airline and accommodation booking and account management systems, and e-government services such as online tax return submission and vehicle licensing.

On a potentially darker note, ubiquitous computing, connectivity, and social technologies also enable lifetime surveillance and data gathering, whether for commercial or intelligence purposes. Furthermore, Web 2.0 services are provided by commercial enterprises which manage the servers and exercise various levels of control—not all transparent—over storage and access, as well as the content of social networking sites. Their longevity is ultimately dependent on the viability of the services and their providers, and long-term ownership, preservation, and accessibility issues are not generally addressed in the frameworks in which the service providers operate.

Social technologies are already changing the way archival services are provided and the ways in which they interact with their users. Eric Ketelaar first highlighted the potentially transforming effects of Web 2.0 technologies in relation to such initiatives in 2003,[63] and has traced the emergence since the 1990s of digital storytelling in institutional archival spaces, including personal narrative and testimony. Early examples cited by Ketelaar include the Library of Congress Veterans History Project and the Centre for Digital Story Telling in California.[64] He also points to more recent examples of the ways in which archival institutions are beginning to use these technologies to engage individual users in interactions which involve contributing their stories; uploading their documents; commenting on or annotating the content of archives; and providing descriptions, metadata, and (potentially) parallel or multiple provenances (for example, the Your Archives initiative of The National Archives in London and the Polar Bear Expedition Digital Collections of the Bentley Historical Library). These "Archives 2.0" applications enable people's individual stories to be connected with public archives "using technologies for social navigation and ubiquitous computing which can transform archives into social spaces of memory"[65]—encompassing both "evidence of me" and "evidence of us." Australian examples include the National Archives of Australia's Mapping our Anzacs site, which provides digitised copies of the World War I service records of Australian Anzacs who fought at Gallipoli, and enables users to add notes and photographs relating to individual servicemen to the scrapbook.[66] The Public Record Office of

Victoria's pilot wiki site features the 1891 Women's Suffrage Petition, and offers users the opportunity to enrich the information available about the collections of the Public Record Office by posting their knowledge and research, either by adding to existing information on this site or creating their own subject streams.[67]

In these examples, digital technologies are enabling the sharing of archival spaces, but the spaces are still under the control of a single archival institution, and multiple perspectives are present within a framework constructed from the perspective of that institution. A recent paper points to parallel developments in the museum world with museums exploring the potential of "Museum 2.0" applications, and discusses the "contradictions [that] must be resolved between museum practices, which privilege the account of the 'expert,' and distributed social technology practices, whose strengths lie in allowing for many, sometimes contradictory, perspectives," with reference to a number of initiatives that explore other ways of representing the knowledge of diverse communities and challenge institutionalised archives/museum boundaries.[68]

In the archival world, digital technologies can enable the coexistence of different perspectives in shared, networked spaces in which all parties are considered co-creators of records and co-formers of the archives. "Evidence of us" in the form of digital communities of records[69] is enabled in networked spaces where personal and corporate archive(s) can be co-located in the intricate webs of the lives of other people, other communities, other organisations. New ways of forming individual and collective archives enable the construction of multiple and contested views, and empower "others" in shared archival spaces. They challenge the conventional roles of the recordkeeping profession and archival institutions, and the singular viewpoint that informs their practice, including appraisal and description. And the emphasis shifts from how to archive blogs to blogging as archiving; from archiving the Internet to the Internet as archive; from how to use digital technologies to make archival collections more accessible to how to use digital technologies to enable the co-creation of records and the co-formation of the archives in spacetime, and assure the preservation and accessibility of these networked, shared archival spaces through time.

In his recent book, *Managing the Crowd: Rethinking Records Management for the Web 2.0 World*, Steve Bailey considers the challenges confronting the records management profession as new technologies expose the inadequacies of existing frameworks, strategies, and tools.[70] One of the most daunting and exciting challenges is concerned with how the recordkeeping profession and archival institutions can work in partnership with organisations, communities, and individuals—and with commercial service providers—to negotiate and implement frameworks, meta-systems, and ontologies for negotiated, shared control of the recordkeeping and archival spacetimes of the future. Recordkeeping and archival expertise is needed to:

- Develop socio-legal frameworks, archival policies, and practice that support co-creatorship of records and co-formation of the archives, enabling shared decisionmaking, and negotiation of rights and responsibilities.

- Provide management, appraisal, metadata, and access services and tools that support the implementation of negotiated, networked recordkeeping and archival arrangements (for example, appraisal policies and tools that address the multiple provenances of records and the different perspectives, recordkeeping requirements, and archival values of the co-creators of records; metadata schemas which support the description of multiple provenances from multiple perspectives; and access services and tools that provide for differentiated access).

- Deliver trusted digital repository services to sustain shared recordkeeping and archival spaces and their infrastructures, enabling the storage, preservation, and accessibility of these spaces through time.

Optimal use of digital technologies, including cloud computing and web services, can only be achieved by partnerships involving archival institutions, organisations, communities, and individuals, as well as standard-setting bodies and the commercial enterprises which manage the grids, servers, and applications. Commercial service providers exercise various levels of control (not all transparent) over storage and access, as well as the content of digital repositories and social networking sites. The sustainability and longevity of these repositories and sites are ultimately dependent on the viability of the services and their providers. Long-term ownership, preservation, and accessibility issues are yet to be addressed in the frameworks in which the service providers operate, and archival policies, strategies and standards are needed to address these critical issues.

Is the recordkeeping profession as we know it equipped to meet these challenges? If not, what is involved in building the required capability? Could a transformed profession and refigured institutions deliver the recordkeeping and archival expertise required, or will the role be taken on by others? An examination of specific archives provides insight into these and related issues.

Parallel Archival Universes: The Mandela Archive

> In the life of any individual, family, community or society, memory is of fundamental importance. It is the fabric of identity . . . the memory of an individual is founded in collective memory, and it is with this ancient wisdom in mind that we inaugurated the Nelson Mandela Centre of Memory and Commemoration . . . to unravel the many silences imposed by our apartheid and colonial pasts, to find space for the memories suppressed by power.[71]

The Mandela Archive is an example of an institutionalised personal public archive that challenges conventional configurations of the archive, the power structures they embody, and the boundaries we have drawn around the forms that archives might take and between personal and public recordkeeping. It addresses many of the questions posed in "Evidence of Me . . ." and here—about the multiple forms and provenances of archives, the relationship between orality and other forms of record, and between individual and collective memory—including the role of personal recordkeeping in the recovery of collective memory, and the role archivists can play in making a personal archive, broadly defined, accessible as collective memory. And it is enabled by digital technologies.

The Nelson Mandela Centre of Memory and Commemoration was launched in Johannesburg in September 2004. It was set up to locate, document, and facilitate access to the many archives that contain traces of Mandela's life and the lives of those who have shared his life: "The Mandela Archive is, in the first instance, defined by Mandela himself, and documents his life and work. He is the centre point of the archive, from which a myriad of threads can be followed."[72] These threads lead out into the intricate webs of other people's lives. This social justice archive is also an exemplar of the concept of parallel provenance.

The archive includes or points to the memories and oral records of Mandela, his family and clan, and of the people whose lives he touched; buildings and landscapes occupied by Mandela, the places where "he has left his trace" (his homeland, the prison cells, workplaces, and homes, the structures and streets that bear his name); artefacts and objects used by or associated with him; Mandela's own records, his writings and speeches, personal notes and correspondence, diaries, medical and legal records; the official records of his trials and imprisonments, and his presidency; the archives of the apartheid government, the African National Congress (ANC), anti-apartheid movements around the world, and the Truth and Reconciliation Commission; media records and archives; websites, publications, literature, song, and art in which he figures:

> Whereas a conventional archive has a single location and a finite number of documents, the Mandela Archive is an infinite one, located in innumerable places. It is also not confined to documents, but includes sites, landscapes, material objects, performances, photographs, artworks, stories and the memories of individuals.[73]

In the Mandela Archive, these records are identified, appraised, contextualised, and described with reference to Mandela's participation in the events they document, as a party to the transactions and activities they evidence, and in the ambient context of his whole life. Simultaneously, the ANC records, the official records of Mandela as president of South Africa, or the foreign government records of involvement in the anti-apartheid movement are located in parallel provenances, in the archival systems of the ANC archive, the National Archives of South Africa, or the government archives of other nations. There they are identified, appraised, contextualised, and described from the perspectives of the ANC, the South African government, or the foreign government with reference to the functions and activities of their "creating" agencies, the organisations that set them aside.

Toward the Archival Multiverse: The Koorie Archiving System

> I think it is very important for us . . . the stories . . . of our family and Ancestors, and also . . . the stories about culture and the law, and the creation stories that are relevant to where we are from, and for our kids as well . . . Probably the most fundamental thing is an individual's identity, where they fit in, and where they belong is really important. Having some way to re-connect with family, community and culture in that way is a really good path to follow.[74]

The Koorie Archiving System (KAS), an outcome of an Australian Research Council-funded project Trust and Technology: Building Archival Systems for Oral Memory, is an initiative that aims to use digital technologies and ideas about archives that derive from both postmodern and Indigenous traditions to move beyond conventional configurations of archives; traditional notions of ownership of and rights in government records based on the construct of a singular records creator; and the boundaries we have drawn between personal records and public records, community and government records. It moves toward an archival multiverse in that it aims to provide an archival space where control is shared and all parties involved can negotiate a meta-framework in which multiple perspectives, provenances, and rights in records coexist. KAS involves a partnership between Monash University, the Public Record Office Victoria, the Koorie Heritage Trust, the Koorie Records Taskforce, the Indigenous Special Interest Group of the Australian Society of Archivists, and the National Archives of Australia.

The Koorie people are the Indigenous people of southeastern Australia who have been subject post-invasion to a repressive colonial and postcolonial regime which robbed them of their heritage, their language, their land, and—in the case of the Stolen Generations—their identity. A major aim of the KAS initiative is to provide a space in which Koorie oral memory can be captured, shared, and linked to archival sources of Koorie knowledge and records about Koorie Victoria. "Oral memory" as used here is broadly defined to encompass traditional stories transmitted orally, contemporary narratives, individual and family stories, and narratives that can be recovered from mainstream archives. It is particularly significant because of the role it plays in the recovery of identity, reconnecting families, and rebuilding communities.[76]

The Koorie Archiving System as a Shared Archive Space

Collaborative Web 2.0 technologies can be deployed to create shared archival spaces. They can enable archival institutions, communities and individuals to work in partnership and exercise mutual rights and responsibilities in relation to archival records in a shared virtual space. In the Koorie Archiving System, government archival records and Koorie community and personal records, the public and the private will co-exist—complementing, completing, balancing and contradicting each other in a shared space. In this collaborative place, Koorie communities and individuals, including members of the Stolen Generations, will be able to archive their records and stories, linking them to related official records and providing a rich, multi-layered resource to support knowledge sharing, the construction of identity, the re-uniting of families and the re-generation of culture and communities. These virtual spaces can be configured to respect the rights in records and protocols of all parties involved, and support differentiated access. The Koorie Archiving System will use web-based technologies to create a shared space for the Public Record Office of Victoria, the Koorie Heritage Trust Inc, the National Archives of Australia, and Koorie communities and individuals to work collaboratively as equal partners to create an archive that operates in both public and personal spacetime, an archive that respects Koorie community requirements relating to Koorie rights in government archival records, and supports Koorie community control of who can use community and personal records and stories according to their access protocols. More broadly, the project will provide a demonstrator of a socially inclusive approach to archiving, showing how government and alternate views can be presented in a harmonious environment, while demonstrating how community organisations can integrate government records into their own knowledge and records systems. It will illustrate how collaborative technologies can support creative and innovative partnerships between archival institutions and communities to build and manage richer archival resources that reflect multiple perspectives of history.[75]

The Trust and Technology Project's findings strongly support the need to refigure the archive, redraw or obliterate the boundaries, and develop alternative, holistic approaches to building a network of personal, family, and community archives and provide gateways to all records in any form relating to a particular family or community.

Many of the Koorie community elders and members interviewed in the Trust and Technology Project see government, church, and other records that relate to them as *their* records, echoing the views of members of communities elsewhere who have been subjected to repressive government regimes and abuse of human rights:

> A recent book . . . contains the poignant story of Rene Baker, who, 4 years old, was literally snatched from the arms of her mother by a missionary. Being a half-caste she was removed to Mount Margaret Mission. Fifty years later, with the help of Bernadette Kennedy, Rene Baker . . . went searching for her file. "They've got *me* up there in Canberra," she explained with a passionate emphasis on the word "me." "They've got something of me up there and I want it back. They're keeping me, but in real life they don't give a stuff because it didn't happen to them and they'll never know the experience that I and other kids went through. They keep these things but they don't respect the experience behind them."[77]

Rene Baker is a member of the Stolen Generation. This quote is a powerful expression of how she identifies with *her* file in the National Archives. As Eric Ketelaar notes, Rene Baker's identification with *her* file reminds one of the slogan "I want *my* file," shouted by civic groups who stormed the offices of the Stasi, the ministry for state security in East German cities on January 15, 1990.[78] The most commonly expressed view of Koorie people in relation to government records is that the so-called subjects of the record or their families have a right to know that there are records relating to them in archival custody, and not only to access them, but to participate as co-creators in decisionmaking about access, ownership, and control. More generally, from a Koorie perspective, Koorie knowledge and narratives are contained in, and recoverable from, all archival records relating to Koorie people, including government records.[79] Eric Ketelaar reminds us:

> "Freedom for my file" means also: liberating the file from the one and only context of the record creator. A different perspective is needed, allowing, what in archival practice is called the *subject* of the record, to become a *party* to the record.[80]

In this context, Chris Hurley's concept of simultaneous multiple provenance becomes an archival imperative.

A constant theme in the interviews was the participants' requests to be able to add their own "stories" to the records held in public archives and other institutions. This is most keenly expressed in these quotations as a desire to put the record straight:

Interview No. 42: "Aboriginal people should have the opportunity to add their oral history versions and an opportunity to say 'This is the way we see it.' So that should be included so that any researcher accessing those archives in the future can be aware of the Aboriginal family's position on the information."

Interview No. 43: "I know a lot of Aboriginal people get very upset when they look at their files and they look at the words that were used by the social workers of the time, or why people were taken away. And it's just purely from the policies of that era and then if Aboriginal people had a chance to be able to say: 'It wasn't like that at all. Yes, I was dirty and I didn't have food, but I was well loved and cherished.' So that you get that equal perspective."

Interview No. 64: "That's right, just to put the record straight. 'That wasn't the way it happened. This is the way it happened.'"[81]

KAS is a response to the need to "put the record straight" and for participation in decisionmaking about, and control of, archival records of Koorie people and communities whatever their source or current location. Capitalizing on the technologies available in the Web 2.0 environment, it will link recordings of oral narratives and memories to other records of Koorie people, including government records. KAS will connect many different archives, organisations, and individuals via suites of web pages collaboratively built by Victorian Koorie communities and individuals, Koorie heritage organisations, and government archival institutions. It will provide family- or community-centred alternative views to current and historical accounts of Victoria's past found in government, church, and other archives. KAS is envisaged as a "cloud archive" that:

- Sources, brings together, integrates, preserves, and makes accessible existing records relating to Koorie communities, families, and individuals from government, community, and personal sources.

- Caters for content in many different forms and media, including official written records, oral testimony, records of Koorie organizations, family and personal records, photographs, audio and video recordings, and so on.

- Enables the negotiation of controls and protocols that respect Koorie community, family, and individual rights in records, and establishes requirements relating to the preservation, storage, accessibility, and use of the content of the cloud archive, including requirements relating to differentiated access.

- Provides a space in which communities, families, and individuals can easily create and add new content linked to the core collection of information.

- Provides a mechanism for annotations that interpret, correct, or provide context for information content sourced from official records, involving a fundamental rethinking of how government archives present the information they contain to communities.[82]

Addressing the challenge of managing, preserving and making accessible such networked, shared archival spaces through time, KAS will model an approach involving a trusted independent community archival organization (in this case the Koorie Heritage Trust) acting as the manager of a shared archival space on behalf of all the parties involved; and separation of the ownership, control, and management of the content of the cloud archive from the provision of the expert technological services involved in running servers and ensuring the archive's long-term preservation and accessibility, drawing in this case on the specialist capacity of the Public Record Office Victoria in digital archives. It is also envisaged that government and church archives, libraries, and museums might in turn link back to the KAS sites so that when users look at the official files they will know that there are other views or counter narratives, and further layers of context. Full implementation of KAS-like systems will also test how well the Australian series system[83] and related metadata schema, with their powerful relational characteristics, might accommodate alternative readings of the records and their contexts and different perspectives, from the point of view of all parties to or participants in the transaction, in and through time, from individual, community, corporate, and societal perspectives.

> Effective democratization can always be measured by this essential
> criterion: the participation in and access to the archive, its constitution,
> and its interpretation.[84]

New digital technologies impact on personal and public recordkeeping and archiving behaviours. They can be employed in socially inclusive, integrated approaches to personal and public recordkeeping and archiving. They enable personal and public records to take new forms and open up new possibilities of archiving. They can represent multiple perspectives, parallel or multiple provenances; enable shared control and the exercise of negotiated rights in records; present government, alternate, and contested views in parallel or together in a shared archival space; allow community organizations to integrate government records into their own knowledge and records systems, and individuals to interact with public and community archives. Ultimately they might even enable incommensurate ontologies to be reconciled in the archival multiverse.

Web-based technologies are increasingly being used by archival institutions to improve the interaction between their collections and their clients, especially through web-based access. But digital technologies support an emerging present and a future that challenge our current institutionalised recordkeeping and archival practices in fundamental ways. Key challenges include building meta-frameworks for integrated personal and public recordkeeping; developing policies, strategies, and tools for managing appraisal and metadata to support multiple simultaneous provenances; providing controlled and differentiated access to sensitive information; enabling the exercise of mutual rights and responsibilities by all partners in collaborative recordkeeping and archiving initatives; and the development of trusted digital repository services that can ensure long-term preservation and accessibility where required.

The emergent new personal and public recordkeeping behaviours, new forms of personal archive and collective archives, the parallel universe of the Mandela Archive, the potential of KAS-like systems to provide and sustain shared, collaborative archival spaces, and the possibility of the archival multiverse exemplify the ways in which new technologies—together with new ways of conceptualising the archive drawn from continuum, postmodernist and postcolonial thinking, and Indigenous ways of knowing—"change not simply the archiving process, but what is archivable . . . the possibility of archiving," as described by Derrida.[85]

A number of other chapters in this book focus on archival or collecting institutions and explore the way new technologies can be deployed to make the archives more accessible. The application of digital technologies as explored in this chapter demonstrates how they may impact on the fundamental nature of personal and public recordkeeping, the personal archive, and the collective archives as we know them. The implications are far-reaching in terms of the recordkeeping profession, what it means to be an archivist, and the role of archival institutions. This chapter has canvassed exciting prospects for integrating personal and public recordkeeping, personal and public archives, transforming our understandings of the relationship between "evidence of me" and "evidence of us," and refiguring the nature of the personal archive and its place in the archives of society. And it suggests ways in which we can move closer to the reality of Derrida's "effective democratisation of the archives," involving not only broad access to the archive, but also extensive "participation in its constitution and interpretation."[86]

Acknowledgments

In reporting on the project, I acknowledge the Indigenous peoples of Australia and the members of the Koorie communities of Victoria who agreed to be interviewed as part of the project, who shared their views and experiences with us, and gave permission for the use of the interview transcripts for the research purposes of the project. I also gratefully acknowledge the others working with me on the ARC Linkage Project *Trust and Technology: Building an Archival System for Indigenous Oral Memory* (T&T Project). The Chief Investigators were Professor Lynette Russell, Centre for Australian Indigenous Studies, Monash University (CAIS); Professor Sue McKemmish, Faculty of Information Technology, Monash University (FIT); Professor Don Schauder (FIT); Dr. Graeme Johanson (from 2005, FIT); and Dr. Kirsty Williamson (2003-4, FIT); with Partner Investigator Justine Heazlewood, Director and Keeper, Public Record Office Victoria (PROV). The industry partners are PROV; the Koorie Heritage Trust Inc. (KHT); the Australian Society of Archivists Indigenous Issues Special Interest Group; and the Victorian Koorie Records Taskforce. Members of the research team included Andrew Waugh (PROV), Rachel U'Ren (FIT and PROV), Emma Toon (PROV), Merryn

Edwards (PROV), Sharon Huebner (KHT and FIT), Diane Singh (CAIS), Dr. Stefanie Kethers (FIT), Fiona Ross (FIT), Carol Jackway (FIT), and Jen Sullivan (FIT). The Australian Postgraduate Award (Industry) PhD researcher was Shannon Faulkhead (CAIS). I also thank our Advisory Committee, in particular the continued support of Aunty Joan Vickery, and especially acknowledge the vital role undertaken by the project's Koorie Liaison Officer, Diane Singh (CAIS).

I acknowledge Frank Upward for providing a key reference point for the article in his model of the records continuum and thank him for his permission to publish the model and extracts from our joint writing. I also thank Michael Piggott for his encouragement and support through our long-time shared interest in personal recordkeeping, and for prompting me to consider how the recordkeeping behaviours referenced in "Evidence of Me . . ." might play out in a digital world. I thank Eric Ketelaar and Andrew Waugh who reviewed early drafts and provided invaluable advice on the development of this chapter.

Notes

[1] Sue McKemmish, "Evidence of Me . . . " *Archives and Manuscripts* 24, no. 1 (1996): 28–45.

[2] Jacques Derrida, "Archive Fever in South Africa," in *Refiguring the Archive,* ed. Carolyn Hamilton, Verne Harris, Jane Taylor, Michele Pickover, Graeme Reid, and Razia Saleh (Dordrecht, Boston, London: Kluwer, 2002), 46.

[3] Graham Swift, *Ever After* (London: Picador, 1992), 52.

[4] Graham Swift, *Waterland* (London: Picador, 1983), 62.

[5] Edmund White, *The Burning Library: Writings on Art, Politics and Sexuality 1969-1993* (London: Picador, 1995), 215.

[6] Swift, *Ever After,* 207.

[7] Anthony Giddens, *Modernity and Self-Identity: Self and Society in the Late Modern Age* (Cambridge: Polity Press, 1991), 54.

[8] Janet Malcolm, *The Silent Woman* (London: Picador, 1994), 110.

[9] Swift, *Ever After,* 52.

[10] Gillian Mears, *The Grass Sister* (Sydney: Knopf, 1995).

[11] Patrick White, quoted in David Marr, *Patrick White: A Life* (Sydney: Vintage, 1992), 323.

[12] Andras Riedlmayer, "Killing the Memory: The Targeting of Libraries and Archives in Bosnia-Herzegovina," *Newsletter of the Middle East Librarians Association* 61 (Autumn 1994): 1.

[13] Derrida, "Archive Fever in South Africa," 44.

14 Sue McKemmish and Frank Upward, "The Archival Document: A Submission to the Inquiry into Australia as an Information Society," *Archives and Manuscripts* 19, no. 1 (1991): 17–32; paper originally prepared as a submission to the Inquiry into Australia as an Information Society in October 1990.

15 Sue McKemmish, "Traces: Document, Record, Archive, Archives," in *Archives: Recordkeeping in Society*, ed. Sue McKemmish, Michael Piggott, Barbara Reed, and Frank Upward (Wagga Wagga: CIS CSU, 2005), 3. Quote from McKemmish, "Evidence of Me . . . ," 29.

16 Extract from McKemmish and Upward, "The Archival Document: A Submission to the Inquiry into Australia as an Information Society," 19-22.

17 Frank Upward and Sue McKemmish, "In Search of the Lost Tiger by way of Saint-Beuve: Reconstructing the Possibilities in 'Evidence of Me . . . ,'" *Archives and Manuscripts* 29, no. 1 (2001): 30.

18 Sue McKemmish, "Are Records Ever Actual?" in *The Records Continuum: Ian Maclean and Australian Archives First Fifty Years*, ed. Sue McKemmish and Michael Piggott (Clayton: Ancora Press in association with Australian Archives, 1994), 200.

19 Frank Upward, "Structuring the Records Continuum Part One: Post-custodial Principles and Properties," *Archives and Manuscripts* 24, no. 2 (November 1996): 268–85; and Frank Upward, "Structuring the Records Continuum Part Two: Structuration Theory and Recordkeeping," *Archives and Manuscripts* 25, no. 1 (1997): 10–35.

20 Upward and McKemmish, "In Search of the Lost Tiger," 27-28.

21 Chris Hurley, "Parallel Provenance: (1) What, If Anything, is Archival Description?" *Archives and Manuscripts* 33, no. 1 (2005): 110–45; and Chris Hurley, "Parallel Provenance: (2) When Something is *Not* Related to Everything Else," *Archives and Manuscripts* 33, no. 2 (2005): 52–91.

22 In physics, spacetime refers to a continuum with four dimensions—three of space and one of time—in which any event takes place. For a discussion of the concept of spacetime as applied to the keeping of records, see Upward and McKemmish, "In Search of the Lost Tiger."

23 Upward and McKemmish, "In Search of the Lost Tiger," 200.

24 Terry Cook, "What Is Past Is Prologue: A History of Archival Ideas Since 1898, and the Future Paradigm Shift," *Archivaria* 43 (1997): 20.

25 Richard Holmes, literary biographer of Stevenson, Shelley, Coleridge and others, uses the powerful metaphor of subatomic particles which are only definable in terms of a wave motion when reflecting on how biographical subjects are witnessed. See Holmes, *Footsteps: Adventures of a Romantic Biographer* (London: Flamingo, 1995), 68–69.

26 Hamilton et al., *Refiguring the Archive*, 7.

27 Ann Laura Stoler discusses the concept of evidentiary paradigms, a term coined by Carlo Ginzburg, in "Colonial Archives and the Arts of Governance: On the Content in the Form," in Hamilton et al., *Refiguring the Archive*.

28 Hurley, "Parallel Provenance: (1)" and "Parallel Provenance: (2)."

29 Hurley, "Parallel Provenance: (2)," 81–82.

30 From 1910 to 1970, up to fifty thousand Indigenous children were forcibly removed from their families. The Australian Human Rights and Equal Opportunity Commission's *Bringing Them Home* report tells their stories. See Human Rights and Equal Opportunity Commission Australia (HREOC), *Bringing Them Home: Report of the National Inquiry into the Separation of Aboriginal and Torres Strait Islander Children from their Families* (Canberra: HREOC, 1997).

31 Hurley, "Parallel Provenance: (1)," 138.

32 Terry Cook, "Fashionable Nonsense or Professional Rebirth: Postmodernism and the Practice of Archives," *Archivaria* 51 (2001): 30–31.

[33] Lynette Russell, "Indigenous Researchers and Archives: Mutual Obligations and Binding Trust," *Archives and Manuscripts* 34, no.1 (2006): 32–43.

[34] I am grateful to colleague Ally Krebs for introducing me to the term *archival multiverse*. According to the Oxford English Dictionary, the term *multiverse* was originally coined in 1895 by psychologist William James, and is now used to refer to the hypothetical set of multiple possible universes.

[35] First Archivists Circle, *Protocols for Native American Archival Materials* (2007), http://www.firstarchivistscircle.org/files/index.html.

[36] Cook, "What Is Past Is Prologue"; Eric Ketelaar, "Recordkeeping and Societal Power," in McKemmish et al., *Archives: Recordkeeping in Society*, 277–98.

[37] Verne Harris, "The Archival Sliver: A Perspective on the Construction of Social Memory in Archives and the Transition from Apartheid to Democracy," in Hamilton et al., *Refiguring the Archive*, 149–51.

[38] Jacques Le Goff, *History and Memory*, trans. Steven Rendall and Elizabeth Claman (New York: Columbia University Press, 1992).

[39] Patrick J. Geary, *Phantoms of Remembrance: Memory and Oblivion at the End of the First Millennium* (New York: Princeton, 1994).

[40] M.T. Clanchy, *From Memory to Written Record: England, 1066-1307*, 2nd ed. (Cambridge, MA: Blackwell, 1993).

[41] For an extensive discussion and referencing of a selection of the memory metatexts from other fields, including those that directly address archival issues, see Cook, "What Is Past Is Prologue," 50, no. 3.

[42] Michel Foucault, *The Archaeology of Knowledge* (New York, 1970; originally published in French in 1966); Jacques Derrida, *Archive Fever: A Freudian Impression* (Chicago and London: University of Chicago Press, 1996); Anthony Giddens, *The Constitution of Society: Outline of the Theory of Structuration* (Cambridge: Polity Press, 1984).

[43] Brien Brothman, "Declining Derrida: Integrity, Tensegrity, and the Preservation of Archives from Deconstruction," *Archivaria* 48 (1999): 64–89.

[44] Terry Cook, "Mind Over Matter: Towards a New Theory of Archival Appraisal," in *The Archival Imagination: Essays in Honour of Hugh A. Taylor*, ed. Barbara Craig (Ottawa: Association of Canadian Archivists, 1992), 38–70; Terry Cook, "Electronic Records, Paper Minds: The Revolution in Information Management and Archives in the Post-custodial and Post-modern Era," *Archives and Manuscripts* 22, no. 2 (1994): 300–29; Terry Cook and Joan M. Schwartz, "Archives, Records, and Power: From (Postmodern) Theory to (Archival) Performance," *Archival Science* 2 (2002): 171–85; and Tom Nesmith, "Still Fuzzy, But More Accurate: Some Thoughts on the 'Ghosts' of Archival Theory," *Archivaria* 47 (1999): 136–50.

[45] Hans Booms, "Uberlieferungsbiblung: Keeping Archives as a Social and Political Reality," *Archivaria* 33 (1991): 25–33.

[46] Verne Harris, "Redefining Archives in South Africa: Public Archives and Society in Transition," *Archivaria* 42 (1996): 6–27; Verne Harris, "Claiming Less, Delivering More: A Critique of Positivist Formulations on Archives in South Africa," *Archivaria* 44 (1997): 132–41; Wendy Duff and Verne Harris, "Stories and Names: Archival Description as Narrating Records and Constructing Meanings," *Archival Science* 2, nos. 3-4 (2002): 263–85.

[47] See, for example, Randall C. Jimerson, *Archives Power: Memory, Accountability and Social Justice*, (Chicago: Society of American Archivists, 2009).

[48] Anne J. Gilliland, Sue McKemmish, Zhang Bin, Kelvin White, Yang Lu, and Andrew Lau, "Pluralizing the Archival Paradigm: Can Archival Education in Pacific Rim Communities Address the Challenge?" *American Archivist* (Spring–Summer 2008): 84–114; Kelvin White and Anne Gilliland, "Promoting Reflexivity and Inclusivity in Archival Education, Research and Practice," *Library Quarterly* 80, no. 3 (July 2010): 231–48.

[49] Kelvin L. White, "*Mestizaje* and Remembering in Afro-Mexican Communities of the Costa Chica: Implications for Archival Education in Mexico," *Archival Science* 9 (2009): 1–2.

[50] Diane Taylor, *The Archive and the Repertoire: Performing Cultural Memory in the Americas* (Durham, NC: Duke University Press, 2003).

[51] Shannon Faulkhead, "Narratives of Koorie Victoria" (PhD dissertation, Faculty of Arts, Monash University, 2008); Matthew Kurtz, "A Postcolonial Archive? On the Paradox of Practice in a Northwest Alaska Project," *Archivaria* 61 (2006): 63–90; Sue McKemmish, Shannon Faulkhead, Livia Iacovino, and Kristen Thorpe, "Australian Indigenous Knowledge and the Archives: Embracing Multiple Ways of Knowing and Keeping," *Archives and Manuscripts* 38, no. 1 (2010): 27–50; and Shauna McRanor, "Maintaining the Reliability of Aboriginal Oral Records and their Material Manifestations: Implications for Archival Practice," *Archivaria* 43 (1997): 64–88.

[52] Upward and McKemmish, "In Search of the Lost Tiger."

[53] Frank Upward and Sue McKemmish, "Somewhere Beyond Custody," special issue, ed. Glenda Acland, *Archives and Manuscripts—Electronic Recordkeeping: Issues and Perspectives* 22, no. 1 (1994): 149.

[54] Christopher A. Lee, "Introduction" in this volume.

[55] Katherine Gallen, "Archiving and Memorialising the Taboo," *Archives and Manuscripts* 36, no. 1 (2008): 46–74.

[56] Derrida, "Archive Fever in South Africa," 46.

[57] Eric Ketelaar, "Archives as Spaces of Memory," *Journal of the Society of Archivists* 29, no. 1 (2008): 9–27.

[58] Emma Berry, Narinder Kapur, Lyndsay Williams, Steve Hodges, Peter Watson, Gavin Smyth, James Srinivasan, Reg Smith, Barbara Wilson, and Ken Wood, "The Use of a Wearable Camera, SenseCam, as a Pictorial Diary to Improve Autobiographical Memory in a Patient with Limbic Encephalitis," *Neuropsychological Rehabilitation* 17, nos. 4/5 (2007): 582–681.

[59] Tim O'Reilly, "What is Web 2.0?" (2005), http://www.oreillynet.com/lpt/a/6228 (accessed August 16, 2009).

[60] Eric Ketelaar, "Everyone An Archivist," in *Managing and Archiving Records in the Digital Era, Changing Professional Orientations,* ed. Niklaus Bütikofer, Hans Hofman, and Seamus Ross (Baden: Hier + Jetzt, Verlag für Kultur und Geschichte, 2006), 9–14.

[61] Ketelaar, "Archives as Spaces of Memory," 14, 18.

[62] Hurley, "Parallel Provenance: (2)," 82.

[63] Eric Ketelaar, "Being Digital in People's Archives," *Archives and Manuscripts* 31, no. 1 (2003): 8–22.

[64] Ketelaar, "Archives as Spaces of Memory."

[65] Ibid., 9.

[66] http://mappingouranzacs.naa.gov.au/default.aspx (accessed August 24, 2009).

[67] http://wiki.prov.vic.gov.au/index.php/PROV_Wiki_-_Home (accessed August 24, 2009).

[68] Ramesh Srinivasan, Robin Boast, Jonathan Furner, and Katherine M. Becvar, "Digital Museums and Diverse Cultural Knowledges: Moving Past the Traditional Catalog," *Information Society* 25, no. 4 (2009): 265. The examples Srinivasan et al. discuss include the Ara Irititja Archive and the Mukurtu Wumpurrarni-kari Archive initiatives of the Pitjantjatjara and Warumungu communities of Northern Australia (see http://www.irititja.com and http://www.mukurtuarchive.org).

[69] Jeannette Bastian coined the term *communities of records,* "imagined as the aggregate of records in all forms generated by multiple layers of actions and interactions between and among the people and institutions within a community." See Jeannette Bastian, *Owning Memory: How a*

Caribbean Community Lost Its Archive and Found Its History (Westport, CT: Libraries Unlimited, 2003), 5.

70 Steve Bailey, *Managing the Crowd: Rethinking Records Management for the Web 2.0 World* (London: Facet, 2008).

71 Nelson Mandela Foundation, *A Prisoner in the Garden: Opening Nelson Mandela's Prison Archive* (London: Viking, 2005), 9.

72 Ibid., 35.

73 Ibid., 41.

74 ARC Linkage Project, *Trust and Technology: Building Archival Systems for Indigenous Oral Memory* (2003–8), transcript of interview no. 42, 4.

75 Public Record Office Victoria, Koorie Heritage Trust, and Monash University, "Koorie Archiving System" (application to the Victorian Government's Collaborative Internet Innovation Fund, prepared by Andrew Waugh, Shannon Faulkhead, and Sue McKemmish, 2009).

76 Fiona Ross, Sue McKemmish, and Shannon Faulkhead, "Indigenous Knowledge and the Archives: Designing Trusted Archival Systems for Koorie Communities," *Archives and Manuscripts* 34, no. 2 (2006): 112–51.

77 Eric Ketelaar, "Access: The Democratic Imperative," *Archives and Manuscripts* 34, no. 2 (2006), quoting Rene Powell and Bernadette Kennedy, *Rene Baker: File #28 /EDP* (Fremantle: Arts Centre Press, 2005), 174.

78 Ketelaar, "Access: The Democratic Imperative," 63.

79 Ross et al., "Indigenous Knowledge."

80 Ketelaar, "Archives as Spaces of Memory," 14, referencing Michael Piggott and Sue McKemmish, "Recordkeeping, Reconciliation and Political Reality," in *Past Caring? What Does Society Expect of Archivists? Proceedings of the Australian Society of Archivists Conference, Sydney, 13–17 August 2002,* ed. Susan Lloyd (Canberra: ASA, 2002).

81 ARC Linkage Project, *Trust and Technology,* 13–14.

82 Public Record Office Victoria et al., "Koorie Archiving System."

83 Chris Hurley, "The Australian ('Series') System: An Exposition," in *The Records Continuum: Ian Maclean and the Australian Archives First Fifty Years,* ed. Sue McKemmish and Michael Piggott (Clayton, Australia: Ancora Press in association with Australian Archives, 1994), 150–72.

84 Derrida, *Archive Fever: A Freudian Impression,* 4.

85 Derrida, *Archive Fever: A Freudian Impression,* (as endnote 16) 17.

86 Derrida, *Archive Fever: A Freudian Impression,* 4.

Part 2

Specific Genres and Document Types

"Three Backups Is a Minimum": A First Look at Norms and Practices in the Digital Photo Collections of Serious Photographers

Kristina M. Spurgin

Serious amateur photographers are largely invisible in the literature on the management of personal photo collections. Leisure practitioners have been of little interest to researchers studying personal collections and the management thereof. The little that is known about leisure-related information behavior suggests that people develop and manage rich personal collections in the pursuit of serious leisure activities. Further, it appears that studying these collections has high potential for advancing research in the areas of personal digital collections and personal information management (PIM).

Bodies of literature exist on the character, management, and use of photo collections by institutions and organizations, casual snapshooters collecting mainly family photos, and unknown individuals sharing, tagging, and annotating photo collections on the Web. Amateur photographers occupy a space sharing fuzzy boundaries with each of these areas. Gaining knowledge of amateur collections and collection-related practices will begin to fill in that space.

This chapter describes first steps exploring these potentials in the domain of amateur photography. It reports on preliminary analysis of a year of discussion threads from an online forum devoted to discussing collection management and digital photography workflow. Themes emerging from the data so far suggest that further study of amateur photographers' collection management practices will indeed uncover rich practices heretofore invisible in the gap between institutional/ organizational, casual family, and publicly shared online photo collections.

Serious Leisure

Serious leisure is a theoretical typology of approaches to leisure activities developed by Robert Stebbins in the context of his Serious Leisure Perspective. In the Perspective, serious leisure is differentiated from two other approaches to leisure: casual and project-based. Note that the Perspective is not a classification of leisure activities; rather it classifies different patterns of engagement with any particular leisure activity. For example, different people may approach photography as a casual activity, part of a project, or a serious pursuit. The Perspective's well-defined descriptions of leisure approaches facilitate clear communication about what kinds of leisure contexts are studied.

Serious leisure is of three types: volunteering, hobbies, and amateur pursuit. It is differentiated from casual or project-based leisure by its six distinguishing characteristics: (1) development of a leisure career in the chosen pursuit; (2) accumulation of knowledge and skills via significant personal effort; (3) perseverance at the activity, even when it is challenging, frustrating, or unpleasant; (4) the formation of a social world and a unique ethos around the activity; (5) strong identification with the serious leisure pursuits; and (6) the enjoyment of eight durable benefits beyond the typical enjoyment found in leisure. The eight benefits—self-actualization; self-enrichment; self-expression; regeneration or renewal of self; feelings of accomplishment; enhancement of self-image; social interaction and belongingness; and lasting physical products of the activity—may or may not be initial motivations for serious participation in an activity, but they are outcomes of participation.[1]

An amateur pursuit is a serious approach to some activity, for leisure, that others pursue professionally.[2] Photography as leisure is typically pursued as an amateur activity. The link between amateur and professional means that the social world of amateur photography is part of a larger social world where expectations and standards of excellence are set by professionals. In the Serious Leisure Perspective, amateurism implies not unskillfulness, but a striving for professional-level results. Amateurs are dedicated and critical members of the professionals' publics.[3] Some amateurs move into professional pursuit of their chosen activity by making it their job and main source of income. Other amateurs remain leisure participants; they may even make some money from their activity, but they do not depend upon that money as income.

Why Study Leisure Contexts?

Relatively little is known about positively construed, non-work information behavior. Most research in library and information science (LIS) focuses on work contexts and problematic life situations.[4] The number of studies inquiring about information behavior outside the workplace, and in unproblematic—even pleasurable—contexts increased in the past two decades, but they still make up a small fraction of the LIS literature.[5]

Research efforts should be directed toward understanding the informational aspects of the higher things of life, including serious leisure activities.[6] Serious leisure is a form of lifelong learning,[7] an activity highly relevant to cultural institutions and their funding agencies.[8] Many serious leisure participants become experts in their areas of interest, and much can be learned from self-motivated experts with successful practices, and from contexts in which things are going right.[9]

A number of the existing studies on information behavior in leisure contexts have introduced findings that run counter to the "common knowledge" in personal information management (PIM) and personal digital collections. The common knowledge about personal collection management paints it as difficult, drab, and undesirable. William Jones briefly describes "information warriors" who proactively take on PIM tasks without being triggered by negative events; however, most PIM research finds that, for most people, information management is a set of tasks that are, at best a low priority, and often indefinitely postponed.[10] At worst, it is characterized as a tedious, unpleasant activity that should be eliminated.[11] The same pattern is seen in home mode photography, where people report intentions of annotating photos and organizing them into albums, but never quite get around to it.[12]

Information management is viewed differently in some leisure contexts. Managing and making sense of found information is a core geneaology activity.[13] Systematic organization of collections is part of many collecting hobbies; the satisfaction of imposing order on some segment of the world is one attraction of serious collecting.[14] Hobbyist gourmet cooks maintain personal culinary libraries requiring routine upkeep; their attitudes to this task range from "unconscious or nonchalant" to "zealous." In large personal culinary libraries, the cook "takes on the sensibility of a trained librarian."[15]

Leisure participants also create information artifacts for other participants. This requires gathering and organizing information. In fandoms—organized subcultures of enthusiasts of phenomena—fans produce information objects organizing information about the phenomenon of interest: bibliographies, directories, chronologies, discographies, catalogs, and listings.[16] Computer and electronics hobbyists spend significant amounts of time and effort producing how-to documentation to share online.[17] Elementary school children create and share hobby or leisure-related information for fun.[18] Information creation and sharing remains a fundamental aspect of leisure activities such as fan fiction[19] and role-playing games.[20]

Amateur Photographers

In this chapter, the term *amateur* refers to the approach to a leisure activity as described by the Serious Leisure Perspective. Existing literature uses the phrase *amateur photographer*, with less precision, to refer to home mode photographers and camera club members.

The home mode is a pattern of interpersonal and small group communication centered around the home and focused on pictorial materials.[21] Home mode photography has no professional counterpart. It documents other leisure pursuits rather than being pursued itself as a leisure activity. In the Serious Leisure Perspective, it would be considered a casual pursuit. In the literature of art, sociology, photowork (information processing of digital photos after capture but prior to end use in order to support the desired use of photos), and PIM, the home mode is variously referred to as *domestic, amateur, family, vernacular,* or *snapshooter* photography.

Camera clubs have existed since soon after the discovery of photography, and have developed their own distinct practices and aesthetic.[22] Though there is no direct linkage between camera club photography and any particular flavor of professional photography, it is included as a subcategory of amateur photography here for two reasons. First, a dynamic exists—present since the early days of camera clubs—between the clubs and the camera and film industry as commodity agent.[23] A commodity agent is a group or individual "involved in the production, facilitation, and exchange of activity related commodities."[24] Stebbins now includes these actors in the complex dynamic between amateurs and professionals.[25] Second, aspects of the camera club aesthetic have many traits of landscape, wildlife, portrait, and some advertising photographies, though there is not a direct connection between those professional practices and the practices of camera clubs.

Barbara Rosenblum described separate social worlds of professional art, advertising, and photojournalist photography with different values and practices.[26] If amateurs by definition are aligned with some professional social world, this suggests the possibility that amateur photographers outside the camera club might exist. If such "free-range" amateurs exist, however, they have until recently been invisible in the literature. Three recent studies of the photo-sharing website Flickr describe participants who seem to fit the profile of the free-range serious amateur without clearly defining them as such.[27]

- Julia Davies examined Flickr as an environment for learning and teaching. Based on email questionnaires sent to the author's Flickr contacts, and her own experiences and observations on Flickr, Davies concluded that some users engage in in-depth social learning about photography, with long-term increase in skills and confidence. This is an example of the acquisition of knowledge and skills through effort, with the durable benefits of self-image enhancement and feelings of accomplishment. Some users develop new ways of seeing through participation in the site. Learning to see like a photographer is a key part of taking on the role of photographer.[28] Davies also reports on the emergence of shared social procedures and values—an indicator of the presence of a shared social world, which can also lead to social interaction (online or off) and a sense of belongingness.[29]

- Jean Burgess investigated Flickr group members' use of new media to articulate vernacular creativity. Some participants were interested in professional standards for photography and devoted significant time and effort to learning about advanced camera techniques and the theory of photography. One participant sought formal photography training. This recalls the amateur's dedication to acquisition of knowledge and skill, as well as his link to the photography professions.[30] Participants had arcs of increasing interest, knowledge, and skill in photography (leisure careers). These were marked by the purchase of digital single lens reflex cameras (DSLRs), investment in lenses, and a desire to regularly upgrade their equipment—a pattern of consumption characteristic of serious leisure.[31] Participants described their photography in terms of art and self-expression (a durable benefit), and reported forming social groups based on photo activities. Burgess identified social worlds of photography with aesthetics, discourses, and best practices. Professionals and nonprofessionals mingled in these social worlds, but professional values and standards ruled.[32]

- Andrew Miller and Keith Edwards intended to explore how the use of Flickr changed people's photo-sharing practices by comparing sharing via Flickr with previous research on photo sharing in the home mode. Half of the participants were recruited via a photography group on Flickr. Researchers were surprised to find that these participants—referred to as Snaprs—had markedly different practices from the other participants whose home mode orientation persisted online. Snaprs took photos more frequently, and processed them more promptly, than home mode photographers. Snaprs considered photography a hobby, were more technologically literate, and expressed no concern about the privacy of their photos. They shared their photos publicly and tagged photos to increase their visibility.[33]

Services like Flickr may simply be increasing the visibility of the existing free-range, solo amateur photographer. An alternate view is that such services are fundamentally changing the landscape of amateur photography by introducing new affordances,[34] eroding or redrawing existing boundaries between kinds of amateur photography, and blurring the line between amateur and professional.[35]

Why Study Amateur Photographers?

Managing photographs presents unique challenges. The choice to study amateur photographers was motivated by the fact that knowledge about their collection management practices will fill a gap in the literature on image organization and retrieval. Further, the collection management practices of amateur photographers will be of interest to archivists, librarians, curators, or others interested in collecting, preserving, and providing access to such collections, and understanding amateurs' information management practices may inform services offered by such professionals.

Many studies exist on the collection, organization, description, and retrieval of images in cultural heritage, organizational, and educational settings.[36] A respectable body of work also exists on how home mode photographers use and manage photographs.[37] Finally, the literature on the use of online tools (primarily Flickr) for sharing and tagging photographs is rapidly expanding.[38] Results of research on amateur photographers can be linked to findings in these three areas because amateur photographers are (1) individuals working with personal collections; (2) working with often vast collections, at least part of which are made public; and (3) using the Web to share photos.

The complexity of providing intellectual access to images is well-documented.[39] The attributes that may be salient for retrieval are numerous and layered. Multiple approaches and facets of image subjects exist. Unlike text documents, photos cannot yet be automatically organized and retrieved semantically. Very recently, some personal photo management applications have added face recognition features;[40] however, this sort of content-based image retrieval is a relatively young technology and we are far from bridging the semantic gap using automated techniques.[41]

Amateur photography collections might be of interest to cultural institutions for various reasons. An amateur photographer's interests may lead him to document various facets of his community over the length of his photography career. For example, one photographer may document architecture and cycles of urban development and decay. Another may document the local visual and performing arts scene. Yet another may capture images of local flora and fauna. Collections of this type may be valuable in local history collections. Description and access of these collections using Semantic Web technologies and linked data could increase their value to researchers and learners beyond local communities. As one example, imagine photographs from a local production of *Hamlet* described using established Uniform Resource Identifiers (URIs) for the characters pictured, linked to the passages in the text of the play being performed in each shot, along with geographic and temporal metadata automatically captured by the camera. These images could be found and used by a researcher studying the costuming of Hamlet and Ophelia, or by a director looking for set design ideas for the final scene. Librarians and archivists who understand the information management practices and the photography-related values of amateur photographers will be better equipped to work with such collections, and to conduct effective precustodial intervention with the content creators.

While amateur photographers possess the standards and ethos of professionals, they are people who make their livings in other ways. They do not have the financial resources or incentives of professionals in managing and protecting their collections. However, their enjoyment of and interest in photography suggests they may pay more attention to the technical aspects of the activity than do home mode photographers. Thus, amateurs' photography-related information practices may include strategies for organizing and maintaining collections that are within the means of and teachable to home mode photographers concerned about the future of their digital photos. This knowledge could inform training sessions for the public—a way of providing a service and making connections in the community. It could also be useful in doing precustodial intervention with creators of important non-amateur collections when the collections include some photographs.

Studying personal collections in leisure contexts is needed to gain a holistic understanding of information practices. Knowledge about how self-motivated, self-supporting experts understand and work with information in their pursuits may help libraries to meet the needs of lifelong learners and those with more casual interests in leisure pursuits in protecting their digital collections. Knowledge of the practices of serious amateur photographers can support the collection of their potentially valuable materials by cultural institutions; it can also inform the provision of educational services to the

"Three Backups Is a Minimum": A First Look at Norms and Practices
in the Digital Photo Collections of Serious Photographers

159

larger community and content creators. In an increasingly visual culture, information professionals must understand photograph collections and how people work with them.[42] While historical and sociological research on amateur photographers and camera clubs exists,[43] the information practices of individuals clearly identified as serious amateur photographers have not been studied in LIS, and so there is a knowledge gap to be filled.

The Study

This chapter reports on an exploratory qualitative analysis of a year's worth of threads on a Photo.net forum devoted to discussing digital photograph collection management and digital photography workflow. The purposes of the study are twofold: to assess the likely contribution of further research into amateur photographers' collections, and to learn about norms and expectations concerning digital collection management in the social world of photography.

An exploratory qualitative analysis of a well-known photography forum was conducted because it allowed initial forward movement on each of the research goals to proceed simultaneously. As the forum threads already existed, it was possible to survey them for the presence of topics and practices in the community's discourse without influencing responses. The presence of previously unseen personal collection management practices and concerns was assumed to be indicative of phenomena of research interest and promising for future research.

Amateur photography is part of a social world[44] in which standards of excellence are set by professional photographers. The dispersed nature of this world requires reliance on mediated communication in order to transmit, maintain, and develop the discourse, values, and norms of the social world. Online photo-sharing services like Flickr provide mediated spaces for social learning about "seeing like a photographer" and technical photography skills.[45] It follows that a primarily text-based service focused on collection management issues provides space for social learning about the norms surrounding collections and their management. The data represent a range of photographers larger and more diverse than could be personally surveyed, so topics and practices could be seen across numerous individuals.

Template analysis and data displays were used to analyze and synthesize the data. Template analysis is a good approach for an unexplored topic with a large body of closely related literature because it lies between the extremes of grounded theory and content analysis.[46] Use of the template in the current study will show whether topics and themes from the literature represented in the template map to real-world issues in the personal collections of amateur photographers. The template can be augmented, refined, and shaped to more realistically reflect the collection management issues faced by amateur photographers.

It should be noted that the methods used in this work have several limitations. The use of one online community potentially biases the results. Voices of those who do not follow the norms of the forum, or who do not have problems or strong opinions, may be silent. The use of forum data means that no follow-up questions could be asked to clarify the meaning of ambiguous or confusing statements. There is no way of knowing who all of the forum authors are, or what their motivations for authoring threads and comments are. Each thread is a vignette torn from an unknown, richer context.

Source Selection

Photo.net was selected as the data source based on the many references to the site encountered in informal exploration of the online world of amateur photography and personal awareness of several amateur photographers active on the site. The Photo.net forums capture candid communication between professional and amateur practitioners sharing information pertinent to real-life photography situations and concerns.

In addition to its thirty-three active forums devoted to a range of photography topics, Photo.net includes articles, galleries, and reviews. A blurb on the site's home page contains several indicators of serious leisure/ professional orientation:

> Photo.net is a site for serious photographers to connect with other photographers, explore photo galleries, discuss photography, share and critique photos, and learn about photography. The site began in 1993 as Philip Greenspun's personal home page at MIT and has grown to become a community of photographers that includes more than 800,000 registered users working to help each other improve.

Our editorial goal is to serve busy readers who want clear answers to questions. When we review equipment, we do it from the perspective of "In what kinds of photographic situations would this be the right choice?" In building community, we value members who provide constructive criticism and helpful assistance to other members.[47]

First, the audience is identified as *serious photographers.* Social connection and desire to learn and improve skills are emphasized. Discussion and critique of photography build and transfer a shared discourse across the community. The mention of *right choices* implies that there are wrong choices, suggesting some level of shared community values, standards, and practice. Finally, while community building and social networking are a goal of the site, the busy users are not coming to the site to hang out and collect friends; the focus remains on efficient, useful sharing of information.

Most of the activity on Photo.net takes place on thirty-five topical forums. The home page claims that more than three thousand new threads are added daily. The forums are placed into five broad forum categories: General Photography; Image Related; Photography Practice and Technique; Photography Equipment; and Other.

The Digital Darkroom forum is the focus of this study because much of its content is directly related to personal digital collections. This forum is in the Photography Practice and Technique category. The threads in the Digital Darkroom forum are divided into forty thread categories. Fourteen thread categories were selected as the most directly relevant to personal digital collection management. (The thread categories are summarized in table 1.) The sample was defined as all threads posted in these fourteen thread categories between January 29, 2008 and January 29, 2009 (n=1008). A year's worth of threads were included in the sample in order to avoid bias by seasonal fluctuation of activity or themes.

Data Acquisition, Processing, and Analysis

Forum data, in the form of 1008 hypertext markup language (HTML) files, were scraped from the Photo.net site over three days, in compliance with the site's terms of use.[48] These files were combined into 26 large text files based on thread category before being cleaned up and structurally coded.

Table 1. Forum categories included in study.

Photo.net label	Study label	Threads in forum	Threads in sample
Computers	Computers	1169	300
Software—Utilities	Utilities	600	128
Software—File Formats	Formats	582	123
Archiving	Archiving	491	108
Storage	Storage	446	82
Images—Libraries	ImageLibs	210	59
Software—Capturing	Capture	280	49
Software—Web Publishing	WebPub	191	36
Books	Books	149	34
Services—Printing	Printing	189	27
Software—Archiving/Billing	ArchBillApps	128	23
Printing—Archival	ArchPrinting	168	20
Migration	Migration	70	16
Services—Hosting	Hosting	29	3
	Total	4702	1008

These files were concatenated into 26 large text files, each containing the HTML of up to 50 threads; HTML files from different thread categories were lumped into separate text files. A series of Emacs macros was used to clean the 26 text files. The HTML and JavaScript code from the Photo.net web pages was stripped; it was replaced with simple markup tags to retain the structure of the data. Each thread and its followup comments were coded as a THREAD, while each original thread posting (minus comments) was coded as an ORIG-THREAD. The preliminary qualitative analysis reported here focused on the original threads posted to the forum. Comments on some threads of particularly direct relevance were analyzed. For example, responses to questions about how people organize their photo directories were coded.

For a broad view of activity on the forum, basic patterns of thread and comment authorship were analyzed using spreadsheet pivot tables. Photo. net requires users to register with a unique user name in order to add forum content. The forum is a communication mechanism for a dispersed social world in which knowledge and expertise are social capital. This would suggest that those sharing their knowledge and expertise on the forum would have little motivation to create multiple user names for themselves. There may, however, be social pressure against asking what might be perceived as stupid questions, especially if one typically presents as an expert or is a newcomer trying to gain status and respect. It is possible that one person is active on the forum under more than one user name, or that multiple people may use the same user name. Teasing out actual personal identity is beyond the scope of this study, so user names are treated as separate authors, following the tradition for persons who inhabit multiple bibliographic identities.

An initial template based on the literature of personal collections, photowork, serious leisure, personal information management (PIM), and image description was constructed before data collection began. The template is divided into five key areas:

- Selected aspects of photography including photographic activities, forms of information in the collection, social aspects, space devoted to or used for photography (physical or digital), and tools and services used. Examples might include a transition from film to digital and learning new skills (photography activities); a laptop hard drive (digital space); a laptop (tool); a spouse to consider (social aspect); a shared office (physical space); friends who also do photography (social aspect); and RAW files (form of information).

- Organization and management activities, including collection organization strategies; metadata creation, manipulation, and use; collection maintenance strategies; and collection storage strategies. Examples might include organizing photos into folders chronologically (organization strategy) by creation year (metadata use); and storage of said files on the laptop hard drive (storage strategy).

- Collection management evaluation criteria, including definitions of concepts such as *archiving* and *backup*, and the characteristics on which collection management-related tools, strategies, and practices are judged. Examples might include portable viewing access to photos, time required for collection management tasks, and physical space required.

- Collection management situations, or the types of situations in which amateur photographers engage in collection management, such as organizing, weeding, backing up, or migrating. This area also includes the kinds of steps taken to develop strategies when in these situations. Examples might include running out of digital storage space, adopting new software tools, or instituting a new backup plan.

- Influences, or the objects, events, and people named as helpful or unhelpful in collection management situations. Examples might include particular books, web resources, help functions, or people.

The first category contains aspects of the larger photography leisure career, while the rest of the categories are focused on collection management practices and decisions. Forum authors tend to describe the specific situations that brought them to ask their questions on the forum, so most aspects of their photography activities remain unknown. For instance, an author asking the forum about organizing digital photos may never mention his many years' worth of film negatives and prints. With this limitation in mind, this category is used to code what authors mention as background information in their forum threads. (Broader data on this topic will be collected in future interview research.)

The data were coded in ATLAS.ti using this template. Topics or practices not included in the initial template were added during analysis if there was a clearly appropriate place for them. Frequently occuring topics or practices that did not easily fit into the template indicated that the template did not fit the reality of the community and should be reorganized.

The Digital Darkroom Forum

Table 1 displays the Digital Darkroom forum thread categories selected for inclusion in this study, the category labels used for these in the study, the number of forum threads in each category at the time of data collection, and the number of threads from each category included in the sample. The table is organized in descending order by number of threads in the sample.

As mentioned above, 14 of the 40 Digital Darkroom forum thread categories were included in the sample because they were topically relevant to the study. The other 26 categories were excluded because the topics they covered were not clearly related to managing collections of photos.[49] Deciding whether to include a category was a subjective decision based on asking whether it was reasonable to expect that much of the discussion in the category would directly pertain to collections management. The first page of posts in each category was skimmed to assess typical recent discussion topics. Excluded categories focused on technical aspects of digital image editing, printing, projection, and scanning.

In contrast, the included categories contained discussion of how to work with images as documents or information objects. Much of the Computers category is concerned with designing computer systems sufficient to manipulate and safely store photographs. Software utilities are often used to automate file management tasks such as renaming or format conversion. The Capture category contained discussions about file formats and workflow management. The Printing category contained discussions about selecting and organizing photos to be printed. The Hosting and WebPub categories contained discussions of using these services for online backup.

Forum authors interpret the boundaries of these categories loosely; similar threads are found in different categories. The forum and the sample are dominated by the Computers category, but many of the threads in this category are about storage, "archiving," and migration. Though, by definition, most digital darkroom activities will require a computer, the discussion on the Digital Darkroom forum is not as skewed to the subject of hardware as a glance at the numbers in table 1 might suggest.

During the year, 718 unique authors (user names) created the 1008 threads in the sample. Authors created between 1 and 23 threads each. Only 5 authors created more than 6 threads, and 572 authors created only one thread. The frequency distribution of number of threads created per author exhibited a Lotka's law-like shape: as the number of threads created by an author increases, the number of authors creating that number of threads decreases.

The same basic pattern emerged among commenters: 1404 unique commenters left 6872 comments. Authors created between 1 and 324 comments each. Only 30 authors created 30 or more comments. Only 18.95 percent of authors (n=266) created 5 or more comments. Nearly half (49.29 percent) of authors (n=692) made a single comment. Again, the distribution took the shape of a power function: as the number of comments made by an author increased, the number of authors making that many comments decreased.

The same person posted the largest number of threads and comments. Only four other authors appear in both top 30 lists. This suggests there is a very small group of core contributors to the forum. The majority of its content is written by a very large number of infrequent or one-time contributors, at least some of whom are regular lurkers [22:56, 12:44].[50] The forum is a mediated communication tool for sharing knowledge within the dispersed social worlds of photography. While most authors do not explain their interest or involvement in photography, some do identify themselves as professionals or amateurs. Presence of both on the forum confirms that this is part of a photography social world with the Professional–Amateur–Public dynamic characteristic of amateur pursuits. The results of this study are not only about amateur photographers, then, but also about serious photographers.

General Themes

What emerges from the analysis is a blend of confirmations of existing knowledge about how people work with photo collections; contradictions to findings in previous photowork and PIM studies; and new themes.

Functions of Personal Collections

Prior research has identified functions of personal collections that include: (1) to support sharing of collection contents; (2) to assuage fears of loss; (3) to support refinding; (4) identity construction; and (5) bearing witness to a legacy.[51] Consideration of these functions in light of the distinguishing characteristics of serious leisure[52] suggests that serious leisure-related personal collections should also serve these functions. The Serious Leisure Perspective suggests that the latter two functions might be the most central in serious leisure-related collections. Personal collection development as identity construction would contribute to the serious leisure characteristic of strong identification with the pursuit. The serious leisure-related personal collection would also bear witness to the legacy of development of a long-term leisure career requiring significant personal effort and perseverance— three distinguishing characteristics of serious leisure. A serious leisure pursuit's social world and unique ethos are related to the durable benefit of social interaction and belongingness. While these suggest that sharing, which itself implies the need to refind, would be an important function of the serious leisure collection, this is not necessarily the case. The social core of some serious leisure pursuits, such as sports or volunteering, centers more on doing activities together rather than sharing activity-related materials from a personal collection. The serious pursuit of liberal arts hobbies is based on reading and is a largely solitary activity. In this case, a feeling of belonging to a social world and holding its unique ethos may be based largely on the one-way transmission of knowledge from author to reader. The reader may or may not share sources and notes with others interested in the topic.

Sharing is a central function of home mode photo collections.[53] The amateur photographers in the Flickr studies previously discussed shared photos, but they did so more openly than home mode photographers. Four kinds of sharing are mentioned by forum authors: with known people [15:180, 19:104]; with the public via photo-sharing sites or the Web at large [27:76, 11:40]; with clients [16:87, 9:24]; and with the art world via exhibition [24:15, 30:30]. The presence of the latter two indicate the Professional–Amateur–Public dynamic of the photography social world.

Many people dread losing their home mode photos; often described as irreplaceable, family photos are among the most cherished objects in the home.[54] Ironically, their digital collection-keeping often contradicts their stated values on this matter. Many people back up their data infrequently or not at all.[55] The spectre of "losing everything" also haunts the forum [12:31, 34:73], but unlike participants in previous studies, authors report going to extensive measures to guard against the possibility.

Previous studies of home mode photographers have found that, to find images, they tend to rely on browsing through recent photos rather than searching the collection.[56] This is consistent with findings that people seem to prefer browsing over searching in personal collections.[57] In contrast, forum authors express a desire for very specific search and filtering functions such as finding images by camera model [22:62, 22:224], focal length [11:143, 22:250], image resolution [22:114], and image ratings [22:16]. This is indicative of the forum's professional values: professional photographers must be able to provide former clients with specific photos on demand. Also, the ability to find images created in a certain way, or of a particular quality, enables the use of the collection as a reflective tool for self-assessment and further learning [22:293].

Lack of Clear Guidelines for Safekeeping

There are few sources of clear advice for forum authors regarding management of their digital photo collections for the long term. The standard source on this topic for forum authors is *The Digital Asset Management (DAM) Book* by Peter Krogh,[58] but some of its advice contradicts existing preservation guidelines. *The Digital Images Archiving Study* provides guidelines for institutional digital image collections and highlights gaps in information professionals' knowledge of how to best handle these materials.[59] The Paradigm project's *Workbook on Digital Private Papers* contains an appendix of guidelines for creators of personal archives, but is not focused on the particular issues for such archives that consist predominantly of photographs.[60] There is a lack of information about managing digital photo collections that: (a) is targeted to serious photographers, rather than home mode photographers or cultural heritage professionals; (b) demonstrates awareness of the social world and values of serious photography; and (c) contains clear guidelines for digital photo preservation from authoritative preservation professionals.

Size and Complexity

The bloated size and complexity of collections, which can be attributed to the low cost of producing digital images and the ease with which they can be edited and duplicated, emerged as a dominant theme of the study. Once one owns a digital camera, taking photos costs nothing but digital storage space, which continually gets cheaper.[61] Why not take "over 100 images of the same sheep on a hillside" [22:294]? What to do with the original file, the one with the touched-up red eyes, the cropped one sent to parents, the low resolution one uploaded to the Web? As Catherine Marshall points out, while lots of copies may keep things safe, they also make it even harder to keep track of what one has.[62]

The situation is more pronounced for serious photographers. Not only do they shoot more images more frequently, but the images they create are often much larger than those of the home mode photographer. This is due to their insistence on the highest quality, and the related tendency to purchase new cameras and other equipment in order to keep up with technological advances.[63] One author writes, "so my final image is saved as a tagged image file format (TIFF) no compression, in 16-bits mode, 360 resolution. I just finished working on an image in those settings, and the file size has come up to 59MB (megabytes) . . . Is this normal?" The first commenter's response: "Yes, that's normal. Hopefully you're also keeping your RAW files" [22:144].[64] The availability of ever-larger storage devices at reasonable prices allows photographers to continue building their collections, even as the file size of RAW files increase; however, large RAW files pose three further challenges. First, the large RAW file itself cannot be used as an image; an image file must be created from the data in the RAW file in order to view, edit, or print the image. This means there will be at least two files for every edited image a photographer would like to save. Second, the size of an image file created from a RAW file may be much larger than the original RAW file, depending on the conversion settings used and the desired format of the image file. Third, powerful software is needed to convert RAW files to images, and to manipulate the resulting image files. The applications are themselves huge, but more importantly, they require powerful hardware to run efficiently.[65]

The challenges of working with large files leads many serious photographers to buy or custom build powerful computers dedicated to working with and storing images. The extreme example was an author asking what kind of computer to build to handle working with large format sheet film scans at 3000 dots per inch (DPI),[66] resulting in images file sizes in the range of 3 gigabytes (GB) each [15:92]. Most of the Computers thread category is given over to questions about choosing and configuring hardware for image collection use and management.

The initial analysis template lacked categories for coding technical discussion about choosing and configuring hardware. It also excluded codes for technical discussions about shooting photos and editing photos for aesthetic reasons—color correcting, sharpening, and retouching, for example. These topics were excluded for two reasons. First, though the Paradigm project's guidelines touch upon them,[67] they are not discussed in the photowork literature. Second, it was assumed that they were not directly related to collection management. Analysis of the forum data proved this assumption partially wrong.

Discussions on the forum show that hardware, shooting, and editing are, in fact, related to serious photographers' collection management. A photographer's plan for capturing images and managing his photo collection influences his hardware choices and configuration decisions.

Conversely, available hardware constrains collection management and shooting decisions. Choosing to shoot RAW images introduces a wide range of collection management issues. Editing images introduces questions about versioning, weeding collections, and file formats. Tools used to edit images are often part of, or tightly integrated with, digital asset management tools used to manage the collection. Choosing and using editing and asset management tools often requires knowledge of and decision making about file formats and metadata.

Based on forum data, the template was updated to reflect the relevance of hardware, shooting, and editing to collection management. A distinction was made between topics relevant to image files as visual objects and topics relevant to image files as information objects to be managed. Categories for coding topics related to images as information objects were added to the template. Topics relevant only to image files as visual objects remain excluded from the template. Examples of irrelevant topics used to clarify the distinction between topics included choice of aperture setting while shooting, how to achieve perfect skin tones in post-processing, and where to buy a certain cable needed for a laptop.

Importance of Workflow

A common forum topic is the development of digital photography workflows: all of the steps required to process and manage photos, from transferring files from the camera, through backing up or archiving. Forum authors are concerned with having the "proper" or best workflow [19:63], where efficiency is a key criterion for evaluation. People ask for help and guidance in developing their own workflows:

> Hopefully someone can recommend a good book on a proper and efficient workflow [9:110].

> I am planning on using Lightroom and wanted a book to walk me through an efficient workflow and for . . . some tips regarding image processing [9:129].

> Is there some better workflow I'm not thinking of? What works for people [13:72]?

One of the milestones of becoming a serious photographer is to learn to shoot and process RAW images. Working with RAW files requires the photographer to perform functions that are otherwise done automatically by the camera when it is set to save files in the joint photographic experts group (JPEG) format—the default setting on most digital cameras. The typical amateur or professional workflow is complex, uses a number of applications, and results in multiple versions of photos in various file formats. Figure 1 illustrates a relatively simple workflow for processing RAW photos. The graphic is derived from a step-by-step description of one author's workflow. The steps explicitly described by the author were broken down into the types of hardware, software, versions of the image, edits made, and image storage locations mentioned. Some of the labels on the arrows were added or reworded for clarity. The author reported all of the image converting, processing, and saving on the laptop as his actual workflow practice. Worried about filling up his hard drive, he proposed a monthly routine of burning of digital negative (DNG) files to recordable compact discs (CD-R) and subsequently deleting them from his laptop, and requested feedback on the present and proposed parts of the workflow. Workflow is at the core of the amateur's personal digital collection management, where a duality[68] is found between workflow and collection: workflow shapes and is shaped by the use and growth of the collection, while tools and services are chosen (or built) to fit into a workflow and shape it via their affordances, functions, and limitations.

Proactive Information Management

Many forum authors proactively assess, reassess, plan, design, redesign and tweak their workflows. Developing a good workflow requires consideration of several activities included in the Paradigm guidelines: naming and structuring files and folders; keywording/tagging or adding other metadata; choosing file formats and software; devising a backup strategy; and, to some extent, system administration and hardware/media management. A number of authors posted on the forum because they decided to catalog their photo collections: "I am about to embark on the arduous task of organizing, cataloguing, and backing up several terabytes of digital images, and would like to get it right the first time" [11:77]. Authors ask for book and software recommendations as well as procedural information regarding the best ways to get organized [11:38, 12:51].

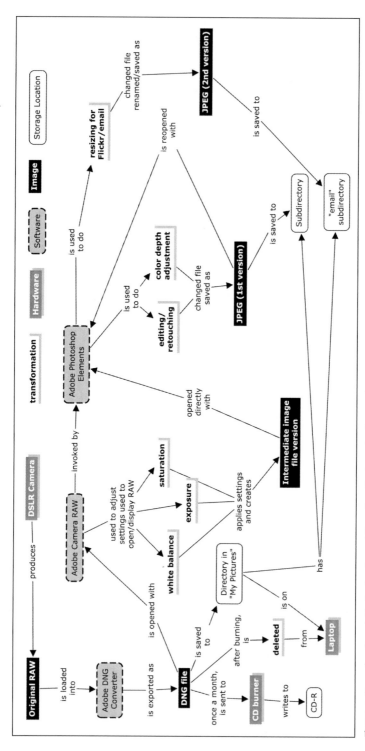

Figure 1. Example of a relatively simple workflow described on the forum. The graphic is derived from a step-by-step description of one forum author's workflow [19:66].

"Three Backups Is a Minimum": A First Look at Norms and Practices
in the Digital Photo Collections of Serious Photographers

173

Finally, many authors write about how to build the best backup systems to avoid data loss. Making sure things are backed up before problems occur is the expected and approved behavior in this social world. Two authors volunteered that they had not backed up their data. One asked how to make backups using a particular tool [11:196], while the other was in a software malfunction/possible data loss situation, vowing to make backups in the future [22:19]. All except the latter are taking proactive steps to manage and maintain their collections before a problem strikes.

In contrast with the participants in many personal collection or PIM studies who do reactive collection management in response to existing problems, forum authors commonly engage in proactive collection management in response to anticipated potential problems. This is most clearly illustrated by the attention that authors have devoted to designing backup systems. Some forum authors report or recommend doing quality testing and benchmarking of systems to make sure they do not simply work, but that they work optimally [9:54, 14:39, 14:200, 16:228].

One important conclusion from this study is that forum authors frequently mention doing proactive collection management activities. Collection management is part of the amateur leisure pursuit. This echos the Snaprs' enjoyment of organizing their collections,[69] but stands in contrast to the findings of most previous photowork and PIM studies.

Technical Knowledge and Skill

Possession of adequate technical knowledge and skill increases the personal collection management strategies available to a collection creator. Previous studies have demonstrated that many who manage personal collections—photo or otherwise—display a lack of the most basic understanding of how computers work, how to use them, and the nature of digital information.[70] Often people rely on others to provide ad hoc technical support.[71]

Technical knowledge and skill on the forum appears to be higher than that reported in the studies mentioned above. A number of forum authors mention that they provide technical support for others. One author does tech support at a summer camp [22:200]. Another mentions that he organizes other people's photos for them, but does not explain in what capacity he provides this service [22:290]. Others claim that they are posting to get answers on an issue they are working on for someone else: a girlfriend [27:38], a friend

[13:67], and parents [12:118, 11:17, 15:235]. Also, a number of forum authors report having jobs or job responsibilities that require advanced technical skills. Some examples include software development [18:97, 31:87], technical support [22:323], building and repairing computer systems [16:226], hardware engineering [17:99], information technology management [14:199], and system administration [37:178, 37:227, 16:227]. Finally, many authors active on the forum demonstrate considerable knowledge of technology by providing technical support and system configuration recommendations.

Of course, this does not mean that everyone on the forum has technology expertise. Many forum threads request technical information or support, and some forum authors mention that they receive offline ad hoc tech support from others [12:77, 15:119, 19:129]. Many forum authors qualify their thread posts with admissions of having little knowledge about computers or technical matters [14:171, 14:180, 15:124, 15:242, 29:73], but most of these are trying to learn more. There are a few examples of lack of basic computing concepts such as installation of Photoshop on an external hard drive [22:101]; uncertainty about whether RAW files could be backed up [33:40]; and asking whether external hard drives need operating systems [37:206]. Most of the authors asking for help, however, appear to be operating at a higher level of technical understanding than the participants described in other studies. The overall tone of the forum is one of comfort with and enthusiasm for technology.

The high level of technical competence shown on the forum is in line with the characteristics of amateur photographers. From the time of the discovery of photography, they have been interested in the technical details of photographic processes. At first this required knowledge of how to prepare plates and work finicky camera equipment. Extensive knowledge of chemistry and properties of light remained key in print photography. Now the necessary high technical skills of the professional and amateur are computer skills. This finding also echoes the 2007 study by Miller and Edwards, in which Snaprs were described as highly technically proficient.[72]

Conceptual Ambiguity

The 2008 "Digital Lives" study found "a certain ambiguity" in use of the terms *backup, storage,* and *archive* by the creators of personal collections. This ambiguity is also noted by Catherine Marshall,[73] and is present on the forum.

A few authors clearly use *backup* to refer to regular duplication of current files to enable recovery of active documents [11:58, 16:146, 22:240]. Others suggest archiving is for long-term storage [12:114, 12:158]. Most authors do not clearly indicate what they mean by these terms, which are used rather loosely and interchangeably, such as in the request for recommendations of "archiving software for incremental backup of image files" [11:145] and the question of whether labeling DVDs would affect the "archivability" of the backups [12:66]. The forum is an inappropriate source of data on which to base inferences about serious photographers' conceptual understandings of these terms, so the remainder of this chapter makes no distinctions among them.

A Unique Ethos

A social world and a unique ethos will form around a serious leisure activity. In the case of an amateur activity, this social world and ethos will be embedded in a Professional-Amateur-Public dynamic informed by professional standards and values.[74] Threads on the Digital Darkroom forum suggest it functions as a mediated communication space for members of the dispersed social world of photography. Forum authors include self-described professionals, semi-pros, and amateur photographers, as well as many who do not describe their level of photography activity. Forum content suggests the existence of a shared set of values in three ways: (1) one book appears to be the authoritative text on managing digital photo collections; (2) norms and best practices are implicitly and explicitly referenced; and (3) common practices and advice emerge.

The forum includes no formal guidelines for managing collections, but *The DAM Book*[75] is considered the most authoritative print source on the matter. In some threads, authors mention that they have already read this book, as though doing so were expected or commonly recommended. Others base their systems on the book's suggestions, or describe plans to do so [37:72, 12:168]. In the comments that have been analyzed, commenters frequently advise thread authors to consult the book [27:80, 22:314, 11:209]. One set of comments suggests that the book is so commonly cited because it is the only book on the subject [11:10].

Norms and best practices are referenced implicitly and explicitly in threads on the forum. Implicit references refer to a right and a wrong way of doing things, often asking the forum to rule on best practice. Examples include: "Is this the correct practice?" [19:63]; "I want to start naming the files correctly RIGHT from the start" [22:307]. Explicit references directly ask about or refer to best practices and norms: "Which DVDs have the consensus of being the best for image archiving and storage?" [22:80]; "I am an avid fan of Apple's Aperture. But I have been considering using Photo Mechanic as it is the industry norm for image archiving and such" [27:29]; "What's the best practice regarding importing using LightRoom?" [27:42].

The existence of an accepted authoritative source for guidance, implicit and explicit references to norms, and evidence of common practices across the community suggest there is a shared ethos in the social world of photography.

Paradigm and the Personal Photo Collection

The Personal Archives Accessible in Digital Media (Paradigm) project was a research initiative designed to "explore the issues involved in preserving digital private papers."[76] The Paradigm project's *Workbook on Digital Private Papers* outlined a set of guidelines for creators of personal archives. The following sections adapt the Paradigm guidelines in order to organize discussion of common collection management practices described on the forum. Each subheading is one of the Paradigm guidelines. Shared common practices indicate some level of consensus regarding best practice across the dispersed community. The remainder of the section is a structured comparison of the photographers' best practices—with both practices recommended by digital preservation professionals (i.e., the Paradigm guidelines) and key findings from the existing photowork and PIM literatures.[77]

Name and File Appropriately

These guidelines are concerned with making it easier to find and manage files, as well as with maintaining the context of documents over time. The desire to get organized drives some forum authors to consider or reconsider workflows, choose tools for managing photos, and develop systems for storing, naming, and otherwise describing photos [11:38, 22:84]. The question of why they feel it is important to develop a very organized system is not discussed; it is unclear whether being organized is a strategy for refinding, part of a long-term keeping plan, part of the ethos of serious photography, a general cultural virtue, or a blend of all of these. Regardless of the motive for doing so, organizing collections as they are built will hopefully make it easier to maintain the collections in the present and for the long term.

Name files and folders. Part of designing a workflow is deciding on a standard directory structure for organizing photos, a standard method of naming directories in the structure, and a standard way of naming files. Strategies for naming files and naming and structuring directories are discussed in detail on the forum, usually when some author asks for advice on the best strategies [22:110, 22:311, 22:97]. Home mode photographers most commonly organize film photos using their photo processing envelopes.[78] In the digital environment, the directory created when photos are transferred from the camera plays the role of the photo envelope. This directory is often automatically created and named with a date—usually the date of file transfer. Such directories are the primary organizing method used by home mode digital photographers, with little renaming of individual files.[79] This method arranges images in chronological order, collocating images from specific events, with very low effort on the part of the photographer.

Most descriptions of organization strategies described by forum authors are more complex. Multilevel directory structures are employed by many. It is most common to arrange top-level directories by date; however, the granularity of date used varies. Some have a YearMonthDay subdirectory at the top level [11:214, 22:97], while others have Year-Month-Day directory structures [22:309]. Other directories are added for aspects such as event [22:97], sub-event [22:309], and project name [22:296, 22:127]. Outside these repeated date-based structures, some authors report having additional special directories. These are used to organize work (in progress, completed, to print, to burn) [22:278], photo format [22:140], or photo quality (best photos, okay photos, bad photos), and may be forced to the top of the directory list by adding appropriate characters to the beginning of the directory names [22:97, 22:127]. If photos are grouped by type (portrait, landscape) at the top level [22:140], date directory structure is added beneath each category [22:97]. These practices echo previous findings on the importance of date for organizing photos, as well as manipulation of directory order and reuse of directory structures.[80]

While some forum authors advise against renaming all individual image files as part of the workflow [22:309, 37:138, 11:215], the practice is reported on the forum more frequently than in the literature on home mode digital photography. Authors who rename all their files report using various scripts and the batch renaming features of photo processing and photo organization tools in order to accomplish renaming [22:324, 28:96, 37:228, 11:214]. As with directory names, it is common to include dates in file names [11:156, 22:311, 19:235]. One author includes the entire creation timestamp, down to the second, in each file name [11:214]. Other information in file names includes photographer name [11:156, 11:213], project name/number [11:194, 11:214], descriptive keyword [11:217], and media card identification (ID) number [11:194]. A unique sequential number is also commonly part of the file name [11:156, 11:214, 20:110, 31:88]. This may be retained from the name generated by the camera, or created by the renaming script.

Overall, discussion on the forum implies that serious photographers are interested in, and often meeting, the Paradigm guidelines' best practices for file organization and naming. They create meaningful names. One author explains, "I designed this naming scheme so that the file name alone is sufficient to contain the critical data necessary to find the picture" [11:214]. These names have standardized forms. One author reports maintaining a list of codes for use in his file names [11:217]. The date format yyyymmdd seems to be most commonly used, and there is some discussion about why it is better than other ways of recording date [11:218]. The main downfall of serious photographers' file naming is that the names and directory structures often become long and/or complex. Using tools with automatic rename capabilities removes some of the difficulties of dealing with this complexity, but it can still be problematic [11:215], as one author attests: "my file names became so long (in Lightroom) that the Seagate would not back up hundreds of files" [11:126].

Establish a version control system. Version proliferation—the existence of multiple versions of the same information, which may also be scattered across locations—is a challenge in personal collections.[81] Forum authors create and sometimes keep several versions of the same image [22:157, 11:217]. Photos may be saved at various stages of processing to allow for rolling back to an earlier state [22:150]. Images color-corrected for specific uses may be saved as different versions [22:129]. The lower-resolution images emailed to friends or posted online might be saved as further versions in different sizes [22:116].

Though version proliferation is present in serious photographers' collections, it does not seem to be a problem. Versions are the products of a carefully planned workflow, so a system for dealing with them without confusion is in place. Making changes to file names is one method used to organize versions [20:85, 11:66, 11:226, 11:217]. Another strategy is to create special directories to contain different versions of an image [19:153, 22:140, 37:161]. One forum author combines both of these strategies [11:215].

Make data self-documenting. This guideline is essentially concerned with creating and managing metadata in order to maintain information about the context of files. We know that home mode photographers generally do not spend much time on metadata-related activities. They may aspire to annotating and labeling all of their photos or arranging them with captions in albums; however, this level of description is not necessary to support the use of the home mode photo collection, and is often deferred until another day.[82]

Forum authors, on the other hand, express much interest in creating and using metadata to describe their photos. This is demonstrated in several ways. First, there are numerous threads asking about the best way to tag, keyword, or otherwise describe images [11:186, 22:123, 12:131]. Second, authors report spending a lot of time and effort describing their images [22:126, 22:191, 27:63]. Third, tagging and keywording are taken seriously. One author refers to "keywording methodology," [22:133] while another suggests a formal approach and use of a controlled vocabulary [22:288]. Fourth, adding keywords to all photos is regularly mentioned as part of workflow [27:70, 27:74]. In short, adding metadata to images appears to be the norm for a well-managed collection: "By mangaed [sic] I mean uniquely named, keyworded and captioned, with my copyright and contact data embedded, rated with either stars and color tags (or both) organized into folders and collections" [27:78].

Home mode photographers typically do not search their collections,[83] preferring to rely on browsing by chronology[84] for images taken recently.[85] Forum authors, however, seem concerned with increasing the findability of their photos [11:192, 22:303]. They report wanting to search their photos on a number of attributes: camera used to shoot image [11:87, 22:62], camera settings used (f-stop, focal length, shutter speed) [11:143, 22:250], pre-digitization file format [22:115], image resolution [22:114, 27:33], and rating of image [22:293, 22:16]. Previous studies found that serious amateur photographers who post photos on Flickr report tagging photos solely for the benefit of others.[86] The amount of time forum authors report spending on image description and their desire to be able to find specific photos in flexible ways highlights the fact that the use of Flickr to manage a subset of an image collection tells us little about what people do with their actual image collections.

A commitment to describing photos as part of a photo workflow lands the serious photographer into metadata issues beyond the ken or care of most people managing personal collections. First, four major metadata standards may be used to manage personal image collections: EXchangeable Image File (Exif) [11:189, 22:225], International Press Telecommunications Council (IPTC) [27:69, 22:50], Extensible Metadata Platform (XMP) [12:123, 22:112], and International Color Consortium (ICC) [11:222, 13:85]. Exif is used to embed information such as camera type, exposure settings, and creation timestamp in a photo when it is captured. IPTC metadata is an industry standard for describing aspects of photos not described by Exif. Some applications still read and write IPTC metadata directly, but recent implementations express the IPTC core standard information using XMP, a standard for embedding content and rights metadata in the documents they describe, which is based on the Resource Description Framework (RDF). ICC profiles describe the color spaces of image input, display, and output devices. They must be managed, but are typically not manipulated by those using them.

Despite the existence of four standards for photo description, elements important to photographers such as tags, ratings, and post-processing data are not standardized, and are implemented differently in different applications. This is problematic for photographers who begin with a basic photo organizing application and later want to upgrade to a more powerful tool. Authors report being unable to transfer keywords/tags and descriptions between applications [12:44, 22:72] or retain album category information when migrating to a new computer [16:62]. When considering organizational strategies and software choice, a number of serious photographers consider the portability of their metadata [12:123, 11:192, 20:42, 20:111, 22:235].

Serious photographers must protect the authenticity of their image metadata from applications that overwrite or delete metadata [27:69]. This usually happens when photos are being migrated from one application to another or from one storage location to another. Sometimes undesired metadata changes are made by the operating system based on either a person or an application accessing the file. A common problem is replacement of creation timestamp with modification or replication timestamp [13:149, 22:100]. This is particularly problematic because creation date is an essential piece of information for sorting and finding photos. Further, the operations that make such changes are often run on large batches of photos, causing widespread damage.

Another layer of metadata complexity stems from the characteristics of most RAW file formats. These formats typically bundle the data representing the light hitting the charge-coupled device (CCD) at the time of an image exposure with file headers containing metadata about camera settings at the time of exposure, the date and time of exposure, camera model, and sometimes geographic coordinates or other information. The applications used to convert RAW files into viewable, editable images cannot modify the RAW image data representing the light. Applications allow photographers to apply settings such as white balance and sharpness that are used to transform the RAW image data into an image on the screen. This generated image must be saved as a new file. This process is partially analogous to film photography: it is as if, in one step, the photographer develops one frame of his film and prints the image using the resultant negative. A major flaw in this analogy is that RAW formats allow the photographer to do the equivalent of developing the original film again using different chemicals or processes as many times as he wishes. The RAW image data remain in a pure, original state, like exposed but undeveloped film. Some tools used to view and convert RAW files will save "new" RAW files with changes applied. This means only that the tool can write the settings chosen by the photographer into the file's headers—the RAW image data remain unchanged.

Of course, the image data in a RAW file may be directly edited with a text editor or other tool; however, unless the encoding of the RAW format has been reverse engineered, editing the data will corrupt the file so that no image could be produced from it. In the case of proprietary RAW file formats, doing this could be illegal. The encryption for some formats would also have to be cracked. On the forum and in texts about digital photography,[87] it is axiomatic that RAW image data remain unchanged.

The benefits of the RAW format for photographers include higher image quality and more control. One of the downsides is that metadata generated post-exposure cannot be embedded in the RAW file unless one of the aforementioned tools that can save conversion settings is used. Use of these tools is constrained by the individual RAW file formats the tools support. Even if these tools are used, valuable metadata such as keywords and descriptions cannot be bundled into RAW files. One solution is to handle and process all images using a digital asset management tool. If this route is taken, the photographer will typically lose all metadata captured by and entered into the tool if he decides to change to another tool. Another solution is to write metadata into a companion file known as a sidecar. The sidecar file usually has the same name as the RAW image file, but a separate extension. The problem with this approach is that sidecars can become disassociated from the files they describe or otherwise lost [19:211]. A large advantage of Adobe's DNG RAW image format is that users have the option to embed XMP metadata directly into the DNG file. XMP metadata can represent information including rights, subject description, image adjustment settings, and ratings [22:112]. DNG is sometimes referred to as the equivalent of the physical film processing envelope, as it contains the digital negative and the metadata necessary to transform it into viewable images [19:219, 19:220].

This metadata complexity and the ways in which serious photographers learn about and deal with it have not been discussed in previous work. The photo industry is aware of the importance of image metadata and has formed a working group to explore metadata issues. The Metadata Working Group has released guidelines for managing image metadata in the design of image creation and manipulation tools.[88] There is a large body of research on image metadata.[89] Of particular interest is the 2006 Digital Images Archiving Study, targeted to professionals working with digital images in cultural heritage.[90] Increasing awareness of the shared interests and overlapping work among these communities could improve the outlook for the future of all digital image collections.

Delete what's not important. The Paradigm guidelines recommend making choices about what materials to keep for the long term. This recommendation is consistent with the values of collection development in libraries and archival appraisal, which acknowledge the importance of winnowing materials to develop substantial collections. In contrast, some in the PIM research community espouse the view that it is probably better to keep everything, since the availability of abundant storage makes it cheaper to do this than to spend time doing the complex signal detection task of making keeping/weeding decisions.[91] Making decisions about what to keep or delete is difficult,[92] complicated by the fact that the value of items in personal collections is nuanced, highly contextual, and changes with time.[93] Yet a collection by definition implies selection,[94] and as difficult as culling is, many people do not want to keep everything;[95] as we gain the capability to record everything in perpetuity, it becomes important to support the emotional necessity of forgetting.[96]

Forum authors report a range of strategies for weeding their collections. It is common practice to delete photos of poor technical quality [22:274, 16:204, 16:221]. Some weed "ruthlessly" [16:46]: "My thinking is to cull out not just ruthlessly but to the point of fanaticism. If you keep your best then this becomes the target to which you have to shoot that quality to in the future. It will over time make you a better photographer and not just a shutter snapper" [16:225]. Others keep nearly everything [16:214, 16:220]. Some point out that as time passes, photos once thought unimportant or even bad may increase in sentimental or monetary value [16:224, 16:203]. Others mention the usefulness of even poor images as source material for photo editing [16:210] or for instructional or entertainment value: "Then there are photos so bad that they're worth keeping. Mine are collected together in a set I call 'When Decisive Moments Go Awry'" [16:224]. Most authors seem to fall somewhere in the middle. They are nervous about the finality of deletion, but see the value of culling the collection: "I view deletion as a cathartic process that much improves my perception of what's left" [16:217]. Culling is typically an iterative process done in multiple stages during the workflow. One author explains, "What persists in my working archive has to survive at least four to five rounds of cutting and grading" [16:210]. If files are to be deleted, general recommended practice is to allow time between shooting and deletion. One strategy is to move files to be deleted into a holding directory for a waiting period before deletion [16:207, 22:231, 32:81].

There are a few reports of deleting images from the camera pre-transfer [16:201, 16:218, 32:80], but some express reservations about making quality judgments based on camera display [32:80]. Instead, most weeding, sorting, and selecting is done post-transfer. Some photographers acquire laptops (and now are considering netbooks [16:127, 16:100]) to use for initial weeding on shoots or when traveling [14:74, 15:80, 15:155, 19:97]. The laptop functions as a larger camera display so that the quality of images can be confidently assessed [16:127]. It may also be used to move images from memory cards (that are used in the camera) to (often multiple) external hard drives for safekeeping [16:127, 15:62, 15:86, 22:216]. At this point, poor quality photos (out of focus, etc.) are often deleted [16:201, 19:225].

After initial transfer, decisions are made about which images to develop from RAW into another format for further editing or other use [13:162, 19:222, 19:223]. Subcollection creation—for example, choosing some photos to add to a Flickr photostream, include in a photobook, or share with a photo club [19:230]—requires sorting. Finally, selection may take place before photos are "archived."

Select Suitable Formats and Software

This Paradigm guideline highlights that choice of software and file formats affects the ease of long-term preservation. The literature on home mode personal photo collections does not treat the topic of file formats at all. One study mentioned in passing that a participant had both JPEG and Photoshop document (PSD) files,[97] but overall a digital photo is described as a digital photo—as though all digital photos are the same.

The situation is very different in serious photography. Forum authors most frequently mention working with JPEG and RAW files. RAW is not itself a specific file format, but a term referring to a family of file formats that encode the raw data representing the light on the image sensor in a digital camera at the time of exposure. In 2005, there were more than one hundred separate formats for encoding this RAW image data. Nikon Electronic Format (NEF), Cannon RAW Version 2 (CR2), and DNG (Adobe) are the most frequently mentioned specific RAW formats. PSD and TIFF are also mentioned a number of times, and a wide array of other formats are mentioned once or twice. Forum authors also mention having film negatives, transparencies, slides, prints from film, gallery prints of digital images, photobooks, and various multimedia objects made using their photos. This underscores a broader need to understand the entire photography-related collection and not only the digital images.

File formats are an important issue on the forum; the topic is presented as its own category, but the topic is also discussed in many other categories. Discussion of file formats roughly falls into five types. First, there are questions about the general advantages and disadvantages of different formats [19:53, 22:322, 27:27]. Longevity of the format is not mentioned. Second, there is discussion of which format(s) to use for active work [19:181, 19:183, 26:28]. This topic centers around quality tradeoffs when editing, saving, and printing images.

The third type of discussion concerns incompatibility of software and file formats [19:102, 20:47, 22:198, 16:117]. These problems stem mainly from the proprietary nature of native camera RAW formats. For example, Nikon uses the NEF RAW format, while Canon has the CR2 raw format. These formats are not equivalent. Some include compression, and others use encryption. New cameras often introduce RAW formats that are not readable by existing software. These issues can sometimes be solved by downloading free software updates. Sometimes introducing new tools or steps into the workflow is necessary to use a new camera. The following quote illustrates the convoluted steps required to open a Canon RAW file in an older version of Photoshop (note that he still cannot open the files):

> I clearly am missing something. I was told that I could convert my .cr2 files to adobe raw and edit them in PS CS (Photoshop Creative Suite). Here's what I did: (1) I have Adobe DNG converter 4.3.1; (2) I have the Camera RAW plugin for CS; (3) I convert my .cr2 file to a .dng file (works fine, no problems); (4) I try to open in PS CS . . . They will not open in PS CS, I get the error "not the right kind of document" [19:19].

Forum authors generate a number of versions of images in several different formats, and the fourth type of question is about which of these formats to retain for the future [19:233]. The final type of discussion centers on whether or not to convert camera RAW files to DNG files [19:63, 19:78]. Learning to work with RAW formats is a milestone in the amateur career. Shooting RAW is the digital equivalent of developing film and enlarging prints in the darkroom, whereas shooting JPEG is like dropping film off at a one-hour photo kiosk. As described above, multiple versions of an image can thus be pulled from a RAW file, as multiple prints can be made from a film negative. The RAW file is the negative of digital photography—the original, authentic representation of the light present at the moment of exposure.[98]

Serious photographers are understandably attached to their digital negatives, but those digital negatives are inherently problematic from an interoperability (and thus preservation) standpoint. Problems opening current RAW files with commonly used software in a straightforward manner bodes ill for the long-term usability of these files. To some extent, this is recognized in the photography community. Adobe created the DNG—a standard format for storing RAW data. The company also released a free tool to convert a variety of proprietary RAW formats into DNG (DNG Converter). As an open format for RAW data that enables embedding of metadata, DNG could greatly increase the long-term safety of digital photographs. However, the question of whether or not DNG has long-term viability as a standard format is still open. While a number of manufacturers of cameras and software have adopted the format in the past year, major players Canon and Nikon still use their own proprietary formats. Also, there is some resistance to the DNG format in the photography community.

Unless all major camera brands begin natively writing DNG, there will be resistance to the format within the photography community. If a camera does not create original images in DNG, transforming its RAW files to DNG is a step away from the authentic negative [20:109]; as a result of manipulating the original RAW data, such a DNG file does not replace the original RAW file. To ensure access to some RAW version of their photos if the camera's native format becomes obsolete, some forum authors retain the camera native and DNG files in long-term storage [12:162, 20:100]. Others view this as unnecessary because it involves retaining another large file and they are not concerned about not being able to open the original file in the future [12:170]. One author believes he has this problem solved:

> A quick trick to make sure you will always be able to open your raw file in the future is to get a cheap mac or pc that can run your needed software . . . put it in a plastic box with cd copy of your software, tape it and put it in the attic. If one day you need to access those raw that are not supported in Vista 28 or in OS 17 . . . just open the box and get your raw from it, that way you will save space, money and hard drive for other use than DNG file . . . and save major time today not converting all your files [19:218].

Another writes:

> I also don't understand the rationality of converting raw into dng [. . .]
> What is the point of making life difficult. Scientifically and logically,
> the most "efficient" way of doing anything is the one that involves
> [the] least step(s) without sacrificing the quality and durability of the
> outcome [19:238].

Unfortunately, this author's attitude may threaten the "durability of the outcome" by valuing today's efficiency over ensuring valuable RAW data will exist in open formats for the future. Native RAW formats are far too numerous and proprietary to depend upon for the long term. Current preservation standards for raster images recommend retention of image files in TIFF or JPEG2000 formats. The latter is not mentioned by forum authors. TIFF is mentioned, but less often than JPEG and various RAW formats.

Some forum authors recognize attractive qualities of the TIFF format: it is an open standard [19:245, 20:84, 20:108], offers lossless compression [20:84], and is recommended by Adobe Lightroom staff as the best target format to use when converting RAW files [19:246]. Authors do report converting RAW files to TIFF for printing [12:90, 19:181] or editing [19:185, 22:150]. Others convert older non-RAW files or digitized images to TIFF [12:116, 12:124, 14:169, 22:168]. A number of authors report "archiving" TIFFs along with their RAW files [19:231, 19:235, 22:278, 36:71]. Sometimes others question their wisdom in doing so [12:169]. Others keeping TIFFs are warned that they should also be keeping their RAW files [22:144]. Among a number of forum members, the attitude toward the safest image format currently available is: "tiff is completely pointless to me" [12:170]; and "I don't keep any TIF anymore as I can just rerun an action from the PSD to get them" [22:321].

The ethos of the photography world is to honor the sanctity of the original image—the digital negative. A common assumption appears to be that retaining the negative—the original RAW file in camera-native format—will ensure access to the high-quality image data in perpetuity. The implications for long-term preservation of these collections are discouraging.

Back Up Files

People fear losing their data and understand that regular backups and taking other steps to safeguard data for the long term are important for protecting data against loss; however, their actions do not always mirror their values. Many people back up infrequently or not at all,[99] or in ways that put files at risk. For example, they may "back up" to a different folder on the same hard drive, or store all backups in the same physical location.[100] As discussed above, forum authors also fear data loss [12:31, 34:73], but the norm is to take extensive steps to guard against the possibility. This supports the finding in the "Digital Lives" report that more technically proficient users are more diligent about backing up. Note that forum authors make no clear distinctions between the terms *backup, archiving,* and *storage,* so they are discussed together here (see "Conceptual Ambiguity," above).

Decide what to back up. Creators of home mode and general personal collections tend toward unsystematic approaches. Reasons include ad hoc backup via email and use of social websites, time and effort required to back up, lack of appropriate storage media, lack of technical knowledge, and unrealistic beliefs about the replaceability of data.[101]

In contrast, creation of a backup routine is part of the well-planned photography workflow for serious photographers. The level of selectivity for backup purposes is unclear from the forum data. There seems to be no typical practice, as preference for selectivity in choosing which files to retain varies widely across individuals.

Make copies on portable media. Use of portable media for backup—floppy disks, zip drives, external drives, CDs, DVDs, and alternative computers—is commonly reported in the literature.[102] Floppies are too small for use with today's photos and zip drives are out of date; their use is not described on the forum. Also, forum authors appear to be technically competent and engaged enough to migrate files from system to system, and they do not mention collecting old computers as external media. Forum authors heavily use external hard drives and, to a lesser extent, optical media.

External hard drives are generally a cheaper, simpler solution for replicating the large image collections of serious photographers, and appear to be the most popular form of portable media for backup on the forum. Optical media are considered by some to be too slow to burn and read, too unreliable, and too small [12:99, 22:176]. Having at least two backup drives is considered the best practice [22:146]. Backup drives need not be portable—some forum authors have multiple internal drives and redundant array of independent disk (RAID) setups to ensure systematic file replication

[12:42, 16:76, 12:133, 13:104]. These systems do not provide physical offsite storage, however. Two authors mention using several hard drives [16:146, 11:177]. One reports using five drives [13:130], and two use six [22:106, 22:77]. Redundancy is a key criterion in evaluating a backup system on the forum [12:42, 12:150]. Drive reliability is another factor important to forum authors [11:125, 12:99, 16:78]. The true test of any backup system is whether it provides an adequate restoration after a loss of data. One forum author did report a mostly successful restore [12:155].

Though external drives are generally considered better for backup, forum authors do back up to DVDs [22:60, 11:105, 12:127], a combination of DVDs and CDs [15:246, 22:141, 22:159], or CDs only [19:157]. A common concern is the long-term, "archival" reliability of optical media. Authors have a sense that some brands are better than others and ask for recommendations [12:159, 22:214, 22:80]; a favorite brand is MAM-A. Forum authors are also concerned with the effect of labeling optical media on their archival properties [13:113, 12:148]. Finally, optical media are also sometimes used in concert with external hard drives to rehouse replicated data [11:159, 12:144].

Store a copy offsite. The guidelines suggest storing a backup at some physical location removed from other backups. This protects against loss due to physical catastrophe. Some creators of general collections do this by keeping important information in safe deposit boxes,[103] and forum authors also report this strategy [22:183]. One provides extensive guidelines for a backup system using safe deposit boxes [37:74]; while others move hard drives to offsite storage locations [11:147, 16:146, 22:155].

Another method of offsite storage is backing up to a remote networked location. Typical personal collection backup strategies, such as using webmail as an offsite repository or uploading images to web services like Flickr, are clearly unfeasible given the scale of the serious photographer's collection.[104] There is some interest on the forum in large-scale web storage hosting services [11:57, 11:190, 12:140, 22:165], but most backup systems rely mainly on physically accessible hard drives and optical media.

Use data synchronization services or software. Some forum authors are using data synchronization services more advanced than what the Paradigm guidelines recommend. Apple's Time Capsule, an automatic backup drive for Macs, is used by several forum authors [22:236, 17:34, 22:31]. Others have automated systems for backing up to an external hard drive [16:146, 22:132]. Still others describe their network attached storage (NAS) automated backup systems using tools such as Drobo [11:54, 12:155, 13:130, 22:177]. These strategies were also observed in a minority of advanced users in the "Digital Lives" report.

Look after Your Hardware and Media

This guideline stresses the fallibility of hardware and media, and gives suggestions on how to minimize the chances of hardware and media failure. Forum authors cite the inevitable fallibility of hard drives as one of the reasons behind their backup plans [11:223, 11:224, 12:171]. The only routine for monitoring and upgrading hardware mentioned so far is a plan to annually replace the primary internal hard drive [11:147]. That said, there are surprisingly few reports of data loss due to hardware failure. Forum authors frequently cite running low on space and increasingly sluggish performance as reasons for replacing hardware [12:42, 12:67, 16:172, 14:196]. The failure rate of optical media is also mentioned by forum authors [12:173, 12:74], and they are aware that things like labeling and brand quality can affect the longevity of the media [11:225]. One author recommends checking burned DVDs on a regular basis [22:213] and another stresses the importance of finding out the best writing speed in order to avoid errors in burning optical media [22:215].

Administer Your System

Much of workflow design falls under this guideline. As discussed above, forum authors report careful planning of their systems and updates. There are no reports of viruses or badware in the forum data analyzed.

Consider Using Passwords and Encryption Devices

There is little discussion of dealing with passwords and encryption on the forum. This is consistent with the findings of the three Flickr studies discussed above. Snaprs did not consider their photos to be private documents.[105] Participants in Julia Davies' study and Jean Burgess's study also shared their photos openly on Flickr.[106] One participant in the latter study also publicly exhibited his photos in a gallery.

Be Aware of Intellectual Property Rights and Privacy

In general personal collections, the inclusion of materials created by others requires care to avoid violation of intellectual property laws. The overwhelmingly self-created composition of the serious amateur's collection means this is not a large concern. As mentioned above, forum authors give little indication that they consider the photos they make viewable to others to be private. They do not report encrypting or password-protecting their images. Instead, forum authors express concern about identifying and protecting their photographs as their own intellectual property. One asks about the proper time in the photo processing workflow to embed watermarks in photos to be shared with others [11:128]. Others discuss the use of copyright/rights metadata [19:221, 27:78, 22:82]. One author expresses concern that the terms of service of a new photo-sharing service gives the service too many rights for use of user-posted photographs [29:41]. Finally, some forum authors asked questions about managing and interpreting software licenses [13:145, 15:175, 16:74, 19:58]. While the applications themselves are not part of the collection, it is good practice to maintain some record of software purchase, licensing, and installation details. This enables photographers to make sure they are using the software legally, and also gives them evidence to use if requesting replacement license codes in the case of hardware failure or theft.

Keep Up to Date

Amateur photographers' thirst for knowledge and attainment of professional standards suggest that they will keep hardware up to date as best they can. High-end cameras, image management and organization software, and the computers needed to run them are expensive. Cost is one of the most frequent criteria mentioned in evaluative statements about tools and services, but amateurs want to have the newest and best they can afford. New hardware can be incompatible with older software. This fact, along with the desire for new features, ensures that software will be kept up to date. Greater danger lurks in the archives, however: old file formats silently become unusable as new applications drop support for them. Keeping file formats fresh by migrating them to newer formats flies in the face of the ethos of photographers. It would be viewed as compromising the original digital negatives.

Handling Legacy Digital Files

Some forum authors have already run into issues of dealing with legacy digital files:

> I have a number of vintage 90's Kodak PhotoCD disks and I realize that the time has come to process them out of that format for archival storage. I noticed it was time to do something, when I went to process an image using Photoshop CS4. I installed the CS3 version of the PhotoCD plugin and processed the image I needed, but this isn't going to work forever [12:115].

Photo CD is a proprietary format no longer readable by current versions of PhotoShop or Lightroom. The author quoted above and one other [19:79] were advised that they would need to copy the files to another form of media and that they would need to process the files individually in order to transform them into an open format. It seems that such problems will become more frequent as proprietary RAW files begin to age.

Ask Digital Archivists for Advice

The Paradigm guidelines encourage collection creators to consult preservation professionals for guidance in maintaining their collections. There is no evidence that forum authors consider doing this. The forum is a place for consulting professional photographers, but as discussed above, their advice sometimes conflicts with what preservation professionals would advise. Forum authors exhibit a hunger for information on how to best take care of personal digital collections. They cite *The Digital Asset Management Book*[107] as a resource, and want to know if similar books exist [11:77]. Development of personal photo collection management guidelines addressing the complexities and values of serious photography in the presentation of current preservation best practice could be a way for archival professionals to reach out to this community.

This chapter reports partial, preliminary analysis of posted threads from a single category of a single photography forum. Practices described on the forum cannot be assumed to represent the practices of serious photographers in general. The content is shaped by those who speak out, ask questions, and share advice—a small subset of serious photographers.

Revisiting the research goals from the beginning of the chapter, however, shows that the study has been successful. The first goal was to determine if there is anything new and important to learn from studying the personal collection management of amateur photographers. The answer to this is clearly *yes*. Many practices are described on the forum that have not been described in previous work on personal photo collections. These include proactive collection management; extensive description of collections using several metadata standards; successful handling of multiple versions of photos; development of extensive backup systems; and design of entire computing systems to support the tasks of processing, organizing, and storing image collections. In particular, further work should explore whether these practices are reported by photographers who do not share their practices on the forum. Other questions include:

- What are photographers' long-term goals or plans for their collections? It is clear that maintaining the collections is important to photographers, but the forum data do not tell how the collections are used or what creators expect or hope for their collections in the long term.

- How do serious photographers learn about and deal with the complexity of the metadata required for managing their personal collections? To what extent do they create, manipulate, and use metadata? How do their image descriptions compare with those seen on photo-sharing sites and institutional collections?

- Is there some metaphor or model in the serious photographer's understanding of and approach to backing up and archiving that could be used to design tools and/or educational materials to help home mode photographers better protect their collections from data loss?

- How do serious photographers devise potential system breakdown scenarios in order to plan for and prevent future collection management problems?

The second research goal was to learn about the norms and expectations of the social world of photography regarding photography-related collection management. A number of forum authors identify themselves as either professionals or amateurs, indicating that the forum is a shared mediated communication space for the social world of photography. Norms and best practices are there to aspire to; whether or not most photographers follow practices recommended on the forum, certain recommended and expected collection management practices were evident. These include maintenance of an organized, well-described collection; using a RAW workflow; having extensive backup plans; and keeping up with new hardware and software.

Finally, there appear to be three areas of difficulty for which information professionals in cultural heritage institutions might be able to help create solutions. First, as one forum author explains [22:289], there are two distinct yet complementary paradigms for organizing image collections. On one hand, there is the vertical, visible, hierarchical file system structure of named directories containing named subdirectories and named files. On the other hand, a horizontal, abstract, flexible structure can be brought to the images using applications that leverage metadata. One problem is that the distinction between and importance of both of these organization methods is rarely explicitly spelled out. New adopters of operating systems and various photo organization and manipulation tools exhibit confusion about exactly how their images are being organized—what the underlying model of the organization system is. This leads to frustration, tedious attempts to force applications to do things they were not designed for, and in the worst cases, data loss. This is an aspect of collection management that applies not just to photos. Explaining these different paradigms, the purposes of each, and what kind of tools manipulates which aspects of photo organization should be incorporated into educational materials for personal collection creators. As experts in organizing information, professionals in institutions that acquire personal collections could contribute to developing such explanations and learning objects.

Second, the image metadata situation highlights the disconnects between the end-user, the photo industry, and cultural heritage image collection communities. Each of these has knowledge and perspective on the issues of organizing images that may be useful to the others, but they do not appear to communicate. LIS professionals could initiate some attempts to bridge these communication gaps, or, at the very least, can incorporate the knowledge of the other two in its own understanding of the problem space.

Finally, the serious photography community's privileging of the RAW format and disregard for preservation-friendly formats is troubling for those of us concerned with the long-term viability of these collections. Photographers will not be convinced to abandon archiving RAW files as digital negatives, nor should anyone try to convince them: to not keep the negative would fly in the face of the ethos of serious photography. What preservation professionals could do is strongly encourage the practice of keeping a high quality TIFF version of an image in addition to the negative. Preservation professionals could also become involved in and advocate for a standard RAW format so that they can be confident of their ability to preserve what is considered the most authentic version of an image. They could also become active in projects such as the OpenRAW Working Group,[108] which aims to encourage camera manufacturers to openly document their RAW formats. There has been very little activity on the OpenRAW website since 2006, but achievement of the group's goal would make it possible to develop third-party tools able to read all of the data in RAW files. The availability of such tools within the preservation community would help to ensure full access to preserved RAW files.

This study also demonstrates that investigating serious leisure activities can uncover interesting new findings that run counter to "common knowledge" about information practices in the literature of information behaviors and practices. Though the study is far from conclusive, it raises a number of new questions and suggests avenues for practical action aimed at helping to ensure the long-term safety of personal image collections.

Notes

1 Robert Stebbins, *Serious Leisure: A Perspective for Our Time* (New Brunswick, NJ: Transaction Publishers, 2007).

2 Robert Stebbins, *After Work: The Search for an Optimal Leisure Lifestyle* (Calgary: Detselig Enterprises, 1998).

3 Robert A. Stebbins, "Serious Leisure: A Conceptual Statement," *Pacific Sociological Review* 25, no. 2, (1982): 251–72.

4 Jarkko Kari and Jenna Hartel, "Information and Higher Things in Life: Addressing the Pleasurable and the Profound in Information Science," *Journal of the American Society for Information Science and Technology* 58, no. 8 (2007): 1131–47.

5 Lynne E. F. McKechnie et al., "Research Method Trends in Human Information Literature," in *The New Review of Information Behavior Research: Studies of Information Seeking in Context*. Vol. 3. (London: Taylor Graham, 2002), 113–126.

6 Kari and Hartel, "Information and Higher Things in Life."

7 Ian Jones and Graham Symon, "Lifelong Learning as Serious Leisure: Policy, Practice and Potential," *Leisure Studies* 20, no. 4 (2001): 269–83.

8 Richard Urban, "Second Life, Serious Leisure, and LIS," *Bulletin of the American Society for Information Science and Technology* (2007): 38–40.

9 Tanja Kotro, "User Orientation through Experience: A Study of Hobbyist Knowing in Product Development," *Human Technology: An Interdisciplinary Journal on Humans in ICT Environments* 3, no. 2, (May 2007): 154–66; David Redmiles, Hiroko Wilensky, Kristie Kosaka, and Rogerio de Paula, "What Ideal End Users Teach Us About Collaborative Software," in *Group '05: Proceedings of the 2005 International ACM SIGGROUP Conference on Supporting Group Work* (New York: ACM Press, 2005), 260–63; and Cristen Torrey, David McDonald, Bill Schilit, and Sara Bly, "How-To Pages: Informal Systems of Expertise Sharing," in *ECSCW 2007: Proceedings of the Tenth European Conference on Computer Supported Cooperative Work*, ed. Liam Bannon, Ina Wagner, Carl Gutwin, Richard Harper, and Kjeld Schmidt (London: Springer, 2007), 391–410.

10 Deborah K. Barreau, "Context as a Factor in Personal Information Management Systems," *Journal of the American Society for Information Science* 46, no. 5 (1995): 327–39; Richard Boardman and M. Angela Sasse, "'Stuff Goes into the Computer and Doesn't Come Out': A Cross-Tool Study of Personal Information Management," in *Proceedings of ACM CHI 2004 Conference on Human Factors in Computing Systems April 24-29, 2004, Vienna, Austria*, 583–90; William P. Jones, *Keeping Found Things Found: The Study and Practice of Personal Information Management* (Amsterdam: Morgan Kaufmann, 2008); and Joseph Kaye, Janet Vertesi, Shari Avery, Allan Dafoe, Shay David, Lisa Onaga, Ivan Rosero, and Trevor Pinch, "To Have and to Hold: Exploring the Personal Archive," in *Proceedings of the SIGCHI Conference on Human Factors in Computing Systems*, ed. Rebecca E. Grinter (New York: ACM Press, 2006), 275–84.

11 Edward Cutrell, Susan T. Dumais, and Jaime Teevan, "Searching to Eliminate Personal Information Management," *Communications of the ACM* 49, no. 1 (2006): 58–64.

12 David Frohlich, Allan Kuchinsky, Celine Pering, Abbe Don, and Steven Ariss, "Collaborating Around Collections: Requirements for Photoware," in *Proceedings of the 2002 ACM Conference on Computer Supported Cooperative Work* (New York: ACM Press, 2002), 166–75; David Kirk, Abigail Sellen, Carsten Rother, and Ken Wood, "Understanding Photowork," in *Proceedings of the SIGCHI Conference on Human Factors in Computing Systems* (New York: ACM Press, 2006), 761–70; and Andrew D. Miller and W. Keith Edwards, "Give and Take: A Study of Consumer Photo-Sharing Culture and Practice," in *Proceedings of the SIGCHI Conference on Human Factors in Computing Systems* (New York: ACM Press, 2007), 347–56.

13 Ronald D. Lambert, "Doing Family History," *Families* 35 (1996): 11–25; Elizabeth Yakel, "Seeking Information, Seeking Connections, Seeking Meaning: Genealogists and Family Historians," *Information Research* 10, no. 1 (2004), http://informationr.net/ir/10-1/paper205.html.

14 Steven M. Gelber, *Hobbies: Leisure and the Culture of Work in America* (New York: Columbia University Press, 1999).

15 Jenna Hartel, "Information Activities, Resources and Spaces in the Hobby of Gourmet Cooking" (PhD dissertation, University of California, Los Angeles, 2007), 197–98.

16 Chris Hart, Michael Shoolbred, and David Butcher, "The Bibliographical Structure of Fan Information" (paper presented at the 64th IFLA General Conference, Amsterdam, August 16–21, 1998).

17 Torrey et al., "How-To Pages: Informal Systems of Expertise Sharing."

18 Ciaran B. Trace, "Resistance and the Underlife: Informal Written Literacies and their Relationship to Human Information Behavior," *Journal of the American Society for Information Science and Technology* 59, no. 10 (2008): 1550.

19 Anne Kustritz, "Slashing the Romance Narrative," *Journal of American Culture* 26, no. 3 (2003): 371–84; Angela Thomas, "Blurring and Breaking Through the Boundaries of Narrative, Literacy, and Identity in Adolescent Fan Fiction," in *A New Literacies Sampler*, ed. Michele Knobel and Colin Lankshear, New Literacies and Digital Epistemologies (New York: Peter Lang, 2007), 137–65.

20 Jessica Hammer, "Agency and Authority in Role-Playing 'Texts,'" in *A New Literacies Sampler*, 67–93.

21 Richard Chalfen, *Snapshot Versions of Life* (Bowling Green, OH: Bowling Green State University Popular Press, 1987).

22 Rebecca E. Grinter, "Words About Images: Coordinating Community in Amateur Photography," *Computer Supported Cooperative Work* 14, no. 2 (2005): 161–88; Dona B. Schwartz and Michael Scott Griffin, "Amateur Photography: The Organizational Maintenance of an Aesthetic Code," in *Natural Audiences: Qualitative Research of Media Uses and Effects*, ed. T. Lindlof (Norwood, NJ: Ablex), 198–224.

23 Michael Scott Griffin, "Amateur Photography and Pictorial Aesthetics: Influences of Organization and Industry on Cultural Production" (PhD dissertation, University of Pennsylvania, 1987); Don Slater, "Consuming Kodak," in *Family Snaps: The Meaning of Domestic Photography*, ed. Jo Spence and Patricia Holland (London: Virago, 1991), 49–59.

24 Daniel G. Yoder, "A Model for Commodity Intensive Serious Leisure," *Journal of Leisure Research* 29, no. 4 (1997): 407–29.

25 Stebbins, *Serious Leisure* (2007).

26 Barbara Rosenblum, *Photographers at Work: A Sociology of Photographic Styles* (New York: Holmes and Meier, 1978).

27 For the purposes of comparing findings in this study, it is assumed that the participants described in the three Flickr studies are indeed serious amateur photographers.

28 Rosenblum, *Photographers at Work*.

29 Julia Davies, "Affinities and Beyond! Developing Ways of Seeing in Online Spaces," *E-Learning* 3, no. 2 (2006): 217–34.

30 Amateur photography is a leisure activity pursued by men much more heavily than by women. (See Andrew M. Cox, Paul D. Clough, and Jennifer Marlow, "Flickr: A First Look at User Behaviour in the Context of Photography as Serious Leisure," *Information Research* 13, no. 1 (2008), http://informationr.net/ir/13-1/paper336.html. See also Don Slater, "Consuming Kodak.") Based on this, I use masculine pronouns unless I am referring to someone clearly identified on the forum as female.

31 Stebbins, *Serious Leisure* (2007).

32 Jean Burgess, "Vernacular Creativity and New Media" (PhD dissertation, Creative Industries Faculty, Queensland University of Technology, 2007), 288, http://eprints.qut.edu.au/archive/00010076/.

33 Miller and Edwards, "Give and Take: A Study of Consumer Photo-Sharing Culture and Practice."

34 Cox, Clough, and Marlow, "Flickr: A First Look at User Behaviour."

35 Nancy A. Van House, "Flickr and Public Image-Sharing: Distant Closeness and Photo Exhibition," in *CHI '07 Extended Abstracts on Human Factors in Computing Systems* (New York: ACM Press, 2007), 2717–22; Susan Murray, "Digital Images, Photo-Sharing, and Our Shifting Notions of Everyday Aesthetics," *Journal of Visual Culture* 7, no. 2 (2008): 147–63.

36 Shelia Anderson, Mike Pringle, Mick Eadie, Tony Austin, Andrew Wilson, and Malcolm Polfreman, *Digital Images Archiving Study* (Arts and Humanities Data Service, 2006), 163; Murtha Baca, *Introduction to Art Image Access: Issues, Tools, Standards, Strategies* (Los Angeles: Getty Research Institute, 2002); Hsin Liang Chen and Edie M. Rasmussen, "Intellectual Access to Images," *Library Trends* 48, no. 2 (1999): 291–302; Corinne L. Jorgensen, *Image Retrieval: Theory and Research* (Lanham, MD: Scarecrow Press, 2003); Diane Neal, "News Photography Image Retrieval Practices: Locus of Control in Two Contexts" (PhD dissertation, University of North Texas, 2006); and Jennifer Hain Teper, "Newspaper Photo Morgues: A Survey of Institutional Holdings and Practices," *Library Collections, Acquisitions, and Technical Services* 28, no. 1 (2004): 106–25.

37 Anne Adams, Sally Jo Cunningham, and Masood Masoodian, *Sharing, Privacy and Trust Issues for Photo Collections* (working paper no. 01/2007 University of Waikato, Department of Computer Science, Hamilton, New Zealand, 2007), http://hdl.handle.net/10289/59; David Frohlich and Jacqueline Fennell, "Sound, Paper and Memorabilia: Resources for a Simpler Digital Photography," *Personal and Ubiquitous Computing* 11, no. 2 (2007): 107–16; Kirk et al., "Understanding Photowork"; Virginia Nightingale, "The Cameraphone and Online Image Sharing," *Continuum: Journal of Media and Cultural Studies* 21, no. 2 (2007): 289–301; and Kerry Rodden and Kenneth R. Wood, "How Do People Manage Their Digital Photographs?" in *Proceedings of the SIGCHI Conference on Human Factors in Computing Systems* (New York: ACM Press, 2003), 409–16.

38 Emma Angus, Mike Thelwall, and David Stuart, "General Patterns of Tag Usage Among University Groups in Flickr," *Online Information Review* 32, no. 1 (2008): 89–101; Cox, Clough, and Marlow, "Flickr: A First Look at User Behaviour"; Pauline Rafferty and Rob Hidderley, "Flickr and Democratic Indexing: Dialogic Approaches to Indexing," *Aslib Proceedings* 59, nos. 4/5 (2007): 397–410.

39 Corinne L. Jorgensen, "Retrieving the Unretrievable: Art, Aesthetics, and Emotion in Image Retrieval Systems," *IS&T/SPIE Human Vision and Electronic Imaging IV*, ed. Bernice Ellen Rogowitz and Thrasyvoulous Pappas (Bellingham, WA: SPIE, 1999), 348–55; Michael G. Krause, "Intellectual Problems of Indexing Picture Collections," *Audiovisual Librarian* 14, no. 2 (1988): 73–81; Sara Shatford Layne, "Some Issues in the Indexing of Images," *Journal of the American Society for Information Science* 45, no. 8 (1994): 583–88.

40 Apple iPhoto '09 (software application), http://www.apple.com/ilife/iphoto/; Google Picasa 3 (software application), http://picasa.google.com/ (both accessed March 21, 2009).

41 Peter G.B. Enser, Christine J. Sandom, Jonathon S. Hare, and Paul H. Lewis, "Facing the Reality of Semantic Image Retrieval," *Journal of Documentation* 63, no. 4 (2007): 465–81.

42 James W. Marcum, "Beyond Visual Culture: The Challenge of Visual Ecology," *Portal-Libraries and the Academy* 2, no. 2 (2002): 189–206.

43 Andrew Birrell, Peter Robertson, Lilly Koltun, Andrew C. Rodger, and Joan M. Schwartz, "Private Realms of Light: Canadian Amateur Photography, 1839-1940: 2. On View: The Evolution of Amateur Photography," *Archivaria* 17 (1983): 115–35; Carole Glauber, "Eyes of the Earth: Lily White, Sarah Ladd, and the Oregon Camera Club," *Oregon Historical Quarterly* 108, no. 1 (1983): 34–67; Griffin, "Amateur Photography and Pictorial Aesthetics"; G. Harthardottir, "Amateur Photography Groups in Reykjavik 1950-70," *History of Photography* 23, no. 1 (1999): 43–48; David L. Jacobs,

"Domestic Snapshots: Toward a Grammar of Motives," *Journal of American Culture* 4, no. 1 (Spring 1981): 93–105; Dona B. Schwartz, "Doing the Ethnography of Visual Communication: The Rhetoric of Fine Art Photography," *Research on Language and Social Interaction* 21 (1987): 229–50; Elizabeth Shove and Mika Pantzar, "Recruitment and Reproduction: The Careers and Carriers of Digital Photography and Floorball," *Human Affairs* 17, no. 2 (2007): 154–67; and Slater, "Consuming Kodak."

44   David R. Unruh, "The Nature of Social Worlds," *Pacific Sociological Review* 23, no. 3 (1980): 271–96.

45   Burgess, "Vernacular Creativity and New Media"; Davies, "Affinities and Beyond."

46   Nigel King, "Template Analysis," in *Qualitative Methods and Analysis in Organizational Research*, ed. Gillian Symon and Catherine Cassell (London: Sage, 1998).

47   Photo.net, http://photo.net/.

48   Josh Root, "Terms and Conditions of Use," Photo.net, http://photo.net/info/terms-of-use (accessed January 30, 2009).

49   Digital Darkroom thread categories excluded from the study were: Color Management—Calibration, —Color Space, —Lighting; Imaging Techniques—Emulating (B&W, IR, filters, etc.), —Other, —Resizing/Sharpening, —Retouching; Monitors; Printing—B&W, —Inkjet Inks/Papers, —Other, —Technique, —Printers—Home, —Printers—Pro/High volume; Projection; Scanning—Other, —Scanners, —Software, —Technique, —Scanners—Drum, —Scanners—Film, —Scanners—Flatbed; Services—Educational, —Scanning; Software—Editing, —Stitching, HDR, compositing.

50   Using an exploratory analysis to develop a template requires no tests to demonstrate the validity or reliability of coding; therefore, the trustworthiness of the present analysis is not statistically demonstrated. To improve the transparency and trustworthiness of this study, an audit trail is provided for statements based on the data. The unique ID of the ATLAS.ti quotation(s) related to the statement is inserted in square brackets. The number before the colon refers to the ID of the primary document. The number after the colon refers to a quotation within the primary document. The data are available from the author in XML or native ATLAS.ti.hu format.

51   Kaye et al., "To Have and to Hold"; Sue McKemmish, "Evidence of Me . . . ," *Archives and Manuscripts* 24, no. 1 (1996): 28–45; José Van Dijck, "From Shoebox to Performative Agent: The Computer as Personal Memory Machine," *New Media and Society* 7, no. 3 (2005): 311–32; and Pete Williams et al., "Digital Lives: Report of Interviews with the Creators of Personal Digital Collections," *Ariadne* 55 (2008), http://www.ariadne.ac.uk/issue55/williamset-al/.

52   Stebbins, *Serious Leisure* (2007).

53   Adams, Cunningham, and Masoodian, *Sharing, Privacy and Trust Issues for Photo Collections;* Frohlich et al., "Collaborating Around Collections"; and Kirk et al., "Understanding Photowork."

54   Mihály Csíkszentmihályi and Eugene Rochberg-Halton, *The Meaning of Things: Domestic Symbols and the Self* (Cambridge: Cambridge University Press, 1981); Greg Noble, "Accumulating Being," *International Journal of Cultural Studies* 7, no. 2 (2004): 233–56.

55   Kirk et al., "Understanding Photowork"; Catherine C. Marshall, "Rethinking Personal Digital Archiving, Part 1," *D-Lib Magazine* 14, nos. 3/4 (2008), http://dx.doi.org/10.1045/march2008-marshall-pt1.

56   Kirk et al., "Understanding Photowork"; Rodden and Wood, "How Do People Manage Their Digital Photographs?"; Frank Bentley, Crysta Metcalf, and Gunnar Harboe, "Personal vs. Commercial Content: The Similarities Between Consumer Use of Photos and Music," *Proceedings of the SIGCHI Conference on Human Factors in Computing Systems* (New York: ACM Press, 2006), 667–76.

57   Ofer Bergman, Simon Tucker, Ruth Beyth-Marom, Edward Cutrell, and Stever Whittaker, "Improved Search Engines and Navigation Preference in Personal Information Management," *ACM Transactions on Information Systems* 26, no. 4 (2008): 1–24.

[58] Peter Krogh, *The DAM Book: Digital Asset Management for Photographers* (Sebastopol, CA: O'Reilly, 2006).

[59] Anderson et al., *Digital Images Archiving Study.*

[60] Paradigm project, *Workbook on Digital Private Papers,* 2007, http://www.paradigm.ac.uk/workbook/.

[61] Neil Beagrie, "Plenty of Room at the Bottom? Personal Digital Libraries and Collections," *D-Lib Magazine* 11, no. 6 (2005), http://dx.doi.org/10.1045/june2005-beagrie.

[62] Marshall, "Rethinking Personal Digital Archiving, Part 1."

[63] Burgess, "Vernacular Creativity and New Media"; Cox, Clough, and Marlow, "Flickr: A First Look at User Behaviour"; Stebbins, *Serious Leisure* (2007).

[64] A RAW file is the original image data directly from the camera with no algorithmic corrections or compression applied.

[65] "Optimize Performance of Photoshop CS3 On Windows XP And Vista," Adobe technical note kb401088, accessed March 25, 2009, http://kb.adobe.com/selfservice/viewContent.do?externalId=kb401088: "Photoshop requires at least 1 GB of free hard-disk space, but more is recommended. If you have more than one hard disk volume, you should specify additional scratch disks. Photoshop CS2 supports up to 64 exabytes (EB) of scratch disk space on a total of four volumes. (An EB is equal to 1 billion gigabytes.) RAID 0 partitions provide the best possible performance as Photoshop scratch disks."

[66] DPI is a measure of image resolution. Capturing an image at a higher DPI increases the quality of prints made of the image, or high-definition projections or displays of the image.

[67] Paradigm, *Workbook on Digital Private Papers.*

[68] See Anthony Giddens, *The Constitution of Society: Outline of the Theory of Structuration* (Berkeley: University of California Press, 1984).

[69] Miller and Edwards, "Give and Take: A Study of Consumer Photo-Sharing Culture and Practice."

[70] Catherine C. Marshall, Sara Bly, and Francoise Brun-Cottan, "The Long Term Fate of Our Personal Digital Belongings: Toward a Service Model for Personal Archives," in *Proceedings of IS&T Archiving 2006* (Springfield, VA: Society for Imaging Science and Technology, 2006), 25–30; Williams et al., "Digital Lives."

[71] Marshall, "Rethinking Personal Digital Archiving, Part 1."

[72] Miller and Edwards, "Give and Take: A Study of Consumer Photo-Sharing Culture and Practice."

[73] Marshall, "Rethinking Personal Digital Archiving, Part 1."

[74] Stebbins, *Serious Leisure* (2007).

[75] Krogh, *The Dam Book: Digital Asset Management for Photographers.*

[76] http://www.paradigm.ac.uk/index.html.

[77] The second guideline, Manage Your Emails, is omitted because the topic is not discussed on the forum.

[78] Rodden and Wood, "How Do People Manage Their Digital Photographs?"; Gilliam Rose, "Family Photographs and Domestic Spacings: A Case Study," *Transactions of the Institute of British Geographers* 28, no. 1 (2003): 5–18; Sander Vroegindeweij, *My Pictures: Informal Image Collections* (tech. rep. HPL-200272R1, Palo Alto, CA: HP Labs, 2001), 105, http://www.hpl.hp.com/techreports/2002/HPL-2002-72R1.pdf.

[79] Frohlich et al., "Collaborating Around Collections"; Kirk et al., "Understanding Photowork"; Rodden and Wood, "How Do People Manage Their Digital Photographs?"; Vroegindeweij, *My Pictures.*

[80] William Jones, Ammy Jiranida Phuwanartnurak, Rajdeep Gill, and Harry Bruce, "Don't Take My Folders Away!: Organizing Personal Information to Get Things Done," in *CHI '05 Extended Abstracts on Human Factors in Computing System* (New York: ACM Press, 2005), 1505–8.

[81] Kirk et al., "Understanding Photowork"; Marshall, "Rethinking Personal Digital Archiving, Part 1"; Williams et al., "Digital Lives."

[82] Frohlich et al., "Collaborating Around Collections"; Rodden and Wood, "How Do People Manage Their Digital Photographs?"; Rose, "Family Photographs and Domestic Spacings."

[83] Bentley, Metcalf, and Harboe, "Personal vs. Commercial Content"; Kirk et al., "Understanding Photowork"; Rodden and Wood, "How Do People Manage Their Digital Photographs?"

[84] Miller and Edwards, "Give and Take: A Study of Consumer Photo-Sharing Culture and Practice."

[85] Sally Jo Cunningham and Masood Masoodian, "Identifying Personal Photo Digital Library Features," in *Proceedings of the 2007 Conference on Digital Libraries* (New York: ACM, 2007), 400–01.

[86] Cox, Clough, and Marlow, "Flickr: A First Look at User Behaviour"; Miller and Edwards, "Give and Take: A Study of Consumer Photo-Sharing Culture and Practice."

[87] Michael Langford and Efthimia Bilissi, *Langford's Advanced Photography*, 7th ed. (Oxford: Focal Press, 2008); Scott Kelby, *The Digital Photography Book* (Berkeley: Peachpit Press, 2006).

[88] Metadata Working Group, *Guidelines for Handling Image Metadata* (Feb. 2009), http://www.metadataworkinggroup.org/pdf/mwg_guidance.pdf (accessed March 21, 2009).

[89] See notes 36–41 for references to this work.

[90] Anderson et al., *Digital Images Archiving Study*.

[91] Desney Tan, Emma Berry, Mary Czerwinski, Gordon Bell, Jim Gemmell, Steve Hodges, Narinder Kapur, Brian Meyers, Nuria Oliver, George Robertson, and Ken Wood, "Save Everything: Supporting Human Memory with a Personal Digital Lifetime Store," in *Personal Information Management*, ed. William P. Jones and Jaime Teevan (Seattle, WA: University of Washington Press, 2007), 90–107.

[92] Harry Bruce, "Personal, Anticipated Information Need," *Information Research* 10, no. 3 (2005), http://informationr.net/ir/10-3/paper232.html.

[93] Marshall, "Rethinking Personal Digital Archiving, Part 1."

[94] Hur-Li Lee, "The Concept of Collection from the User's Perspective," *Library Quarterly* 75, no. 1 (2005): 67–85.

[95] Marshall, "Rethinking Personal Digital Archiving, Part 1."

[96] Martin Dodge and Rob Kitchin, "'Outlines of a World Coming into Existence': Pervasive Computing and the Ethics of Forgetting," *Environment and Planning B-Planning and Design* 34, no. 3 (2007): 431–45.

[97] Marshall, "Rethinking Personal Digital Archiving, Part 1."

[98] Karl Lang, *Rendering the Print: The Art of Photography* (technical paper, Adobe, 2007), http://wwwimages.adobe.com/www.adobe.com/products/photoshop/family/prophotographer/pdfs/pscs3_renderprint.pdf.

[99] Kaye et al., "To Have and to Hold"; Kirk et al., "Understanding Photowork"; Marshall, "Rethinking Personal Digital Archiving, Part 1."

[100] Williams et al., "Digital Lives."

[101] Kaye et al., "To Have and to Hold"; Marshall, "Rethinking Personal Digital Archiving, Part 1."

[102] Kirk et al., "Understanding Photowork"; Marshall, "Rethinking Personal Digital Archiving, Part 1"; Williams et al., "Digital Lives."

[103] Marshall, "Rethinking Personal Digital Archiving, Part 1."

[104] Marshall, "Rethinking Personal Digital Archiving, Part 1"; Williams et al., "Digital Lives."

[105] Miller and Edwards, "Give and Take: A Study of Consumer Photo-Sharing Culture and Practice."

[106] Davies, "Affinities and Beyond"; Burgess, "Vernacular Creativity and New Media."

[107] Krogh, *The DAM Book: Digital Asset Management for Photographers*.

[108] See http://www.openraw.org/.

Collecting the Externalized Me: Appraisal of Materials in the Social Web

Christopher A. Lee

With the adoption of highly interactive web technologies (frequently labeled "Web 2.0"), forms of individual documentation and expression also often are inherently social and public. Such online environments allow for personal documentation, but they also engage external audiences in ways not previously possible. This opens up new opportunities and challenges for collecting personal materials, particularly within the context of archival appraisal. This chapter explores various ways in which principles of archival appraisal can be operationalized in an environment in which collecting takes the form of submitting queries and following links.

Algernon. Do you really keep a diary? I'd give anything to look at it. May I?

Cecily. Oh no. [Puts her hand over it.] You see, it is simply a very young girl's record of her own thoughts and impressions, and consequently meant for publication. When it appears in volume form I hope you will order a copy.

— *The Importance of Being Earnest,* Oscar Wilde[1]

Western man has become a confessing animal.

—Michel Foucault[2]

Your identity on the computer is the sum of your distributed presence.

—Sherry Turkle[3]

The Traces We Choose

Human activities leave traces: doors left open, footprints in the sand, receipts, browser cache contents, temp files, headers of Internet Protocol (IP) packets, pixels on the screen of a Global Positioning System (GPS) device, voice mail messages, flight prices on an airline website. All of the traces can convey information. The vast majority of traces play a role only in their immediate context and then disappear. However, we occasionally want the traces to stick around for a while.

Any time we purposely increase the chance of use across contexts, we are engaging in selection. Selection always involves some cost, whether that is time, attention, money or technical resources. There are various criteria that guide individual and organizational selection activities. Because of the diversity of activities in which they are involved, individuals' criteria for selecting materials within their personal collections can range from tacit heuristics, habits, and gut feelings to highly codified policies and procedures. Table 1 provides examples of common selection actions by individuals and collectors.

Many of the traces of individuals are now being created and distributed through the Web. To be available for future use, web content must be (1) continuously maintained by the party who is hosting it, (2) preserved by a distributed set of individuals involved in the activities that leave the traces, or (3) harvested by someone with an interest in collection building (e.g., amateur enthusiast, interested scholar, archivist, or librarian). This chapter discussed the nature of personal online traces and issues involved in selecting them for continuing use.

Table 1. Individual and collector selection activities.

Selection actor	Examples of selection actions
Individual	• Creating richer traces of some moments (e.g., taking a high-resolution photo of an event) • Making extra copies in multiple places • Storing information in multiple ways (e.g., online services, formats, systems) • Exporting information to reduce the risk of lock-in • Sharing with other people, so they also have copies
Collector (e.g., librarian, archivist)	• Capturing information from dynamic environments (e.g., web archiving) • Developing and maintaining long-term collections • Value-added actions on parts of collections (e.g., search and analysis capabilities, technical support, sophisticated transformations)

The Personal Moves Online

Individuals leave their personal traces in various places. One of the major issues in the literature on personal information management (PIM) is the "fragmentation" of information across a diversity of locations, devices, and media. Archivists have recognized for a long time that the collective traces (fonds) of a given individual or organization are often spread across numerous storage locations and caretakers. A current manifestation of this issue is the distribution of information across desktop applications and applications that are accessed through the Web.[4]

According to the Pew Internet and American Life Project, the percentage of adult Internet users who have a profile on an online social network site rose from 8 percent in 2005 to 35 percent in December 2008. This percentage is much higher (75 percent) for those eighteen to twenty-four years of age. Even more relevant to the discussion in this chapter is the finding that "personal use of social networks seems to be more prevalent than professional use of networks, both in the orientation of the networks that adults choose to use as well as the reasons they give for using the applications." Online social networking systems are primarily being used "for explaining and maintaining personal networks."[5]

Many of the places where individuals generate a substantial amount of user-generated content are called Social Network Sites (SNSs).

> The rise of SNSs indicates a shift in the organization of online communities. While websites dedicated to communities of interest still exist and prosper, SNSs are primarily organized around people, not interests. Early public online communities such as Usenet and public discussion forums were structured by topics or according to topical hierarchies, but social network sites are structured as personal (or "egocentric") networks, with the individual at the center of their own community.[6]

Although social connections are a driving force in an SNS, the activities are often enacted and documented through documentary artifacts. For example, Facebook, which is primarily a space for managing personal connections, is reportedly "the world's largest photo-sharing service."[7]

Some other Web 2.0 environments can be characterized in the opposite way: they involve numerous individual contributions, but those are dispersed across the space as micro-contributions, rather than existing together in one coherent place. For example, a wiki—a collaborative website where individual users add and edit content—includes a page that lists all of the contributions from a given account, but those contributions only make sense within the context of other users' contributions, that is, as an individual article.

Consider the implications of the following scenario for an archivist responsible for personal collections:

> In the very near future an archivist might enter the office of a deceased writer and find *no electronic files of personal significance*: the author's appointment calendar might split between her organization's Microsoft Exchange server and Yahoo Calendar; her unfinished and unpublished documents stored on Google Docs; her diary stored at the online LiveJournal service; correspondence archived on the Facebook "walls" of her close friends; and her most revealing, insightful and critical comments scattered as anonymous and pseudonymous comments on the blogs of her friends, collaborators, and rivals.[8]

The above scenario does not reflect the current reality, but personal recordkeeping does appear to be moving quickly in the direction that it suggests. Archivists may discover "that content from the first twenty-five years or so of personal computing represents an anomalous window of opportunity where the archivist has reasonable prospects for access to the original storage media."[9] Collection of personal archives may increasingly become a matter of capturing the "externalized me" that individuals have left in various online locations.

Opportunities to Document those Beyond the "Usual Suspects"

Howard Zinn has called on archivists "to compile a whole new world of documentary material about the lives, desires and needs of ordinary people."[10] Adrian Cunningham has argued that existing archival collections fail to reflect all segments of society because of "differing recordkeeping practices between different categories of individuals (creative writers create more records and are better recordkeepers than boilermakers)" and "the biased collecting interests of manuscript curators which, at least in part, is a reflection of their perceived research demands."[11] As a result, social historians have often "resorted to parish registers, censuses and personnel files in order to document social characteristics and changes."[12] Another mechanism for documenting "the lives of the anonymous" has been oral histories.[13] Collecting materials from the Web opens up numerous new mechanisms for documenting the lives and experiences of individuals.

New opportunities for documentation do not only include traditionally disempowered populations; they also include leaders of business. Documenting businesses has been a persistent weak point for archives. Collection of material from the Web that was generated by individuals associated with a company (e.g., blog postings by executives, professional forums to which employees regularly contribute) is a promising way to reflect information that would not otherwise be available to archivists. This can compliment other important information collection techniques, such as solicitation of records from companies[14] and oral histories of influential employees.[15]

The Nature of User-Generated Content on the Web

Personal online presence takes the form of both completely new documentary forms and the movement of existing documentary forms onto the Internet. Many, for example, have characterized blogs as the digital equivalent of journals and diaries, and sites such as Flickr as the digital equivalent of photo albums. Such comparisons can be useful, but it is also important to recognize numerous differences between offline personal records and user-generated content on the Web.

Networks of Micro-Contributions

A great deal of user-generated content is being disseminated through what Rich Skrenta has called the "incremental web."[16] In contrast to web content that is structured around a page metaphor (with logical flow from introduction to body to conclusion), the incremental web is experienced as a flow of relatively small chunks of content that appear over time—either arranged in reverse chronological order on a page or streamed through various "feed" mechanisms.

The characterization of user-generated content in terms of relatively fast interchange of small content contributions is not only true of text, but also of video. The emergence of user-generated online video sharing has shortened both content length and production time by "two orders of magnitude." For example, "it only takes 15 days in YouTube to produce the same number of videos as all IMDb [Internet Movie Database] movies."[17]

Blogs—websites that are composed of (usually short) individual postings arranged in reverse chronological order— are very common venues for user-generated content on the Web. Meg Hourihan, cofounder of Pyra Labs, describes blogs as "post-centric" rather than "page-centric."[18] Personal online contributions can be used as a way to stay in touch with others, which is a role that written correspondence has played for centuries. However, web-based communications can have the advantage of semi-persistent access while not forcing the content onto all potential recipients. One early blogger explained, "I don't clutter my friends' in-boxes and folks who know me well also know they can check out my website to see if anything truly noteworthy has come my way."[19] Another early blogger, Justin Hall, explained his motivations as an "urge to share of oneself" and "a deep geek archivist's urge to experiment with documenting and archiving personal media and experience."[20]

Three aspects of inter-blog conversation make them difficult to systematically identify and collect: contributions to the conversation are fragmented and distributed; links are often not bidirectional; and available tracking technologies often do not afford the identification of conversation threads over time.[21] Stated in archival terms, multiple items in a "series" of correspondence are usually widely distributed and can be difficult to bind together. When receiving someone's personal papers, a large body of correspondence will be all in one place—whether that is in a cardboard box or an email inbox. In order for the dialog that is carried out through the Web to be available to future generations, it must either be preserved by a distributed set of individuals who were party to the correspondence or actively harvested by someone with an interest in collection building (amateur enthusiast, interested scholar, archivist, or librarian). Even if one were able to capture the entire series of blog posts, this would be only a small sliver of the entire fonds of the individuals involved. For example, individuals often continue "discussions of blog topics in other media including instant messaging, phone, and email, as well as face to face," including cases in which "these exchanges involved delicate topics in which feelings could easily be hurt."[22] Capturing only the blog content from all of the interactions between individuals will generate a heavily filtered collection, but it may also reflect the subset of interactions that individuals would be most comfortable disclosing to future researchers. Archivists still have a great deal to learn about the intentions and expectations of individuals in regard to the long-term retention of their digital traces.

The amount and type of personal expression and disclosure varies considerably across different types of Web 2.0 spaces. For example, the blogosphere is built on software that allows an individual to frequently post items, but the affordances of the specific software can have a major impact. A widely-cited account of the history of blogs points out that the availability of Blogger software helped to spark a shift "from the filter-style weblog to journal-style blog"; whereas the data input interface of Metafilter (with boxes provided only for Uniform Resource Locator (URL), title, and short commentary), facilitates much more of a telegraphic set of external pointers.[23]

There has been considerable discussion—within the literature about blogs and in the blogosphere itself—about differences and relative merits of (1) the filter blog (emphasizing pointers to external resources), and (2) the blog that focuses on personal narrative and disclosure. This is an important distinction for an archivist focusing on personal papers, but it is also important to recognize that the two are not mutually exclusive. To the extent that individuals live much of their lives online and enact many of their social network connections online, links are much more than ways to lead readers to interesting news items; they are often an essential form of self-disclosure:

> You can write up what you did with your real-life friend yesterday, but you can't link to that experience. You can link to what your online friend blogged yesterday. The annotated-list-of-links Weblog form, then, becomes one and the same with the diaristic form for Webloggers in the Internet demimonde: Links are diaries because life is the Web.[24]

An additional characteristic of user-generated web content that makes it quite different from previous forms of correspondence is that it can significantly "desituate" the conversation while or shortly after it has taken place. A blog entry, for example, written primarily to be read by the blogger herself, her family, other known bloggers, or some other specific audience may actually be read, linked to, and aggregated or reused by others.[25] This does not imply that all blog entries will be widely exposed to "the public"— in fact, most blog entries are not likely to be read by anyone beyond their authors—but it does change the dynamics of interaction when uncontrolled dissemination is possible. Given the affordances of digital content for re-aggregation and reuse, digital conversations can also be dramatically desituated through the movement of records that were created in relatively closed forums (e.g., email lists and Usenet news groups) onto the Web.[26]

There are multiple methods for obtaining micro-content in the form of feeds; current examples are Really Simple Syndication (RSS), Atom, and Twitter. Such content feeds can be a huge boon for collecting archivists, but they can also miss much of the contextual information that is so important to archivists and (presumably) future users. For example, the RSS feed from a blog often "undoes the idiosyncratic feel of many weblogs by stripping them of visual elements such as layout or logos, as well as eliminating the context produced by blogrolls (blog authors' links to other weblogs) or the author's biographical information (and any advertising)."[27]

One of the forms of micro-content that has received considerable discussion among Web 2.0 advocates is tagging. Tags are small, discrete labels applied by users, and they usually do not conform to a preconceived controlled vocabulary. Instead, patterns in the use of tag terminology tend to be exploited after the fact. Tags have the potential to be more accurate representations of an item's "ofness" or "aboutness" than more formal descriptions, because they have been applied voluntarily by people who are often very close to the items in question. "As the old saying goes, 'one volunteer is worth ten pressed men,' the records management version of which might be 'one optional tag is worth ten mandatory keywords.'"[28] Some social network spaces provide "community-based tagging," which allows users to assign tags to objects, while others provide a more limited "self-tagging" system, which allows only those uploading items (and possibly a select set of approved others) to assign tags; in the latter, tags often serve as "secondary activity or side effect" rather than being a primary focus of user activity.[29]

The Personal Becomes More Public

Social network sites—forums through which individuals interact online—are often referred to collectively as social media or the social web. danah boyd has identified four fundamental features of social network sites that allow them to act as "networked publics:"

- Persistence: in contrast to the "ephemeral quality of speech."

- Searchability: "because expressions are recorded and identity is established through text."

- Replicability: "expressions can be copied from one place to another verbatim such that there is no way to distinguish the 'original' from the 'copy.'"

- Invisible audiences: "it is virtually impossible to ascertain all those who might run across our expressions in networked publics." [30]

Personal records—even nominally "private" diaries—have always been embedded in social contexts and have often been shared with others. However, the networked and potentially interactive characteristics of online content do tend to make them qualitatively more "shared" resources than their offline predecessors. For example, many bloggers began blogging because someone else asked them to do so, and "consciousness of audience is central to the blogging experience."[31] According to Doc Searls, "For us readers, it's actually a bit like eavesdropping. Who do I want to drop in on unannounced?"[32]

Inequality of Attention and Interaction

Online environments that allow users to contribute content tend to have very unequal participation across users.[33] Clay Shirky explains, "In systems where many people are free to choose between many options, a small subset of the whole will get a disproportionate amount of traffic (or attention, or income), even if no members of the system actively work towards such an outcome."[34] The result is a power law distribution,[35] in which a small number of sources gain the majority of traffic and attention. Within the blogosphere, the power law is manifested as a small set of "mainstream media blogs" with a large number of views and in-links, and a much larger number of "conversational blogs" with a very small number of views and in-links.[36]

Investigation of structures and patterns of the Web reveals that "although the range of online content is vast, the range of sites that users actually visit is small."[37] A small percentage of pages accounts for a great deal of the linking and clicking on the Web, and the two phenomena (in-links to pages and the traffic to pages) are closely correlated.[38] Among websites in general, the top ten sites account for 62 percent of total traffic; while the top ten blogs account for 38 percent of blog traffic.[39] Other research also reports "only a small number of high-influence blogs which command high levels of attention, complemented by a much larger group of smaller blogs which do not have any real impact beyond their local peer networks."[40] David Weinberger states the situation more bluntly: "on the Web, everyone will be famous to fifteen people."[41]

The geographic representation of the blogosphere is also quite uneven. Posts to blogs "appear to concentrate on countries well covered in mainstream media—China, Iraq, the USA, France—and ignore the same regions neglected by the media—Central Asia, Sub-Saharan Africa and Central America."[42] If one is interested in building collections that reflect the issues and perspectives of populations from across the globe, then one may need to adopt collecting strategies that specifically target underrepresented populations (rather than simply following links from popular English-language sources), in order to ensure that those populations are reflected in the collections.

There is also major variance in levels of activity. Since 2002, the blog search site Technorati has indexed 133 million blog records. Technorati data from 2008 reveal that 7.4 million blogs posted in the last 120 days (5.56 percent), 1.5 million blogs posted in the last 7 days (1.13 percent), and 900,000 blogs posted in the last 24 hours (.68 percent).[43] In short, while there are many bloggers who post every day and receive many visitors, this is certainly not the case for most blogs.

Table 2 summarizes the twenty most popular blogs. It illustrates that the most popular blogs are largely dominated by political news and commentary, information technology, and celebrity gossip (roughly in that order). The most frequent tags applied in the popular social bookmarking service Delicious also reveal a strong emphasis on information technology, especially web technology.[45]

Table 2. Ten most popular blogs as ranked by Technorati, November 22, 2008.[44]

Blog Title	Language	Focus	Responsibility for posts
1. Huffington Post	English	News and commentary on contemporary events, with a heavy focus on politics	Core group of regular writers and larger set of invited contributors, with oversight by a team of editors
2. Gizmodo	English	Consumer electronics	Team of editors, contributing editors, reporters, and columnists
3. TechCrunch	English	Internet products and companies	Core group of regular contributors, several other occasional contributors, some "guest posts," a paid Writer/Analyst, with oversight by two co-editors
4. Engadget	English	Consumer electronics	Team of editors, contributing editors, and columnists
5. Ars Technica	English	"Original news and reviews, analysis of technology trends, and expert advice on topics ranging from the most fundamental aspects of technology to the many ways technology is helping us enjoy our world"	Team of editors, staff writers, and contributing writers; OpenForum area allows registered users to post, with oversight by a team of moderators
6. Boing Boing	English	Various aspects of popular culture, with a heavy emphasis on information technology	Team of editors and series of "guest bloggers"; registered users can submit comments on posts, which are moderated
7. Lifehacker	English	"Life hacks," which are personal productivity suggestions, often based on creative use of software	Team of editors, occasional guest contributors
8. Daily Kos	English	Political discussion, commentary, and advocacy	Team of contributing editors, featured writers, and "guest bloggers" post to the front page; registered users can comment on postings and can post "diaries"; "trusted users" can hide comments from public view; system administrators can edit comments and block problematic accounts
9. The Official Google Blog	English	Google "products, technology, and the Google culture"	Google employees
10. Smashing Magazine	English	Web design and development trends and techniques	Two editors and paid guest authors
11. Mashable	English	Web 2.0, social networking and social media	Team of editors, to whom users can submit suggested stories
12. Gawker	English	Manhattan media news and gossip	Team of editors; invited authors; invited users can post comments but can later be banned by editors

13. I Can Has Cheezburger	English	Collection of "lolcats," which are pictures with captions intended to be humorous, often featuring cats	All items (images) are submitted by site users, then rated by other users
14. ReadWriteWeb	English	"Web Technology news, reviews and analysis"	Team of writers and guest writers; anyone can comment
15. GIGAZINE	Japanese	Popular culture, technology, and various oddities	Co-editors; users can suggest news items
16. Seth's Blog	English	Personal perspectives on contemporary issues and events	Seth Godin
17. CNN Political Ticker	English	Political news	Cable News Network (CNN) staff; users can submit comments, which are vetted and moderated by CNN staff
18. PerezHilton.com	English	Celebrity gossip	Mario Armando Lavandeira Jr.; registered users can post comments
19. Threat Level	English	Current events related to security and individual liberties	Team of Wired News editors; anyone can post comments
20. The Caucus –New York Times Politics Blog	English	Political news	New York Times staff; anyone can post comments, which must be approved by New York Times staff and are occasionally copyedited (when included in an article or "Comment of the Moment")

If the archivist's goal is to document the topics and issues that receive the most widespread attention, then the top blogs are important to address. However, if the archivist's goal is to collect blogs as a way to document the lives of individuals or to collect a cross-section of blogs that are more representative of the blogosphere as a whole, then it is important to note that, at least in the U.S., the "blogosphere is dominated by those who use their blogs as personal journals. Most bloggers do not think of what they do as journalism."[46] The majority of blogs have been found to be "of the personal journal type . . . in which authors report on their lives and inner thoughts and feelings,"[47] and on "topics of personal interest."[48] A study of several million Japanese blog entries found that only 16.3 percent of entries had any hyperlinks, only 1.25 percent included links to other blogs in the data set, and 1.15 percent had in-links from other blogs in the data set,[49] suggesting that the blog entries in the study "are less like journalism and more like diaries or letters–they're intended to be read by the author alone, or by a small set of friends. Rather than documenting links and stories found online, they document daily life."[50]

Active vs. Passive Interactions

One of the most widely proclaimed characteristics of Web 2.0 is that it allows users to post content to the Web as well as annotate the content of others (e.g., through tagging, comments, bookmarking, and other annotations). However, it is important to recognize that the wide popularity of many Web 2.0 sites does not necessarily mean that most users are actively contributing their own responses to the things they encounter in such spaces.

Jakob Nielsen points out that participation patterns in online spaces often reflect a "90-9-1 rule":

- 90 percent of users are lurkers (i.e., read or observe, but don't contribute).

- 9 percent of users contribute from time to time, but other priorities dominate their time.

- 1 percent of users participate a lot and account for most contributions: it can seem as if they don't have lives because they often post just minutes after whatever event they're commenting on occurs.[51]

Archivists who are collecting materials for the social web in order to reflect the views, sentiments, and lives of individuals should heed Nielsen's warning: "The problem is that the overall system is *not representative* of average web users. On any given user-participation site, you almost always hear from the same 1 percent of users, who almost certainly differ from the 90 percent you never hear from."[52] Rather than holding out hope that some new, more representative online space is on the horizon, Nielsen adds: "The first step to dealing with participation inequality is to recognize that it will always be with us. It's existed in every online community and multi-user service that has ever been studied."[53]

Bill Tancer reports very similar findings within the specific context of Web 2.0 sites:

> Based on our data, less than 1 percent of all Internet visits to Web 2.0 sites are attributable to consumer-generated media (such as a video uploaded to YouTube); 9 percent (this actually can vary between 3 and 9 percent based on complexity) are visits where users interact with consumer-created content through either editing an entry or adding comments; and 90 percent remain lurker visits, where Internet users are passively viewing content without interacting at all.[54]

For example, on YouTube, "active contribution, such as video uploading and rating of videos, is much less prevalent than passive use."[55] Only 0.22 percent of views in YouTube result in user ratings of videos, and only 0.16 percent of views generate comments.[56]

Most bloggers allow for comments to their blog entries.[57] However, a very small percentage of blog entries ever receive comments.[58] Some bloggers report that they value the lack of rapid interchange associated with most blog posts, which makes blogs a more self-reflective and narrative form of expression than more interactive online media.[59]

As of December 2006, "28 percent of online Americans say they have tagged content like a photo, a news story or a blog post."[60] User tagging may have already increased significantly since then and may also increase in the future. However, the fact that less than one-third of American Internet users were engaging in tagging at the time of the Pew study does suggest that adding metadata to their content has not been one of the primary drivers for individuals posting personal content online.

Fragility of Online Content in "Public but Private" Spaces

There are numerous risk factors associated with reliance on web service providers for persistent access to personal materials. These include:

- Expiration of service
- Changes in service offerings
- Automatic deletion of content after a given period of inactivity (e.g., no user logins or purchases)[61]
- Companies going out of business
- Take-down of data based on complaints from other parties (e.g., confidentiality, obscenity, intellectual property, right to publicity, national security)
- Mergers of sites/companies that result in major displacement or complete loss of existing content
- Accidental loss due to drive failure with insufficient backup
- Purposeful destruction of data by malicious attackers

There have been many widely publicized cases of all of these types of data loss in recent years.

Appraisal Priorities: The Why and What of Collecting

There are numerous conceptual approaches for an archivist to use in determining appraisal priorities. Much of the professional appraisal literature is based on the idea of identifying some entities (e.g., functions, individuals, organizational units, types of transactions) that warrant documentation over time, and then focusing on the subset of the overall universe of documentation that is most likely to serve as documentation of those entities. Three figures who arguably had the strongest influence on the formation of appraisal thinking in the English-speaking world are Hilary Jenkinson (in the UK), T. R. Schellenberg (in the U.S.), and Peter Scott (in Australia). All three men were responding to massive, unruly bodies of records, primarily generated by government activities. As a result, much of their focus was on the selection of records from government units. Aside from issues of defining the proper documentary units (e.g., record groups, fonds, or series), a significant consideration in the major appraisal frameworks over the years has been to convey to the future an archival record that reflects the present in meaningful ways. In the words of Jenkinson, "we wish to ensure that the future (whose exact needs we do not know) shall be provided at least with as *representative* a body of unimpeachable Archives as the past has left to us."[62]

Booms 2.0

Hans Booms brought a new perspective to North American archival thought when his work was translated into English in the 1980s. Booms argued that appraisal should be based on best (i.e., most informed by empirical evidence) judgments of the "value ascribed by those contemporary to the material,"—what members of society judged most valuable or important at the time documents were created.[63] This includes "what was debated, what was controversial, what provoked society, and what moved it."[64] If one accepts this approach, then a natural next question is how best to reflect the emphasis that people were placing on issues or materials at a given time. There is no single monolithic set of values or perceptions of "society," but one can use various data sources to infer what is most influential, viewed, discussed, and cited. When conducting archival appraisal based on notions of representativeness, it is important to determine "whether this record is intended to be 'representative' of all of recorded memory, or 'representative' of the activities of members of the society, or 'representative' of those aspects of social activity perceived by members of the society at the time as important to the understanding of the culture."[65] One answer to this question is that archivists should aim for collections that represent "the broad spectrum of human experience."[66]

Booms assumed that the most likely sources about public sentiment would be "published statements." The archivist should consult the literature in order to compile a chronology of important events from a given period, and then select records (not the published literature originally consulted) that can be acquired and preserved by the archive in order to serve as "raw social data for historical research."[67] In the appraisal of content from the Web, the distinction between "publications to consult" and "records to collect" is often not very clear. There are various sources of data from the Web that reflect trends and patterns, and there are likely to be many cases in which the archivist will then acquire those same sources of data to be preserved in a repository. Likewise, materials from the Web that have already been acquired by an archivist will often provide valuable data about "value ascribed by those contemporary to the material," which can inform decisions about what else should or should not be collected.

One of the dangers of relying too heavily on public sentiment to drive appraisal is that it risks overemphasizing uncommon, but spectacular events and phenomena, while underemphasizing more pervasive but mundane aspects of life. According to Gustave Le Bon:

> A hundred petty crimes or petty accidents will not strike the imagination of crowds in the least, whereas a single great crime or a single great accident will profoundly impress them, even though the results be infinitely less disastrous than those of the hundred small accidents put together. The epidemic of influenza, which caused the death but a few years ago of five thousand persons in Paris alone, made very little impression on the popular imagination.[68]

Popularity on the Web can also have a reinforcing quality that does not necessarily reflect more fundamental qualities of the materials. For example, knowledge of the number of previous downloads of music files skews the popularity of those songs: "meaning popular songs are more popular and unpopular songs are less popular—than [they are in] the world in which individuals make decisions independently."[69]

The Value of Reflecting Links and Bridges

> To forget a period of one's life is to lose contact with those who then surrounded us.
>
> —Maurice Halbwachs[70]

More than twenty-five years ago, Harold Naugler expressed "potential for record linkage" as an important factor in the appraisal of machine-readable records.[71] This can become a particularly important criterion when collecting materials from the Web, given the significant role of hyperlinks. An important part of one's identity can be tied up in the symbolically encoded relations that are enacted through her online links to others, for example, blogrolls and "friendings." However, links are ephemeral, and one will never be able to fully recreate the state of a given individual (or even a given page) within the entire universe of hyperlinked resources. The curation of web content involves strategies and heuristics for reflecting the sets of associations that are most likely to have continuing value.

In cases when public attention to content is a major appraisal criterion, collecting blogs can be particularly important for two reasons. First, because search engines use link structure to help predict useful pages, bloggers, as the most prolific and timely linkers, have a disproportionate role in shaping search engine results. Second, because the blogging community is so highly self-referential, bloggers paying attention to other bloggers magnifies their visibility and power.[72]

Online Demographics: Who Would Be Reflected in Collections of User-Generated Content?

If one is attempting to collect materials from the Web in order to provide a reflection of human activities, it is important to recognize the different populations that different sites represent. While there is often a diverse range of participants within a given site, a comparison of the site's statistics does reveal notable patterns. See table 3 for a compilation of data about users of several of the most popular social media sites. Two important observations from the data are that social media users are not a completely representative slice of humanity, and the various social media sites do not represent the same slices of humanity.

One can identify further differences between those who visit sites and those who contribute content to them. For example, eighteen- to twenty-four-year olds constitute almost 25 percent of the visitors to *Wikipedia*, but only 17 percent of those who edit entries. Conversely, those over age forty-five constitute only 33 percent of *Wikipedia* visitors, but 41 percent of those who edit the entries are over the age of forty-five. Interestingly, middle-class users from the suburbs are also more likely to edit entries than other visitors, including the urban middle class. YouTube, on the other hand, shows differences between visitors and contributors (those who upload videos) along both gender and age lines. Although the overall YouTube user base is only slightly tipped toward males, men constitute 58 percent of video uploaders to the site. The most represented age group among those who upload videos to YouTube is forty-five- to fifty-four-year-olds. Small town and rural users of YouTube are also more likely to upload videos than are urban or suburban visitors.[73] Another important factor is level of proficiency with Internet technology; for example, "medium specific proficiency" is a much stronger predictor of online political activity than "traditional civic skills."[74]

Such differences in representation can have important implications for appraisal. An archivist interested in documenting what particular populations *were mostly likely exposed to* would make very different collecting choices than an archivist who had a goal of collecting what particular populations *created.*

Although the blogosphere is widely heralded as a two-way medium that allows all Internet users to be publishers, 2006 statistics show that only a small percentage of Internet users create blogs: 19 percent of Internet users age twelve to seventeen and 8 percent of Internet users age eighteen and older.[75]

Table 3: Demographics of users of popular social media services, November 5, 2009.[76]

Site	Data source	Age group most represented	Gender most represented	Education level most represented	Salary range most represented	Ethnicity most represented
Blogger	Quantcast	35-49: 60%	Female: 55%	No college: 40%	$30-60k: 40%	Caucasian: 84%
Daily Motion	Quantcast	18-34: 41%	Male: 61%	No college: 53%	$30-60k: 34%	Caucasian: 63%
DeviantART	Quantcast	18-49	Male	No college	$0-30k	Caucasian
Facebook	Quantcast	18-34: 46%	Female: 54%	No college: 44%	$60-100k: 29%	Caucasian: 78%
Flickr (Yahoo!)	Quantcast	18-34: 39%	Male: 59%	No college: 43%	$30-100k+: 27%	Caucasian: 75%
hi5	hi5	18-34: 67%	Male: 59%			
	Quantcast	18-34: 55%	Male: 59%	No college: 65%	$0-30k: 46%	Hispanic: 46%
Hubpages	Quantcast	35-49: 36%	Female: 52%	No college and college: 44%	$30-60k: 32%	Caucasian: 77%
ImageShack	Quantcast		Male: 56%	No college: 54%	$0-60k: 32%	Caucasian: 67%
Linkedin	Quantcast	35-49: 48%	Male: 53%	College: 46%	$100k+: 38%	Caucasian: 85%
LiveJournal	LiveJournal	29	Female: 64.9%			
LiveJournal	Quantcast	18-34: 51%	Female: 58%	College: 45%	$30-60k: 27%	Caucasian: 79%
Metacafe	Quantcast	18-34: 39%	Male: 60%	No college: 52%	$30-60k: 34%	Caucasian: 70%
Myspace	Quantcast	18-34: 58%	Male: 51%	No college: 64%	$30-60k: 44%	Caucasian: 61%
Ning	Quantcast	18-49: 34%	Female: 54%	No college and college: 43%	$60-100k: 28%	Caucasian: 61%

Table 3 continued.

Site	Data source	Age group most represented	Gender most represented	Education level most represented	Salary range most represented	Ethnicity most represented
Photobucket	Photobucket	18-34: 47%	Female: 55%		$60k: 59%	
	Quantcast	18-34: 41%	Female: 54%	No college: 53%	$30-60k: 27%	Caucasian: 67%
Scribd	Quantcast	35-49: 37%	Male: 55%	No college: 43%		
Snapfish	Quantcast	18-34: 35%	Female: 62%	College: 43%	$60-100k: 32%	Caucasian: 87%
	Tagged	25-35: 22%	Female: 52%			
Tagged	Quantcast	35-49: 62%	Female: 59%	No college: 61%	$30-60k: 41%	Caucasian: 54%
Twitpic	Quantcast	18-34: 54%	Female: 51%	College: 47%	$30-60k: 43%	Caucasian: 79%
Twitter	Quantcast	18-34: 44%	Female: 53%	No college: 44%	$30-60k: 28%	Caucasian: 76%
TypePad	Quantcast	35-49: 45%	Male: 52%	College: 47%	$100k+: 28%	Caucasian: 78%
Wordpress	Quantcast	35-49: 38%	Male: 53%	College: 46%	$30-60k: 28%	Caucasian: 78%
	YouTube	"Our user base is broad in age range, 18-55"	"evenly divided between males and females"			
YouTube	Quantcast		50-50	No college: 48%	$30-100k+: 27%	Caucasian: 70%

Translating Appraisal Criteria into Web Collecting Strategies

There are two distinct selection strategies for honing in on materials related to an individual:

- Work from the individual outward (e.g., ask the person or find information on his/her computer that helps to identify points of entry to his/her online presence, such as logins, browsing histories, and favorite sites).[77]

- Work from the wider web inward toward the individual (e.g., use web searches to locate information that leads to elements of his/her web presence).

T.R. Schellenberg made a distinction between two types of value of archival records: informational and evidential. The archival literature—especially in the United States—has frequently cited Schellenberg's two types of value. The boundary between informational and evidential value is not absolute, but it does raise an important distinction. In the realm of collecting traces of individuals from the Web, the archivist should ask whether it is the content of particularly digital objects that is most important, or instead the transactional information associated with the posting, exchange, and use of the objects that matters. An extreme case of the latter situation is the retention of anonymized search log data, which can reveal many very interesting trends and correlations in individual interests,[78] but cannot be identified as belonging to the fonds of any particular individual.

Three factors make appraisal of personal archives from the Web dramatically different from the appraisal of personal papers from the homes and offices of individuals:

- The *massive volume* of individually-generated content on the Web.

- The potential access to (i.e., ability to harvest and collect) material from a large and *diverse population* of creators.

- The unlikelihood that an archivist (or even the individual himself) will be able to identify and collect all or even most of an individual's most valuable and representative materials from a *distributed and unintegrated* "cloud" of services and micro-contributions.

Personae as Provenance

Online profiles often reveal numerous things about individuals—both attributes (things about the person) and relations (things about the person's connections with others). While many details may seem relatively shallow as characterizations of people, they do reveal elements that could be of considerable interest to future researchers. For example, someone doing genealogical research in the year 2100 could be interested in the movie, music, and product preferences of her grandparents in 2010.

Relational characteristics can often say a lot about the person. This is a fairly obvious point when it comes to relations such as one's spouse, but less direct relations, such as being a fan of a particular celebrity, can also carry considerable meaning. Margaret Gibson notes: "Many people can feel they know someone on television better than a neighbour or family member. This is a peculiar feature of our highly modern existence, the fact that billions of people spend considerable amounts of time watching 'persons' or 'personalities' projected from television and computer screens."[79]

One of the primary challenges of collecting information about or by given individuals from the Web is "web presence identification"[80]—determining what pages on the Web are actually by or about a given individual. Online activities involve numerous "boundary regulation" processes,[81] in which individuals disclose varying amounts of information about themselves. These characteristics of online profiles reflect well-established human tendencies toward selective disclosure.

As both effect and enabling cause of this kind of commitment to the part one is currently performing, we find that "audience segregation" occurs; by audience segregation the individual ensures that those before whom he plays one of his parts will not be the same individuals before whom he plays a different part in another setting.[82]

There is a wide spectrum of potential information disclosure within Web 2.0 environments. First, people can decide how much of their personal information to disclose within a given space. There are varying levels of control, from simply not linking to a page, to using robot exclusions, to explicitly indicating who can see something, to setting up private social networks. Second, they can create separate accounts across various spaces, in which they disclose different things. Third, they can either actively promote the content they have created or simply post it and see what happens.

Users of social networks often maintain multiple profiles and apply varying levels of restriction on the content of their profiles. A Pew study found that 51 percent of social network users have two or more online profiles, 60 percent of adult social network users restrict access to their profiles to only their friends, and 58 percent of adult social network users restrict access to certain content within their profiles.[83] The study revealed that 55 percent of online teens have profiles, 66 percent of whom report that they have placed some restrictions on access to the profiles.[84] Of the teens with completely open profiles, 46 percent reported including at least some false information.[85]

A 2004 study found that roughly a third of bloggers were providing their personal names on their blogs, while 54 percent provided "some other explicit personal information (e.g., age, occupation, geographic location)." Only 17.5 percent presented "graphical representations of the author (including photos) on the first page, and only 10.9 percent link to such representations elsewhere."[86] Another study found that 55 percent of bloggers reported using their real names, with 20 percent using "some variant of their name (only first name, a nickname that friends knew, initials, etc.)."[87] Another study found 55 percent of bloggers using a pseudonym, and 46 percent blogging under their own names.[88] The use of first name or full name among blog authors—in contrast to use of pseudonyms—does appear to have increased somewhat over time.[89] A more recent study reports that about two-thirds of bloggers "openly expose their identities on their blogs" (presumably within either profiles or blog entries).[90]

The degree to which and the ways in which users actively and consciously engage in "identity management" can vary dramatically. For example, a high school student may not be as concerned as a forty-year-old professional about differentiating a personal persona from a work persona, but she may pay significant attention to which channel of communication (e.g., social network site, online chat, phone) is most appropriate for conducting a given conversation among friends,[91] and maintain a "mirror profile," which is designed to prevent her parents from easily discovering information in her "true" profile.[92]

There are notable differences in identity management across demographic groups, which is strongly related to the ways in which one has experienced personal disclosure in the past. For example, "social networking sites typically display as standard precisely the personal information that previous generations often have regarded as private (notably age, politics, income, religion, sexual preference)."[93] However, there can also be considerable diversity of attitudes and behavior within a given segment of the population. Employees who all work in the same company, for example, have revealed major differences in what information they share with whom within a given social network space, reflecting different attitudes and expectations about the boundaries between personal and professional life.[94] Among college students, research has also revealed differences in whether or not they have made their online profiles private, with major predictors being gender, amount of online activity, and whether their friends and roommates have private profiles.[95] It is worth noting that the actual behavior of online social network users does not necessarily reflect their stated attitudes about self-disclosure. For example, despite stating strong concerns about privacy, many Facebook users report that they are not aware of and have not used the available features for controlling access to their personal information.[96]

Logistics of Collecting Web Content of Individuals

The "archiving" of websites—capturing web content remotely by making requests to the servers that host the content—has received a great deal of professional and commercial attention in recent years. The basic technical challenges and many collection strategies are now well-documented.[97] Table 4 outlines five ways to collect web content. All five approaches involve multiple selection decisions: which sources to engage, how often to collect content, what collecting parameters to use, and how much effort to invest in fixing specific problem cases.

Stated more simply, there are two fundamental approaches to capturing web content for purposes of building digital collections: recursive link-following and query submission. The former has been the most common and involves the identification of a set of seed uniform resource locators (URLs) and then recursively following links within a specified set of constraints (e.g., number of hops, specific domains). When collecting content from specific, database-driven web spaces, query submission is often the most effective approach. For example, the VidArch project has collected videos and their associated pages from YouTube by submitting daily queries to YouTube and then downloading the results.[99]

Effective web collecting strategies will often involve a combination of link-following and text-based queries. For example, several projects have demonstrated methods for further scoping a topic-based crawl, based on automated analysis of the content of pages or their place within a larger network of pages.[100] There have also been many successful efforts to automatically populate web entry forms in order to collect pages that cannot be reached directly through link-following.[101] Four fundamental parameters for any web collecting initiative are: environments crawled (e.g., blogosphere, YouTube); access points from those environments used as crawling or selection criteria (e.g., number of views, primary relevance based on term matching, number of in-links, channel or account from which an item was submitted); threshold values for scoping capture within given access points

Table 4. Strategies for collecting web content.

Approach	Explanation	Advantages	Disadvantages
Ask the provider	Through direct contact, the collector can request and negotiate for a direct transfer of the data that reside on the server(s) of the provider	Can yield information not directly accessible through other means, and can get data directly from the source (e.g., whole database, high-res images) rather than what is served through the Web	Requires cooperation of the provider
See if someone else has it[98]	If content has been cached by a search service, harvested by the Internet Archive, or collected by a peer institution, obtain a copy of content from them	Allows for post hoc recovery	Coverage and success of recovery are subject to the systems and priorities of systems that were designed for other purposes
Follow links	Start with seed URLs, then recursively follow them— possibly feeding new URLs back into seed list (used by search engine bots and many web crawlers)	Tools and techniques are very well established and well understood	Many dimensions of interest (e.g., provenance, topic, time period) are not reflected in the link patterns of web content
Pull results of queries	Collecting institution issues queries to known sources (e.g., collecting videos from YouTube by queries for specific named individuals)	Can benefit from the structure and standardized interfaces of the content providers	Strongly dependent on interface and ranking algorithms of the content provider's system
Receive results of pushed queries	Subscription model of tapping into alert services or "feeds" that are pushed to the collecting institution	Particularly good for communication forms (e.g., blogs) that are "post-centric" rather than "page-centric"	Feeds of content will often lose formatting and contextual information that could be important to retain

(e.g., one hundred most relevant query results, at least five in-links);[102] and frequency of crawls. It is very likely that the most appropriate approaches will vary the environments, access points, and thresholds in different ways, depending on the materials and collecting goals. For example, different types of web materials change or disappear from the Web at very different rates, which implies the need for different crawl frequencies.[103]

As mentioned earlier, a great deal of content on the Web is now being generated, distributed, and used outside of the context of discrete, consistently predefinable "pages." Instead, chunks of content are being displayed and presented in various ways, through mechanisms such as RSS feeds, dashboard interfaces (e.g., iGoogle), and various aggregators. For the archivist, this means that collection will not always involve downloading pages of a website like collecting the pages in a box. Instead, web extraction technology will play an important role,[104] with archivists needing to define the parameters for capture of data elements from various sources. After identifying specific web pages, extracting structured data can require "extracting relevant pieces of data from these pages (data extraction problem), distilling the data and improving its structuredness (structure synthesis problem), ensuring data homogeneity (data mapping problem), and merging data from separate hypertext markup language (HTML) pages (data integration problem)."[105]

As discussed above, a major challenge of collecting content related to given individuals can be the identification of the person's online web presence. This can be greatly facilitated by having background knowledge about the person's online activities and interactions, rather than conducting simple web searches using the person's name. Ideally the individual herself can serve as a source of information about her online presence (e.g., personae created, sites frequented, forums to which she contributed). Conversations with an individual or her family are an obvious way to collect such information, though the individual could also use a tool to aggregate her personal information in advance. A service called ClaimID was designed for this specific purpose.[106]

Further information about a person's online presence can be gleaned from the Web, the person's email, or the storage media used by her computer, especially the hard drive.[107] The most fruitful sources of personal content are likely to vary by individual, but there might be predictable patterns that could assist the archivist in tracking down content. For example, those working in academia are probably more likely to have home pages or curricula vitae that point to many materials related to their professional lives, because promotion of their own research is an important part of career advancement. However, a prominent individual working in the private sector may not have such an obvious single point of entry to her online presence. Today's professors are also quite likely to rely heavily on email, which makes the inbox a rich source of both information and pointers to relevant sources of online material; but today's teenager is likely to rely more heavily on other modalities of communication (those that directly support audio and video, and many of which afford short and quick interchanges, using mobile devices). The hard drive from the one computer that was used exclusively for many years will serve as a much richer source of personally relevant information than would the hard drive from just one of dozens of computers that someone used at a given point in time, as devices to access sources and services that were all provided through "the cloud."

Data mining for pointers to online materials opens up unprecedented opportunities for archivists to document individuals, but it also raises important ethical and logistical issues about informed consent and respecting the rights and interests of various stakeholders who are represented within the data. For example, an archivist might reasonably infer that a Facebook account that is linked off a donor's ClaimID page is a good candidate for acquisition by the archives to include in that person's personal papers. However, another online account that is discovered through mining of data on the person's hard drive may or may not be something that individual would like to disclose to future researchers.

Depth-First vs. Breadth-First Appraisal

Traditional archival practice in relation to personal papers and manuscripts has been to devote a relatively large amount of effort (identification, research, field work, donor negotiation, processing, description) to materials donated by a relatively small number of individuals who are deemed to be especially important. In short, archivists have practiced depth-first appraisal of personal archives.

A very different model for appraisal is based on identifying specific selection criteria that are likely to yield a substantial body of valuable materials that are of or by individuals but without focusing on the individuals themselves as the primary unit of collecting. For example, one could establish a crawling "campaign" that collected the top one hundred results of a Technorati search once per week using query terms that reflect one's selection criteria. In order to document the provenance of the blog entries being collected, one could also run scripts that attempted to:

- Capture the profile information from the blog that generated the entry.

- Collect all other postings to the blog that generated the entry.

- Send email to the most likely blog author to ask for confirmation of authorship and inform him or her of the intention to include his or her material in an archival collection.

- Use "query by example" to determine if there is other content online that is sufficiently similar to suggest that it might have come from the same source.

Such collecting strategies would result in collections that reflect many more voices than traditional collecting of relatively large collections from a few individuals. This need not violate the archival notion that collections should provide provenance and other contextual information. New forms of archival description could provide information about the authors, sources, and various other aspects of the provenance of items. A relatively wide and shallow selection of personal content from the Web could also advance the sort of "insight into the lives and experiences of broad cross-sections of society"[108] that many social historians seek.

From a postcustodial[109] or records continuum[110] perspective, record-keeping—including selection and appraisal—should not be seen as a set of activities that begin at the moment that records are transferred to an archival repository and end at the moment that records enter the hands of users. Instead, selection of records for ongoing care based on continuing value can and should occur at many points throughout (and even before) the existence of records. Transfer to an archive (crossing the "archival threshold") is an important moment, for many professional and institutional reasons, but it is not the only transition point that matters.[111] If one accepts a postcustodial orientation toward archives, then one can begin to make many creative and fruitful connections between previous distinct areas of archival appraisal literature.

For the purposes of appraisal of web materials, one connection worth considering is the application of sampling techniques to collecting activities. Sampling has long been recognized as a potential approach to reducing the volume of large collections.[112] Schellenberg was quite insistent about the differences between statistical sampling and the "special selection" carried out by archivists.[113] There has been continuing discussion about the extent to which archivists can rely on standard statistical methods for sampling, or must instead use more subjective criteria based on the archivist's personal judgment and domain knowledge.[114] A frequently espoused position in the archival literature is:

> When one employs statistical sampling, one must choose a series that is as homogenous as possible and in which the individual file is not important. The statistical sample will target typical cases. If the spectacular cases are to be culled, then a subjective sample should be employed.[115]

The pieces related to statistical sampling in the archives and records management literature generally focus on sampling from existing aggregations of records, in order "to reduce the bulk" of a body of records "that has been appraised as having some research value but whose immense size presents serious problems to repositories and researchers."[116] In order to support secondary use, sampling can recover some records from what would otherwise be the "discard pile" from a primary use perspective.[117]

Sampling is a "practical solution for the typically large homogeneous collections of the 20th century,"[118] with many published examples from large government agencies,[119] courts,[120] businesses,[121] and members of Congress.[122] One of the driving factors in the adoption of sampling as a method of appraisal is that any selection based on the contents of analog records would require human inspection of individual folders or items, which is not feasible with large collections. The use of sampling as a collecting strategy is addressed in the archival literature as part of the "Minnesota Method." This appraisal strategy includes the assignment of desired "documentation levels" to different companies or business sectors, in order to determine "those sectors and businesses that should be actively solicited."[123] However, in a web archiving context, the archivist is much more directly shaping the boundaries of the original aggregation, based on the selection of sources, crawling criteria, and criteria thresholds.

Dangers and Responsibilities of Relying on Wisdom of the Crowds

Much has been written in the archival literature about the danger of relying solely on the whim of user interest as a basis for archival appraisal. Those same concerns apply when collecting web materials related to individuals. There are numerous possibilities for identifying the retention value of content in new and exciting ways based on use and link patterns, and these are all possibilities which archivists should pursue. However, such techniques should be monitored, revisited, and supplemented by qualified archivists who can place the results within the context of larger collecting goals.

Another important consideration when engaging in selective web capture is that the content obtained could do a serious disservice to the individuals involved. Archival theory and practice have long been driven by the importance of contextual information. On the Web, a serious concern is that "when intimate information is removed from its original context and revealed to strangers, we are vulnerable to being misjudged on the basis of our most embarrassing, and therefore most memorable, states and preferences." The resulting "impressions are likely to oversimplify and misrepresent our complicated and often contradictory lives."[124] For example, if one were to collect a popular YouTube video featuring a given individual, and then collect hundreds of blog pages that link to and discuss that video, it is quite likely that the future researcher will have a pretty good sense of the video's cultural impact and how it was perceived by many Internet users of the time. However, the video is simply one sliver of exposure into the life of the individual featured in the video. This can be particularly problematic in cases when the associated buzz takes the form of gossip, slander, and salacious rumors.[125] Simply understanding a rumor in its full detail is a far cry from understanding the lives of the individuals involved.

According to Vance Packard, "When the details of our lives are fed into a central computer or other vast file-keeping systems, we all fall under the control of the machine's managers to some extent."[126] When amassing collections of personal material from the Web, archivists become the "controllers of the machine," and with this role comes considerable responsibility.

Notes

[1] Oscar Wilde and Richard Allen Cave, *The Importance of Being Earnest and Other Plays*, Penguin Classics (London: Penguin Books, 2000), 329.

[2] Michel Foucault, *The History of Sexuality*, trans. Robert Hurley, 1st Vintage Books ed., vol. I: An Introduction (New York: Vintage Books, 1990), 59.

[3] Sherry Turkle, *Life on the Screen: Identity in the Age of the Internet* (New York: Touchstone Books, 1997), 13.

[4] Stefania Leone, Michael Grossniklaus, and Moira C. Norrie, "Architecture for Integrating Desktop and Web 2.0 Data Management" (paper presented at the 7th International Workshop on Web-Oriented Software Technologies, IWWOST 2008, Yorktown Heights, NY, July 14, 2008); Moira C. Norrie, "PIM Meets Web 2.0," in *Conceptual Modeling: ER 2008: 27th International Conference on Conceptual Modeling, Barcelona, Spain, October 20-24, 2008: Proceedings*, ed. Qing Li, Stefano Spaccapietra, Eric Yu, and Antoni Olivé (Berlin: Springer, 2008), 15–25.

[5] Amanda Lenhart, "Adults and Social Network Websites" (Washington, DC: Pew Internet and American Life Project, 2009).

[6] danah m. boyd and Nicole B. Ellison, "Social Network Sites: Definition, History, and Scholarship," *Journal of Computer-Mediated Communication* 13, no. 1 (2007): 219.

[7] Tom Vanderbilt, "Data Center Overload," *New York Times*, June 14 2009, MM30.

[8] Simson Garfinkel and David Cox, "Finding and Archiving the Internet Footprint" (paper presented at the First Digital Lives Research Conference: Personal Digital Archives for the 21st Century, London, UK, February 9–11, 2009).

[9] Matthew G. Kirschenbaum, Erika Farr, Kari M. Kraus, Naomi L. Nelson, Catherine Stollar Peters, Gabriela Redwine, and Doug Reside, "Approaches to Managing and Collecting Born-Digital Literary Materials for Scholarly Use" (May 2009), 23, http://neh.gov/ODH/Default.aspx?tabid=111&id=37.

[10] Howard Zinn, "The Archivist and Radical Reform" (unpublished manuscript, 1970), as quoted in Randall C. Jimerson, "The Future of Archives and Manuscripts," *OCLC Systems and Services* 20, no. 1 (2004): 11–14.

[11] Adrian Cunningham, "The Mysterious Outside Reader," *Archives and Manuscripts* 24, no. 1 (1996): 132.

[12] Tom Nesmith, "Archives from the Bottom Up: Social History and Archival Scholarship," *Archivaria* 14 (1982): 10.

[13] Linda Henry, "Collecting Policies of Special Subject Repositories," *American Archivist* 43 (1980): 59.

[14] Mark A. Greene and Todd J. Daniels-Howell, "Documentation with an Attitude: A Pragmatist's Guide to the Selection and Acquisition of Modern Business Records," in *The Records of American Business*, ed. James O'Toole (Chicago: Society of American Archivists, 1997), 161–229.

[15] James E. Fogerty, "Facing Reality: Oral History, Corporate Culture, and the Documentation of Business," in O'Toole, *The Records of American Business*, 251–73.

[16] Rich Skrenta, "The Incremental Web," *Topix.net Weblog*, February 12, 2005, http://blog.topix.com/archives/000066.html.

[17] Meeyoung Cha, Haewoon Kwak, Pablo Rodriguez, Yong-Yeol Ahn, and Sue Moon, "I Tube, You Tube, Everybody Tubes: Analyzing the World's Largest User Generated Content Video System," in *IMC '07: Proceedings of the 2007 ACM SIGCOMM Internet Measurement Conference, San Diego, California, USA, October 24-26, 2007* (New York: Association for Computing Machinery, 2007), 1–14.

18 Dan Gillmor, *We the Media: Grassroots Journalism by the People, for the People*, 1st ed. (Sebastopol, CA: O'Reilly, 2004), 29.

19 Brad L. Graham, "Why I Weblog: A Rumination on Where the Hell I'm Going with This Website," in *We've Got Blog: How Weblogs Are Changing Our Culture*, ed. John Rodzvilla (Cambridge, MA: Perseus, 2002) , 34–40; originally posted to Bradlands, June 16, 1999.

20 Gillmor, *We the Media*, 12.

21 Lilia Efimova and Aldo de Moor, "Beyond Personal Webpublishing: An Exploratory Study of Conversational Blogging Practices" (paper presented at the 38th Hawaii International Conference on System Sciences, Big Island, HI, January 3–6, 2005).

22 Bonnie A. Nardi, Diane J. Schiano, and Michelle Gumbrecht, "Blogging as Social Activity, or, Would You Let 900 Million People Read Your Diary?" in *CSCW 2004: Computer Supported Cooperative Work: Conference Proceedings, November 6–10, 2004, Chicago* (New York: Association for Computing Machinery, 2004), 222–31.

23 Rebecca Blood, "Weblogs: A History and Perspective," in Rodzvilla, *We've Got Blog*, 7–16; originally posted to Rebecca's Pocket, September 7, 2000.

24 Joe Clark, "Deconstructing 'You've Got Blog,'" in Rodzvilla, *We've Got Blog*, 59; originally posted to fawny.com, November 16, 2000, updated on January 25, 2002.

25 Fernanda B. Viégas, "Bloggers' Expectations of Privacy and Accountability: An Initial Survey," *Journal of Computer-Mediated Communication* 10, no. 3 (2005), http://jcmc.indiana.edu/vol10/issue3/viegas.html.

26 Jonathan Grudin, "Desituating Action: Digital Representation of Context," *Human-Computer Interaction* 16, no. 2/4 (2001): 269–86.

27 Gillmor, *We the Media*, 40.

28 Steve Bailey, *Managing the Crowd: Rethinking Records Management for the Web 2.0 World* (London: Facet, 2008), 152.

29 Ying Ding, Elin K. Jacob, James Caverlee, Michael Fried, and Zhixiong Zhang, "Profiling Social Networks: A Social Tagging Perspective," *D-Lib Magazine* 15, no. 3/4 (2009), http://dx.doi.org/10.1045/march2009-ding.

30 danah boyd, "Why Youth ♥ Social Network Sites: The Role of Networked Publics in Teenage Social Life," in *Youth, Identity, and Digital Media*, ed. David Buckingham (Cambridge, MA: MIT Press, 2008), 126.

31 Nardi et al., "Blogging as Social Activity," 225.

32 J. D. Lasica, "Weblogs: A New Source of News," in Rodzvilla, *We've Got Blog,* 179; originally published in *Online Journalism Review*, May 31, 2001.

33 Steve Whittaker, Loren Terveen, Will Hill, and Lynn Cherny, "The Dynamics of Mass Interaction," in *CSCW '98: Proceedings: ACM 1998 Conference on Computer Supported Cooperative Work, Seattle, Washington, November 14–18* (New York: Association for Computing Machinery, 1998), 257–64.

34 Clay Shirky, "Power Laws, Weblogs and Inequality," in *Extreme Democracy*, ed. Jon Lebkowsky and Mitch Ratcliffe (Lulu, 2005), 46.

35 Henry Farrell and Daniel W. Drezner, "The Power and Politics of Blogs," *Public Choice* 134, no. 1-2 (2008): 15–30.

36 Shirky, "Power Laws, Weblogs and Inequality."

37 Matthew Hindman, "A Mile Wide and an Inch Deep: Measuring Media Diversity Online and Offline," in *Localism and Media Diversity: Meaning and Metrics*, ed. Philip Napoli (Mahwah, NJ: Lawrence Erlbaum Associates, 2006), 328.

38 Ibid., 332.

[39] Ibid.

[40] Lars Kirchhoff, Axel Bruns, and Thomas Nicolai, "Investigating the Impact of the Blogosphere: Using Pagerank to Determine the Distribution of Attention" (paper presented at the Annual Conference of the Association of Internet Researchers, Vancouver, Canada 2007).

[41] David Weinberger, *Small Pieces Loosely Joined: A Unified Theory of the Web* (Cambridge, MA: Perseus, 2002), 104.

[42] Ethan Zuckerman, "Meet the Bridgebloggers," *Public Choice* 134 (2008): 60.

[43] Michele Madansky and Polly Arenberg, "State of the Blogosphere," Technorati, 2008, http://www.technorati.com/blogging/state-of-the-blogosphere/.

[44] Technorati rankings are based on the number of blogs linking to a website in the previous six months. Information on responsibility for posts was inferred from information on the sites themselves. Site administrators have not confirmed the accuracy of this information. Quoted material is from respective websites.

[45] Ding et al., "Profiling Social Networks."

[46] Amanda Lenhart and Susannah Fox, "Bloggers: A Portrait of the Internet's New Storytellers" (Washington, DC: Pew Internet and American Life Project, 2006), ii.

[47] Susan C. Herring, Lois Ann Scheidt, Sabrina Bonus, and Elijah Wright, "Bridging the Gap: A Genre Analysis of Weblogs" (paper presented at the 37th Annual Hawaii International Conference on System Sciences, HICSS '04, Big Island, Hawaii, January 5–8, 2004); and Susan C. Herring, Lois Ann Scheidt, Inna Kouper, and Elijah Wright, "A Longitudinal Content Analysis of Weblogs: 2003-2004," in *Blogging, Citizenship, and the Future of Media*, ed. Mark Tremayne (London: Routledge, 2007), 3–20.

[48] Madansky and Arenberg, "State of the Blogosphere."

[49] Ko Fujimura, Takafumi Inoue, and Masayuki Sugisaki, "The EigenRumor Algorithm for Ranking Blogs (paper presented at the 14th International World Wide Web Conference, Chiba, Japan, May 10–14, 2005).

[50] Zuckerman, "Meet the Bridgebloggers," 51.

[51] Jakob Nielsen, "Participation Inequality: Encouraging More Users to Contribute," *Alertbox*, October 9, 2006, http://www.useit.com/alertbox/participation_inequality.html.

[52] Ibid., emphasis in original.

[53] Ibid.

[54] Bill Tancer, *Click: What Millions of People Are Doing Online and Why It Matters* (New York: Hyperion, 2008), 125–6.

[55] Siddharth Mitra, "Characterising Online Video Sharing and Its Dynamics" (Master's thesis, Indian Institute of Technology, 2009).

[56] Cha et al., "I Tube, You Tube."

[57] Lenhart and Fox. "Bloggers: A Portrait of the Internet's New Storytellers."

[58] Herring et al., "Bridging the Gap"; Gilad Mishne and Natalie Glance, "Leave a Reply: An Analysis of Weblog Comments" (paper presented at the 3rd Annual Workshop on the Weblogging Ecosystem: Aggregation, Analysis and Dynamics, Edinburgh, UK, May 23, 2006); Herring et al., "Longitudinal Content Analysis of Weblogs."

[59] Nardi et al., "Blogging as Social Activity."

[60] Lee Rainie, "Tagging" (Washington, DC: Pew Internet and American Life Project, 2007).

[61] This has been common practice for many online photo-sharing sites; see William M. Bulkeley, "The Downside of Photo-Storage Sites," *Wall Street Journal*, February 1, 2006.

[62] Hilary Jenkinson, *A Manual of Archive Administration* (Oxford: Clarendon Press, 1922), 130, emphasis added.

[63] Hans Booms, "Society and the Formation of a Documentary Heritage: Issues in the Appraisal of Archival Sources," *Archivaria* 24 (1987): 69–107.

[64] Hans Booms, "Überlieferungsbildung: Keeping Archives as a Social and Political Activity," *Archivaria* 33 (1991–92): 31.

[65] David Bearman, "Selection and Appraisal," in *Archival Methods* (Pittsburgh, PA: Archives and Museum Informatics, 1989), 13.

[66] F. Gerald Ham, "The Archival Edge," *American Archivist* 38 (1975): 5–13; F. Gerald Ham, "Archival Strategies for the Post Custodial Era," *American Archivist* 44 (1981): 207–16.

[67] Booms, "Überlieferungsbildung," 28.

[68] Gustave Le Bon, *The Crowd: A Study of the Popular Mind*, The Criminology Series (New York: Macmillan, 1896), 59–60.

[69] Mathew J. Salganik, Peter Sheridan Dodds, and Duncan J. Watts, "Experimental Study of Inequality and Unpredictability in an Artificial Cultural Market," *Science* 311 (2006): 855.

[70] Maurice Halbwachs, *The Collective Memory*, 1st ed. (New York: Harper and Row, 1980), 30.

[71] Harold Naugler, *The Archival Appraisal of Machine-Readable Records: A RAMP Study with Guidelines* (Paris: General Information Programme and UNISIST United Nations Educational Scientific and Cultural Organization, 1984), 41.

[72] Tim O'Reilly, "What Is Web 2.0: Design Patterns and Business Models for the Next Generation of Software," *Communications and Strategies* 65 (2007): 26.

[73] Tancer, *Click*, 126–7.

[74] Samuel J. Best and Brian S. Krueger, "Analyzing the Representativeness of Internet Political Participation," *Political Behavior* 27, no. 2 (2005): 193.

[75] Lenhart and Fox. "Bloggers: A Portrait of the Internet's New Storytellers."

[76] Data were obtained from Quantcast and the sites themselves, as noted. I would like to thank Brian Leaf and Christine Cheng for helping me to compile this information. Another valuable resource that is not reflected in table 3 is Alexa, which reports demographic data in relative terms (e.g., "relative to the general internet population, females are over-represented at livejournal.com").

[77] Garfinkel and Cox, "Finding and Archiving the Internet Footprint."

[78] Tancer, *Click*. For a selected assortment of observations based on search data, see also "Hitwise Intelligence—Analyst Weblogs," http://www.ilovedata.org.

[79] Margaret Gibson, "Some Thoughts on Celebrity Deaths: Steve Irwin and the Issue of Public Mourning," *Mortality* 12, no. 1 (2007): 2.

[80] Ron Bekkerman and Andrew McCallum, "Disambiguating Web Appearances of People in a Social Network," in *Proceedings of the 14th International Conference on World Wide Web, WWW 2005: Chiba, Japan, May 10–14, 2005*, ed. Allan Ellis and Tatsuya Hagino (New York: ACM Press, 2005), 463–70.

[81] Leysia Palen and Paul Dourish, "Unpacking 'Privacy' for a Networked World," in *CHI 2003: New Horizons: Conference Proceedings, Conference on Human Factors in Computing Systems*, ed. Gilbert Cockton and Panu Korhonen (New York: Association for Computing Machinery, 2003), 129–36.

[82] Erving Goffman, *The Presentation of Self in Everyday Life* (Garden City, NY: Doubleday, 1959), 49.

[83] Lenhart, "Adults and Social Network Websites."

[84] Amanda Lenhart and Mary Madden, "Social Networking Websites and Teens: An Overview" (Washington, DC: Pew Internet and American Life Project, 2007).

[85] danah m. boyd and Nicole B. Ellison, "Social Network Sites: Definition, History, and Scholarship," *Journal of Computer-Mediated Communication* 13, no. 1 (2007): 222.

[86] Herring et al., "Bridging the Gap."

[87] Viégas, "Bloggers' Expectations."

[88] Lenhart and Fox, "Bloggers: A Portrait of the Internet's New Storytellers," ii.

[89] Herring et al., "Longitudinal Content Analysis of Weblogs."

[90] Madansky and Arenberg, "State of the Blogosphere."

[91] Sonia Livingstone, "Taking Risky Opportunities in Youthful Content Creation: Teenagers' Use of Social Networking Sites for Intimacy, Privacy and Self-Expression," *New Media and Society* 10, no. 3 (2008): 393–411.

[92] boyd, "Why Youth ♥ Social Network Sites."

[93] Livingstone, "Taking Risky Opportunities."

[94] Joan Morris DiMicco and David R. Millen, "Identity Management: Multiple Presentations of Self in Facebook," in *Group'07: Proceedings of the 2007 International ACM Conference on Supporting Group Work*, ed. Tom Gross and Kori Inkpen (New York: Association for Computing Machinery, 2007), 383–86.

[95] Kevin Lewis, Jason Kaufman, and Nicholas Christakis, "The Taste for Privacy: An Analysis of College Student Privacy Settings in an Online Social Network," *Journal of Computer-Mediated Communication* 14, no. 1 (2008): 79–100.

[96] Allessandro Acquisti and Ralph Gross, "Imagined Communities: Awareness, Information Sharing, and Privacy on the Facebook," in *Privacy Enhancing Technologies*, ed. G. Danezis and P. Golle (Berlin: Springer, 2006), 36–58.

[97] Jennifer Marill, Andrew Boyko, and Michael Ashenfelder, "Web Harvesting Survey" (International Internet Preservation Coalition, 2004); Adrian Brown, *Archiving Websites: A Practical Guide for Information Management Professionals* (London: Facet, 2006); Julien Masanès, *Web Archiving* (New York: Springer, 2006); Bernhard Pollak and Wolfgang Gatterbauer, "Creating Permanent Test Collections of Web Pages for Information Extraction Research," in *Proceedings of SOFSEM 2007: Theory and Practice of Computer Science, Volume II ICS AS CR, Prague, 2007* (Prague: Institute of Computer Sciences, 2007), 103–15.

[98] See Warrick, Recover Your Lost Website, http://warrick.cs.odu.edu/.

[99] Robert Capra, Christopher A. Lee, Gary Marchionini, Terrell Russell, Chirag Shah, and Fred Stutzman, "Selection of Context Scoping for Digital Video Collections: An Investigation of YouTube and Blogs" in *JCDL 2008: Proceedings of the 8th ACM/IEEE Joint Conference on Digital Libraries: Pittsburgh, Pennsylvania, June 15–20, 2008*, ed. Ronald L. Larsen, Andreas Paepcke, José Luis Borbinha and Mor Naaman (New York: ACM Press, 2008), 211–20; Christoper A. Lee and Helen R. Tibbo, "Capturing the Moment: Strategies for Selection and Collection of Web-Based Resources to Document Important Social Phenomena," in *Archiving 2008: Final Program and Proceedings, June 24–27, 2008, Bern, Switzerland* (Springfield, VA: Society for Imaging Science and Technology, 2008), 300–305.

[100] Soumen Chakrabarti, Martin van den Berg, and Byron Dom, "Focused Crawling: A New Approach to Topic-Specific Resource Discovery," in *Proceedings of the Eighth International World Wide Web Conference: Toronto, Canada, May 11–14, 1999* (Amsterdam: Elsevier, 1999), 545–62; Donna Bergmark, "Collection Synthesis," in *Proceedings of the Second ACM/IEEE-CS Joint Conference on Digital Libraries: July 14–18, 2002, Portland, Oregon*, ed. Gary Marchionini and William R. Hersh (New York: ACM Press, 2002), 253–56; Donna Bergmark, Carl Lagoze, and Alex Sbityakov; "Focused Crawls, Tunneling, and Digital Libraries," in *Research and Advanced Technology for*

Digital Libraries: 6th European Conference, ECDL 2002, Rome, Italy, September 2002: Proceedings, ed. Maristella Agosti and Constantino Thanos (Berlin: Springer, 2002), 91–106; Gautam Pant and Padmini Srinivasan, "Learning to Crawl: Comparing Classification Schemes," *ACM Transactions on Information Systems* 23, no. 4 (2005): 430–62; and Gautam Pant, Kostas Tsioutsiouliklis, Judy Johnson, and C. Lee Giles, "Panorama: Extending Digital Libraries with Topical Crawlers," in *JCDL 2004: Proceedings of the Fourth ACM/IEEE Joint Conference on Digital Libraries: Global Reach and Diverse Impact: Tucson, Arizona, June 7–11, 2004*, ed. Hsinchun Chen, Michael Christel, and Ee-Peng Lim (New York: ACM Press, 2004), 142–50.

101 Sriram Raghavan and Hector Garcia-Molina, "Crawling the Hidden Web," in *Proceedings of 27th International Conference on Very Large Data Bases, September 11–14, 2001, Roma, Italy*, ed. Peter M. G. Apers, Paolo Atzeni, Stefano Ceri, Stefano Paraboschi, Kotagiri Ramamohanarao, and Richard T. Snodgrass (Orlando, FL: Morgan Kaufmann, 2001), 129–38; Alexandros Ntoulas, Petros Zerfos, and Junghoo Cho, "Downloading Textual Hidden Web Content through Keyword Queries," in *Proceedings of the 5th ACM/IEEE Joint Conference on Digital Libraries: Denver, Co, USA, June 7–11, 2005: Digital Libraries, Cyberinfrastructure for Research and Education* (New York: ACM Press, 2005), 100–109; and Xiang Peisu, Tian Ke, and Huang Qinzhen, "A Framework of Deep Web Crawler," in *2008 Proceedings of the 27th Chinese Control Conference: Kunming, China, 16–18 July 2008*, edited by Dai-Zhan Cheng and Min Wu (Piscataway, NJ: IEEE Service Center, 2008), 582–86.

102 Capra et al., "Selection of Context Scoping."

103 Bernard Reilly, Carolyn Palaima, Kent Norsworthy, Leslie Myrick, Gretchen Tuchel, and James Simon, "Political Communications Web Archiving: Addressing Typology and Timing for Selection, Preservation and Access" (paper presented at the Third ECDL Workshop on Web Archives, Trondheim, Norway, August 21, 2003); Wallace Koehler, "A Longitudinal Study of Web Pages Continued: A Consideration of Document Persistence," *Information Research* 9, no. 2 (2004), http://informationr.net/ir/9-2/paper174.html.

104 Chia-Hui Chang, Mohammed Kayed, Moheb Ramzy Girgis, and Khaled F. Shaalan, "A Survey of Web Information Extraction Systems," *IEEE Transactions on Knowledge and Data Engineering* 18, no. 10 (2006): 1411–28.

105 Jussi Myllymaki, "Effective Web Data Extraction with Standard XML Technologies," *Computer Networks* 39 (2002): 637.

106 Frederic Stutzman and Terrell Russell, "ClaimID: A System for Personal Identity Management," in *Opening Information Horizons: 6th ACM/IEEE-CS Joint Conference on Digital Libraries: June 11–15, 2006, Chapel Hill, NC, USA: JCDL 2006* (New York: ACM Press, 2006), 367.

107 Garfinkel and Cox, "Finding and Archiving the Internet Footprint"; Aron Culotta, Ron Bekkerman, and Andrew Mccallum, "Extracting Social Networks and Contact Information from Email and the Web" (paper presented at the First Conference on Email and Anti-Spam, Mountain View, CA, July 30–31, 2004).

108 Melinda Van Wingen and Abigail Bass, "Reappraising Archival Practice in Light of the New Social History," *Library Hi Tech* 26, no. 4 (2008): 577.

109 It is important to note that *postcustodial* does not mean *noncustodial*. Ham argued that archivists need to think of their professional role much more broadly than simply managing physical artifacts. Rather than saying "don't take stuff," the postcustodial position is to say "don't fixate on taking stuff as the main focus of your job"; see Ham, "Archival Strategies for the Post Custodial Era." See also Terry Cook, "The Concept of the Archival Fonds: Theory, Description, and Provenance in the Post-Custodial Era," in *The Archival Fonds: From Theory to Practice*, ed. Terry Eastwood (Bureau of Canadian Archivists, 1992), 31–85.

110 Jay Atherton, "From Life Cycle to Continuum: Some Thoughts on the Records Management-Archives Relationship," *Archivaria* 21 (1985-86): 43–51; Sue McKemmish, "Placing Records Continuum Theory and Practice," *Archival Science* 1, no. 4 (2001): 333–59; Frank Upward, "The

Records Continuum," in *Archives: Recordkeeping in Society*, ed. Sue McKemmish, Michael Piggott, Barbara Reed, and Frank Upward (Wagga Wagga, N.S.W.: Centre for Information Studies, Charles Sturt University, 2005), 197–222.

[111] Christopher A. Lee, "Matrix of Digital Curation Knowledge and Competencies" (2009), http://ils.unc.edu/digccurr/digccurr-matrix.html.

[112] William Jerome Wilson, "Analysis of Government Records an Emerging Profession," *Library Quarterly* 16, no. 1 (1946): 1–19.

[113] T. R. Schellenberg, "The Appraisal of Modern Public Records," in *A Modern Archives Reader: Basic Readings on Archival Theory and Practice*, ed. Maygene F. Daniels and Timothy Walch (Washington, DC: National Archives and Records Service, 1984), 57–70.

[114] Paul Lewinson, "Archival Sampling," *American Archivist* 20 (1957): 291–312; Frank Boles, "Sampling in Archives," *American Archivist* 44, no. 2 (1981): 125–30; David R. Kepley, "Sampling in Archives: A Review," *American Archivist* 47, no. 3 (1984): 237–42; and Joseph Carvalho III, "Archival Application of Mathematical Sampling Technique," *Records Management Quarterly* 18 (1984): 60–62.

[115] Kepley, "Sampling in Archives: A Review," 239.

[116] Ibid., 238.

[117] Felix Hull, "The Use of Sampling Techniques in the Retention of Records: A RAMP Study with Guidelines" (Paris: UNESCO, 1981), 1.18.

[118] Carvalho, "Archival Application," 60.

[119] Lewinson, "Archival Sampling"; Emmet J. Leahy, "Reduction of Public Records," *American Archivist* 3, no. 1 (1940): 25; Carl Kulsrud, "Sampling Rural Rehabilitation Records for Transfer to the National Archives," *American Archivist* 10 (1947): 328–34; James Gregory Bradsher, "The FBI Appraisal," *Midwestern Archivist* 13 (1988): 51–66.

[120] Michael Stephen Hindus, Theodore M. Hammett, and Barbara M. Hobson, *The Files of the Massachusetts Superior Court, 1859-1959: An Analysis and a Plan for Action: A Report of the Massachusetts Judicial Records Committee of the Supreme Judicial Court, Boston, 1979* (Boston: G.K. Hall, 1980); Evelyn Kolish, "Sampling Methodology and Its Application: An Illustration of the Tension between Theory and Practice," *Archivaria* 38 (1994): 61–73.

[121] Robert W. Lovett, "The Appraisal of Older Business Records," *American Archivist* 15, no. 1 (1952): 231–39; Lary Steck and Francis Blouin, "Hannah Lay and Company: Sampling the Records of a Century of Lumbering in Michigan,"*American Archivist* 39, no. 1 (1976): 15–23; and Boles, "Sampling in Archives."

[122] Eleanor McKay, "Random Sampling Techniques: A Method of Reducing, Large, Homogeneous Series in Congressional Papers," *American Archivist* 41, no. 3 (1978): 281–89; Faye Phillips, "Sampling and Electronic Records," in *Congressional Papers Management: Collecting, Appraising, Arranging, and Describing Documentation of United States Senators, Representatives, Related Individuals and Organizations* (Jefferson, NC: McFarland, 1996), 163–81.

[123] Greene and Daniels-Howell, "Documentation with an Attitude," 199.

[124] Jeffrey Rosen, *The Unwanted Gaze: The Destruction of Privacy in America*, 1st ed. (New York: Random House, 2000), 8–9.

[125] Daniel J. Solove, *The Future of Reputation: Gossip, Rumor, and Privacy on the Internet* (New Haven, CT: Yale University Press, 2007).

[126] Vance Packard, "Don't Tell It to the Computer," *New York Times Magazine*, January 8, 1967, 90.

Part 3

Implications for Memory Institutions

Take It Personally: The Implications of Personal Records in Electronic Form

Rachel Onuf and Thomas Hyry

Changes in technology have profoundly affected the ways that people create, transmit, and store documentation of their lives. These changes, in turn, create profound challenges and opportunities for archives that have traditionally collected, preserved, and provided access to personal papers. In this essay, Hyry and Onuf revisit their 1997 article in Archival Issues *on personal papers in electronic form, exploring the evolving meanings of "personal" and "papers" within the archival profession and within a larger societal context. They call on archivists to engage with issues related to electronic records in personal collections by explicitly collecting the digital, developing enhanced access systems, and embracing and acquiring new skills. This engagement, the authors contend, will help archivists and others to succeed in serving as effective custodians of born-digital material and to serve the archival mission and users in new ways.*

If you were a student in one of the pioneering electronic records courses taught in archival education programs in the mid-1990s, you read and discussed strategies for handling records rooted in organizations. Although the archives profession had identified the challenges of records created in machine-readable form many years earlier, a new group of theorists and practitioners emerged during this period to tackle issues surrounding electronic records. The two most prominent initiatives, the Pittsburgh Project[1] and the diplomatics framework originating out of the University of British Columbia,[2] carried an assumption that archives served first and foremost (and perhaps exclusively) evidentiary functions within the organizations they served, be they governments, corporations, universities, or nonprofit organizations. These projects articulated strategies such as precustodial intervention, postcustodial management of archival records, and the inclusion of records management functionality in recordkeeping systems, which all presumed that archives existed only within institutional frameworks where archivists could have a significant impact in the record creation environment and on the behavior of creators. These were heady times—there was wide recognition that there were essential records being created solely in electronic form and archivists were creating the new approaches necessary to handle an evolving records environment.

Whether for ideological or pragmatic reasons, the major electronic records research of the 1990s omitted a significant segment of materials that have historically been included in archives in the United States. The American archival tradition has been an amalgamation of the public archives tradition, which mandates archives to collect and preserve records created by their parent institutions; and the historical manuscripts tradition, which directs archives to collect materials for their broader cultural, societal, and historical value.[3] As students drawn to archives more for their cultural values, we found virtually no representation of the concerns of collecting repositories in the burgeoning electronic records literature of the mid-1990s. Up to that point, the only articles that had been published on the topic of personal electronic records were written by Australian archivists.[4] We found this lacuna to be a significant problem, knowing that the ways in which individuals were creating personal records were evolving as quickly as records created in organizational settings.

For a graduate seminar, we decided to examine the issues surrounding personal electronic records in a paper that we subsequently published as an article titled "The Personality of Electronic Records" in 1997.[5] A contemporary reading of that article reveals it to be an artifact of its time and place, and some of its arguments have proven less than timeless. We believe that the main thesis does hold true, however: changes in technology have profoundly affected the ways that people create, transmit, and store documentation of their lives, and these changes produce profound challenges for archives that have traditionally collected, preserved, and provided access to personal papers. In the world of electronic records and technological development in general, a dozen years is an eternity. Today, the problems of personal electronic records persist and proliferate, but so do exciting developments and opportunities for archivists and others to succeed in serving as effective custodians of born-digital material.

This essay revisits our 1997 article in light of subsequent technological evolution and developments in electronic records theory and practice, and considers the current landscape and future prospects for archiving personal digital records. Our original article has three components relevant to a contemporary discussion of personal electronic records: (1) the exhortation that the profession needs to engage with issues related to electronic records in personal collections; (2) the contention that electronic records provide *Serve in new ways* not only a difficult set of challenges for archivists but also significant opportunities to serve the archival mission and users in new ways; and (3) a careful consideration of the changes to personal documentation, which we structured by exploring the concepts of *personal* and *papers*. The last point is where we would like to begin, for the definitions of both *personal* and *papers* have continued to evolve dramatically in the intervening years.

So What's So Great about Paper Anyway?

The 1997 article posited that creators of personal "papers" collections were moving away from paper and into digital media. Email was replacing correspondence (and many phone conversations), word processing software replaced paper drafts, and there was a whole new platform for self expression and transmission—the World Wide Web. Since then, people have increased their use of digital media in an even broader way. Email and the Web have only become more prominent and new media have emerged. Digital photography has almost completely replaced film.[6] The proliferation of cellular telephones has led to the widespread use of text messaging. Digital audio recording technologies come preloaded on most personal computers and can easily be used to record the spoken word, music, and other sounds, which can then be quickly and easily disseminated as podcasts. Video has become almost entirely digital as well. Digital video cameras are ubiquitous, whether handheld, pocket-sized, or built into cellular phones. Blogging software has emerged, allowing the traditional personal journal to move to an online public forum.[7] In recent years, social networking sites have gone mainstream, providing not only new methods for online self-expression, but ones that are explicitly interactive. Even personal finance has gone digital, with wide adoption of online banking and bill receipt and payment. To top it off, data storage is now relatively cheap, with inexpensive terabyte capacity external hard drives and a myriad of companies and services emerging to allow one to back up data in the "cloud," for a reasonable price. It is now clearer than ever that digital tools and formats have become the rule, rather than the exception, in how individuals create and store the records of their lives.

But while personal record creation and personal recordkeeping have continued to assume a more digital profile, archivists who have collected these types of materials in their more traditional formats have, with only a few notable exceptions, failed to adjust to this reality. Susan Davis found in a 2006 research study that archivists working in collecting repositories "realize the magnitude of the issues and that they are making efforts to evolve their practices, and, sometimes, policies . . . It is clear, however that archivists are incorporating born-digital records and papers into their collections without necessarily altering existing policies to do so."[8] Archivists have been well aware of the widespread use of new media to create personal records, so one must ask the question: Why have we been so slow to act? One major reason is a technical gap: the skills necessary to manage electronic records differ considerably from those necessary for managing analog collections. As has been widely lamented in the electronic records literature in the archival field, digital media remains a moving target with new tools and formats emerging at a dizzying pace. While many recent graduates of archival education programs have received intensive training in electronic records management, most mid-career and late career archivists have never received adequate training in this field. Many initiatives have addressed this problem, but the technological gap remains wide. Another reason is that archives routinely experience a lag in time between when records are created and when they are collected and processed by a repository. Creators often donate or sell their personal papers near the end of their lives, meaning that many archives, even those that document contemporary times, have not yet experienced the coming deluge of digital records, as materials created over the past several years might still be considered "active" by creators. Many archivists (and creators) also remain most comfortable with paper and instinctively believe paper to be the medium on which "permanent" records should be recorded. When faced with computer discs or other digital files, archivists have often opted to print files as a long-term solution for preserving the information they store.

Finally, we remain comfortable with paper because there is still so much of it. Ironically, even as documentation of the human experience becomes more complex and is recorded on a growing number of formats, archivists are also confronted with more paper than at any other point in history. The ubiquity of the laser printer and the photocopier has made it easier than ever to print or copy paper. In their book *The Myth of the Paperless Office*, Abigail Sellen and Richard Harper found that paper consumption has increased dramatically in the age of email and the Web.[9] While Sellen and Harper's work focused primarily on the use of paper in work environments, those archivists who collect the records of academics, writers, politicians, and others have experienced a trend of larger and larger modern archival collections, which tend to require more resources to acquire, process, preserve, store, and access. The photocopier and printer cause other problems for an archivist as collections are now clogged with redundant copies and near copies of the same information.[10]

The reality of our present and future donors' transition to digital records creation gives archivists enough incentive to evolve our practices. But we should move out of our paper comfort zone for strategic reasons as well, as digital materials provide many advantages over their analog counterparts. First of all, in the right access system, digital records can be served over networks, freeing researchers from the need to travel to our repositories for certain types of inquiries. Patrons increasingly want and expect to access archival holdings in digital form. Any archivist who has worked at a reference desk knows the common question, "Can I get that online?"—which is almost always followed by an exasperated response. Dan Santamaria has noted "increasing incredulousness" on the part of researchers as he attempts to explain access policies:

> Why is very little available online or in any electronic form? Why do
> they need to travel to the library to conduct research? Why can't

> we just email them the photocopies they requested 4 weeks ago
> instead of making them pay for shipping? Our traditional responses
> to these questions—the cost of digitization, staffing resources, digital
> preservation issues—are increasingly falling on deaf ears. Our users
> expect to find information quickly, at whatever time they happen to
> need it.[11]

We all increasingly live in a world where information not available online may as well be information that does not exist. In a 2007 article in the *New York Times*, Katie Hafner argued, "As more museums and archives become digital domains, and as electronic resources become the main tool for gathering information, items left behind in nondigital form, scholars and archivists say, are in danger of disappearing from the collective cultural memory, potentially leaving our historical fabric riddled with holes."[12] Many archives have been digitizing selections from their holdings for years and others have recently begun aggressively to scan entire manuscript collections and provide access to them over the Web.[13] While archivists are ever unlikely to digitize all or even most paper-based collections, there exists compelling evidence that doing so would provide a significant benefit to researchers, who increasingly see the limits of paper. Most pertinent to this discussion is the fact that if we collect materials in digital form in the first place, they can be added to the online flow of information far more easily than analog holdings that first must be digitized.

Records in digital form have other potential benefits over their paper counterparts. In addition to their portability, most digital records have their own embedded metadata, and text-based records can themselves be searched, if access is provided in the right system. A future access system will allow the blurring of the lines between data and metadata for archival records, much in the same way that David Weinberger suggests is happening in the broader world of information management.[14] In fact, it is increasingly clear that the development and use of research tools that incorporate digital technologies may be the only way for users to make sense of and harness the overabundance of records.

The Beinecke Library, for example, recently acquired a significant portion of the papers of playwright and Acquired Immune Deficiency Syndrome (AIDS) activist Larry Kramer.[15] Kramer has used personal computers for his writing since at least the mid-1980s, and one portion of the acquisition included no fewer than twenty paper drafts of just one of his plays, *The Normal Heart*. The large number of drafts was made possible by the computer and printer, and while the play evolved dramatically over the course of its writing, the variations from one draft to the next were relatively minor. In the print world, a scholar studying Kramer's process of creating *The Normal Heart* might want to examine carefully each draft to find the differences, particularly those that were unmarked by the editorial pen. Having digital copies of each draft would allow a researcher to use any number of programs to identify with ease the differences from one to the next. The scholar's time could then be put toward the important and difficult process of interpreting the significance of the drafts' variations.[16]

In addition to using digital tools to help researchers navigate the over-abundance of modern records, electronic records have the potential of enabling new forms of scholarship. Matthew Kirschenbaum has written:

> But for every problem that electronic documents create—problems for preservation, problems for access, problems for cataloging and classification and discovery and delivery—there are equal, and potentially enormous, opportunities. What if we could use machine-learning algorithms to sift through vast textual archives and draw our attention to a portion of a manuscript manifesting an especially rich and unusual pattern of activity, the multiple layers of revision captured in different versions of the file creating a three-dimensional portrait of the writing process? What if these revisions could in turn be correlated with the content of a Web site that someone in the author's MySpace network had blogged?[17]

From the perspective of a historian, Roy Rosenzweig suggests a foundational shift in research methodology, writing

> Future graduate programs will probably have to teach . . . social-scientific and quantitative methods as well as such other skills as "digital archaeology" (the ability to "read" arcane computer formats), "digital diplomatics" (the modern version of the old science of authenticating documents), and data mining (the ability to find the historical needle in the digital hay). In the coming years, "contemporary historians" may need more specialized research and "language" skills than medievalists do.[18]

The now established field of digital humanities has busily begun, as Tom Scheinfeldt has put it, to shift "the work of a rapidly growing number of scholars away from thinking big thoughts to forging new tools, methods, materials, techniques, and modes of work which will enable us to harness the still unwieldy, but obviously game-changing, information technologies now sitting on our desktops and in our pockets."[19] Archivists who work in research settings need to be collecting in formats that will facilitate scholars' use of emerging techniques.

A final note about the potential benefit of born-digital records versus paper collections relates to cost. While a great deal is appropriately made of the cost of developing digital repositories and preserving digital assets, paper collections provide their own enormous and at times hidden or assumed costs for archives and archivists. Archivists must not forget that they spend a great deal of money preserving, processing, and housing paper collections. The cost of paper storage and retrieval will be evident to anyone who has recently planned and implemented offsite shelving facilities, maintained constant temperature and humidity in stack areas, and retrieved dozens of boxes of a modern collection for researcher use in a reading room. The cost of providing granular processing to paper collections has been at the heart of the archival profession's recent dialogue related to the "More Product, Less Process" approach to arrangement, description, and preservation of holdings.[20] As archivists make the necessary shift to a less granular level of description for archival holdings, they also must acknowledge the desirability of a finer level of access for some collections. With born-digital holdings, archivists may be able to have their cake and eat it too, by providing descriptive information on the collection and/or series level, and then allowing the records themselves to be searched and mined at a more granular level. If an access platform such as this were employed, it could also be adapted to allow archivists to engage users to provide enhanced descriptions of specific holdings to complement the higher-level, less granular archival description.

Though we argue that archivists should begin to privilege collecting digital records over their analog counterparts, this is not a call to entirely replace paper with the digital; contemporary collections will continue to be created in hybrid form, and archivists absolutely will and should include appropriate paper holdings in their repositories. In particular, paper records that have high artifactual value should be sought, collected, cared for, and made accessible. But over time, as our hybrid collections pitch toward the digital and away from paper, archivists should not cling to paper as a preferred medium just because we have centuries of experience in how to preserve it. Rather, we should be orienting our attention, techniques, and even preferences toward the digital forms in which our documentary heritage is increasingly being created. Archivists need to be moving strategically—not grudgingly—to digital preservation solutions. The profession should change descriptive standards so they refer to collections as "personal records" rather than "papers" in order to reflect their hybrid form and to break the habits of paper-based thinking.[21]

[handwritten: Change name from personal papers to personal records]

Nothing Personal?

The meaning of *personal* has also undergone radical transformation over the past fourteen years. In 1997 we were primarily concerned with the impersonality of the new digital media, and how the sameness of email communications and home pages effectively suppressed individual expression. The remarkable growth of new media and its use for self-expression has made this early critique unfounded. New tools allow people to provide access to all sorts of creative works: text-based, still and moving image, audio, and any imaginable combination. There are even companies working on providing online access to smells and tastes.[22] Loosed from the constraints of "traditional" web formats, people have much more control over the look and feel of their Internet-based forms of self-expression. So if electronic records now have the capability of expressing personality, of exuding individuality, what else has changed?

As defined by the *Oxford English Dictionary*, the word *personal* means: "Of, pertaining to, concerning, or affecting the individual self (as opposed, variously, to other persons, the general community, etc., or to one's office, rank, or other attributes); individual; private; one's own." Largely due to technological innovation, there has been a decoupling of the personal from the private. Personal no longer presumes private, as personal production and documentation increasingly takes place in public forums, sometimes with the opportunity to self-select the audience; but in other cases, available literally to the entire wired world.

We do not mean to insinuate that people will no longer accumulate over a lifetime a record of that life, write letters or email meant only to be read by a lover, or diaries they share with no one, all stored in data silos like file cabinets and thumb drives. Increasingly, however, much of life takes place on the Internet, or is placed on the Internet: instead of writing letters or emails back and forth, friends may write on each other's Facebook walls or follow each other on Twitter; instead of being siloed in a shoebox or on a hard drive, family photos might be uploaded to Flickr. Interestingly, many people—especially those digital natives who have grown up using technology (and specifically the Internet)—seem to have few qualms about placing personal information that would traditionally have been understood as private online.[23]

Much has been made of the superficiality of much of this personal information, perhaps best epitomized by Twitter's limit of each tweet to 140 characters or fewer. In many virtual spaces, however, people can *and do* create or provide access to rich and robust materials: thoughtful blogs, original music, still images, and videos. The banal personal home page we bemoaned back in 1997 has developed into something far more interesting, not only because of its content, but also because of the kinds of audience participation the Internet allows. Once the productions of the individual are placed within these networks, they can be viewed by others, who can comment, caption, tag, and otherwise augment the original posting with material from their own personal digital collections. Again, many have been quick to disparage the quality of such collaboration, but even if the "cool!" comments and incorrect identifications are legion, there is great potential for contributions that enhance the original. Arguably the quality of this collective documentation will improve over time, as the personal home page has, and the development of tag clouds and collabularies will improve the ability to search for and find information.[24]

To push this a bit further, because personal production increasingly takes place within multiple large networks, the creation and documentation of the individual ought to be preserved within those larger contexts in order to be understood by future researchers. Much of this production may be small packets of data, insubstantial on its own, and only gaining substance within the call and response of a community. Substance ("depth and breadth") is a traditional criterion for assessing research value, the reason archivists preserve materials in the first place. If removed from the original contexts, a collection of an individual's responses to blogs, contributions to wikis, unidentified photos, and outgoing email will be diminished. It is within the contextual webs that individual lives will resonate.

This is not a new idea: context has always been critical to understanding documentary evidence. What is new is the tremendous opportunity to capture these digital contexts, and future social historians and others invested in documenting regular folk could benefit from capturing the contexts. No more arduous quests for the other half of a correspondence or for critical responses to a creative work. Archivists have the ability to document the human experience as never before. For better or worse, the more real time people spend online or documentation of offline life they place online, the greater the chance that archivists can capture, preserve, and make available that information in the aggregate and in its particulars. So the newest challenges lie in determining how to capture the interconnected digital documentation of individual lives. Arguably the profession has come full circle, back to the idea that the records we need to preserve are rooted in larger systems—but now in online networks, rather than organizational recordkeeping systems—and archivists need to focus on holistic capture of this data in order to meaningfully document the individual.

This opportunity—and this charge—is laid at the feet of the archival profession as a whole. The Library of Congress has taken a leading role, tweeting its intention to "acquire ENTIRE Twitter archive" in April 2010.[25] But these social networks do not necessarily need to live within a traditional archival repository to be preserved. Archivists should impress upon service providers the importance of preserving the interconnected content on their networks, and encourage the networks themselves to develop and implement long-term retention plans. We must persuade them to hire electronic records archivists.[26] In addition to the need to appraise and preserve materials at the network level, there are steps archivists can take when working with individual donors. At collecting repositories, archivists must make sure to cast a wide net when negotiating for personal records: do not just take the "easy" box of floppies; probe into what sorts of digital creation, collaboration, and interaction the potential donor has produced and discuss ways to capture it for the archives. It may be that the richer materials are in these more fugitive forms.

Another challenge is not to lose sight of those who do not participate in the online world; there must be documentation strategies in place to preserve some record of their various individual and collective experiences. While our focus in this piece has been on the increased ways that individuals use digital technologies to create documentation of their lives, we remain cognizant of the "digital divide" and must point out that a digital-only approach would create as many holes in our future heritage as its alternative.

So What's Next?

One pleasant aspect of returning to the theme of personal electronic recordkeeping is that we can now say that a multitude of archivists, curators, preservationists, and scholars have been working on the myriad issues posed by personal digital records, and we have seen real progress in the development of acquisition, preservation, and processing techniques and systems. In particular, British initiatives, including the Paradigm project (and its spinoff, futureArch) and the Digital Lives Research Project, serve as models *and provide tools* for archives moving into collecting, preserving, processing, and making accessible personal digital records.[27] We see three specific areas for action for archivists working with personal digital records in collecting repositories, and the following recommendations partially echo and build upon the work of these projects.

Explicitly collect the digital. When working with contemporary individuals and organizations, many of whom have rooms of paper and audiovisual records to offer, archivists should, as a routine, target their digital files. Doing so will not only allow archives to collect a fuller (and at times, better) record, but it will also encourage the archivist to learn the new tools necessary to handle the digital. Archivists should do this fearlessly and opportunistically, and share what they accomplish with their colleagues. To quote the editor of this volume, "it will only break if we don't play with it," because ignored electronic records will disappear anyway.[28] When working with creators, archivists must also contact them early in their careers, and strive to influence how they create and keep records. Adrian Cunningham made this argument in the earliest article on the topic of personal electronic archives[29] and it remains true fifteen years later. What has changed since then is that research projects, such as InterPARES2 and Paradigm, and repositories themselves have developed tools for working with donors, including guidelines for creators that can be used and/or repurposed by individual archives and archivists.[30] Finally, when working with creators, archivists need to be as explicit as possible about the potential new uses of holdings in digital form. Creators must be made aware of all of the potential ways their records might be searched, delivered over networks, and otherwise repurposed, making individuals' records more widely and immediately accessible than ever before.

Develop enhanced access systems. Perhaps rightly so, the current research relating to personal digital records has focused on acquisition, preservation, and processing. Looking forward, archivists need to utilize the chief benefits of electronic media by devising and developing access systems that allow records and their embedded metadata to be searched and mined, as well as served to users over the Internet. In other words, archivists need to develop a next generation of archival access systems that combine and index metadata for physical and digitized holdings along with the full text of electronic records, and allow users to access the results from wherever they do their research. When copyright and privacy concerns prevent us from delivering records over the Web, archivists should strive to create virtual spaces that mirror our reading rooms, where readers must register and agree to a set of access rules before they can use material. The creation of these spaces may also encourage users to help us describe our holdings further, by adding comments and tags to records and finding aids.

Embrace and acquire new skills. Many have spoken over the past few decades of the need for archivists to learn the new skills necessary to succeed at managing electronic records, and the call bears repeating.[31] As the tools for records creation continue to evolve, so must our awareness of and familiarity with those new tools and with technologies for capturing, preserving, and providing access to personal digital archives.[32] Archivists working within collecting repositories must not lag behind in developing new technology skills and working with others in their home repositories to implement new systems. As a profession, we need to continue to develop training aimed not only at graduate students and younger archivists, many of whom may have a more natural affinity for new technologies, but at mid-career professionals as well, many of whom still have decades of service left to the profession. Educators and experts need to develop new and enhance existing training opportunities, professionals need to take them and incorporate their lessons into their daily work, and managers need to prioritize support for such training.[33]

The profession needs to continue to engage with issues related to electronic records in personal collections. These digital records are out there, proliferating at awesome rates, but archivists should not be awed into inertia. Instead, take that awe and seize opportunities to expand collections, expand access to collections, and expand archival expertise.

Notes

1 Wendy Duff, "Ensuring the Preservation of Reliable Evidence: A Research Project Funded by the NHPRC," *Archivaria* 42 (1996): 28–45.

2 Luciana Duranti and Heather MacNeil, "The Protection of the Integrity of Electronic Records: An Overview of the UBC-MAS Research," *Archivaria* 42 (1996): 46–67.

3 See Luke J. Gilliland-Swetland, "The Provenance of a Profession: The Permanence of the Public Archives and Historical Manuscripts Traditions in American Archival History," *American Archivist* 54, no. 2 (1991): 160–75.

4 Adrian Cunningham, "The Archival Management of Personal Records in Electronic Form: Some Suggestions," *Archives and Manuscripts* 22, no. 1 (1994): 94–105.

5 Tom Hyry and Rachel Onuf, "The Personality of Electronic Records: The Impact of New Information Technology on Personal Papers," *Archival Issues* 22, no. 1 (1997): 37–44.

6 See Jochen Runde, Matthew Jones, Kamal Munir, and Lynne Nikolychuk, "On Technological Objects and the Adoption of Technological Product Innovations: Rules, Routines and the Transition from Analogue Photography to Digital Imaging," *Cambridge Journal of Economics* 33, no. 1 (2008): 1–24. This article reports that digital still camera sales overtook analog camera sales in the United States in 2003, and that analog camera, film, and film processing sales have been greatly reduced.

7 Catherine O'Sullivan, "Diaries, On-line Diaries, and the Future Loss to Archives; or Blogs, and the Blogging Bloggers who Blog Them," *American Archivist* 68, no. 1 (2005): 53–73. O'Sullivan discusses the similarities and differences between traditional diaries and blogs and online journals.

8 Susan E. Davis, "Electronic Records Planning in 'Collecting' Repositories," *American Archivist* 71, no. 1 (2008): 185.

9 Abigail J. Sellen and Richard H. R. Harper, *The Myth of the Paperless Office* (Cambridge, MA: MIT Press, 2002).

10 This reality evokes Gerald Ham's point from the 1990s that "today's information-laden world has lessened the value of any single set of records; the documents may be unique but the information is usually not"; the statement rings even more true in contemporary times. F. Gerald Ham, *Selecting and Appraising Archives and Manuscripts* (Chicago: Society of American Archivists, 1993), 72.

11 Dan Santamaria (untitled paper presented at the Legal and Ethical Implications of Large-Scale Digitization of Manuscript Collections Symposium, University of North Carolina–Chapel Hill, February 13, 2009), available at http://shc2009symposia.pbwiki.com/Dan-Santamaria.

12 Katie Hafner, "History, Digitized (And Abridged)," *New York Times*, March 10, 2007.

13 The Smithsonian Archives of American Art provides an excellent example of this: http://www.aaa. si.edu/collectionsonline/.

14 David Weinberger, *Everything Is Miscellaneous: The Power of the New Digital Disorder* (New York: Times Books, 2007).

15 Beinecke Rare Book and Manuscript Library, Yale University, http://www.library.yale.edu/ beinecke/.

16 In this case, the Beinecke Library would like to preserve and make available each of Kramer's drafts, as his literary work, activism, and connection to Yale make him a high priority for its collecting initiatives. In other cases, however, archivists do not and would not collect quite so comprehensively. While beyond the scope of this essay, issues related to archival appraisal of personal digital records remain a fertile ground for inquiry.

17 Matthew Kirschenbaum, "Hamlet.doc: Literature in a Digital Age," *Chronicle of Higher Education* (August 17, 2007), B8.

18 Roy Rosenzweig, "Scarcity or Abundance? Preserving the Past in a Digital Era," *American Historical Review* 108, no. 3 (2003): 758.

19 Tom Scheinfeldt, "Sunset for Ideology, Sunrise for Methodology?" post on Found History blog, March 18, 2008, available at http://www.foundhistory.org/2008/03/13/sunset-for-ideology-sunrise-for-methodology/.

20 Mark A. Greene and Dennis Meissner, "More Product, Less Process: Revamping Traditional Archival Processing," *American Archivist* 68, no. 2 (2005): 208–63.

21 For U.S. archivists, this would necessitate a revision of rule 2.3.18 of *Describing Archives: A Content Standard (DACS)* (Chicago: Society of American Archivists, 2007).

22 Even though DigiScents' iSmell peripheral device never made it beyond the prototype phase and was voted one of the "25 Worst Tech Products of All Time" by *PC World* magazine in 2006, other companies continue to develop olfactory tools, like the Scent Dome from TriSenx (http://www. trisenx.com).

23 See the Digital Natives project (http://www.digitalnative.org), an interdisciplinary collaboration of the Berkman Center for Internet and Society at Harvard University and the Research Center for Information Law at the University of St. Gallen. *Born Digital: Understanding the First Generation of Digital Natives*, by John Palfrey and Urs Gasser (New York: Basic Books, 2008) is one of the publications to come out of the project.

24 Tag clouds are defined as "visual presentations of a set of words, typically a set of tags, in which attributes of the text such as size, weight or colour can be used to represent features (e.g., frequency) of the associated terms" (Martin Halvey and Mark T. Keane, "An Assessment of Tag Presentation Techniques," in *Proceedings of the 16th international conference on World Wide Web* (New York: Association for Computing Machinery), 1313–4). Collabularies are conceived as a compromise between a folksonomy and a controlled vocabulary: a team of classification experts collaborates with content consumers to create rich, but more systematic content tagging systems. See also Paul Anderson's JISC Technology and Standards Watch report, "What is Web 2.0? Ideas, technologies, and implications for education," http://www.jisc.ac.uk/media/documents/techwatch/tsw0701b.pdf.

25 The April 14, 2010 tweet in its entirety: "Library to acquire ENTIRE Twitter archive—ALL public tweets, ever, since March 2006! Details to follow." (http://twitter.com/librarycongress/status/12169442690.)

26 Admittedly, there are significant copyright and privacy concerns at work here and the entities who collect and preserve this information should have careful policies that respect individual rights.

27 The Personal Archives Accessible in Digital Media (Paradigm) project was a collaboration of the major research libraries of the Universities of Oxford and Manchester, 2005-2007 (http://

www.paradigm.ac.uk/). A Bodleian Library project funded by the Andrew W. Mellon Foundation, futureArch, seeks to build upon the work of the Paradigm project (http://futurearchives.blogspot. com/). The Digital Lives Research Project was a collaboration of the British Library, University College London, and the University of Bristol, 2007-2009 (http://www.bl.uk/digital-lives/index. html).

[28] Christopher A. Lee, "Guerilla Electronic Records Management: Lessons Learned," *Records and Information Management Report* 18, no. 5 (2002): 1–13.

[29] Cunningham, "Archival Management of Personal Records."

[30] The InterPARES2 project developed "Creator Guidelines," an exhaustive 10-page guide for records creators to follow, found at http://www.interpares.org/display_file. cfm?doc=ip2%28pub%29creator_guidelines_booklet.pdf. The Paradigm project also developed approaches for working with active donors, described in the Paradigm workbook: http://www. paradigm.ac.uk/workbook/. Facing the reality of working with authors with little technical skill and less interest, the Beinecke Rare Book and Manuscript Library created a stripped-down version of these documents, available at http://beineckepoetry.wordpress.com/digital-preservation/.

[31] See, for instance, Richard Pearce-Moses, "Janus in Cyberspace," *American Archivist* 70, no. 1 (2007): 13–22.

[32] The New Skills for a Digital Era colloquium and report provide a useful discussion of these skills: http://rpm.lib.az.us/NewSkills/index.asp.

[33] There are an increasing number of training opportunities available, including the DigCCurr Professional Institute and the Society of American Archivists continuing education offerings, most notably the Electronic Records "Summer Camp."

Making It Usable: Developing Personal Collection Tools for Digital Collections

Leslie Johnston

Scholars are increasingly engaging in born-digital scholarship in which the digital nature of their teaching and research is inherent to the scholarship itself. A key assumption identified by the University of Virginia (UVa) Library while developing its Digital Collections Repository was that the library was responsible not only for collection and repository building, but also for the creation of tools for collection use. Input from faculty and librarians led to the development of a User Collection Tool to organize personal digital media collections, a PageComber tool to gather images from the open Web, and the Collectus digital object collector tool to develop portfolios of all object types and create presentations. This chapter examines the development of this suite of gathering and authoring tools that make personal and library digital collections integrable into new forms of scholarly output.

It is very likely that every person reading these words has some form of personal digital collection. It may be a collection of website bookmarks; images from a digital camera; pages saved from websites; files sent by friends and family; music; citations stored in citation management software; downloaded ejournal articles; ebooks; or every letter, lecture, paper, article, or book that you have written over time—with associated data, spreadsheets, and images—in multiple versions and multiple locations. Neil Beagrie distinguishes personal digital collections from other forms of personal records:

> The term "personal digital collection" is used here to distinguish these informal, diverse, and expanding collections accumulated and maintained by individuals. It focuses on what is maintained and accumulated by an individual, and excludes, for example, information on individuals that may be held in government sources such as census records or reviews of an individual's work created and maintained by third parties. Personal digital collections therefore may in part be an informal "personal archive" of record; a "personal library" of externally generated articles, PowerPoint slides, music, video and monographs; or other materials such as working papers or family photographs intended either solely for personal access or for sharing with others. Although in many ways similar to past personal papers and collections, there are radical divergences emerging in a digital environment.[1]

The process of building and organizing personal digital collections is a recognized activity in all areas of research and teaching. Such collections are sets of digital artifacts assembled by known criteria, placed in one or more contexts, and organized by one or more wildly varying ontologies—subject(s), event(s), media type, etc. The process of selection and organization assists in later recall, but the inevitable issue of scale makes this increasingly challenging. Such personal collections might also be shared using a variety of social media, but how is a personal organizational scheme extrapolated without appearing chaotic? What tools can be developed to aid in the organization, presentation, and sharing of personal collections in teaching and research?

Context for the Work at UVa

In 2002, the University of Virginia Library began planning the development of a Digital Collections Repository to manage and deliver its digital collections. The process began with a set of assumptions which framed all work on the repository. There were six key assumptions about the architecture:

- The repository will be a part of a global network.
- All media and all content types will be integrated into one repository collection.

- There will be simple objects and complex objects with many relationships, and we will need to manage the objects, their relationships to one another, and their relationships to their contexts.

- We will be faced with born-digital scholarship incorporating both digital materials and context.

- Any given resource can be associated with and presented in any number of contexts.

- The repository will have a public discovery interface, for which the architecture and metadata must support both searching and browsing.

There were six key assumptions about services:

- The repository will be a curated repository, where all content is selected using the same criteria as for the print collections.

- Members of the UVa community are the primary users of the repository. This does not mean that the repository will be closed; it will support open access to content and public accessibility whenever possible.

- All of the UVa Library's digital collections will eventually be managed and delivered by the repository.

- The repository will be part of the solution to create a single point-of-access for both the library's print and digital collections.

- The repository will have a public interface to support discovery and use of the collections by the UVa community.

- The repository will provide tools for the use of the collections in instruction and research.

It is the final assumption about services that in many ways made this project stand out. The UVa Library had extensive experience in working with scholars to develop digital collections and resources through its Electronic Text Center and Geospatial and Statistical Data Center, now part of the Scholars' Lab.[2] Faculty members were building extensive digital corpora such as the Valley of the Shadow, the Rossetti Archive, the Tibetan and Himalayan Library, the Salem Witch Trials Documentary Archive, and the Salisbury

Project.[3] Each of these projects, and many more like them, began with a personally-amassed digital collection and a desire to use digital resources in teaching and research and to share them with as broad an audience as possible.

In 2002 there were only a few options for managing personal digital collections. For images and multimedia the commonly used personal tools were iView, Canto Cumulus, and Extensis Portfolio.[4] The enterprise Luna Insight and EmbARK products were in place at some institutions.[5] These supported creation of persistent, personal image sets built from institutional collections, but no easy integration of personal images at the time. A number of universities had developed tools: James Madison University developed its Madison Digital Image Database (MDID) tool, UVa had its first User Collection Tool, Princeton University developed Almagest, and the University of Washington developed ContentDM, later licensed to OCLC.[6] Documentum was the standard for document management.[7] Presto was prototyped at Xerox PARC (Palo Alto Research Center), but never went into widespread production.[8]

Course management systems such as WebCT and Blackboard were not yet in widespread use for the management of personal digital media in teaching. Most faculty managed and presented collections using HTML (hypertext markup language) pages: sets of low-resolution images for courses, lists of links to websites, or bibliographies that most likely did not link to online publications.

The local mantra "If digital collections cannot be used, then they have not been preserved" was foremost in our minds when we declared that the library had to develop both discovery services and end-user tools for the repository.

First Steps

In 2001, the Digital Media Lab launched its User Collection Tool (UCT), a web-based application used for managing personal digital media files: images, video, and audio.[9] This was an application—built on top of the mySQL relational database management system and PHP (Hypertext Processor) programming language—which allowed users to point to their own media files. Functionality included searching; viewing files in a light table; organizing files or batches

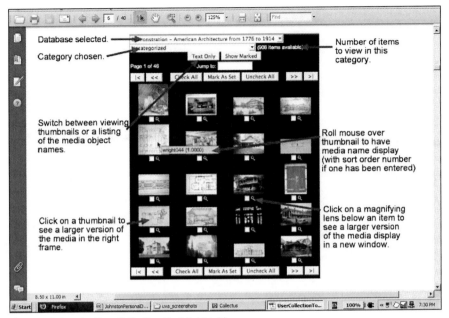

Figure 1. Using the User Collection Tool light table.

of files into sets; creating categories and sort orders; assigning descriptive metadata in any of twenty fields for individual files or batches; and publishing the sets as web pages that optionally included search functionality.

The UCT required that the files be available on a web server in a persistent location, because the tool pointed to the files rather than copying them into the application. Users could import their personal files into collections themselves, or ask a library staff member to import the files for them. Access permissions were set by the owner for each collection and each website.

Understanding the Use of Digital Collections

When building the initial repository image collection interface in 2003, the team held a focus group with media and image librarians and instructional technology staff from the Fine Arts Library and its Image Collections, the Art Department Visual Resources Collections, and the Digital Media Lab. Their comments guided the development of online image services and the initial idea of what we then referred to as the "shopping cart" for the collections. The identified priorities were:

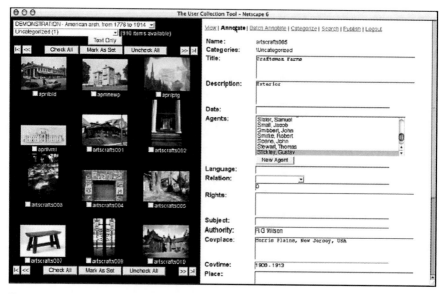

Figure 2. Annotating an image with metadata in the User Collection Tool.

- Users should be able to conduct both simple and advanced searches across and within collections.

- Search sort options should be available, including title, creator, medium, and date. The default should be sorting by title. This group stated that relevance ranking was a lower priority than customizable sorting. They felt that relevance rules that would please all potential audiences would be difficult to codify.

- There should be a browse interface to find lists of collections. Clicking on a collection to browse should take users to the individual collection page with the option to search or browse. Browsing should support the same sorting as a search.

- Multiple options to view search results were required. Mentioned were titles only, thumbnails with titles, and thumbnails only.

- When viewing resources found through a search, the words or phrase from the search must be highlighted in context.

- Image metadata must include contextual collection affiliation(s).

- Online image viewing tools must support panning and rotating. Users must be able to view descriptive and possibly technical metadata.

- There must be a shopping cart that supports the creation of persistent sets, allow batch downloading, and integrate images from other sources.

By fall 2004, a fully functional Digital Collections Repository built on top of the Flexible and Extensible Digital Object and Repository Architecture (Fedora) launched for selective testing.[10] This included a combined metadata-only discovery search for images, electronic texts, and finding aids, full-text searches for the electronic texts and finding aids, and a page-turner for reading books online. The page-turner let a user read a book online, moving through the pages in order or allowing the user to skip to selected pages. The page-turner could be used to view either full text or page images, depending upon what was available for individual texts. An ImageViewer supported zooming, rotation, and other on-the-fly image manipulation such as brightness and contrast.

This was the first release of the Collector Tool, later called Collectus, which allowed users to create personal portfolios of objects. All images discovered through a repository search were "collectable" through the imbedding of a small chunk of JavaScript in the results page. This was a Java application for client machines (updated automatically via Java WebStart) that provided the

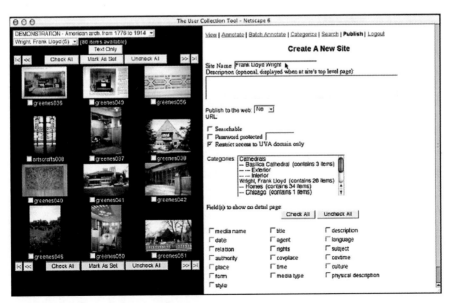

Figure 3. Creating a collection website in the User Collection Tool.

ability to collect images into personal portfolios and generate slide shows or electronic reserve websites that included pointers to the images and metadata in the repository. Java was selected for its presumed ease of development of a single application for use on Microsoft Windows or Apple Macintosh. This proved to be not entirely the case, as the Apple implementation of Java at that time required that more Java imaging libraries be installed on a Mac than on a Windows machine. Over time, this issue was resolved as the Macintosh Operating System evolved. A wide range of installers for various permutations of the MacOS System continued to be documented on the Collectus Help page to support users in all possible environments.

Java WebStart was selected to simplify support for users. Initial installation of the tool was handled through a link on a web page, with no installer to download, unzip, or manage. With Java WebStart, as long as the user had live network access, every time he or she launched the tool the WebStart connection checked for a newer version and, if one was found, automatically updated the software without any action being required of the user. In that way, users would always have the most up-to-date software without having

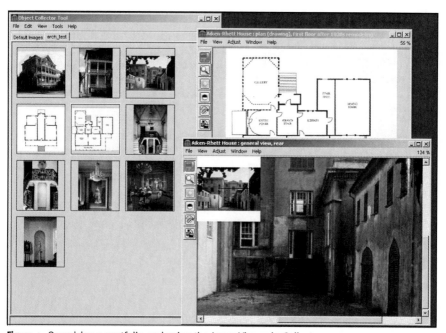

Figure 4. Organizing a portfolio and using the ImageViewer in Collectus.

Aiken-Rhett House : exterior, Corner of the piazza

Aiken-Rhett House : general view, rear

Figure 5. Displaying dual carousel side-by-side images in Collectus.

to check for new versions. Library staff would also always know that users had the most recent version when providing any assistance in using the tool.

The portfolios could be saved by users to any location that they chose—on their own machines, portable drives, or on any accessible UVa network directory. The portfolios are small XML (Extensible Markup Language) files that record the order of the resources, the URLs (Uniform Resource Locators) for the resources (the actual media files themselves are not saved as part of the portfolio), and any custom settings. This made the personal portfolios portable to any location where the user had access to an Internet connection. An Internet connection was required because the resources were online, not saved locally, and if any of the resources were restricted the user had to be able to authenticate as a member of the UVa community. Since the resources were served out of the repository, access rights were managed there and required that authentication. At this point the tool only supported images, and only images from the repository.

Users worked with images in a lightbox, where they could organize image order and add custom titles to use in place of the title from the library's collection. Slide shows could be created for a single image, split screens, or two projector classrooms. Web pages could be formatted in varying grid configurations, or as a sort of slide show with one image per page. The slide shows and electronic reserves delivered the images wrapped in the same ImageViewer as was used in the online environment. The electronic reserve web pages that were generated by the Collector Tool contained the same chunk of JavaScript as the repository search results, allowing any images on the pages to be themselves collectable by any other user with the tool.

Four faculty members were invited to test the Image Collection and tools in classroom use. One made sets of images available as a study set for a course; two built collections and used the Collector Tool to teach in class; and one used the tool in the classroom and also asked students to build their own image collections for use in class projects. The testers provided vital feedback in the development of the tools. They requested the following:

- That additional data elements, including all associated dates and rights, be included in the metadata view for images.

- The ability to selectively include certain types of metadata when creating web pages, such as checkboxes where the user could make selections such as: *Title, Agent, Location information, Subjects,*

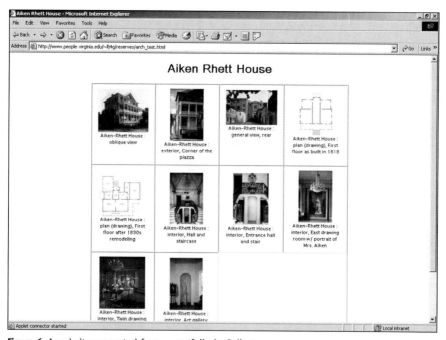

Figure 6. A website generated from a portfolio in Collectus.

All information (or just *Brief information* or *Full information*), with preselected subsets.

- The ability to place duplicates of digital images within a collection that they create.

- That blank placeholders be available in constructing their digital slideshows.

- The ability to see a URL for an individual image to use as a persistent pointer.

- The ability to see a formatted citation for an image with a URL.

- A list printing feature, to provide an ordered list of what is in a collection/slide show for reference use in the classroom.

- The ability to integrate personal digital images and those from licensed collections with repository images for use in slide shows and web pages.

Two focus groups were held with architecture, history, and art history faculty. They were presented with a demonstration of the image and text interfaces, and asked to provide feedback. Findings from the focus groups included the following:

- Some wondered why certain categories of metadata—such as when the image was taken and who took it—were not displayed. Documenting the context of the individual images, such as showing images of sites or buildings over time, was important to them.

- They asked for the ability to create a different format of web page when viewing a larger image with associated metadata. They were looking for "tombstone" metadata: creator, title, location, and date. *Tombstone* is a term commonly used to describe a minimally descriptive metadata set, such as one might find on a brief wall label in a museum or in an exhibition catalog inventory. Additionally, they requested the ability to more selectively choose a custom set of metadata elements for inclusion in any of the web pages.

- When organizing images in the light box for use in split screen or two-screen slide shows, they wanted to be able to see them in two separate physical spaces, not just all in one with the slide carousel numbers. They wanted to identify and organize only the images that would appear on the left of the screen, or only the images that would appear on the right of the screen, in addition to viewing all the images together, identified with their left (1) and right (2) carousel numbers.

- They requested the ability to place duplicates of digital images within a collection, as well as blanks. Where blanks would be inserted, some wanted the option of creating a text label that would appear instead of the blank, like a title slide.

- They wanted to be able to add not only a custom label to an image, but also a lengthier annotation, and to provide an annotation to describe the collection itself.

- They wanted to be able to print lists of what was included in a collection, with options for metadata to be included in the list, and the option to include thumbnails in printouts.

- The issue that was most troublesome to the group was that Internet access was required for use. They all wanted an option to work offline, and create offline slide shows for use in rooms where there is no network access, or at remote locations.

- Their top, unanimous request was to be able to integrate personal digital images into collections for use in slide shows and web pages. Many architecture faculty used iView, which was licensed by the Architecture School, to manage their collections.

In preparing for the release of the tools to the entire university in January 2007, almost all of the feedback was translated into new functionality. Texts and finding aids could be collected in addition to images. The lightbox was updated for improved splitscreen and dual projector organization. Duplicate images and blanks could be added into display presentations. URLs for individual objects could be more easily discovered. Object citations could be generated. Lists for image sets could be printed. Thumbnail images could be cached for offline work. A concept called "asset actions"—a method for objects to identify themselves and express information about available functionality—was integrated into the tool. An object could be called upon to identify itself—I am an image or a text or a finding aid; here is my descriptive metadata; I have multiple component files, such as pages; I have multiple deliverables, such as a thumbnail and a screen-sized image; I have these rights associated with me—using a consistently structured URL interface shared by all objects.

Some functionality was not in place. Because the underlying Fedora repository managed the access controls, offline slideshows could not be implemented. There were also some Fedora infrastructure restrictions that made the ability to selectively include metadata more technically challenging than expected. The ability to include personal images was not in place, but work was under way to develop improved integration. It was also at this time that the collector tool was formally named "Collectus." The source code was released in spring 2007.

Moving Toward Integration of Personal Collections

In 2007 the library started down a path to integration of objects from multiple sources: the library's repository, personal collections, instructional scanning, and images from the Web. This effort was part of a larger University of Virginia initiative called the Academic Information Space (AIS), with the goal of providing an environment for users to easily collect digital objects and incorporate them into virtual presentations and exhibitions.

The first step was the selection of Collectus as the tool in which the objects could be aggregated. Its ability to add any object with an asset action package into a personal portfolio made the asset action package a standard for interchange that could be used across many tools. As well, the basic JavaScript "connector" code for "collecting" objects from the repository could easily be added into any web application.

The greatest limiter in adding the ability to incorporate personal collections was the architectural requirement that the media exist in a web-addressable space. Collectus does not store media files, it merely points to them. The most sensible place to begin was to take advantage of an existing web-based tool for the management of personal media: the User Collection Tool. The JavaScript connector for collectability was added into the UCT, which meant that any media files managed in a faculty member's online UCT collection could be added to a Collectus set. The downside was that this meant that integration required the prior loading of personal media into the

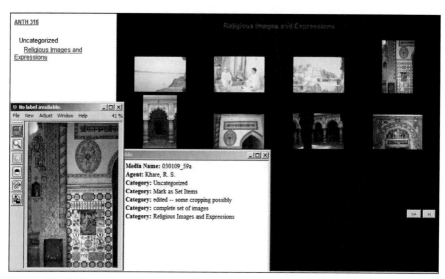

Figure 7. A website made with the User Collector Tool.

UCT, but this was balanced by lack of significant redevelopment of an existing tool and infrastructure to support a pathway to collection integration.

Collectus as implemented at UVa requires that objects be in a web-addressable location. An early win was the realization that these objects could be saved in the My Workspace portal that each user was automatically granted in UVa's implementation of the open-source learning management tool Sakai, called UVaCollab.[11] UVaCollab encompasses course content management and group and community collaborative sites with functionality that includes—in addition to communication, event management, and testing and grading tools—digital resource management. The Resources tool allows users to upload files of any type; the files can be shared with and downloaded by specific users, or be made available to the general public (including those without privileged access to Collab) through a URL. Users can also upload links to URLs, essentially functioning as a tool for sharing bookmarks. The Sakai Collab tool provided a secure location where users could keep their personal media files. By making changes to the code in the Resources module, functionality was added to collect one file or batches of files into Collectus for subsequent use in presentations or research. Any file in the Collab Resources space could be integrated with UVa Library collection objects.

Figure 8. Resources in a Collab site with checkboxes and Send to Collectus function.

The missing element was an easy path to incorporate images from the open Web. Even though there are known issues of authenticity in personal collection building from the often undocumented Web,[12] this is a known collection building strategy that had to be supported. While building the Collectus integration into Collab—any file in Collab could be incorporated into Collectus—it seemed sensible to develop a tool to easily capture images from the open Web and integrate them as well.

PageComber is a tool that examines the web page the user is currently viewing and searches for images that exist on that page, allowing the selection and collection of images for future use. PageComber is similar to a browser bookmark or favorite: it is a "bookmarklet" that is added to and used from a web browser's bookmark or favorites menu. While viewing a web page containing desired images, a user invokes PageComber. It examines the page and displays a new page with a list of images that it found on the original page. Each image is represented as follows:

- A scaled-down version of the image is displayed.

- A set of checkboxes (unchecked by default) is available to choose the image(s) to be collected.

- A *Title* label and text field with a title for the collected image is displayed. The default is the file name, but this can be edited by the user. Title text values must be unique for collected images.

After selecting the image(s), the user can click on the Collect Selected Images button. If a Collectus set is already open, the images are added to that set. If not, Collectus starts a new set and adds the images. The user can save the set, modify its contents, and display collected items as a slide show or web pages.

There are two caveats. First, the image that a user selects can be any size or resolution, and may not be of equal quality to images that are available from the library's collection or that have been digitized for instructional use. Clicking on a thumbnail will collect the thumbnail, not a larger image that the thumbnail might link to. Following a thumbnail to the largest image available will provide the best results. Second, no images are actually downloaded. Collectus stores URLs, not files, so if an image that is collected is deleted or moved, that image is lost to Collectus. Downloading is not supported out of concern for potential rights issues in making use of files when the rights status is not known. Legally, linking is a much less risky feature to support, because it falls within fair use. Unfortunately, this is not an optimal personal information preservation strategy.

In 2008 the UVa Library's Instructional Scanning unit began offering the option to load digitized course materials directly into Collab. The Scholarly Resources unit also began offering services to scan personal faculty

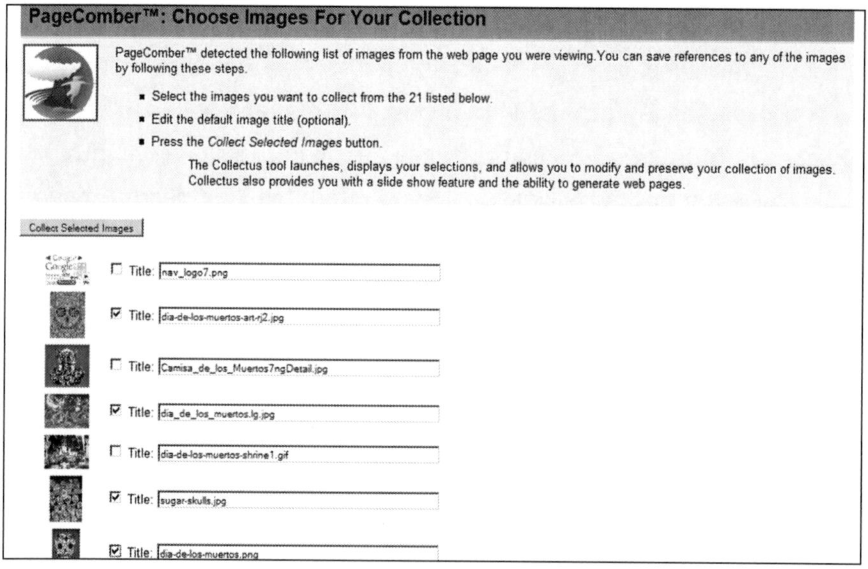

Figure 9. Selecting images to collect from a web page using PageComber.

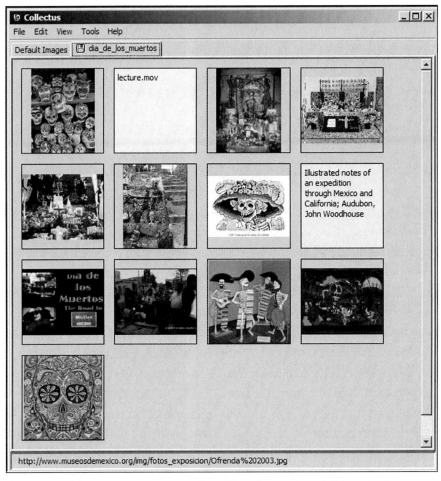

Figure 10. Portfolio containing resources collected from the repository, Collab, and using PageComber.

collections (with proper copyright clearances) directly into Collab. For the first time, faculty could mingle images found on the Web, images downloaded from licensed databases such as ARTstor, personal digital media files, and items from the library's digital collection in a single tool for organization, annotation, and sharing.

Planned Directions

The ultimate goal for the Academic Information Space is a "scholar's workbench"—an integrated framework where faculty store, create, collect, manage, and use digital objects in their full range of scholarly and teaching activities. The suite of tools would include easy-to-use tools for the capture, organization, editing, and presentation of the most commonly used media by faculty.

The conceptual similarity between the process of creating born-digital scholarly projects and online exhibition building at cultural heritage organizations is frequently noted. The Virtual Exhibition Tool (VET) was one possible next-generation tool to make it easier for faculty to do more sophisticated presentations in either web pages or slide show formats. It would also allow faculty to pass data between all the tools in the suite to better support their scholarship and teaching. In 2008, the project considered Pachyderm, an open source tool originally developed by the San Francisco Museum of Modern Art, which allows users to organize and design their own slide shows.[13] As originally implemented, Pachyderm assumed that the user has imported images into Pachyderm itself. UVa developers planned to update the application so faculty can build collections and create slide shows using a variety of source material. The goal was to make it possible for Pachyderm not just to store files, but also to point to resources elsewhere online in the same way that Collectus did. This would give faculty a useful tool to do lectures and presentations without potentially violating fair use with a copied file. In addition, this would represent gains in both efficiency and productivity for faculty, as they would be able to integrate materials from a variety of sources into a single presentation. Pachyderm could support more media types than the current tools, extending the usefulness into true multimedia instruction. The next logical step could be to open up the code so that lecture presentations can be saved and reused, making it possible for a faculty member to iterate and to elaborate on earlier work.

Strategies for finding information have been the subject of considerable study in the field of information retrieval. But what does one do with that information once one has found it? How does one organize and retain what he or she found without knowing how and when it might be used it in the future? The ability to manage information for use over time is the single most vital component of what is commonly called personal information management, which, not surprisingly, is indeed very personal in nature.[14] The realm of personal information management studies encompasses all acquisition of information, its organization into personal management systems, and strategies for rediscovery and use. In many Keeping Found Things Found (KFTF) studies, participants often expressed frustration over the need to maintain multiple organizational strategies and locations in parallel.[15] Which is used under what circumstances? What is the cost of employing multiple schemes in multiple locations? How are resources assembled later when needed?

> The assembly of task–relevant information can be a problem even if people know where to look for each item. Considerable time may be required to retrieve information from different places and across several different information forms (e-mail, e-documents, Web references, paper) in order to complete a task. When information is scattered, there is also increased danger that some information relevant to a task is simply overlooked or forgotten about altogether.[16]

Of recent note in the body of research into personal digital management strategies is the Digital Lives project coordinated by the British Library:

> Not surprisingly, given the inexorable march of technological innovation, individuals are capturing and storing an ever-increasing amount of digital information about or for themselves, including documents, articles, portfolios of work, digital images, and audio and video recordings. People can now correspond by email, have personal Web pages, blogs, and electronic diaries. Many issues arise from this increasingly empowered landscape of personal collection, dissemination, and digital memory, which will have major future impacts on librarianship and archival practice as our lives are increasingly recorded digitally rather than on paper. Not only the media and formats but, as we discovered in our research into digital collections, also the contents of works created by individuals are changing in their exploitation of the possibilities afforded them by the various software applications available. We need to understand and address these issues now if future historians, biographers and curators are to be able to make sense of life in the early twenty-first century. There is a real danger otherwise that we will lose whole swathes of personal, family and cultural memory.[17]

The work at the University of Virginia Library is less focused on keeping found things found, information management, or preservation, than it is on making personal collections more usable. Of course, the suite of tools is designed to support multiple strategies for aggregating information from multiple sources, allowing the management and organization of the aggregated resources in place of disparate sets. But personal collections should be coupled with tools that support their use, such as tools to create personal portfolios of objects, analyze texts, tag and annotate objects, generate slide shows or web pages, and otherwise author and share digital work.

The issues of information gathering and management strategies and preservation should in no way be downplayed. Information gathering and management are often-studied topics. One of the most important research topics in this realm is that of preservation: file format documentation and sustainability; standards for metadata and data exchange; and format transformation and migration strategies. And the most basic questions of all remains: where will all these growing personal digital collections be stored and how will that storage be maintained?

The work of tool building must itself also be openly shared and collaborative. The UVa Library created the Collectus digital object collector tool as a generalizable tool for any type of repository. For example, it was integrated into a proof-of-concept project for the Digital Library Federation's Aquifer initiative.[18] The source code for Collectus is readily available. The UVa use of Collab as a gathering point is extensible to other Sakai environments.

One of the most interesting tools to come out of this problem space was the prototype Scholar's Box from the Interactive University Project at the University of California, Berkeley.[19] Their mantra was "Gather. Create. Share." The tool supported the collection of resources from California Digital Library collections and its metasearch, amazon.com, Google, NSDL (National Science Digital Library), RSS (Really Simple Syndication) feeds, METS (Metadata Encoding and Transmission Standard) files, the open Web, and local file systems. Files could be organized and annotated, and then shared as IMS-CP (IMS Content Packaging), an OpenOffice.org presentation, PDF (Portable Document Format), HTML, a METS document, a set of Endnote references, a Chandler parcel, or sent to a blog via the Blogger API (Application Program

Interface). The tool never went into full production, but was approved for release as a SourceForge project.[20] The concept has since inspired tools for new projects.[21]

In more recent work, Omeka is emerging as a tool for making collections usable.[22] Omeka is a free and open source collections-based, web-based publishing platform developed by the Center for History and New Media at George Mason University. Omeka is designed with scholars and librarians in mind, allowing users to focus on content and interpretation rather than programming. It brings new interactive technologies to the creation of academic and cultural websites to foster user participation by employing a flexible templating system. Omeka supports the building of collections as a way to organize items, and the building of an exhibition that presents a contextual story around collections to better share them. While this is a tool optimized for individual use, it is not a desktop tool or a generally available web tool—it requires hosting on a web server and requires image manipulation software. This is a tool worth following.

Faculty have a sense of vision and expectation as to the use of new technologies in higher education: all forms of digital media, aggregated from a variety of sources or created by themselves, made reusable to be mixed and remixed in multiple contexts for teaching, research, and scholarly communication. For as long as cultural heritage and higher education institutions have been creating digital resources, faculty members have been building extensive personal digital collections using a wide variety of means. Fostering innovation requires that scholars have available to them a set of flexible tools and services not only to gather resources from every appropriate source, including institutional digital libraries, but also to manipulate those resources for their own purposes. For those personal collections to be made more useful and usable, such tools that support the transformation of such collections into new forms of scholarly output are of critical importance.

Notes

[1] Neil Beagrie, "Plenty of Room at the Bottom? Personal Digital Libraries and Collections," *D-Lib Magazine* 11, no. 6 (June 2005), http://dx.doi.org/10.1045/june2005-beagrie.

[2] http://www2.lib.virginia.edu/scholarslab/.

[3] See Valley of the Shadow at http://valley.vcdh.virginia.edu/; the Rossetti Archive at http://www.rossettiarchive.org/; the Tibetan and Himalayan Library at http://www.thlib.org/; the Salem Witch Trials Documentary Archive at http://etext.virginia.edu/salem/witchcraft/; and the Salisbury Project at http://salisbury.art.virginia.edu/.

[4] For information on these tools see iView at http://www.iview-multimedia.com/mediapro/; Canto Cumulus at http://www.canto.com/en/products/; and Extensis Portfolio at http://www.extensis.com/en/products/asset_management/product_information.jsp?id=2000.

[5] For information on Luna Insight see http://www.lunaimaging.com/insight/index.html; for EmbARK see http://www.gallerysystems.com/products/embark.html.

[6] See James Madison University's MDID at http://mdid.org/; UVa's User Collection Tool at http://iris.lib.virginia.edu/dmmc/collectiontool/; Princeton's Almagest at http://www.princeton.edu/~almagest/opensource/; and OCLC's ContentDM at http://www.contentdm.com/.

[7] See http://www.emc.com/products/family/documentum-family.htm.

[8] See Paul W. Dourish, W. Keith Edwards, Anthony LaMarca, and Michael Salisbury, "Presto: An Experimental Architecture for Fluid Interactive Document Spaces," *ACM Transactions on Computer-Human Interaction* 6, no. 2 (1999): 133–61.

[9] See http://iris.lib.virginia.edu/dmmc/collectiontool/.

[10] See the library website at http://lib.virginia.edu/digital/collections/. See also Leslie Johnston, "An Overview of Digital Library Repository Development at the University of Virginia Library," *OCLC Systems and Services* 20, no. 4 (2004): 170–73; and Leslie Johnston, "Development and Assessment of a Public Discovery and Delivery Interface for a Fedora Repository," *D-Lib Magazine* 11, no. 10 (2005), http:// dx.doi.org/10.1045/october2005-johnston.

[11] See http://sakaiproject.org/; https://collab.itc.virginia.edu/portal.

[12] Abby Smith, "Authenticity and Affect: When Is a Watch not a Watch?" *Library Trends* 52 (Summer 2003): 172–82.

[13] See http://www.pachyderm.org/.

[14] M. Lansdale, "The Psychology of Personal Information Management," *Applied Ergonomics* 19, no. 1 (March 1988): 55–66.

[15] William Jones, Harry Bruce, and Susan Dumais, "Keeping Found Things Found on the Web," in *Proceedings of the 2001 ACM CIKM: Tenth International Conference on Information and Knowledge Management: November 5–10, 2001, Atlanta, Georgia, USA*, ed. Henrique Paques, Ling Liu, and David A. Grossman (New York: Association for Computing Machinery, 2001), 119–26; William Jones, Susan Dumais, and Harry Bruce, "Once Found, What Then? A Study of 'Keeping' Behaviors in the Personal Use of Web Information," in *Proceedings of the 65th Annual Meeting of the American Society for Information Science and Technology (ASIST 2002), Philadelphia, PA*, ed. Edie Rasmussen and Elaine G. Toms (Medford, NJ: Information Today, 2002), 391–402; William Jones, "Finders, Keepers? The Present and Future Perfect in Support of Personal Information Management," *First Monday* 9, no. 3 (March 2004), http://firstmonday.org/article/view/1123/1043; and William Jones, *Keeping Found Things Found: The Study and Practice of Personal Information Management* (San Francisco: Morgan Kaufmann, 2007).

[16] Jones, "Finders, Keepers?"

17 Pete Williams, Katrina Dean, Ian Rowlands, and Jeremy Leighton John, "Digital Lives: Report of Interviews with the Creators of Personal Digital Collections," *Ariadne* 55 (April 2008), http://www.ariadne.ac.uk/issue55/williams-et-al/.

18 Robert Chavez, Timothy W. Cole, Muriel Foulonneau, Thomas G. Habing, Jon Dunn, William Parod, and Thornton Staples, "DLF-Aquifer Asset Actions Experiment: Demonstrating Value of Actionable URLs," *D-Lib Magazine* 12, no. 10 (October 2006), http://dx.doi.org/10.1045/october2006-cole.

19 See http://interactiveu.berkeley.edu:8000/IU/SB.

20 See http://sourceforge.net/projects/scholarsbox/.

21 See http://okapi.wordpress.com/projects/fipse-the-scholars-box/ and http://mediavault.wordpress.com/.

22 See http://omeka.org/.

Curating the I, Digital: Experiences at the Bodleian Library

Susan Thomas

This chapter examines how the University of Oxford's Bodleian Library has begun to develop its traditional role as a repository of private papers to enable it to cope with the realities of the way individuals create their archives today. It provides an overview of a research library's engagement with digital archiving to date, illustrating some of the processes and problems involved through the library's day-to-day experiences of building and managing hybrid collections. It also touches on new developments made possible by the futureArch project, including the use of digital forensics tools for capture and analysis of digital archives.

On the 8th of November 1602, the Bodleian Library opened its doors to scholars. This was a re-founding of the University of Oxford's library, whose history can be traced back to the early fourteenth century. It was in this former existence that the library received its first major gift of manuscripts: more than 280 from Humfrey, Duke of Gloucester, between 1439 and 1444.[1] The library's Western Manuscripts department cares for the second largest collection in Britain, with manuscripts spanning a chronological spectrum from the third century BC to the here and now.

With such a bedrock of manuscript collections, it is no surprise that born-digital manuscripts form but an infinitesimal proportion of total manuscript holdings, and this picture will hold true for some time. Nonetheless, like archival repositories the world over, the Bodleian has been the recipient of odd bits of digital media in its archival deposits for more than a decade. By and large, these have entered the stacks alongside their analogue counterparts; decisions about how to manage them being put on hold until such a time as the archive is processed for research use, as closure periods cease and funding permits.

Heightened understanding of digital preservation concerns, including media degradation and technical obsolescence, means that it would be negligent to continue overlooking the needs of the library's existing born-digital manuscript holdings in this way. What should perhaps be of more concern to scholars is the relative *lack* of digital material in the library's late twentieth- and early twenty-first-century manuscript holdings. The documentary footprint for almost anyone born in the West from the mid-twentieth century onwards will be partly digital; and for those "digital natives" coming of age now, and their successors, it will be predominantly so.[2] To continue collecting rich personal archives, research libraries like the Bodleian must grapple with the impact of social and technical change on the personal record, and respond with greater agility to the realities of contemporary and future personal archives. This response must speak to the hybridity of personal archives—a jumble of the digital and the analogue—and it must be evident in all aspects of archival work including collection development, preservation, processing, and access services.

The Bodleian has begun to craft its response to the evolution of the personal record. In a first step, the library led a collaborative, hands-on project named Paradigm.[3] This project drew on traditional archival and records management practices, as well as techniques emerging from the digital curation and preservation communities, to curate sample hybrid archives of contemporary politicians.[4] Paradigm's sphere of enquiry encompassed the entire life of personal archival material, from inception to reuse by a researcher. The work exposed the project team—a multidisciplinary group of two archivists and a software engineer—to a wide range of cultural, legal, and technical issues, shaping the library's future development priorities in the process. Paradigm also produced an online workbook, which introduces the topics confronted in the project, setting these in the context of an institution collecting the (partly digital) footprints of individuals.[5] Subsequent to Paradigm, the library undertook some follow-up work on capturing metadata about digital archives. This work—the Cairo project—was another collaborative venture. Few archival institutions have a critical mass of skills and experience in this arena; exchanging ideas, stories and tools among like-minded institutions can be a fruitful and enjoyable means of making progress.[6]

During these two digital curation projects, the Bodleian established a prototype stand-alone digital archive and some limited processes for accepting born-digital manuscript material. Inevitably, as work on the projects unfolded, colleagues involved in the acquisition and processing of manuscript collections were encountering more in the way of digital material. This set the scene for useful interaction between project work and the day-to-day activities of the Western Manuscripts department: the projects enabled the library to acquire and process materials in ways that would previously have been impossible, and the departmental work provided a useful reality check for project activities, as well as an opportunity to widen the pool of colleagues getting more actively involved with digital manuscripts.

The Paradigm and Cairo projects were made possible through grant funding.[7] This has proven an excellent means of getting started, but if curating the "I, Digital" is to become a norm at any research library, then commitment to underwriting the activities involved is necessary. In the autumn of 2008, the Bodleian set the futureArch project in motion.[8] This project is again sponsored by an outside agency—on this occasion, the Andrew W. Mellon Foundation—but it is an implementation project, with a remit to go beyond exploratory and prototyping work. Through futureArch, the library will begin to embed hybrid archivy—and its subdomain, digital curation—into the everyday life of its archives and manuscripts work. To do so entails policy and budgetary alterations, as well as changes in procedures and infrastructure. The project builds on previous projects, departmental work, interdepartmental work and external collaborations, all of which have contributed to the library's vision of what might be desirable and possible where curating the I, Digital is concerned. When futureArch draws to a close in 2012, the Bodleian Electronic Archives and Manuscripts (BEAM) repository should be established as integral to the systems—both human and machine—which curate digital manuscripts at the library.

Selecting and Collecting

Collection development will always be a subject of ideological debate among archivists and scholars. This discussion will leave aside the question of *whose* archives the library should be collecting, and *what* it intends to document for *whom*. Instead, the focus will be on adjustments that the library is making to cater for the I, Digital: the question of *how*, insofar as this can be divorced from the question of *what*.

Initial experiences with hybrid archives have compelled the library's curatorial staff to imagine a blend of different approaches to collection development. One of these is the proactive approach advocated by a number of writers, perhaps most evocatively in Adrian Cunningham's ghost train depiction:

> Failure to pursue a more active agenda will leave us patiently waiting at the railway station for the goods train of life to deliver the unreliable electronic leavings of our society's movers and shakers. Years of passive and patient pacing of the platform will come to an end, I fear, when the whistle blows and the train pulls in to the station and we finally come to the realization that it is full of ghosts and that ghosts do not satisfy our researchers' need for solid, reliable, and authentic evidence of the past.[9]

One of the Paradigm project's curatorial aims was to evaluate the efficacy of a proactive approach to collection development, largely motivated by the perception that personal digital archives are more volatile and vulnerable than their analogue counterparts. Because of the library's reputation as a major repository for the private papers of politicians, Paradigm was able to identify politicians who would act as potential depositors, contributing materials to Paradigm's testbed.[10] Working with creators through Paradigm provided useful lessons, but it was not an ideal test case for proactive archival engagement with them; the "project" nature of the activity did not reflect the reality of a long-term depositor-library relationship, and gaining access to working politicians and contemporary materials was challenging, especially during the election year of 2005.[11] The library is increasingly applying a proactive approach as one strand of its regular collection development activity, however, and the relationships and collections formed during everyday departmental activity are more informative than Paradigm's artificial scenario.

Record surveys are a useful tool for proactive collection development and form part of more opportunistic collection development practices, too. Surveys provide a window on the lives of record creators and permit the archivist to glean something of the recordkeeping personalities[12] of those whose archives are, or will be, collected. It is sometimes necessary to visit multiple sites in order to survey materials and environments that reflect professional and personal capacities; similarly to surveying "physical" archives, there are numerous containers to consider: local hard disks, networked storage, online stores, and offline media. Hybrid archives surveyed to-date include those of an academic, a book trader, a diplomat, a designer, a writer, a publisher, and a few politicians. In most cases, the creator of the archive surveyed is middle aged and well-established in his or her field, although the library has also surveyed a few hybrid archives after the death of their creators. When surveying the digital portion of a hybrid archive, the digital archivist records technical information about how the material has been created and organized, including data about hardware, software, and online services that have shaped the nature of the archive, and its processing requirements. To record at least a little technical metadata is instinctive to archivists and manuscript curators: while processing a digital archive for ingest to BEAM recently, the digital archivist consulted notes relating to the deposit's file formats made by the accessioning curator in 2001.[13] Technical information of this nature is invaluable and can save considerable technical detective work once the digital material is transferred to the library.

Much that has been encountered in the library's survey work may be familiar to those who conduct research in the areas of human-computer interaction or personal information management.[14] Archivists see a great deal of variety in technical sophistication, specialized applications, organization of personal and professional information, and other aspects of personal recordkeeping behavior. Common trends are also evident, including copious amounts of email, office type documents, and images; growth in the use of web-based storage and services ("the cloud"); and a proliferation of mobile devices and peripherals. Issues of concern include absence of backup facilities; email storage quotas that encourage deletion; changes in circumstance or technology that result in inadvertent losses; disinterest in continuing accessibility beyond short-term needs; poor intellectual control of digital information; old materials now semi-mysterious and inaccessible;

and ignorance of terms and conditions of online services. Good practices are observed too; these are often prompted by the experience of losing data, whether that loss is wholesale or merely a glitch of personal memory or systems availability. An awareness of the technological persuasions and information management habits of the library's potential depositors not only helps in the processing of their particular archive, but it also informs a wider "technology watch" function, which will assist the library as it attempts to identify and act upon trends that have implications for forthcoming accessions.

In an ideal scenario, record surveys include extensive discussion with the creator of the archive and/or the creators' significant others. Conversations address what could and should form part of the archive, so the depositor can make informed decisions about what he or she wishes to convey to the library, and when and how (copies of) material should be transported. Such discussions provide an opportunity for archivists to gather valuable contextual information that will support future arrangement, description, administration, and use of the archive, including the identities and interests of individuals and organizations represented in the archive. The library's experiences of proactive collection development to-date suggest that while individuals may be willing to discuss their archive with the library, many wish to defer the transfer of materials until a much later date. In some cases individuals are more willing to deposit material in portions, although more personal materials may be withheld for substantial periods of time. For digital materials, the library is keen to shrink the time lag between the creation of material and its deposit at a research library. Digital material accessioned closer to its time of creation is more likely to be viable and in a contemporary and familiar format; earlier accessioning also presents the option of returning to the creator with questions about the material should this be necessary.

The library accepts digital material via a number of routes. This includes whole computers and old media, acquired largely through more traditional "bulk" accessions. During the Paradigm project, the library began offering archivist-mediated transfer from live systems using removable media. Such transfers require knowledge of authentic extraction techniques, including familiarity with relevant applications and services; by way of example, the library has encountered creators managing email in CompuServe, Microsoft Outlook, Mozilla Thunderbird, and Qualcomm Eudora clients.[15] On one occasion, the creator's IT support facility was called upon to extract material at the server side and to provide this in a suitable format. The library also receives material copied to removable media by creators, delivered either in person or via a secure courier. For small deposits, it is becoming more common for depositors known to the library to email attachments to specific curators. Some of these methods are not ideal from the perspective of maintaining contextual information and metadata, but they have parallels in the analogue domain and collecting archivists are seldom afforded the luxury of being overly picky in their transfer requirements. To facilitate more regular acquisitions from some creators, the library is investigating secure web-based deposit and email deposit mechanisms for BEAM as part of the futureArch project. However depositors wish to transfer their materials, developing relationships with them at an earlier stage can assist in identifying and mitigating risks to components of the archive.

Problems with Proactive Collection Development

While the approach of working proactively with contemporary creators has a number of advantages, it is undoubtedly complex and requires care. Some of the creators the library has worked with are content to pass on older paper materials, but do not see their more contemporary digital files as "archives." Providing access to, or copies of, more recent digital material can be nerve-racking for creators; it is often while guiding the archivist through their systems and materials that the realities of "being archived" shifts from being an abstract concept to something more concrete in the creator's mind. At this point, depositors may stumble on forgotten or sensitive materials, or materials created by, or for, another family member or close friend. The ease with which the digital may be distributed and interrogated inspires uncertainty in some. Depositors must be confident that the library can manage their digital material appropriately; security for digital materials must be trustworthy and curatorial practices ethical.

Some depositors of personal archives are quite hostile to the idea of researchers interpreting their life's work posthumously through examination of their personal lives and the personal lives of those whom they live alongside. For this reason, the Bodleian contains many personal archives that reveal much more about the professional lives of their creators than their personal lives. These may not be optimal from the biographer's perspective, but they are perfectly valid archives for many other kinds of research, including work related to particular topics or events. The intermingling of data documenting both personal and more public personas can be problematic for individuals and their families.[16] Digital technologies are not yet able to make such human distinctions, and even those making special efforts to segregate aspects of their lives are subject to the reconstruction of their multiple selves through analyses of primary desktop computers, laptops, and web services. There are many traces which can assist archivists and researchers to connect the dots, if they have a mind to do so. It will be important to discuss these issues up front and agree on the scope and content of the archive as well as how material is to be made available to researchers.[17] Archivists could employ redaction techniques to publish some items while obscuring confidential snippets. The library does not employ redaction for paper collections and must consider whether it is appropriate to do so for digital archives; for the near-future it seems likely that curatorial staff will continue to apply closure periods to whole items and/or series of materials in consultation with important parties.

Flexibility and capacity are two further considerations for repositories thinking of adopting more proactive approaches to collection development. When judging the effectiveness of a proactive approach, it is necessary to make this assessment relative to a particular individual. Consideration of domain-specific issues—the different circumstances of a politician, a scientist, and a writer—may also be useful. Regular contact between the library and potential depositors is worth striving for where both parties see a benefit, but the regularity and nature of the contact will vary according to the needs and wishes of the depositor. Libraries must also attend to the obvious management issues associated with maintaining relationships with several creators over extended periods of time.[18] Personal and organizational upheavals may occur on either side of the creator-library relationship, and curators will be more reliant than ever on the library's own records, which are themselves increasingly born digital.

When approaching creators at an earlier stage in their lives it is usually necessary to consider the "physical" element of a hybrid archive alongside the digital. While libraries may wish to accession portions of digital material sooner after their creation, the same desire may not apply to paper materials so readily. Unless paper material is at risk in its current environment, libraries may prefer to defer the accession of this bulky material rather than storing it for extended periods of time before it can be considered for processing and research use.

Questions of monetary value must also be examined for those manuscript collections that are offered for sale rather than gifted. It is thought-provoking to hear representatives of the trade in archives and manuscripts discuss some of the factors that determine an archive's price tag.[19] The value attributed to archives of similar quality is often cited as an important consideration in valuation, but at present it is unclear whether dealers have a working definition for *quality* in a digital context. Creators and vendors appear hesitant to perceive a market for digital archives, perhaps thinking that libraries and private collectors are either uninterested or ill-prepared to purchase born-digital material. A knowledge-base to support valuation of born-digital manuscripts will be slow to evolve while digital material is absent from collections presented for sale, or present only in tiny proportions at the chronological periphery of the material.

The adoption of a collecting strategy that favors working with creators to accession materials earlier could have implications for value. The total paid for a sequence of accessions could turn out to be rather more (or less) than the value of the resulting archive as a whole, depending on the career trajectory of the creator and the quality of the material deposited. How would a depositor feel having discovered that selling later could have been more profitable? Would an arrangement to sell regular installments of an individual's archive generate more, less, or different, material for the archive? These are delicate concerns which could complicate depositor-library relations.

While there continues to be much ambivalence surrounding digital manuscripts, firmer resolutions regarding value and the process of valuation are some way off. In the meantime, it will be useful for curators to know whether or not the born-digital component has been actively considered in the valuation of a larger hybrid archive. Arguably, curators and dealers should also begin discussing the mechanics of appraising digital material, if only to ensure that materials held on read/write media are not inadvertently modified during the valuation process.

The library's experiences during the Paradigm project suggest that any form of proactive collection must be combined with capacity for dealing with collections acquired through more reactive, opportunistic, means.[20] The library will be offered hybrid archives that it has not planned for, but wishes to accession. Among that material will be a mixture of physical media, from which data must be authentically captured. Increasingly, there will also be materials online—in "the cloud"—that are vulnerable. Some cloud services expire user accounts if they have been inactive or if payments have been missed. There are also risks associated with the novelty of cloud services: the products offered could be prone to change as business models are refined and the sector sees some participating businesses merge or fail.

Dealing with Legacy Born-Digital Material and Managing New Arrivals

It is not currently possible to name the Bodleian's first hybrid archive with any certitude, but it might well be an accession containing six computer tapes and hundreds of datacards received at the Rhodes House Library in 1996. This uncertainty exists because the library has not, until very recently, consistently recorded information about the formats of materials received in archive and manuscript collections.

In the past few years the need for an accurate picture of the library's born-digital archive and manuscripts has become increasingly obvious, and to that end a number of activities have taken place. An important first measure has been to survey current curatorial staff, asking them about born-digital material in the holdings for which they are responsible; in doing so a number of legacy hybrid collections have been identified and it has been possible to record information concerning the range, quantity, and condition of the born-digital material they contain. Alongside this activity, the library is gradually embedding digital considerations in the everyday accessions workflow. This is largely thanks to a working group established to reexamine accessioning procedures for archives and manuscripts; the group designed a model for a new collections management database for archives and manuscripts. Each new accession arriving at the library is recorded in the database, and it is now also possible to record the physical format of the incoming material using an extensible vocabulary of analogue and digital forms. The database also records whether digital material has been diverted to BEAM so that the processes applicable to digital accessions can be set in motion. Curators may record that "all," "all known," or "some" digital material has been transferred to BEAM, or state that the question is "not applicable" for those collections which do not contain digital material. This flexibility caters for a range of scenarios, including accessions of such magnitude that each box must be examined before it can be ascertained that all digital material has been transferred to BEAM.

Capture and Ingest of Born-Digital Material

Digital materials require more active preservation than paper. For newly accessioned digital manuscripts, a process of triage, capture, and stabilisation close to the time of accession is optimal, and sometimes vital. This involves the creation of authentic representations of the data stored on digital media, and its submission to BEAM's repository where bit-level integrity can be properly monitored. As well as tweaking the larger accessioning workflow, futureArch is refining the sub-workflow applicable to the capture and ingest of digital content into BEAM and is applying this process retrospectively in order to capture legacy digital archives within the library's collections.

BEAM will incorporate different flavours of digital "capture," depending on the nature of the material. Born-digital materials may be a relatively recent phenomenon, but the category contains a degree of diversity belied by a catch-all term. It is worth developing an appreciation of how computing norms have developed over time to place the materials received in context.[21] Much of the digital material the library receives in posthumous deposits, or deposits from individuals whose working life has ceased, is from the 1980s and early 1990s. Word-processed files predominate in all BEAM's accessions created during this time. Some three hundred word processing applications existed for the IBM PC in 1983; BEAM holds very few word processing formats in comparison, but examples accessioned so far include versions of: Locomotive Locoscript (not for the IBM PC), Samna Word, Ami, WordPerfect, Wordstar, WriteNow, and MS Word.[22] The files have been generated on home computers; many represent the drafting of literary works, although other documentary forms, such as correspondence, are present. It is clear that print was the intended destination for much of the material.

For pertinent older digital media and file formats, BEAM is gradually accumulating hardware, software, licences, and documentation to rebuild the stacks that form part of rescue operations. Some of this supporting infrastructure arrives with the collections themselves; some of it is acquired from other sources. An example of this kind of capture is the retrieval of data from the three-inch Amstrad disks received as part of British Labour politician Barbara Castle's personal archive in 2006. These disks mainly contained drafts of Castle's memoirs, which were written using an Amstrad PCW—a personal computer designed with word processing in mind. The deposit also included two personal computers used by Castle's personal secretaries in the 1990s. The Castle archive is typical of the kind of hybrid deposit that appears to be on the increase at the Bodleian: a collection which is substantially traditional in format, but includes digital artefacts from the adoption of computing technologies in the 1980s and early 1990s, typically representing the later years of the individual's lifetime.

To liberate the data on the three-inch disks, the Digital Archivist drew on the knowledge of the Amstrad enthusiast community and sought out a working Amstrad PCW, application software, and manuals. The final solution involved a migration technology—a special linking cable and software (for the PC and the PCW)—originally created to facilitate the move from the Amstrad PCW platform to the PC. The PC version of the migration software ran on the MS Windows 95 operating system which was supplied as a "virtual machine" running on a contemporary SUSE Linux laptop. The migration software was also able to migrate the files originally created in Locomotive Locoscript format to American Standard Code for Information Interchange (ASCII) or Rich Text Format (RTF), thus creating documents that could be read on a modern system.[23] This solution is now documented and can be reapplied; in fact, it was partially reapplied in 2008 when the library undertook some file format migration on behalf of the Wellcome Library, and will be used again for materials in the Bodleian's United Nations Career Records Project archive. Further extraction and migration processes will be recorded in a digital curation manual initiated through the futureArch project.

There are myriad issues associated with the use of obsolescent computing environments to rescue digital data created in corresponding environments. Such work is often called "digital archaeology," and it raises questions of durability, expertise, and scalability that are addressed elsewhere and will not be repeated in detail here.[24] One unfortunate consequence of digital archaeology that may be less well known is that the metadata associated with a file, including its creation and last modified dates, may be obliterated in the process of rescue. Digital archaeology acts as a component in BEAM's capture workflow, but that is not to say that BEAM intends to equip itself to rescue any kind of digital data; with permissions from the depositor's representatives and the help of trusted partners, some of this work may be outsourced to other libraries and reputable data rescue companies.

The library does not expect to provide researchers with access to functioning obsolescent hardware or media to access "originals," but is considering providing researchers with access to emulators. These tools simulate earlier computing environments and permit the viewing of digital files in their original formats. In order to provide such access mechanisms, BEAM will require ongoing access to some of the software elements (such as operating systems and application software) associated with digital archaeology. The development of "emulation services" suggests that such infrastructure could be shared between archival institutions, although software licensing issues may hinder this.[25]

During the Paradigm project, the library began using the Unix dd tool and Accessdata's Forensic Toolkit (FTK) Imager tool to create "images" of removable media, logical file systems, and directory structures. An "image" may contain the structure and content of the source data—(e.g., the data stored on a Universal Serial Bus (USB) key or recordable compact disc (CD-R)—in a single file; storing the data in this way provides an efficient means of retaining the original order and it may be possible to mount the "image" read-only for exploration purposes. The FTK Imager tool was also used as a means of generating disk inventories, including unique hash values—a kind of digital fingerprint—for files. In futureArch the library is seeking to adopt more precise forensic techniques to capture modern materials.[26] Earlier this year BEAM obtained a forensics workstation, including write-blocking devices, which can acquire forensically sound "images" from a variety of modern removable media and whole hard disks. The write blocker is an essential component, which prevents the archivist from accidentally writing data back to the disk supplied by the depositor. Additionally, BEAM has sourced a robotic forensic imager for optical media, which can be used to image CDs and DVDs en masse. In the future, the library may look to expand this capacity to cater for mobile devices, such as smartphones, personal digital assistants (PDAs), and personal satellite navigation devices.[27]

A further capture technique the library is seeking to add to its armoury is the extraction of personal materials from the plethora of web services typically employed by private individuals. Research data published by the UK's independent regulator for the communications industry (OFCOM) in August 2010 showed that 71 percent of British households had access to broadband (whether fixed or mobile) and that the average download speed obtained through broadband connections was 5.2 megabits per second.[28] The UK government's desire is to further widen participation and improve the infrastructure available.[29] As more individuals are able to tap into a good network connection, there may be little reason to use a local hard disk for storage any longer. Entrusting materials to online services provides access to data at several locations using a range of devices, while leaving basic data maintenance to the professionals. Material is likely to be distributed among private and shared spaces, with the nature of that distribution determined by the privacy preferences, or awareness, of the individual.

Cyberspace presents a raft of additional considerations for archivists. The interactivity in certain online spaces—the social networks, blogs, sharing sites (documents, photos, slides, and videos), microblogging and others—potentially enriches the material, but could prove problematic, too. Ironically, while relationships between people can be made explicit online, the use of opaque screen names can make it difficult to attribute content to a creator who may be traced offline.[30] There are abundant feedback mechanisms such as comments, tagging, and video (sometimes called 'vlog') responses, which give rise to questions of third parties' rights. The concentration of links inevitably prompts us to ask where the boundaries between personal archives fall: where does one begin and the other end? The instinct to compare with the offline world also leads us to question how different this online world really is. Social networks are not new to archives after all; analogue primary sources such as correspondence, diaries, and journals document them, and the fact that one personal archive connects to another is often a factor in selecting it for preservation. It is the nature of the links that differ: paper links between individuals are not so readily surfaced and manipulated, and the content generated by different parties in the archive is perhaps less intertwined.

How much of the unpublished materials archivists seek to collect will find a home online? Will public figures really use Web 2.0 tools with the level of personal detail and honesty that digital natives do?[31] Maintaining a public online persona can be a significant piece of work: some public figures who use the Twitter microblogging service have employed ghost writers to "tweet" on their behalf.[32] The substitution of the ghost writer's voice for the creator's may be little different from a politician using a speech writer, but it seems inauthentic. In a digital world, it may be all the more interesting to compare the private aspects of a personal digital archive with those that have been published. The personal archives the library seeks to acquire and curate in the next few years may be more concerned with acquiring data from the less public online spaces—the chats, calendaring, general private storage, sharing sites, text messages, and webmail services. It is difficult to know how soon curators will be called upon to archive an individual's social network profile or Twitter feed; much will depend on the individuals whose archives the library collects in the coming years.

An important aspect of futureArch is to explore the issue of acquiring content from online services in more depth. The project will draft a model of the ethical, legal, technical, and content-related considerations that come into play and seek to populate that model with data about some services. Flux in the terms and conditions and programming interfaces of services will render any collated data outdated in short order, but the results should serve as a guide to the kinds of issues at stake. Two of many areas that require further exploration are whether the creators have the rights and the means to give the library their data (and data shared with them by others), and how the creators' data structures and metadata can be acquired alongside their data. One thing is certain: during discussions with creators and families, it is imperative that archivists sketch a detailed map of the creators' online data stores, and determine with them which aspects of their online presence will form part of their archives. This entails making provisions that enable the library to acquire the specified digital content from third-party web services at the right time; it may require some form of interaction with the service provider as well as a mechanism for the creator to pass on relevant uniform resource locators (URLs) and account credentials.

Appraisal, Selection, and Arrangement

Forensic tools may be applied to archival processes beyond capture, including appraisal, selection, and arrangement tasks. The futureArch project is employing many useful tricks built on the concept of hashing—the process of generating a unique signature for a file through an algorithm such as MD5 or SHA-1. Hashes are used as means of managing authenticity and monitoring bit-level preservation, but they also have other uses. Using a library of hash values associated with software files, it is possible to filter out a good deal of "noise"—known software or system files—when examining a hard disk.[33] Experience of examining relatively small hard disk images (up to 2.1 gigabyte) without the assistance of filtering has confirmed its utility. With bigger hard disks encouraging the addition of more software, and software bloat, yet more filtering will be required to focus on the data that really matters.[34] Another use for hashing is identifying duplicates. These duplicates may exist in different locations on the same media, as identical copies on different media (common in backup scenarios, or instances of PC migration), or they might be on media sourced from different depositors who form part of the same social network (not necessarily in the online sense; perhaps only in the sense of being socially connected). Files identical in content, but with different file names, can also be identified as duplicates. In collections the library has processed so far this occurs where material has been "deleted" on an MS Windows machine and the operating system has simply moved and renamed the file according to a DC##.ext convention (e.g., DC28.doc). Fuzzy hashing is another promising tool that may be capable of expediting the identification of similar files created in the drafting process.[35]

The futureArch project's exploration of forensic software tools is two-pronged. Initially the focus is on open source tools, such as those available in the bootable Linux distributions, and a proprietary product known as Forensic Toolkit.[36] The Toolkit's interface, which sits above an Oracle database, contains powerful indexing, filtering, and exploration tools, including the ability to view a great many formats using Oracle Outside In technology. The Toolkit also permits the archivist to explore the contents of several images, which is useful when multiple storage devices are associated with a collection, and to bookmark and export select files. This functionality has proven extremely useful to the digital archivist in preparing data and metadata for use by the library's cataloguing archivists, who are responsible for generating an Encoded Archival Description (EAD) finding aid for the entire hybrid archive.

The use of digital forensics analysis tools has introduced some additional ethical and technical dimensions to the library's work that require further thought. On the ethical front, the archivist must understand what additional data a disk image might contain that is unlikely to be obvious to the creator or his or her family. Such issues also exist for email archives, where depositors forget about the inclusion of previous messages, sent mail, and deleted mail. Archivists must discuss these issues with creators and their families to decide what materials should form part of the archive and what materials should be expunged. The kinds and quantity of unexpected data present is subject to a few variables, including the file system, operating system, and application software in use. Part of the processing may well be the selection, or deselection, of materials in keeping with the depositor's wishes. On the technical front, BEAM needs the capacity to deal with different kinds of media. Additionally, as the disks (or cloud stores) requiring imaging and processing get bigger, and encryption technologies more popular, BEAM will require a good deal more storage and processing power, as well as permission to decrypt from creators or their families. Archivists have an advantage in being a little behind the curve here—we can benefit from decline in storage and processing costs as well as advancements in computer forensics.

Bit-Level Preservation Storage and Beyond

Among the technical aspects of the Paradigm project was the creation of a small digital accessions and archive system to store born-digital archives. Inspired by the set-up at the National Archives in the UK,[37] the Paradigm store was isolated from the network. This eliminated security concerns about uncontrolled proliferation of copies and exposure to hacking, but effectively constrained real access to the onsite project team. Moving away from this system is vital for the library's digital curation activity to scale; with that in mind, incorporating the BEAM repository into the wider library architecture forms a foundation step in the current programme of work on the futureArch project.

There are several genres of digital material within Oxford's libraries, and indeed the wider University, in need of curation. For the libraries' part, these include: published digital content, whether purchased or licensed, hosted at Oxford or elsewhere by a third party; the products of digitization projects, from small "boutique" projects to mass digitization initiatives, such as the GoogleBooks project; the library's own institutional records and archives; the research data and publications produced by the university's academic staff; and the born-digital materials acquired by the Bodleian's Western Manuscripts department. The curatorial requirements of these streams of content differ in important ways, but there are nonetheless significant commonalities that are ripe for exploitation. The development of the Digital Asset Management System (DAMS)—a virtual stack—for the Bodleian Libraries is designed to achieve this by bringing together digital curators and software engineers to build a core common infrastructure for the library's digital library applications.[38]

Conceptually speaking, the DAMS consists of four layers: persistent storage, object management, tools and services (indexing, scheduling, etc.), and applications (such as BEAM). Principles include a focus on generic components, which can more easily be applied to a range of applications. That is to say, if a tool being developed for BEAM purposes has wider application, it ought to be developed as generically as possible, and sit in the tools and services layer, where it can be drawn on by other applications. The library aims to build the DAMS as a series of loosely coupled components, which can be retired and replaced piecemeal. In effect, part of the implementation process should be a consideration of how that component may be retired. The modular architecture gives more flexibility to evolve, rather than forcing the library down a path of radical overhaul when changes are needed. Curators can be reasonably certain that the core content to be preserved will not change, though the environment in which it is processed and consumed can be expected to evolve. A key requirement for BEAM is the implementation of security mechanisms that protect materials from unauthorized access while enabling access to curators and cataloguing archivists on multiple sites. The futureArch project's software engineers are working on this, as well as secure ingest and retrieval mechanisms and coordination of metadata extraction and editing tools.

A related issue that must be tackled is the consolidation of thinking around digital preservation strategy in Paradigm into a digital preservation policy for BEAM, which references real strategies for preservation planning and the execution of preservation actions. The library is looking to the outcomes of the Planets project, a collaborative digital preservation project funded by the European Union, and other third-party developments, to support this work.[39]

Interfaces for Arrangement and Description

The creation of interfaces for curators is fundamental to BEAM's integration in the everyday curation of archives and manuscripts. Curatorial staff need to be able to view machine-generated metadata at all levels of the hierarchy, understand its provenance, and correct versions based on human judgment if necessary. In addition to retaining the material's original order, it should be possible to incorporate the digital material into the intellectual arrangement for the entire hybrid archive, as developed in the finding aid for the collection. Additionally, curators must be able to review files and series to assign closure periods, and to publish (components of) an archive to the reading room access system or the wider open Web. Curatorial interfaces supporting these tasks are not currently available, so a number of manual work-arounds are being used to support the arrangement and description of hybrid archives. As the quantity of digital material being processed and managed grows, these methods will not work for much longer.

Barbara Castle's archive is an example of a hybrid archive that has been catalogued at the Bodleian.[40] To accomplish this, working copies were supplied to the cataloguer along with a spreadsheet containing the filepath and hash value of each data item; for each item a series was recorded, as well as information about the file's access status, its shelfmark, and any other notes. With the exception of the Locoscript files, material was supplied in native file formats (mainly MS Office and WordPerfect 5.1) and viewed using OpenOffice or MS Office.[41] Using spreadsheets for the arrangement process is common practice at the library, and it may be desirable to mimic this ability to allocate material to series and assign shelfmarks in BEAM's curatorial interface. For the purpose of the overall archival catalogue, digital material in the archive appears alongside its paper counterparts and the entire archive is arranged along functional lines with series arranged chronologically. This approach was chosen not only to reflect the hybridity of the archive, but also because the original order was poor: the arrangement of data on the hard disk demonstrated the adoption of the default MS Windows storage locations, and the hierarchy and naming conventions used by Castle's secretaries did not lend meaning. It was also decided to eliminate duplicates, which were found within the same hard disk (evidence of a previous PC migration) and on various floppy disks used for transport or backup. The library has not, however, lost the information which records the original logical location of each file in Castle's digital filing system. With the ability to construct different views of the same data, it is possible to allow readers to discover what material was saved alongside a particular item on a disk. With the depositor's permission, it is also possible to mount hard disk drive images allowing the computer environment to be seen as it was used by the creator, though the absence of shelfmarks could frustrate citation.[42]

Access for Researchers

Researcher access is ultimately the driving force behind all the library's endeavors, and as such, it forms an important part of the development roadmap for BEAM under the futureArch project. Initially, the library foresees that it will need the ability to make some materials available onsite only, with avenues of moving materials out of the system appropriately controlled. On occasion it may be necessary to provide select individuals with access to particular items when they have the depositor's express permission to view otherwise restricted material. As it becomes possible to move material into the public domain, it will be desirable to make some of BEAM's material available online and perhaps if not the material itself, its metadata record if appropriate. To service these requirements, BEAM will need to support sophisticated authentication and authorization models and create publication pathways that may be used by curators to make born-digital material available to researchers at the appropriate level. Services for supplying legitimate copies to researchers must also be devised.

BEAM's interfaces and metadata must also make it possible for the researcher to distinguish between variants of the same item, and to cite these accurately in their works. This could become increasingly important over time if researchers wish to ensure that their work is based on the same variant as used by a predecessor; libraries will need to provide support to researchers and ensure that interfaces are clear in their labeling of originals and derivatives. The ways in which digital archives could be presented and interrogated are potentially very exciting. Imagine the provision of annotation and tagging tools, the ability to browse different facets of one or more collections or series, to compare files, to view originals in emulators, to undertake full-text searching, integration with citation managers, pattern matching, data mining, data visualization—whether chronological, geographical, by relationship, or by frequency of interaction. Researchers may wish to configure their own environments according to their needs, which may vary from those who prefer to have access to the content in modern forms, together with powerful interrogative tools, to those wishing to experience authentic representations of the original versions of digital manuscripts.[43] With so many possibilities and limited resources, the futureArch project will need to prioritise to put its resources to the best use. A major challenge will be catering for the numerous genres—audio, documents, email, images, presentations, spreadsheets, video, webpages—and formats that could exist within a single personal archive.

Beyond the user interface, another consideration is how the physical spaces of the library's reading rooms should evolve to cater for those reading a hybrid archive. At a time when few hybrid archives are available to readers, and few readers are requesting those available, the library needs reader spaces that are flexible enough to cope with a predicted growth in demand, without damaging provision of services to the majority of those reading modern archives and manuscripts.[44]

Perhaps most important of all, curators need a better understanding of what researchers need to work with digital archives. The library began exploring researcher requirements through the Paradigm project's Academic Advisory Board, and further discussion and testing will take place as futureArch develops researcher interfaces for BEAM's repository.

Final Thoughts

While the Bodleian's digital manuscript holdings remain small, they are growing; and as the library puts the right systems and processes in place, curators expect to accommodate more vigorous growth in this area in the near future. The library has much to do before digital curation is truly integrated with archives and manuscripts work, but it is making inroads. Digital curation is not a problem with a final solution; archivists must learn to live with ongoing change in the documentary form and in archiving methodologies. In futureArch, the library has provision for two one-year graduate trainees who will enter the profession from the hybrid perspective, while those archivists already working with modern collections adjust. The issue of resourcing for archives and libraries wanting to expand their capabilities for the digital era may be the most complex. The digital preservation community's understanding of digital curation requirements and cost modeling has improved, but budgeting remains a difficult prospect as the landscape continues to change.[45] New challenges rarely equate with additional resources, forcing institutions to make difficult decisions about the allocation of resources between old and new activities. Staff also need support in acquiring and practicing new skills more often than may have been the case historically. Institutions do not yet know what the profile of roles and responsibilities should be. At the Bodleian, it is anticipated that these will be distributed among existing curatorial staff, the newly created (and developing) BEAM repository, and core IT infrastructure services, but the actual division of roles and responsibilities remains to be seen.

The Bodleian is by no means alone in beginning to curate the I, Digital. Many archives and libraries are engaging with digital curation on some scale; some are tentatively dabbling at the edges, while others are taking the plunge with more gusto. There is a perceptible increase in archivists and curators working with digital archives, as well as a growing developer community supporting the work of some institutions. With the development of these networks emerges a broader and deeper pool of case studies and tools; a bridging of theory and practice. In defiance of the scare stories about digital black holes—a history devoid of the personal—perhaps the phenomenon of the personal archive in the research library may yet survive, even thrive, once the digital tipping point truly hits us.[46]

Notes

[1] Duke Humfrey's manuscripts were dispersed during the 1550s. A very small proportion of the manuscripts are known to have survived; of these, three now reside at the Bodleian (MSS. Duke Humfrey b.1, d.1-2), having been reacquired at a later date. See A. C. de la Mare and Stanley Gillam, *Duke Humfrey's Library and the Divinity School 1488-1988* (exhibition catalogue, Bodleian Library, 1988).

[2] John Palfrey and Urs Gasser use the term *digital natives* to describe those born after 1980, who will never know a predigital world. Their book, *Born Digital: Understanding the First Generation of Digital Natives* (New York: Basic Books, 2008), is a perceptive overview of the ways in which their lives may be different from those who came before.

[3] Paradigm project http://www.webarchive.org.uk/wayback/archive/20081001092838/http://www.paradigm.ac.uk/. See also Susan Thomas and Janette Martin, "Using the Papers of Contemporary British Politicians as a Testbed for the Preservation of Digital Personal Archives," *Journal of the Society of Archivists* 27, no. 1 (April 2006): 29–56.

[4] In the UK, the Digital Preservation Coalition and the Digital Curation Centre act as hubs for institutions interested in digital curation and digital preservation activity.

[5] Paradigm project, *Workbook on Digital Private Papers*, 2007, http://www.webarchive.org.uk/wayback/archive/20081001092937/http://www.paradigm.ac.uk/workbook.

[6] Paradigm was a collaboration with colleagues at the John Rylands Library, University of Manchester. In Cairo, the Bodleian collaborated with colleagues from the Rylands once more, as well as colleagues from the Wellcome Library in London. The library has also benefited from more informal collaborations, including with colleagues at the British Library.

[7] The library is thankful to the Joint Information Systems Committee (JISC) and Oxford University's Research Development Fund for their support of these projects.

[8] futureArch project webpage, http://www.bodleian.ox.ac.uk/beam/projects/futurearch ; futureArch project blog, http://futurearchives.blogspot.com.

[9] Adrian Cunningham, "Waiting for the Ghost Train: Strategies for Managing Electronic Personal Records Before it is Too Late," *Archival Issues: Journal of the Midwest Archives Conference* 24, no. 1 (1999): 55–64.

[10] The word *depositor* is used in this chapter to signify the many kinds of relationships a collecting research library may have with the individual(s) responsible for entrusting an archive to a library's care. The depositor could be the creator, the creator's spouse or children, or a literary estate; the depositor could be gifting, loaning, or selling the archive to the library. Helen Langley provides an introduction to the library's political holdings in "Major Political Collections in the Bodleian Library, Oxford," *Primary Sources and Original Works* 3 (1994): 93–112.

[11] Chapter 2 of the Paradigm *Workbook*, "Collection Development Strategies," contains more information on Paradigm's exploration of this topic.

[12] Sue McKemmish, "Evidence of Me . . . " *Archives and Manuscripts* 24 (1996): 28–45.

[13] This particular archive is that of the British politician Edmund Dell. It was accessioned by the library's curator of modern political papers, Helen Langley, and contains some 3500 files, mainly in Samna Word and Lotus Ami Pro formats. The material is being processed as part of the futureArch project.

[14] Probably the most well known to the archive and library community are Catherine C. Marshall's "Rethinking Personal Digital Archiving, Part 1: Four Challenges from the Field" (http://dx.doi.org/10.1045/march2008-marshall-pt1) and "Rethinking Personal Digital Archiving, Part 2: Implications for Services, Applications, and Institutions" (http://dx.doi.org/10.1045/march2008-marshall-pt2), both published in *DLib* 14, no. 3/4 (March/April 2008). Also worth a look is Joseph Kaye, Janet Vertesi, Shari Avery, Allan Dafoe, Shay David, Lisa Onaga, Ivan Rosero, and Trevor

Pinch, "To Have and To Hold: Exploring the Personal Archive," in *CHI 2006: Interact, Inform, Inspire: Conference Proceedings: Conference on Human Factors in Computing Systems: Montreal, Quebec, Canada, April 22–27, 2006,* ed. Rebecca E. Grinter (New York: Association for Computing Machinery, 2006), 275–84; and Pete Williams, Katrina Dean, Ian Rowlands, and Jeremy Leighton John, "Digital Lives: Reports of Interviews with the Creators of Personal Digital Collections," *Ariadne* 55 (April 2008), http://www.ariadne.ac.uk/issue55/williams-et-al/.

15 The Paradigm *Workbook* includes some thoughts on accessioning practicalities, http://www.webarchive.org.uk/wayback/archive/20081001092937/http://www.paradigm.ac.uk/workbook/record-creators/accessioning.html.

16 The author has been asked to segregate personal and professional materials on a computer hard disk, with a view to excluding all personal items from the archive. Such work is seldom clear cut and can be incredibly time consuming.

17 Neil Beagrie, "Plenty of Room at the Bottom? Personal Digital Libraries and Collections," *D-Lib Magazine* 11, no. 6 (June 2005), http://dx.doi.org/10.1045/june2005-beagrie, includes a definition of what personae a personal digital collection might represent and the private and shareable aspects of such collections.

18 This is especially true if the library intends to offer support to creators in curating their own archive for later deposit. The Paradigm project did develop some guidance for potential depositors, but the library's experiences to date have shown that it is most helpful to relate these to the individual circumstances of the creator. The guidelines are available at http://www.webarchive.org.uk/wayback/archive/20081001092937/http://www.paradigm.ac.uk/workbook/appendices/guidelines.html.

19 Examples of panel sessions include: "Trade Perspectives": Joan Winterkorn (chair), Ed Maggs, Rick Gekoski, Manuscripts Matter Conference, British Library (October 2006); "The Archive on The Market": Thomas F. Staley (chair), Rick Gekoski, Glenn Horowitz, and Breon Mitchell, Flair Symposium, Creating a Usable Past: Writers, Archives and Institutions, Harry Ransom Center (November 2008); "On the Monetary Value of Personal Digital Objects": Gabriel Heaton, Julian Rota, and Joan Winterkorn, Digital Lives Conference, British Library (February 2009). See also Tom Simonite, "How Do You Value a Historical Email?" *New Scientist*, February 13, 2009, http://www.newscientist.com/article/dn16589-how-do-you-value-a-historical-email.html.

20 See Chapter 2 of the Paradigm *Workbook on Digital Private Papers,* "Collection Development," for an overview of collection development strategies identified by the project. Chapter 3, "Working with Creators," contains more information about the project's experiences of proactive collection development.

21 Lucie Paquet makes some interesting observations about different generations of technology in her article "Appraisal, Acquisition and Control of Personal Electronic Records: From Myth to Reality," *Archives and Manuscript* 28, part 2 (2000): 73. See also Tom Hyry and Rachel Onuf, "The Personality of Electronic Records: The Impact of New Information Technology on Personal Papers," *Archival Issues* 22 (1997): 37–44, which describes a technological landscape significantly different from the one we now occupy.

22 Martin Campbell-Kelly and William Aspray, *Computer: A History of the Information Machine,* 2nd ed. (Boulder, CO: Westview, 2004), 234.

23 Locomotive software, http://www.locoscript.com/.

24 For an interesting introduction, see Seamus Ross and Ann Gow, *Digital Archaeology? Rescuing Neglected or Damaged Digital Collections* (London: British Library, 1999).

25 The GRATE (Global Remote Access To Emulation) emulation service developed through the EU Planets project could be viable in the future. See Dirk von Suchodoletz and Jeffrey van der Hoeven, "Emulation: From Digital Artefactto Remotely Rendered Environments," *International Journal of Digital Curation* 3, no. 4 (2009): 146–55. Repositories of old software are also useful,

although their legal status can be ambiguous; http://www.oldversion.com/ is a useful resource which distributes freeware and shareware.

[26] The library only had limited experience with data recovery until Jeremy Leighton John of the British Library introduced the digital archivist to digital forensics proper, and its application to archives and manuscripts work. Jeremy kindly imaged a hard disk for the library in 2007. See Jeremy Leighton John, "Adapting Existing Technologies for Digitally Archiving Personal Lives: Digital Forensics, Ancestral Computing, and Evolutionary Perspectives and Tools" (paper presented at iPRES 2008: The Fifth International Conference on Preservation of Digital Objects, London, UK, September 29–30, 2008). The Forensics wiki is another useful source of information about open source and proprietary forensic software: http://www.forensicswiki.org.

[27] Mobile and Global Positioning System (GPS) forensics appears to be a growth area in forensics, with much diversity to negotiate. Consider the range of hardware and operating systems—Android, Blackberry, iPhone, OpenMoko, PalmOS, Symbian, Windows Mobile, etc.—on the market that must be supported. There is a conference to support those working in this area entitled "Mobile Forensics World."

[28] Ofcom, *Communications Market Report* (August 2010), 19; Ofcom, *UK Broadband Speeds: The Performance of Fixed-line Broadband Delivered to UK Residential Consumers* (May 2010), 24; see http://stakeholders.ofcom.org.uk/binaries/research/cmr/753567/CMR_2010_FINAL. pdf; and http://stakeholders.ofcom.org.uk/binaries/research/telecoms-research/bbspeeds2010/ bbspeeds2010.pdf.

[29] This previous Labour government expressed this desire in its "Digital Britain" report (see Department for Culture, Media and Sport and Department for Business, Innovation and Skills, "Digital Britain" (June 2009), http://webarchive.nationalarchives.gov.uk/+/http://www.culture.gov. uk/images/publications/digitalbritain-finalreport-jun09.pdf). The agreement developed by the current Conservative/Liberal Democrat coalition government suggests that "superfast broadband" remains a priority, although available resources may slow the progress toward universal access to higher broadband speeds. See HM Government, "The Coalition: Our Programme for Government" (Cabinet Office, May 2010) and Jeremy Hunt (Secretary of State for Culture, Olympics, Media and Sport, speech to Broadband Industry Event, London, July 15, 2010), http://www.culture.gov.uk/ news/ministers_speeches/7245.aspx.

[30] When users have to find a unique screen name (or handle) for multiple online services, the result is often a complex web of identities. Some users may even prefer to fragment their identities, adopting different identities for different purposes. Sherry Turkle, "Cyberspace and Identity," *Contemporary Sociology* 28, no. 6 (November 1999): 643–48, offers an interesting sociological perspective on this. From a practical point of view, archivists and researchers will need to relate email addresses and screen names with personal names.

[31] In fact a number of public figures are using Twitter, although it is not always clear who is writing and whether the Twitter feed is sanctioned by the person in whose name it is published. In 2009, Twitter began experimenting with a verification system to mark accounts as "verified" when additional checks have been made and have also introduced policies forbidding name squatting and non-parody impersonation. At the time of this writing, the "verified account" service is in beta and Twitter has verified 3,816 accounts (see https://twitter.com/verified/lists for an up-to-date list of verified accounts).

[32] Noam Cohen, "When Stars Twitter a Ghost May Be Lurking," *New York Times*, March 26, 2009.

[33] See the National Software Reference Library maintained by the National Institute of Science and Technology (NIST) at http://www.nsrl.nist.gov/.

[34] The PC on which much of this chapter was written has an 80 gigabyte hard disk. The standard PC rolled out to new staff at the library currently contains a 160 gigabyte hard disk.

[35] Jesse Kornblum, "Identifying Almost Identical Files Using Context Triggered Piecewise Hashing," *Digital Investigation* 3, Supplement 1, Proceedings of the 6th Annual Digital Forensic Research Workshop (DFRWS '06) (2006): 91–97.

[36] CAINE Live forensics is an example of a bootable Linux distribution, http://www.caine-live.net/; AccessData is the producer of Forensic Toolkit, http://www.accessdata.com/.

[37] The National Archives' Digital Preservation Department, http://www.nationalarchives.gov.uk/preservation/digital.htm.

[38] In addition to BEAM, this includes staff from the library's digitization programme (Oxford Digital Library, http://www.odl.ox.ac.uk/) and the library's institutional repository for academic outputs (Oxford University Research Archive, http://ora.ouls.ox.ac.uk/).

[39] Chapter 8 of the Paradigm *Workbook on Digital Private Papers,* "Digital Preservation Strategies," examines digital preservation from the perspective of an institution collecting personal digital archives; see http://www.paradigm.ac.uk/workbook/preservation-strategies/index.html. The Planets project is a large collaborative digital preservation project funded by the European Union; see http://www.planets-project.eu/.

[40] Matthew Neely, *Catalogue of the Papers of Barbara Anne Castle, Baroness Castle of Blackburn, 1968-2002* (Bodleian Library, 2009).

[41] OpenOffice supports a number of file formats; see http://www.openoffice.org/.

[42] Emory University has provided researchers with access to an emulated version of Salman Rushdie's Mac Performa 5400, which was deposited as part of his archive. See Mary J. Loftus, "The Author's Desktop," *Emory Magazine* (Winter 2010), http://www.emory.edu/EMORY_MAGAZINE/2010/winter/authors.html.

[43] Matthew Kirschenbaum is a new media scholar with an interest in experiencing the material in its fullest form. See his book *Mechanisms: New Media and the Forensic Imagination* (Cambridge, MA: MIT Press, 2008).

[44] Schools are remodeling their classrooms for the digital age, with monitors now often embedded in desks.

[45] Assessments and audits can use a variety of toolkits, including Assessing Institutional Assets (AIDA) (http://aida.jiscinvolve.org/toolkit/) and Digital Repository Audit Method Based on Risk Assessment (DRAMBORA) (http://www.repositoryaudit.eu/). There are some projects which have attempted to explore digital preservation costs too, but not in the context of collecting personal digital materials. See Life Cycle Information for E-Literature (LIFE) at http://www.life.ac.uk/, which in its third phase will look to build on the DRAMBORA toolkit.

[46] Further recent published case studies not already referenced include: Catherine Stollar Peters, "When Not All Papers are Paper: A Case Study in Digital Archivy," *Provenance* 24 (2006): 23–35; Sarah Kim, Lorrie Dong, and Megan Durden, "Automated Batch Archival Processing: Preserving Arnold Wesker's Digital Manuscripts," http://repositories.lib.utexas.edu/handle/2152/6003; Matthew G. Kirschenbaum, Erika Farr, Kari M. Kraus, Naomi L. Nelson, Catherine Stollar Peters, Gabriela Redwine, and Doug Reside, "Approaches to Managing and Collecting Born-Digital Literary Materials for Scholarly Use" (May 2009), http://www.neh.gov/ODH/Default.aspx?tabid=111&id=37; Erika Farr, "Rushdie's Born-Digital Archive: Updates and Prospects" (paper presented at New Covenants in Special Collections: A Symposium on Obligations and Opportunities, Atlanta, GA, USA, February 2008); Chris Hilton and Dave Thompson, "Collecting Born-Digital Archives at the Wellcome Library," *Ariadne* 50 (2007), http://www.ariadne.ac.uk/issue50/hilton-thompson/; and Chris Hilton and Dave Thompson, "Further Experiences in Collecting Born-Digital Archives at the Wellcome Library," *Ariadne* 53 (2007), http://www.ariadne.ac.uk/issue53/hilton-thompson/. Searches of the archives-nra@jiscmail.ac.uk and the archives@forums.archives.org lists suggest that several institutions are working with digital archives even if they have not (yet) published about their experiences.

Bibliography

Abbott, Andrew Delano. *The System of Professions: An Essay on the Division of Expert Labor.* Chicago: University of Chicago Press, 1988.

Acland, Glenda. "Archivist: Keeper, Undertaker or Auditor." *Archives and Manuscripts* 19 (1991): 9–15.

Acquisti, Alessandro, and Ralph Gross. "Imagined Communities: Awareness, Information Sharing, and Privacy on the Facebook." In *Privacy Enhancing Technologies*, edited by G. Danezis and P. Golle, 36–58. Berlin: Springer, 2006.

Adams, Anne, Sally Jo Cunningham, and Masood Masoodian. "Sharing, Privacy and Trust Issues for Photo Collections." Working paper no. 01/2007, Department of Computer Science, University of Waikato, Hamilton, New Zealand, 2007. http://hdl.handle.net/10289/59.

Adar, Eytan, David Karger, and Lynn Andrea Stein. "Haystack: Per-User Information Environments." In *Proceedings of the Eighth International Conference on Information Knowledge Management: CIKM '99, November 2–6, 1999, Kansas City, Missouri*, edited by Susan Gauch, 413–22. New York: ACM Press, 1999.

Adatto, Kiku. *Picture Perfect: Life in the Age of the Photo Op.* New ed. Princeton, NJ: Princeton University Press, 2008.

Albrechtslund, Anders. "Online Social Networking as Participatory Surveillance." *First Monday* 13, no. 3 (2008). http://firstmonday.org/article/view/2142/1949.

Aldrich, Howard. *Organizations Evolving.* London: Sage, 1999.

Allison, Arthur, James Currall, Michael Moss, and Susan Stuart. "Digital Identity Matters." *Journal of the American Society for Information Science and Technology* 56, no. 4 (2004): 364–72.

Allman, Thomas Y. "Fostering a Compliance Culture: The Role of the Sedona Guidelines." *Information Management Journal* 39, no. 2 (2005): 54–61.

Ambacher, Bruce I., ed. *Thirty Years of Electronic Records.* Lanham, MD: Scarecrow Press, 2003.

Anderson, Paul. "What is Web 2.0? Ideas, Technologies, and Implications for Education." *JISC Technology and Standards Watch Report.* Joint Information Systems Committee, 2007.

Anderson, Sheila, Mike Pringle, Mick Eadie, Tony Austin, Andrew Wilson, and Malcolm Polfreman. "Digital Images Archiving Study." Arts and Humanities Data Service, 2006.

Angus, Emma, Mike Thelwall, and David Stuart. "General Patterns of Tag Usage Among University Groups in Flickr." *Online Information Review* 32, no. 1 (2008): 89–101.

ARC Linkage Project. *Trust and Technology: Building Archival Systems for Indigenous Oral Memory.* Transcripts of Interviews, 2003.

Assistant Secretary of Defense for Networks and Information Integration. "Electronic Records Management Software Applications Design Criteria Standard." DoD 5015.02-STD. Arlington, VA: U.S. Department of Defense, 2007.

Assurance and Control Assessment Audit: Recordkeeping. Audit Report No. 45 2001–02. Canberra: Australian National Audit Office, 2002.

Atherton, Jay. "From Life Cycle to Continuum: Some Thoughts on the Records Management-Archives Relationship." *Archivaria* 21 (1985–86): 43–51.

Australian Law Reform Commission. Australia's Federal Record: A Review of the Archives Act 1983. Canberra: AGPS, 1998.

Baca, Murtha, ed. *Introduction to Art Image Access: Tools, Standards, and Strategies.* Los Angeles: Getty Research Institute, 2002.

Bailey, Catherine. "From the Top Down: The Practice of Macro-Appraisal." *Archivaria* 43 (1997): 89–128.

Bailey, Steve. *Managing the Crowd: Rethinking Records Management for the Web 2.0 World.* London: Facet Publishing, 2008.

Bantin, Philip C. *Understanding Data and Information Systems for Recordkeeping.* New York: Neal-Schuman, 2008.

Barreau, Deborah "Context as a Factor in Personal Information Management Systems." *Journal of the American Society for Information Science* 46, no. 5 (1995): 327–39.

Barreau, Deborah. "Listserv as Boundary Object: Implications for Personal Information Management and Organizational Learning." In *Knowledge Management: Nurturing Culture, Innovation and Technology: Proceedings of the 2005 International Conference on Knowledge Management, October 27–28, 2005, North Carolina, USA,* edited by Suliman Hawamdeh, 377–83. Singapore: World Scientific Publishing, 2005.

Barreau, Deborah. "The Persistence of Behavior and Form in the Organization of Personal Information." *Journal of the American Society for Information Science and Technology* 59, no. 2 (2007): 307–17.

Barreau, Deborah, and Bonnie A. Nardi. "Finding and Reminding: File Organization from the Desktop." *SIGCHI Bulletin* 27, no. 3 (1995): 39–43.

Bartlett, Nancy. "*Respect Des Fonds:* The Origins of the Modern Archival Principle of Provenance." *Primary Sources and Original Works* 1, no. 1/2 (1991): 107–15.

Bastian, Jeannette. *Owning Memory: How a Caribbean Community Lost Its Archive and Found Its History.* Westport, CT: Libraries Unlimited, 2003.

Bauer, G. Philip. *The Appraisal of Current and Recent Records.* National Archives Staff Informational Circulars, No. 13. Washington, DC: National Archives and Records Service, 1946.

Beagrie, Neil. "Plenty of Room at the Bottom? Personal Digital Libraries and Collections." *D-Lib Magazine* 11, no. 6 (2005). http://dx.doi.org/10.1045/june2005-beagrie.

Bearman, David, ed. *Archival Management of Electronic Records,* Archives and Museum Informatics Technical Report No. 13. Pittsburgh, PA: Archives and Museum Informatics, 1991.

Bearman, David. *Electronic Evidence: Strategies for Managing Records in Contemporary Organizations.* Pittsburgh, PA: Archives and Museum Informatics, 1994.

Bearman, David. "Selection and Appraisal." In *Archival Methods.* Pittsburgh, PA: Archives and Museum Informatics, 1989.

Bearman, David A., and Richard H. Lytle. "The Power of the Principle of Provenance." *Archivaria* 21 (1985): 14–27.

Bekkerman, Ron, and Andrew McCallum. "Disambiguating Web Appearances of People in a Social Network." In *Proceedings of the 14th International Conference on World Wide Web, WWW 2005: Chiba, Japan, May 10–14, 2005*, edited by Allan Ellis and Tatsuya Hagino, 463–70. New York: ACM Press, 2005.

Bell, Gordon, and Jim Gemmell. *Total Recall: How the E-Memory Revolution Will Change Everything.* New York: Dutton, 2009.

Bentley, Frank, Crysta Metcalf, and Gunnar Harboe. "Personal vs. Commercial Content: The Similarities between Consumer Use of Photos and Music." In *Proceedings of the SIGCHI Conference on Human Factors in Computing Systems,* 667–76. New York: ACM Press, 2006.

Bergman, Ofer, Ruth Beyth-Marom, and Rafi Nachmias. "The Project Fragmentation Problem in Personal Information Management." In *CHI 2006: Interact, Inform, Inspire: Conference Proceedings: Conference on Human Factors in Computing Systems: Montreal, Quebec, Canada, April 22–27, 2006,* edited by Rebecca E. Grinter, 271–74. New York: Association for Computing Machinery, 2006.

Bergman, Ofer, Ruth Beyth-Marom, Rafi Nachmias, Noa Gradovitch, and Steve Whittaker. "Improved Search Engines and Navigation Preference in Personal Information Management." *ACM Transactions on Information Systems* 26, no. 4 (2008): 1–24.

Bergman, Ofer, Simon Tucker, Ruth Beyth-Marom, Edward Cutrell, and Steve Whittaker. "It's Not That Important: Demoting Personal Information of Low Subjective Importance Using GrayArea." In *Proceedings of the 27th International Conference on Human Factors in Computing Systems,* 269–78. New York: Association for Computing Machinery, 2009.

Bergmark, Donna. "Collection Synthesis." In *Proceedings of the Second ACM/IEEE-CS Joint Conference on Digital Libraries: July 14–18, 2002, Portland, Oregon,* edited by Gary Marchionini and William R. Hersh, 253–62. New York: ACM Press, 2002.

Bergmark, Donna, Carl Lagoze, and Alex Sbityakov. "Focused Crawls, Tunneling, and Digital Libraries." In *Research and Advanced Technology for Digital Libraries: 6th European Conference, ECDL 2002, Rome,*

Italy, September 2002: Proceedings, edited by Maristella Agosti and Constantino Thanos, 91–106. Berlin: Springer, 2002.

Berner, Richard C. *Archival Theory and Practice in the United States: A Historical Analysis*. Seattle: University of Washington Press, 1983.

Berner, Richard C. "Manuscript Collections, Archives, and Special Collections: Their Relationships." *Archivaria* 18 (1984): 248–54.

Berners-Lee, Tim, James Hendler, and Ora Lassila. "The Semantic Web." *Scientific American* 284, no. 5 (2001): 35–43.

Bernstein, Michael, Max Van Kleek, David Karger, and M. C. Schraefel. "Information Scraps: How and Why Information Eludes Our Personal Information Management Tools." *ACM Transactions on Information Systems* 26, no. 4 (2008): Article 24, 1–46.

Berry, Emma, Narinder Kapur, Lyndsay Williams, Steve Hodges, Peter Watson, Gavin Smyth, James Srinivasan, Reg Smith, Barbara Wilson, and Ken Wood. "The Use of a Wearable Camera, SenseCam, as a Pictorial Diary to Improve Autobiographical Memory in a Patient with Limbic Encephalitis." *Neuropsychological Rehabilitation* 17, no. 4/5 (2007): 582–681.

Best, Samuel J., and Brian S. Krueger. "Analyzing the Representativeness of Internet Political Participation." *Political Behavior* 27, no. 2 (2005): 183–216.

Bikson, Tora K., and Erik. J. Frinking. *Preserving the Present: Toward Viable Electronic Records*. The Hague: Sdu Publishers, 1993.

Birrell, Andrew, Peter Robertson, Lilly Koltun, Andrew C. Rodger, and Joan M. Schwartz. "Private Realms of Light: Canadian Amateur Photography, 1839–1940: 2. On View: The Evolution of Amateur Photography." *Archivaria* 17 (1983): 115–35.

Blood, Rebecca. "Weblogs: A History and Perspective." In *We've Got Blog: How Weblogs Are Changing Our Culture*, edited by John Rodzvilla, 7–16. Cambridge, MA: Perseus, 2002. [Originally posted to: Rebecca's Pocket. September 7, 2000.]

Boardman, Richard. "Improving Tool Support for Personal Information Management." PhD dissertation, Imperial College, London, 2004.

Boardman, Richard, and M. Angela Sasse. "'Stuff Goes into the Computer and Doesn't Come out': A Cross-Tool Study of Personal Information

Management." In *CHI 2004: Connect: Conference Proceedings: April 24–29, Vienna, Austria: Conference on Human Factors in Computing Systems*, edited by Elizabeth Dykstra-Erickson and Manfred Tscheligi, 583–90. New York: Association for Computing Machinery, 2004.

Boles, Frank. "Sampling in Archives." *American Archivist* 44, no. 2 (1981): 125–30.

Bolger, Niall, Anita DeLongis, Ronald C. Kessler, and Elaine Wethington. "The Contagion of Stress across Multiple Roles." *Journal of Marriage and the Family* 51 (1989): 175–83.

Booms, Hans. "Society and the Formation of a Documentary Heritage: Issues in the Appraisal of Archival Sources." *Archivaria* 24 (1987): 69–107.

Booms, Hans. "Überlieferungsbildung: Keeping Archives as a Social and Political Activity." *Archivaria* 33 (1991–92): 25–33.

Bowker, Geoffrey C., and Susan Leigh Star. *Sorting Things Out: Classification and Its Consequences.* Cambridge, MA: MIT Press, 1999.

boyd, danah. "Why Youth ♥ Social Network Sites: The Role of Networked Publics in Teenage Social Life." In *Youth, Identity, and Digital Media*, edited by David Buckingham, 119–42. Cambridge, MA: MIT Press, 2008.

boyd, danah, and Nicole B. Ellison. "Social Network Sites: Definition, History, and Scholarship." *Journal of Computer-Mediated Communication* 13, no. 1 (2007): 210–30.

Bradley, John. "Pliny: A Model for Digital Support of Scholarship." *Journal of Digital Information* 9, no. 26 (2008). http://journals.tdl.org/jodi/article/view/209/198.

Bradsher, James Gregory. "The FBI Appraisal." *Midwestern Archivist* 13 (1988): 51–66.

Brichford, Maynard. "The Provenance of Provenance in Germanic Areas." *Provenance* 7, no. 2 (1989): 54–70.

Brothman, Brien. "Declining Derrida: Integrity, Tensegrity, and the Preservation of Archives from Deconstruction." *Archivaria* 48 (1999): 64–89.

Brothman, Brien. "The Past That Archives Keep: Memory, History, and the Preservation of Archival Records." *Archivaria* 51 (2001): 48–80.

Brown, Adrian. *Archiving Websites: A Practical Guide for Information Management Professionals.* London: Facet, 2006.

Bruce, Harry. "Personal, Anticipated Information Need." *Information Research* 10, no. 3 (2005). http://informationr.net/ir/10-3/paper232.html.

"Building Partnerships: Developing New Approaches to Electronic Records Management and Preservation." Albany: New York State Archives and Records Administration, 1995.

Bulkeley, William M. "The Downside of Photo-Storage Sites." *Wall Street Journal*, February 1, 2006, D1.

Buneman, Peter, Sanjeev Khanna, and Wang-Chiew Tan. "Why and Where: A Characterization of Data Provenance." In *Database Theory–ICDT 2001: 8th International Conference, London, UK, January 2001, Proceedings*, edited by Jan van den Bussche and Victor Vianu, 316–30. Berlin: Springer, 2001.

Burgess, Jean E. "Vernacular Creativity and New Media." PhD dissertation, Creative Industries Faculty, Queensland University of Technology, 2007.

Burke, Frank G. *Research and the Manuscript Tradition.* Lanham, MD: Scarecrow Press, 1997.

Burrows, Toby. "Personal Electronic Archives: Collecting the Digital Me." *OCLC Systems and Services* 22, no. 2 (2006): 85–88.

Butters, Geoff, Amanda Hulme, and Peter Brophy. "Supporting Creativity in Networked Environments: The COINE Project." *Ariadne* 51 (2007). http://www.ariadne.ac.uk/issue51/brophy-et-al/.

Caloyannides, Michael A. "Digital 'Evidence' Is Often Evidence of Nothing." In *Digital Crime and Forensic Science in Cyberspace*, edited by Panagiotis Kanellis, 334–39. Hershey, PA: Idea Group, 2006.

Campbell-Kelly, Martin, and William Aspray. *Computer: A History of the Information Machine.* Second ed. Boulder, CO: Westview, 2004.

Cappon, Lester J. "Historical Manuscripts as Archives: Some Definitions and Their Application." *American Archivist* 19 (1956): 101–10.

Capra, Robert. "Studying Elapsed Time and Task Factors in Re-Finding Electronic Information." Paper presented at the Personal Information Management, CHI 2008 Workshop, Florence, Italy, April 5–6, 2008.

Capra, Robert, Christopher A. Lee, Gary Marchionini, Terrell Russell, Chirag Shah, and Fred Stutzman. "Selection of Context Scoping for Digital Video Collections: An Investigation of YouTube and Blogs." In *JCDL 2008: Proceedings of the 8th ACM/IEEE Joint Conference on Digital Libraries: Pittsburgh, Pennsylvania, June 15–20, 2008*, edited by Ronald L. Larsen, Andreas Paepcke, José Luis Borbinha, and Mor Naaman, 211–20. New York: ACM Press, 2008.

Capra, Robert G., III, and Manuel Pérez-Quiñones. "Factors and Evaluation of Refinding Behaviors." Paper presented at Personal Information Management—A SIGIR 2006 Workshop, Seattle, Washington, August 10–11, 2006.

Capra, Robert G., III, and Manuel Pérez-Quiñones. "Using Web Search Engines to Find and Refind Information." *IEEE Computer* 38, no. 10 (2005): 36–42.

Carr, Nicholas. *The Big Switch: Rewiring the World, from Edison to Google*. New York: W.W. Norton, 2008.

Carrier, Brian D. "A Hypothesis-Based Approach to Digital Forensic Investigations." PhD dissertation, Purdue University, 2006.

Carvalho, Joseph, III. "Archival Application of Mathematical Sampling Technique." *Records Management Quarterly* 18 (1984): 60–62.

Cha, Meeyoung, Haewoon Kwak, Pablo Rodriguez, Yong-Yeol Ahn, and Sue Moon. "I Tube, You Tube, Everybody Tubes: Analyzing the World's Largest User Generated Content Video System." In *IMC '07: Proceedings of the 2007 ACM SIGCOMM Internet Measurement Conference, San Diego, California, USA, October 24–26, 2007*, 1–14. New York: Association for Computing Machinery, 2007.

Chakrabarti, Soumen, Martin van den Berg, and Byron Dom. "Focused Crawling: A New Approach to Topic-Specific Resource Discovery." In *Proceedings of the Eighth International World Wide Web Conference: Toronto, Canada, May 11–14, 1999*, 545–62. Amsterdam: Elsevier, 1999.

Chalfen, Richard. *Snapshot Versions of Life*. Bowling Green, OH: Bowling Green State University Popular Press, 1987.

Chandler, Alfred D. *The Visible Hand: The Managerial Revolution in American Business*. Cambridge, MA: Belknap Press, 1977.

Chandler, Alfred Dupont, and Takashi Hikino. *Scale and Scope: The Dynamics of Industrial Capitalism*. Cambridge, MA: Belknap Press, 1990.

Chang, Chia-Hui, Mohammed Kayed, Moheb Ramzy Girgis, and Khaled F. Shaalan. "A Survey of Web Information Extraction Systems." *IEEE Transactions on Knowledge and Data Engineering* 18, no. 10 (2006): 1411–28.

Chatfield, Helen L. "The Problem of Records from the Standpoint of Management." *American Archivist* 3, no. 3 (1940): 93–101.

Chavez, Robert, Timothy W. Cole, Muriel Foulonneau, Thomas G. Habing, Jon Dunn, William Parod, and Thornton Staples. "DLF-Aquifer Asset Actions Experiment: Demonstrating Value of Actionable URLs." *D-Lib Magazine* 12, no. 10 (October 2006). http://dx.doi.org/10.1045/october2006-cole.

Chen, Hsin Liang, and Edie M. Rasmussen. "Intellectual Access to Images." *Library Trends* 48, no. 2 (1999): 291–302.

Cheyer, Adam, Jack Park, and Richard Giuli. "IRIS: Integrate. Relate. Infer. Share." Paper presented at the Workshop on the Semantic Desktop: Next Generation Personal Information Management and Collaboration Infrastructure, ICSC 2005, Galway, Ireland, November 6, 2005.

Clanchy, M.T. *From Memory to Written Record: England 1066-1307*. 2nd ed. Cambridge: Blackwell, 1993.

Clark, Joe. "Deconstructing 'You've Got Blog.'" In *We've Got Blog: How Weblogs Are Changing Our Culture*, edited by John Rodzvilla, 57-68. Cambridge, MA: Perseus, 2002. [Originally posted to: fawny.com on November 16, 2000. Updated on January 25, 2002.]

Cochran, Thomas C., Howard K. Beale, Katharine E. Brand, George E. Mowry, and Alice E. Smith. "Report of Ad Hoc Committee on Manuscripts Set Up by the American Historical Association in December 1948." *American Archivist* 14 (1951): 229–40.

Cohen, Daniel J. "Zotero: Social and Semantic Computing for Historical Scholarship." *Perspectives* 45, no. 5 (2007).

Cohen, Daniel J., and Roy Rosenzweig. *Digital History: A Guide to Gathering, Preserving, and Presenting the Past on the Web*. Philadelphia, PA: University of Pennsylvania Press, 2005.

Cohen, Noam. "When Stars Twitter a Ghost May Be Lurking." *New York Times*, March 26, 2009.

Cohen, Patricia. "Fending Off Digital Decay, Bit by Bit." *New York Times,* March, 16, 2010, C1.

Cole, I. "Human Aspects of Office Filing: Implications for the Electronic Office." In *Proceedings of the Human Factors Society 26th Annual Meeting, Seattle, Washington, October 25-29, 1982,* edited by Richard E. Edwards and Philip Tolin, 59-63. Santa Monica, CA: Human Factors Society, 1982.

Cook, J. Frank. "The Blessings of Providence on an Association of Archivists." *American Archivist* 46 (1983): 374-99.

Cook, Terry. "Beyond the Screen: The Records Continuum and Archival Cultural Heritage." Paper presented at the Australian Society of Archivists Conference, Melbourne, Australia, August 18, 2000.

Cook, Terry. "The Concept of Archival Fonds and the Post-Custodial Era: Theory, Problems and Solutions." *Archivaria* 35 (1993): 24-37.

Cook, Terry. "The Concept of the Archival Fonds: Theory, Description, and Provenance in the Post-Custodial Era." In *The Archival Fonds: From Theory to Practice,* edited by Terry Eastwood, 31-85. Ottawa: Bureau of Canadian Archivists, 1992.

Cook, Terry. "Documenting Society and Institutions: The Influence of Helen Willa Samuels." In *Controlling the Past: Documenting Society and Institutions: Essays in Honor of Hellen Willa Samuels,* edited by Terry Cook, 1-28. Chicago: Society of American Archivists, 2011.

Cook, Terry. "Electronic Records, Paper Minds: The Revolution in Information Management and Archives in the Post-custodial and Post-modern Era." *Archives and Manuscripts* 22, no. 2 (1994): 300-29.

Cook, Terry. "Fashionable Nonsense or Professional Rebirth: Postmodernism and the Practice of Archives." *Archivaria* 51 (2001): 14-35.

Cook, Terry. "Mind over Matter: Towards a New Theory of Archival Appraisal." In *The Archival Imagination: Essays in Honor of Hugh A. Taylor,* edited by Barbara Lazenby Craig, 38-70. Ottawa: Association of Canadian Archivists, 1992.

Cook, Terry. "What Is Past Is Prologue: A History of Archival Ideas since 1898, and the Future Paradigm Shift." *Archivaria* 43 (1997): 17-63.

Cook, Terry, and Joan M. Schwartz. "Archives, Records, and Power: From (Postmodern) Theory to (Archival) Performance." *Archival Science* 2 (2002): 171–85.

Cox, Andrew M., Paul D. Clough, and Jennifer Marlow. "Flickr: A First Look at User Behaviour in the Context of Photography as Serious Leisure." *Information Research* 13, no. 1 (2008). http://informationr.net/ir/13-1/paper336.html.

Cox, Richard J. "The End of Collecting: Towards a New Purpose for Archival Appraisal." *Archival Science* 2, no. 3-4 (2002): 287–309.

Cox, Richard J. *The First Generation of Electronic Records Archivists in the United States: A Study in Professionalization*. Edited by Lawrence J. McCrank. Primary Sources and Original Works, vol. 3. New York: Haworth Press, 1994.

Cox, Richard J. *Personal Archives and a New Archival Calling: Readings, Reflections and Ruminations*. Duluth, MN: Litwin Books, 2008.

Cox, Richard J. "The Record in the Manuscript Collection." *Archives and Manuscripts* 24, no. 1 (1996): 46–61.

Cox, Richard J. "Searching for Authority: Archivists and Electronic Records in the New World at the Fin-De-Siécle." *First Monday* 5, no. 1 (2000). http://firstmonday.org/article/view/721/630.

Cox, Richard J., and Helen W. Samuels. "The Archivist's First Responsibility: A Research Agenda for the Identification and Retention of Records of Enduring Value." *American Archivist* 51 (1988): 28–42.

Craig, Barbara. "Serving the Truth: The Importance of Fostering Archives Research in Education Programmes, Including a Modest Proposal for Partnerships with the Workplace." *Archivaria* 42 (1996): 105–17.

Crampton, Thomas. "Reporter to NY Times Publisher: You Erased My Career." *Thomas Crampton: China, Internet and New Media Seen from Asia*. May 8, 2009. http://www.thomascrampton.com/newspapers/reporter-to-ny-times-publisher-you-erased-my-career/.

Cresswell, Anthony M., and G. Brian Burke. "The Washington State Digital Archives (Case Study)." Albany, NY: Center for Technology in Government, 2006.

Csikszentmihalyi, Mihaly, and Eugene Rochberg-Halton. *The Meaning of Things: Domestic Symbols and the Self.* Cambridge: Cambridge University Press, 1981.

Culotta, Aron, Ron Bekkerman, and Andrew Mccallum. "Extracting Social Networks and Contact Information from Email and the Web." Paper presented at the First Conference on Email and Anti-Spam, Mountain View, CA, July 30–31, 2004.

Cunningham, Adrian. "The Archival Management of Personal Records in Electronic Form: Some Suggestions." *Archives and Manuscripts* 22, no. 1 (1994): 94–105.

Cunningham, Adrian. "Editorial: Beyond Corporate Accountability." *Archives and Manuscripts* 24, no. 1 (1996): 6–11.

Cunningham, Adrian. "The Mysterious Outside Reader." *Archives and Manuscripts* 24, no. 1 (1996): 130–44.

Cunningham, Adrian. "Waiting for the Ghost Train: Strategies for Managing Electronic Personal Records Before It Is Too Late." *Archival Issues* 24, no. 1 (1999): 55–64.

Cunningham, Sally Jo, and Masood Masoodian. "Identifying Personal Photo Digital Library Features." In *Proceedings of the 2007 Conference on Digital Libraries*, 400–401. New York: ACM Press, 2007.

Cutrell, Edward, Susan T. Dumais, and Jaime Teevan. "Searching to Eliminate Personal Information Management." *Communications of the ACM* 49, no. 1 (2006): 58–64.

Cutrell, Edward, Daniel Robbins, Susan Dumais, and Raman Sarin. "Fast, Flexible Filtering with Phlat." In *CHI 2006: Interact, Inform, Inspire: Conference Proceedings: Conference on Human Factors in Computing Systems: Montreal, Quebec, Canada, April 22–27, 2006,* edited by Rebecca E. Grinter, 261–70. New York: Association for Computing Machinery, 2006.

Czerwinski, Mary, Douglas W. Gage, Jim Gemmell, Catherine C. Marshall, Manuel A. Pérez-Quiñones, Meredith M. Skeels, and Tiziana Catarci. "Digital Memories in an Era of Ubiquitous Computing and Abundant Storage." *Communications of the ACM* 49, no. 1 (2006): 44–50.

Davies, Julia. "Affinities and Beyond! Developing Ways of Seeing in Online Spaces." *ELearning* 3, no. 2 (2006): 217–34.

Davis, Susan E. "Electronic Records Planning in 'Collecting' Repositories." *American Archivist* 71, no. 1 (2008): 167–89.

Dearstyne, Bruce W., ed. *Effective Approaches for Managing Electronic Records and Archives.* Lanham, MD: Scarecrow Press, 2002.

Demerouti, Evangelia, Arnold B. Bakker, and Wilmar B. Schaufeli. "Spillover and Crossover of Exhaustion and Life Satisfaction among Dual-Earner Parents." *Journal of Vocational Behavior* 67 (2005): 266–89.

Derrida, Jacques. *Archive Fever: A Freudian Impression.* Chicago: University of Chicago Press, 1996.

Derrida, Jacques. "Archive Fever in South Africa." In *Refiguring the Archive*, edited by Carolyn Hamilton, Verne Harris, Jane Taylor, Michele Pickover, Graeme Reid, and Razia Saleh, 38–80. Dordrecht, Netherlands: Kluwer Academic Publishers, 2002.

Describing Archives: A Content Standard. Chicago: Society of American Archivists, 2004.

Dey, Anind K., Gregory D. Abowd, and Andrew Wood. "CyberDesk: A Framework for Providing Self-Integrating Context-Aware Services." In *IUI '98: 1998 International Conference on Intelligent User Interfaces, San Francisco, California, January 6–9, 1998*, edited by Peter Johnson, 47–54. New York: Association for Computing Machinery, 1998.

Dibbell, Julian. "Portrait of the Blogger as a Young Man." In *We've Got Blog: How Weblogs Are Changing Our Culture*, edited by John Rodzvilla, 69–77. Cambridge, MA: Perseus, 2002.

Digital Curation Centre. "Digital Curation and Preservation: Defining the Research Agenda for the Next Decade." Report of the Warwick Workshop, November 7–8, 2005.

DiMicco, Joan Morris, and David R. Millen. "Identity Management: Multiple Presentations of Self in Facebook." In *Group'07: Proceedings of the 2007 International ACM Conference on Supporting Group Work*, edited by Tom Gross and Kori Inkpen, 383–86. New York: Association for Computing Machinery, 2007.

Ding, Ying, Elin K. Jacob, James Caverlee, Michael Fried, and Zhixiong Zhang. "Profiling Social Networks: A Social Tagging Perspective." *D-Lib Magazine* 15, no. 3/4 (2009). http://dx.doi.org/10.1045/march2009-ding.

Dittrich, Jens-Peter, Lukas Blunschi, Markus Färber, Olivier René
    Girard, Shant Kirakos Karakashian, and Marcos Antonio Vaz Salles.
    "From Personal Desktops to Personal Dataspaces: A Report on
    Building the iMeMex Personal Dataspace Management System."
    In *Datenbanksysteme in Business, Technologie Und Web (BTW
    2007), 12. Fachtagung Des Gi-Fachbereichs "Datenbanken Und
    Informationssysteme" (DBIS), Proceedings, 7–9 März 2007, Aachen,
    Germany*, edited by Alfons Kemper, Harald Schöning, Thomas
    Rose, Matthias Jarke, Thomas Seidl, Christoph Quix, and Christoph
    Brochhaus, 292–308. Bonn: Ges. für Informatik, 2007.

Dix, Alan, Tiziana Catarci, Benjamin Habegger, Yannis Ioannidis, Azrina
    Kamaruddin, Akrivi Katifori, Giorgos Lepouras, Antonella Poggi, and
    Devina Ramduny-Ellis. "Intelligent Context-Sensitive Interactions on
    Desktop and the Web." In *Proceedings of the International Workshop
    in Conjunction with AVI 2006 on Context in Advanced Interfaces*, 23–27.
    New York: Association for Computing Machinery, 2006.

Dodge, Martin, and Rob Kitchin. "'Outlines of a World Coming into
    Existence': Pervasive Computing and the Ethics of Forgetting."
    Environment and Planning B: Planning and Design 34, no. 3 (2007):
    431–45.

Dollar, Charles M. *Archival Theory and Information Technologies: The
    Impact of Information Technologies on Archival Principles and Methods*.
    Edited by Oddo Bucci. Vol. 1, Informatics and Documentation Series.
    Macerata, Italy: Università degli studi di Macerata, 1992.

Dollar, Charles M. *Authentic Electronic Records: Strategies for Long-Term
    Access*. Chicago: Cohasset Associates, 1999.

Dollar, Charles M. *Electronic Records Management and Archives in
    International Organizations: A RAMP Study with Guidelines*. Paris:
    General Information Programme and United Nations Education
    Scientific and Cultural Organization, 1986.

Dollar, Charles, M., and Deborah S. Skaggs. *Using Information Technology to
    Build Strategic Collaborations: The State of Alabama as a Test Case—
    A Case Study in Archives Management*. Chicago: Society of American
    Archivists, 1996.

Dourish, Paul, W. Keith Edwards, Anthony LaMarca, and Michael Salisbury.
    "Presto: An Experimental Architecture for Fluid Interactive Document
    Spaces." *Transactions on Computer-Human Interaction* 6, no. 2 (1999):
    133–61.

Dow, Elizabeth H. *Electronic Records in the Manuscript Repository.* Lanham, MD: Scarecrow Press, 2009.

Dryden, Jean E. *Implementing Descriptive Standards at the United Church Central Archives: A Case Study in Automated Techniques for Archives.* Chicago: Society of American Archivists, 1997.

Duchein, Michel. "The History of European Archives and the Development of the Archival Profession in Europe." *American Archivist* 55, no. 1 (1992): 14–25.

Duchein, Michel. "Theoretical Principles and Practical Problems of *Respect Des Fonds* in Archival Science." *Archivaria* 16 (1983): 64–82.

Duff, Wendy. "Ensuring the Preservation of Reliable Evidence: A Research Project Funded by the NHPRC." *Archivaria* 42 (1996): 28–45.

Duff, Wendy. "Increasing the Acceptance of the Functional Requirements for Electronic Evidence." *Archives and Museum Informatics* 10, no. 4 (1996): 326–51.

Duff, Wendy. "Steadying the Weathervane: Use as a Factor in Appraisal Criteria." *Provenance* 12, no. 1-2 (1994): 83–129.

Duff, Wendy, and Verne Harris. "Stories and Names: Archival Description as Narrating Records and Constructing Meanings." *Archival Science* 2, no. 3-4 (2002): 263–85.

Dumais, Susan, Edward Cutrell, J.J. Cadiz, Gavin Jancke, Raman Sarin, and Daniel C. Robbins. "Stuff I've Seen: A System for Personal Information Retrieval and Re-Use." In *SIGIR 2003: Proceedings of the Twenty-Sixth Annual International ACM SIGIR Conference on Research and Development in Information Retrieval, Toronto, Canada, July 28 to August 1, 2003*, edited by Jamie Callan, 72–79. New York: Association for Computing Machinery, 2003.

Duranti, Luciana, ed. *Long-Term Preservation of Authentic Electronic Records: Findings of the InterPARES Project.* San Miniato, Italy: Archilab, 2005.

Duranti, Luciana, Terence M. Eastwood, and Heather MacNeil. *Preservation of the Integrity of Electronic Records.* Dordrecht: Kluwer Academic Publishers, 2002.

Duranti, Luciana, and Heather MacNeil. "The Protection of the Integrity of Electronic Records: An Overview of the UBC-MAS Research." *Archivaria* 42 (1996): 46–67.

Efimova, Lilia, and Aldo de Moor. "Beyond Personal Webpublishing: An Exploratory Study of Conversational Blogging Practices." Paper presented at the 38th Hawaii International Conference on System Sciences, Big Island, HI, January 3–6, 2005.

Electronic Records Management and E-Discovery: Leading Lawyers on Navigating Recent Trends, Understanding Rules and Regulations, and Implementing an E-Discovery Strategy. Boston: Aspatore, 2010.

Elford, Douglas, Nicholas Del Pozo, Snezana Mihajlovic, David Pearson, Gerard Clifton, and Colin Webb. "Media Matters: Developing Processes for Preserving Digital Objects on Physical Carriers at the National Library of Australia." Paper presented at the 74th IFLA General Conference and Council, Québec, Canada, August 10–14, 2008.

Ellis, Judith A., ed. *Selected Essays in Electronic Recordkeeping in Australia.* O'Connor, ACT, Australia: Australian Society of Archivists, 2000.

Emory University Libraries. *Preserving Salman Rushdie's Digital Life.* 2008. http://www.youtube.com/user/emorylibraries#grid/user/8A1D63F362925EA9.

Engst, Elaine D., and H. Thomas Hickerson. *Developing Collaborative Structures for Expanding the Use of University Collections in Teaching and Research.* Chicago: Society of American Archivists, 1998.

Enser, Peter G.B., Christine J. Sandom, Jonathon S. Hare, and Paul H. Lewis. "Facing the Reality of Semantic Image Retrieval." *Journal of Documentation* 63, no. 4 (2007): 465–81.

Entlich, Richard. "Blog Today, Gone Tomorrow? Preservation of Weblogs." *RLG DigiNews* 8, no. 4 (2004).

Evans, Frank, Donald Harrison, and Edwin Thompson. "A Basic Glossary for Archivists, Manuscript Curators, and Records Managers." *American Archivist* 37 (1974): 415–33.

Farr, Erika. "Rushdie's Born-Digital Archive: Updates and Prospects." Paper presented at New Covenants in Special Collections: A Symposium on Obligations and Opportunities, Atlanta, GA, USA, February 2008.

Farrell, Henry, and Daniel W. Drezner. "The Power and Politics of Blogs." *Public Choice* 134, no. 1–2 (2008): 15–30.

Faulkhead, Shannon. *Narratives of Koorie Victoria.* PhD dissertation, Faculty of Arts, Monash University, 2008.

Fidel, Raya, Harry Bruce, Annelise Mark Pejtersen, Susan Dumais, Jonathan Grudin, and Steven Poltrock. "Collaborative Information Retrieval (CIR)." In *The New Review of Information Behaviour Research: Studies of Information Seeking in Context,* 235–47. Cambridge, UK: Taylor Graham, 2000.

First Archivists Circle. "Protocols for Native American Archival Materials." 2007. http://www.firstarchivistscircle.org/files/index.html.

Fogerty, James E. "Facing Reality: Oral History, Corporate Culture, and the Documentation of Business." In *The Records of American Business,* edited by James O'Toole, 251–73. Chicago: Society of American Archivists, 1997.

Foote, Kenneth. "To Remember and Forget: Archives, Memory, and Culture." *American Archivist* 53 (1990): 378–93.

Forstram, Michael. "Managing Electronic Records in Manuscript Collections: A Case Study from the Beinecke Rare Book and Manuscript Library." *American Archivist* 72, no. 2 (2009): 460–77.

Foucault, Michel. *The Archaeology of Knowledge.* Translated by A.M. Sheridan Smith. New York: Pantheon Books, 1972.

Foucault, Michel. *The History of Sexuality.* Translated by Robert Hurley. 1st Vintage Books ed. Vol. 1: An Introduction. New York: Vintage Books, 1990.

Fowler, Jeffrey J., and William H. Dance. *Preserving Electronically Stored Information: A Practical Approach,* E-Discovery Portfolio Series. Arlington, VA: BNA Books, 2009.

Franklin, Michael, Alon Halevy, and David Maier. "From Databases to Dataspaces: A New Abstraction for Information Management." *ACM SIGMOD Record* 34, no. 4 (2005): 27–33.

Frohlich, David, and Jacqueline Fennell. "Sound, Paper and Memorabilia: Resources for a Simpler Digital Photography." *Personal and Ubiquitous Computing* 11, no. 2 (2007): 107–16.

Frohlich, David, and Robert Kraut. "The Social Context of Home Computing." In *Inside the Smart Home*, edited by Richard Harper, 127–62. London: Springer, 2003.

Frohlich, David, Allan Kuchinsky, Celine Pering, Abbe Don, and Steven Ariss. "Collaborating Around Collections: Requirements for Photoware." In *Proceedings of the 2002 ACM Conference on Computer Supported Cooperative Work*, 166–75. New York: ACM Press, 2002.

Fujimura, Ko, Takafumi Inoue, and Masayuki Sugisaki. "The EigenRumor Algorithm for Ranking Blogs." Paper presented at the 14th International World Wide Web Conference, Chiba, Japan, May 10–14, 2005.

Gallen, Katherine. "Archiving and Memorialising the Taboo." *Archives and Manuscripts* 36, no. 1 (2008): 46–74.

Galvin, Thomas J., and Russell L. Kahn. *Electronic Records Management as Strategic Opportunity: A Case Study of the State University of New York, Office of Archives and Records Management.* Chicago: Society of American Archivists, 1996.

Gantz, John F., Christopher Chute, Alex Manfrediz, Stephen Minton, David Reinsel, Wolfgang Schlichting, and Anna Toncheva. *The Diverse and Exploding Digital Universe: An Updated Forecast of Worldwide Information Growth through 2011.* Framingham, MA: IDC, 2008.

Garfinkel, Simson. *Database Nation: The Death of Privacy in the 21st Century.* Beijing: O'Reilly, 2000.

Garfinkel, Simson, and David Cox. "Finding and Archiving the Internet Footprint." Paper presented at the First Digital Lives Research Conference: Personal Digital Archives for the 21st Century, London, UK, February 9–11, 2009.

Garrett, R. Kelly, and James N. Danziger. "Which Telework? Defining and Testing a Taxonomy of Technology-Mediated Work at a Distance." *Social Science Computer Review* 25, no. 1 (2007): 27–47.

Garrison, Curtis W. "The Relation of Historical Manuscripts to Archival Materials." *American Archivist* 2, no. 2 (1939): 97–105.

Gates, Charles M. "The Administration of State Archives." *American Archivist* 1, no. 3 (1938): 130–41.

Gavrel, Katharine. *Conceptual Problems Posed by Electronic Records: A RAMP Study*. Paris: United Nations Educational, Scientific and Cultural Organization, 1990.

Geary, Patrick J. *Phantoms of Remembrance: Memory and Oblivion at the End of the First Millennium*. Princeton, NJ: Princeton University Press, 1994.

Geda, Carolyn L., Erik W. Austin, and Francis X. Blouin, eds. *Archivists and Machine-Readable Records: Proceedings of the Conference on Archival Management of Machine-Readable Records, February 7–10, 1979, Ann Arbor, Michigan*. Chicago: Society of American Archivists, 1980.

Geitgey, Adam. "The Kaycee Nicole (Swenson) FAQ." In *We've Got Blog: How Weblogs Are Changing Our Culture*, edited by John Rodzvilla, 89–98. Cambridge, MA: Perseus, 2002.

Gelber, Steven M. *Hobbies: Leisure and the Culture of Work in America*. New York: Columbia University Press, 1999.

Gibson, Margaret. "Some Thoughts on Celebrity Deaths: Steve Irwin and the Issue of Public Mourning." *Mortality* 12, no. 1 (2007): 1–3.

Giddens, Anthony. *The Constitution of Society: Outline of the Theory of Structuration*. Berkeley: University of California Press, 1984.

Giddens, Anthony. *Modernity and Self-identity: Self and Society in the Late Modern Age*. Cambridge: Polity Press, 1991.

Gilliland, Anne J., Sue McKemmish, Zhang Bin, Kelvin White, Yang Lu, and Andrew Lau. "Pluralizing the Archival Paradigm: Can Archival Education in Pacific Rim Communities Address the Challenge?" *American Archivist* 71, no. 1 (2008): 84–114.

Gilliland-Swetland, Anne. *Policy and Politics: The Archival Implications of Digital Communications and Culture at the University of Michigan*. Chicago: Society of American Archivists, 1996.

Gilliland-Swetland, Luke J. "The Provenance of a Profession: The Permanence of the Public Archives and Historical Manuscripts Traditions in American Archival History." *American Archivist* 54, no. 2 (1991): 160–75.

Gillmor, Dan. *We the Media: Grassroots Journalism by the People, for the People*. 1st ed. Sebastopol, CA: O'Reilly, 2004.

Gladney, Henry M. "Principles for Digital Preservation." *Communications of the ACM* 49, no. 2 (2006): 111–16.

Glauber, Carole. "Eyes of the Earth: Lily White, Sarah Ladd, and the Oregon Camera Club." *Oregon Historical Quarterly* 108, no. 1 (2007): 34–67.

Glisson, William Bradley. "Use of Computer Forensics in the Digital Curation of Removable Media." In *Proceedings of DigCCurr2009: Digital Curation: Practice, Promise, and Prospects*, edited by Helen R. Tibbo, Carolyn Hank, Christopher A. Lee, and Rachael Clemens, 110–11. Chapel Hill: University of North Carolina, School of Information and Library Science, 2009.

Goffman, Erving. *The Presentation of Self in Everyday Life*. Garden City, NY: Doubleday, 1959.

Golder, Hilary. *Documenting a Nation: Australian Archives, the First Fifty Years*. Canberra: Australian Government Publishing Service, 1994.

Graham, Brad L. "Why I Weblog: A Rumination on Where the Hell I'm Going with This Website." In *We've Got Blog: How Weblogs Are Changing Our Culture*, edited by John Rodzvilla, 34–40. Cambridge, MA: Perseus, 2002. [Originally posted to: Bradlands. June 16, 1999.]

Green, Richard, and Chris Awre. "RepoMMan: Delivering Private Repository Space for Day-to-Day Use." *Ariadne* 54 (2008). http://www.ariadne.ac.uk/issue54/green-awre/.

Green, Richard, and Chris Awre. "Towards a Repository-enabled Scholar's Workbench: RepoMMan, REMAP and Hydra." *D-Lib Magazine* 15, no. 5/6 (2009). http://dx.doi.org/10.1045/may2009-green.

Greene, Mark A. "The Power of Meaning: The Archival Mission in the Postmodern Age." *American Archivist* 65, no. 1 (2002): 42–55.

Greene, Mark A. "'The Surest Proof': A Utilitarian Approach to Appraisal." *Archivaria* 45 (1998): 127–69.

Greene, Mark A., and Todd J. Daniels-Howell. "Documentation with an Attitude: A Pragmatist's Guide to the Selection and Acquisition of Modern Business Records." In *The Records of American Business*, edited by James O'Toole, 161–229. Chicago: Society of American Archivists, 1997.

Greene, Mark A., and Dennis Meissner. "More Product, Less Process: Revamping Traditional Archival Processing." *American Archivist* 68, no. 2 (2005): 208–63.

Greifeneder, Michael, Stephan Strodl, Petar Petrov, and Andreas Rauber. "HOPPLA—Archiving System for Small Institutions." *ERCIM News* 80 (2010): 18–19.

Griffin, Michael Scott. "Amateur Photography and Pictorial Aesthetics: Influences of Organization and Industry on Cultural Production." PhD dissertation, University of Pennsylvania, 1987.

Grinter, Rebecca E. "Words about Images: Coordinating Community in Amateur Photography." *Computer Supported Cooperative Work* 14, no. 2 (2005): 161–88.

Grudin, Jonathan. "Desituating Action: Digital Representation of Context." *Human-Computer Interaction* 16, no. 2/4 (2001): 269–86.

Grudin, Jonathan. "Groupware and Social Dynamics: Eight Challenges for Developers." *Communications of the ACM* 37, no. 1 (1994): 92–105.

Guercio, Maria. "Archival Theory and the Principle of Provenance for Current Records: Their Impact on Arranging and Inventorying Electronic Records." In *The Principle of Provenance: Report from the First Stockholm Conference on Archival Theory and the Principle of Provenance, September 2-3, 1993*, edited by Kerstin Abukhanfusa and Jan Sydbeck, 75-84. Stockholm: Swedish National Archives, 1994.

Gwizdka, Jacek. "Finding to Keep and Organize: Personal Information Collections as Context." Paper presented at Personal Information Management—A SIGIR 2006 Workshop, Seattle, Washington, August 10-11, 2006.

Hafner, Katie. "History, Digitized (And Abridged)." *New York Times*, March 10, 2007.

Halbwachs, Maurice. *The Collective Memory*. 1st ed. New York: Harper and Row, 1980.

Halevy, Alon. "Why Your Data Won't Mix." *Queue* 3, no. 8 (2005): 50–58.

Halvey, Martin, and Mark T. Keane. "An Assessment of Tag Presentation Techniques." In *Proceedings of the 16th International Conference on World Wide Web*, 1313-4. New York: Association for Computing Machinery, 2007.

Ham, F. Gerald. "The Archival Edge." *American Archivist* 38 (1975): 5–13.

Ham, F. Gerald. "Archival Strategies for the Post Custodial Era." *American Archivist* 44 (1981): 207–16.

Ham, F. Gerald. *Selecting and Appraising Archives and Manuscripts.* Chicago: Society of American Archivists, 1993.

Hamilton, Carolyn, Verne Harris, Jane Taylor, Michele Pickover, Graeme Reid, and Razia Saleh, eds. *Refiguring the Archive.* Dordrecht, Netherlands: Kluwer Academic Publishers, 2002.

Hammer, Jessica. "Agency and Authority in Role-Playing 'Texts.'" In *A New Literacies Sampler*, edited by Michele Knobel and Colin Lankshear, 67–93. New York: Peter Lang, 2007.

Hank, Carolyn, Songphan Choemprayong, and Laura Sheble. "Blogger Perceptions on Digital Preservation." In *Proceedings of the 7th ACM/ IEEE Joint Conference on Digital Libraries: Vancouver, British Columbia, Canada, June 18-23, 2007: Building and Sustaining the Digital Environment: JCDL 2007*, 477. New York: ACM Press, 2007.

Hanna, Jannette, and Daniel Burge. "Preserving Digital Memory Files." The Archival Advisor. Image Permanence Institute, 2007. http://www. archivaladvisor.org/shtml/art_presdigmem.shtml.

Hanna, Jannette, and Daniel Burge. "Saving Digital Prints." The Archival Advisor. Image Permanence Institute, 2007. http://www.archivaladvisor. org/shtml/art_savdigprint.shtml.

Hanna, Jannette, and Daniel Burge. "Saving Digital Storage Media." The Archival Advisor. Image Permanence Institute, 2007. http://www. archivaladvisor.org/shtml/art_savdigmedia.shtml.

Harris, Verne. "The Archival Sliver: A Perspective on the Construction of Social Memory in Archives and the Transition from Apartheid to Democracy." In *Refiguring the Archive*, edited by Carolyn Hamilton, Verne Harris, Jane Taylor, Michele Pickover, Graeme Reid, and Razia Saleh, 135–59. Dordrecht, Netherlands: Kluwer Academic Publishers, 2002.

Harris, Verne. "Claiming Less, Delivering More: A Critique of Positivist Formulations on Archives in South Africa." *Archivaria* 44 (1997): 132–41.

Harris, Verne. "On the Back of a Tiger: Deconstructive Possibilities in 'Evidence of Me . . . '" *Archives and Manuscripts* 29, no. 1 (2001): 8–21.

Harris, Verne. "Redefining Archives in South Africa: Public Archives and Society in Transition." *Archivaria* 42 (1996): 6–27.

Hart, Chris, Michael Schoolbred, and David Butcher. "The Bibliographical Structure of Fan Information." Paper presented at the 64th IFLA General Conference, Amsterdam, August 16–21, 1998.

Hartel, Jenna. "Information Activities, Resources and Spaces in the Hobby of Gourmet Cooking." PhD dissertation, University of California, Los Angeles, 2007.

Harthardottir, G. "Amateur Photography Groups in Reykjavik 1950–70." *History of Photography* 23, no. 1 (1999): 43–48.

Hedstrom, Margaret. "Archives, Memory, and Interfaces with the Past." *Archival Science* 2, no. 1–2 (2002): 21–43.

Hedstrom, Margaret. *Archives and Manuscripts: Machine-Readable Records.* Basic Manual Series. Chicago: Society of American Archivists, 1984.

Hedstrom, Margaret. "Understanding Electronic Incunabula: A Framework for Research on Electronic Records." *American Archivist* 54 (1991): 334–54.

Hedstrom, Margaret, ed. *Electronic Records Management Program Strategies.* Archives and Museum Informatics Technical Report No. 18. Pittsburgh, PA: Archives and Museum Informatics, 1993.

Henning, Jeffrey. "The Blogging Iceberg." Perseus Development Corporation, 2003.

Henry, Linda J. "Collecting Policies of Special Subject Repositories." *American Archivist* 43 (1980): 57–63.

Herring, Susan C., Lois Ann Scheidt, Sabrina Bonus, and Elijah Wright. "Bridging the Gap: A Genre Analysis of Weblogs." Paper presented at the 37th Annual Hawaii International Conference on System Sciences (HICSS '04), Big Island, Hawaii, January 5–8, 2004.

Herring, Susan C., Lois Ann Scheidt, Inna Kouper, and Elijah Wright. "A Longitudinal Content Analysis of Weblogs: 2003–2004." In *Blogging, Citizenship, and the Future of Media,* edited by Mark Tremayne, 3–20. London: Routledge, 2007.

Higgs, Edward, ed. *History and Electronic Artefacts.* Oxford, England: Clarendon Press, 1998.

Hill, William C., James D. Hollan, Dave Wroblewski, and Tim McCandless. "Edit Wear and Read Wear." In *CHI '92 Conference Proceedings: ACM Conference on Human Factors in Computing Systems: Striking a Balance, May 3-7, 1992, Monterey, California*, edited by John Bennett, Penny Bauersfeld, and Gene Lynch, 3-9. New York: Association for Computing Machinery, 1992.

Hilton, Chris, and Dave Thompson. "Collecting Born-Digital Archives at the Wellcome Library." *Ariadne* 50 (2007). http://www.ariadne.ac.uk/issue50/hilton-thompson/.

Hilton, Chris, and Dave Thompson. "Further Experiences in Collecting Born-Digital Archives at the Wellcome Library." *Ariadne* 53 (2007). http://www.ariadne.ac.uk/issue53/hilton-thompson/.

Hinding, Andrea. "Inventing a Concept of Documentation." *Journal of American History* 80, no. 1 (1993): 168-78.

Hindman, Matthew. "A Mile Wide and an Inch Deep: Measuring Media Diversity Online and Offline." In *Localism and Media Diversity: Meaning and Metrics*, edited by Philip Napoli, 327-47. Mahwah, NJ: Lawrence Erlbaum Associates, 2006.

Hindus, Michael Stephen, Theodore M. Hammett, and Barbara M. Hobson. *The Files of the Massachusetts Superior Court, 1859-1959: An Analysis and a Plan for Action: A Report of the Massachusetts Judicial Records Committee of the Supreme Judicial Court, Boston, 1979*. Boston, MA: G.K. Hall, 1980.

Hobbs, Catherine. "The Character of Personal Archives: Reflections on the Value of Records of Individuals." *Archivaria* 52 (2001): 126-35.

Holmes, Oliver W. "Archival Arrangement—Five Different Operations at Five Different Levels." *American Archivist* 27, no. 1 (1964): 21-41.

Holmes, Richard. *Footsteps: Adventures of a Romantic Biographer*. London: Flamingo, 1995.

Horrigan, John B. "Use of Cloud Computing Applications and Services." Washington, DC: Pew Internet and American Life Project, 2008.

Horsman, Peter. "Dirty Hands: A New Perspective on the Original Order." *Archives and Manuscripts* 27, no. 1 (1999): 42-53.

Horsman, Peter. "The Last Dance of the Phoenix, or the De-Discovery of the Archival Fonds." *Archivaria* 54 (2002): 1-23.

House, Nancy A. Van. "Flickr and Public Image-Sharing: Distant Closeness and Photo Exhibition." In *CHI '07 Extended Abstracts on Human Factors in Computing Systems*, 2717-22. New York: ACM Press, 2007.

Hull, Felix. *The Use of Sampling Techniques in the Retention of Records: A RAMP Study with Guidelines.* Paris: UNESCO, 1981.

Human Rights and Equal Opportunity Commission Australia (HREOC). "Bringing Them Home: Report of the National Inquiry into the Separation of Aboriginal and Torres Strait Islander Children from their Families." Canberra: HREOC, 1997.

Hurley, Chris. "The Australian ('Series') System: An Exposition." In *The Records Continuum: Ian Maclean and Australian Archives First Fifty Years*, edited by Sue McKemmish and Michael Piggott, 150-72. Clayton: Ancora Press, 1994.

Hurley, Chris. "Parallel Provenance: (1) What, If Anything, is Archival Description?" *Archives and Manuscripts* 33, no. 1 (2005): 110-45.

Hurley, Chris. "Parallel Provenance: (2) When Something is *Not* Related to Everything Else." *Archives and Manuscripts* 33, no. 2 (2005): 52-91.

Hurley, Chris. "Problems with Provenance." *Archives and Manuscripts* 23, no. 2 (1995): 234-59.

Hyry, Tom, and Rachel Onuf. "The Personality of Electronic Records: The Impact of New Information Technology on Personal Papers." *Archival Issues* 22, no. 1 (1997): 37-44.

Indratmo, and Julita Vassileva. "A Review of Organizational Structures of Personal Information Management." *Journal of Digital Information* 9, no. 26 (2008). http://journals.tdl.org/jodi/article/view/251/200.

International Council on Archives. "Principles and Functional Requirements for Records in Electronic Office Environments, Module 1: Overview and Statement of Principles." 2008.

International Organization for Standardization. "Information and Documentation—Records Management." ISO 15489. 2001.

Jacobs, David L. "Domestic Snapshots: Toward a Grammar of Motives." *Journal of American Culture* 4, no. 1 (1981): 93-105.

Janssen, William C., Jeff Breidenbach, Lance Good, and Ashok Popat. "Making UpLib Useful: Personal Document Engineering." PARC Technical Report. Palo Alto, CA: Palo Alto Research Center, 2005.

Jenkinson, Hilary. *A Manual of Archive Administration: Including the Problems of War Archives and Archive Making.* Oxford: Clarendon Press, 1922.

Jimerson, Randall C. "Archives and Memory." *OCLC Systems and Services* 19, no. 3 (2003): 89–95.

Jimerson, Randall C. *Archives Power: Memory, Accountability, and Social Justice.* Chicago: Society of American Archivists, 2009.

Jimerson, Randall C. "The Future of Archives and Manuscripts." *OCLC Systems and Services* 20, no. 1 (2004): 11–14.

John, Jeremy Leighton. "Adapting Existing Technologies for Digitally Archiving Personal Lives: Digital Forensics, Ancestral Computing, and Evolutionary Perspectives and Tools." Paper presented at iPRES 2008: The Fifth International Conference on Preservation of Digital Objects, London, UK, September 29–30, 2008.

John, Jeremy Leighton. "Because Topics Often Fade: Letters, Essays, Notes, Digital Manuscripts and Other Unpublished Works." In *Narrow Roads of Gene Land: The Collected Papers of W. D. Hamilton*, edited by Mark Ridley, 399–422. Oxford: Oxford University Press, 2005.

John, Jeremy Leighton. "Digital Manuscripts: Capture and Context." Presented at Email Curation: Practical Approaches for Long-Term Preservation and Access, Newcastle, April 24–25, 2006.

John, Jeremy Leighton, Ian Rowlands, Peter Williams, and Katrina Dean. "Digital Lives: Personal Digital Archives for the 21st Century >> An Initial Synthesis." A Digital Lives Research Paper. March 3, 2010.

Johnston, Leslie. "Development and Assessment of a Public Discovery and Delivery Interface for a Fedora Repository." *D-Lib Magazine* 11, no. 10 (2005). http:// dx.doi.org/10.1045/october2005-johnston.

Johnston, Leslie. "An Overview of Digital Library Repository Development at the University of Virginia Library." *OCLC Systems and Services* 20, no. 4 (2004): 170–73.

Jones, Ian, and Graham Symon. "Lifelong Learning as Serious Leisure: Policy, Practice and Potential." *Leisure Studies* 20, no. 4 (2001): 269–83.

Jones, William. "Finders, Keepers? The Present and Future Perfect in Support of Personal Information Management." *First Monday* 9, no. 3 (2004). http://firstmonday.org/article/view/1123/1043.

Jones, William. "How People Keep and Organize Personal Information." In
Personal Information Management, edited by William P. Jones and Jaime
Teevan, 35–56. Seattle: University of Washington Press, 2007.

Jones, William P. Keeping Found Things Found: The Study and Practice of
Personal Information Management. Amsterdam: Morgan Kaufmann
Publishers, 2008.

Jones, William. "Personal Information Management." Annual Review of
Information Science and Technology, edited by Blaise Cronin, 453–504.
Medford, NJ: Information Today, 2007.

Jones, William, Harry Bruce, and Susan Dumais. "Keeping Found Things
Found on the Web." In Proceedings of the 2001 ACM CIKM: Tenth
International Conference on Information and Knowledge Management:
November 5–10, 2001, Atlanta, Georgia, USA, edited by Henrique
Paques, Ling Liu, and David A. Grossman, 119–26. New York:
Association for Computing Machinery, 2001.

Jones, William, Susan Dumais, and Harry Bruce. "Once Found, What Then?
A Study of 'Keeping' Behaviors in the Personal Use of Web Information."
In Proceedings of the 65th Annual Meeting of the American Society for
Information Science and Technology (ASIST 2002), Philadelphia, PA,
edited by Edie Rasmussen and Elaine G. Toms, 391–402. Medford, NJ:
Information Today, 2002.

Jones, William, Ammy Jiranida Phuwanartnurak, Rajdeep Gill, and Harry
Bruce. "Don't Take My Folders Away! Organizing Personal Information
to Get Things Done." In CHI 2005: Technology, Safety, Community:
Conference Proceedings: Conference on Human Factors in Computing
Systems: Portland, Oregon, USA, April 2–7, edited by Wendy Anne
Kellogg, Shumin Zhai, Carolyn Gale and G.C. van der Veer, 1505–8. New
York: Association for Computing Machinery, 2005.

Jones, William, and Jaime Teevan, eds. Personal Information Management.
Seattle: University of Washington Press, 2007.

Jörgensen, Corinne L. Image Retrieval: Theory and Research. Lanham, MD:
Scarecrow Press, 2003.

Jörgensen, Corinne L. "Retrieving the Unretrievable: Art, Aesthetics, and
Emotion in Image Retrieval Systems." In Proceedings of SPIE, edited by
Bernice E. Rogowitz and Thrasyvoulos N. Pappas, 348–55. San Jose,
CA: International Society for Optical Engineering, 1999.

Kaptelinin, Victor, and Mary Czerwinski. "Introduction: The Desktop Metaphor and New Uses of Technology." In *Beyond the Desktop Metaphor: Designing Integrated Digital Work Environments*, edited by Victor Kaptelinin and Mary P. Czerwinski, 1–12. Cambridge, MA: MIT Press, 2007.

Karat, Clare-Marie, John Karat, and Carolyn Brodie. "Management of Personal Information Disclosure: The Interdependence of Privacy, Security, and Trust." In *Personal Information Management*, edited by William P. Jones and Jaime Teevan, 249–60. Seattle: University of Washington Press, 2007.

Karger, David, Karun Bakshi, David Huynh, Dennis Quan, and Vineet Sinha. "Haystack: A General Purpose Information Management Tool for End Users of Semistructured Data." In *Proceedings of the Second Biennial Conference on Innovative Data Systems Research, Asilomar, CA, USA, January 4–7, 2005*, 13–26.

Kari, Jarkko, and Jenna Hartel. "Information and Higher Things in Life: Addressing the Pleasurable and the Profound in Information Science." *Journal of the American Society for Information Science and Technology* 58, no. 8 (2007): 1131–47.

Kaye, Joseph, Janet Vertesi, Shari Avery, Allan Dafoe, Shay David, Lisa Onaga, Ivan Rosero, and Trevor Pinch. "To Have and To Hold: Exploring the Personal Archive." In *CHI 2006: Interact, Inform, Inspire: Conference Proceedings: Conference on Human Factors in Computing Systems: Montreal, Quebec, Canada, April 22–27, 2006*, edited by Rebecca E. Grinter, 275–84. New York: Association for Computing Machinery, 2006.

Keith, Jeremy. "Magnoliloss." *Adactio*. February 17, 2009. http://adactio.com/journal/1552/.

Kelby, Scott. *The Digital Photography Book*. Berkeley, CA: Peachpit Press, 2006.

Kelly, Liadh, Yi Chen, Marguerite Fuller, and Gareth J. F. Jones. "A Study of Remembered Context for Information Access from Personal Digital Archives." In *Proceedings of the Second International Conference on Interaction Context: October 14–17, 2008, London, United Kingdom*, edited by Mounia Lalmas and Anastasios Tombros, 4–50. New York: ACM Press, 2008.

Kepley, David R. "Sampling in Archives: A Review." *American Archivist* 47, no. 3 (1984): 237–42.

Ketelaar, Eric. "Access: The Democratic Imperative." *Archives and Manuscripts* 34, no. 2 (2006): 62–81.

Ketelaar, Eric. "Archives as Spaces of Memory." *Journal of the Society of Archivists* 29, no. 1 (2008): 9–27.

Ketelaar, Eric. "Being Digital in People's Archives." *Archives and Manuscripts* 31, no. 2 (2003): 8–22.

Ketelaar, Eric. "Everyone an Archivist." In *Managing and Archiving Records in the Digital Era. Changing Professional Orientations,* edited by Niklaus Bütikofer, Hans Hofman, and Seamus Ross, 9–14. Baden: Hier + Jetzt, Verlag für Kultur und Geschichte, 2006.

Ketelaar, Eric. "Recordkeeping and Societal Power." In *Archives: Recordkeeping in Society,* edited by Sue McKemmish, Michael Piggott, Barbara Reed, and Frank Upward, 277–98. Wagga Wagga, N.S.W.: Centre for Information Studies, Charles Sturt University, 2005.

Kindberg, Tim, Mirjana Spasojevic, Rowanne Fleck, and Abigail Sellen. "The Ubiquitous Camera: An In-Depth Study of Camera Phone Use." *IEEE Pervasive Computing* 4, no. 2 (2005): 42–50.

King, Nigel. "Template Analysis." In *Qualitative Methods and Analysis in Organizational Research,* edited by Gillian Symon and Catherine Cassell, 118–34. London: Sage, 1998.

Kirchhoff, Lars, Axel Bruns, and Thomas Nicolai. "Investigating the Impact of the Blogosphere: Using Pagerank to Determine the Distribution of Attention." Paper presented at the Annual Conference of the Association of Internet Researchers, Vancouver, Canada, 2007.

Kirk, David, Abigail Sellen, Richard Harper, and Ken Wood. "Understanding Videowork." In *CHI 2007: Reach Beyond: Conference Proceedings: Conference on Human Factors in Computing Systems, San Jose, California, USA, April 18–May 3, 2007,* edited by James Begole, 61–70. New York: Association for Computing Machinery, 2007.

Kirk, David, Abigail Sellen, Carsten Rother, and Ken Wood. "Understanding Photowork." In *CHI 2006: Interact, Inform, Inspire: Conference Proceedings: Conference on Human Factors in Computing Systems: Montreal, Quebec, Canada, April 22–27, 2006,* edited by Rebecca E. Grinter, 761–70. New York: Association for Computing Machinery, 2006.

Kirschenbaum, Matthew G. "Hamlet.Doc? Literature in a Digital Age." *Chronicle of Higher Education* 53, no. 50 (2007): B8.

Kirschenbaum, Matthew G. *Mechanisms: New Media and the Forensic Imagination.* Cambridge, MA: MIT Press, 2008.

Kirschenbaum, Matthew G., Erika Farr, Kari M. Kraus, Naomi L. Nelson, Catherine Stollar Peters, Gabriela Redwine, and Doug Reside. "Approaches to Managing and Collecting Born-Digital Literary Materials for Scholarly Use." College Park, MD: University of Maryland, 2009.

Koehler, Wallace. "A Longitudinal Study of Web Pages Continued: A Consideration of Document Persistence." *Information Research* 9, no. 2 (2004). http://InformationR.net/ir/9-2/paper174.html.

Kolish, Evelyn. "Sampling Methodology and Its Application: An Illustration of the Tension between Theory and Practice." *Archivaria* 38 (1994): 61–73.

Kolowich, Steve. "Alumni Try to Rewrite History on College-Newspaper Web Sites." *Chronicle of Higher Education,* May 15 2009, A1.

Koontz, Linda D. "Electronic Records Management and Preservation Pose Challenges." Washington, DC: U.S. General Accounting Office, 2003.

Kornblum, Jesse. "Identifying Almost Identical Files Using Context Triggered Piecewise Hashing." *Digital Investigation* 3, Supplement 1, Proceedings of the 6th Annual Digital Forensic Research Workshop (DFRWS '06) (2006): 91–97.

Kotro, Tanja. "User Orientation through Experience: A Study of Hobbyist Knowing in Product Development." *Human Technology: An Interdisciplinary Journal on Humans in ICT Environments* 3, no. 2 (2007): 154–66.

Krause, Michael G. "Intellectual Problems of Indexing Picture Collections." *Audiovisual Librarian* 14, no. 2 (1988): 73–81.

Krawcyzk, Bob. "Cross Reference Heaven: The Abandonment of the Fonds as the Primary Level of Arrangement for Ontario Government Records." *Archivaria* 48 (1999): 131–53.

Krogh, Peter. *The DAM Book: Digital Asset Management for Photographers.* Sebastopol, CA: O'Reilly, 2006.

Kuan, Christine. "ARTstor: Collections and the New Curatorial Workspace." Paper presented at International Federation of Library Associations and Institutions, Florence, Italy, 2009.

Kulsrud, Carl. "Sampling Rural Rehabilitation Records for Transfer to the National Archives." *American Archivist* 10 (1947): 328–34.

Kurtz, Matthew. "A Postcolonial Archive? On the Paradox of Practice in a Northwest Alaska Project." *Archivaria* 61 (2006): 63–90.

Kustritz, Anne. "Slashing the Romance Narrative." *Journal of American Culture* 26, no. 3 (2003): 371–84.

Kwasnik, Barbara H. "The Importance of Factors That Are Not Document Attributes in the Organization of Personal Documents." *Journal of Documentation* 47, no. 4 (1991): 389–98.

Lagoze, Carl. "Keeping Dublin Core Simple: Cross-Domain Discovery or Resource Description?" *D-Lib Magazine* 7, no. 1 (2001). http://dx.doi.org/10.1045/january2001-lagoze.

Lakoff, George. *Women, Fire, and Dangerous Things: What Categories Reveal About the Mind.* Chicago: University of Chicago Press, 1987.

Lambert, Ronald D. "Doing Family History." *Families* 35 (1996): 11–25.

Lang, Karl. "Rendering the Print: The Art of Photography." Adobe technical paper. 2007.

Lange, Michele C. S., and Kristin M. Nimsger. *Electronic Evidence and Discovery: What Every Lawyer Should Know Now.* 2nd ed. Chicago: Section of Science and Technology Law, American Bar Association, 2009.

Langford, Michael, and Efthimia Bilissi. *Langford's Advanced Photography.* 7th ed. Oxford: Focal Press, 2008.

Lansdale, M. "The Psychology of Personal Information Management." *Applied Ergonomics* 19, no. 1 (1988): 55–66.

Lasica, J. D. "Weblogs: A New Source of News." In *We've Got Blog: How Weblogs Are Changing Our Culture*, edited by John Rodzvilla, 171–82. Cambridge, MA: Perseus, 2002.

Lavagnino, John. "The Analytical Bibliography of Electronic Texts." Paper presented at the Joint Annual Conference of the Association for Literary and Linguistic Computing and the Association for Computers and the Humanities, Bergen, Norway, 1996.

Lavoie, Brian F. *The Incentives to Preserve Digital Materials: Roles, Scenarios, and Economic Decision-Making.* Dublin, OH: OCLC Research, 2003.

Layne, Sara Shatford. "Some Issues in the Indexing of Images." *Journal of the American Society for Information Science* 45, no. 8 (1994): 583–88.

Leahy, Emmett J. "Reduction of Public Records." *American Archivist* 3, no. 1 (1940): 13–38.

Le Bon, Gustave. *The Crowd: A Study of the Popular Mind.* New York: Macmillan, 1896.

Lee, Christopher A. "Defining Digital Preservation Work: A Case Study of the Development of the Reference Model for an Open Archival Information System." PhD dissertation, University of Michigan, 2005.

Lee, Christopher A. "A Framework for Contextual Information in Digital Collections." *Journal of Documentation* 67, no. 1 (2011): 95–143.

Lee, Christopher A. "Guerilla Electronic Records Management: Lessons Learned." *Records and Information Management Report* 18, no. 5 (2002): 1–13.

Lee, Christopher A. "Matrix of Digital Curation Knowledge and Competencies." 2009. http://ils.unc.edu/digccurr/digccurr-matrix.html.

Lee, Christopher A. "Never Optimize: Building and Managing a Robust Cyberinfrastructure." Paper presented at History and Theory of Infrastructure: Distilling Lessons for New Scientific Cyberinfrastructures, Ann Arbor, MI, September 28–October 1, 2006.

Lee, Christopher A., and Helen R. Tibbo. "Capturing the Moment: Strategies for Selection and Collection of Web-Based Resources to Document Important Social Phenomena." In *Archiving 2008: Final Program and Proceedings, June 24–27, 2008, Bern, Switzerland,* 300–305. Springfield, VA: Society for Imaging Science and Technology, 2008.

Lee, Hur-Li. "The Concept of Collection from the User's Perspective." *Library Quarterly* 75, no. 1 (2005): 67–85.

Le Goff, Jacques. *History and Memory.* Translated by Steven Rendall and Elizabeth Claman. New York: Columbia University Press, 1992.

Lehikoinen, Juha, Antti Aaltonen, Pertti Huuskonen, and Ilkka Salminen. *Personal Content Experience: Managing Digital Life in the Mobile Age.* Chichester, England: John Wiley, 2007.

Lenhart, Amanda. "Adults and Social Network Websites." Washington, DC: Pew Internet and American Life Project, 2009.

Lenhart, Amanda, and Susannah Fox. "Bloggers: A Portrait of the Internet's New Storytellers." Washington, DC: Pew Internet and American Life Project, 2006.

Lenhart, Amanda, and Mary Madden. "Social Networking Websites and Teens: An Overview." Washington, DC: Pew Internet and American Life Project, 2007.

Leone, Stefania, Michael Grossniklaus, and Moira C. Norrie. "Architecture for Integrating Desktop and Web 2.0 Data Management." Paper presented at the 7th International Workshop on Web-Oriented Software Technologies (IWWOST 2008), Yorktown Heights, New York, July 14, 2008.

Levy, David M. "Heroic Measures: Reflections on the Possibility and Purpose of Digital Preservation." In *Digital Libraries 98: The Third ACM Conference on Digital Libraries, June 23–26, 1998, Pittsburgh, PA*, edited by I. H. Witten, Robert M. Akscyn, and Frank M. Shipman, 152–61. New York: Association for Computing Machinery, 1998.

Levy, David M., and Catherine C. Marshall. "Going Digital: A Look at Assumptions Underlying Digital Libraries." *Communications of the ACM* 38, no. 4 (1995): 77–83.

Lewinson, Paul. "Archival Sampling." *American Archivist* 20 (1957): 291–312.

Lewis, Kevin, Jason Kaufman, and Nicholas Christakis. "The Taste for Privacy: An Analysis of College Student Privacy Settings in an Online Social Network." *Journal of Computer-Mediated Communication* 14, no. 1 (2008): 79–100.

Light, Michelle, and Tom Hyry. "Colophons and Annotations: New Directions for the Finding Aid." *American Archivist* 65, no. 2 (2002): 216–30.

Livingstone, Sonia. "Taking Risky Opportunities in Youthful Content Creation: Teenagers' Use of Social Networking Sites for Intimacy, Privacy and Self-Expression." *New Media and Society* 10, no. 3 (2008): 393–411.

Lorie, Raymond. "A Methodology and System for Preserving Digital Data." In *Proceedings of the Second ACM/IEEE-CS Joint Conference on Digital Libraries: July 14–18, 2002, Portland, Oregon*, edited by Gary Marchionini and William R. Hersh, 312–19. New York: ACM Press, 2002.

Lovett, Robert W. "The Appraisal of Older Business Records." *American Archivist* 15, no. 1 (1952): 231–39.

Lukesh, Susan S. "E-Mail and Potential Loss to Future Archives and Scholarship or the Dog That Didn't Bark." *First Monday* 4, no. 9 (1999). http://firstmonday.org/article/view/692/602.

Lutters, Wayne G., Mark S. Ackerman, and Xiaomu Zhou. "Group Information Management." In *Personal Information Management*, edited by William P. Jones and Jaime Teevan, 236–48. Seattle: University of Washington Press, 2007.

Mackenzie, Maureen L. "Storage and Retrieval of E-Mail in a Business Environment: An Exploratory Guide." *Library and Information Science Research* 24, no. 4 (2002): 357–72.

Malcolm, Janet. *The Silent Woman.* London: Picador, 1994.

Malone, Thomas W. "How Do People Organize Their Desks? Implications for the Design of Office Information Systems." *ACM Transactions on Information Systems* 1, no. 1 (1983): 99–112.

Marchionini, Gary, Chirag Shah, Christopher A. Lee, and Robert Capra. "Query Parameters for Harvesting Digital Video and Associated Contextual Information." In *Proceedings of the 9th ACM/IEEE-CS Joint Conference on Digital Libraries*, 77–86. New York: ACM Press, 2009.

Marcum, James W. "Beyond Visual Culture: The Challenge of Visual Ecology." *Portal: Libraries and the Academy* 2, no. 2 (2002): 189–206.

Marill, Jennifer, Andrew Boyko, and Michael Ashenfelder. "Web Harvesting Survey." International Internet Preservation Coalition, 2004.

Markus, M. Lynne. "Toward a Theory of Knowledge Reuse: Types of Knowledge Reuse Situations and Factors in Reuse Success." *Journal of Management Information Systems* 18, no. 1 (2001): 57–93.

Marmor, Max. "The ARTstor Digital Library: A Case Study in Digital Curation." Paper presented at DigCCurr 2007, An International Symposium on Preservation, Chapel Hill, NC, April 18–20, 2007.

Marr, David. *Patrick White: A Life.* Sydney, Australia: Vintage, 1992.

Marshall, Catherine C. "From Writing and Analysis to the Repository: Taking the Scholars' Perspective on Scholarly Archiving." In *JCDL 2008: Proceedings of the 8th ACM/IEEE Joint Conference on Digital Libraries:*

Pittsburgh, Pennsylvania, June 15–20, 2008, 251–60. New York: ACM Press, 2008.

Marshall, Catherine C. "Rethinking Personal Digital Archiving, Part 1: Four Challenges from the Field." *D-Lib Magazine* 14, no. 3/4 (2008). http://dx.doi.org/10.1045/march2008-marshall-pt1.

Marshall, Catherine C. "Rethinking Personal Digital Archiving, Part 2: Implications for Services, Applications, and Institutions." *D-Lib Magazine* 14, no. 3/4 (2008). http://dx.doi.org/10.1045/march2008-marshall-pt2.

Marshall, Catherine C., and Sara Bly. "Saving and Using Encountered Information: Implications for Electronic Periodicals." In *CHI 2005: Technology, Safety, Community: Conference Proceedings: Conference on Human Factors in Computing Systems: Portland, Oregon, USA, April 2–7, 2005,* edited by Wendy Anne Kellogg, Shumin Zhai, Carolyn Gale, and G. C. van der Veer, 111–20. New York: Association for Computing Machinery, 2005.

Marshall, Catherine C., Sara Bly, and Francoise Brun-Cottan. "The Long Term Fate of Our Digital Belongings: Toward a Service Model for Personal Archives." In *Archiving 2006: Final Program and Proceedings, May 23–26, 2006, Ottawa, Canada,* edited by Stephen Chapman and Scott A. Stovall, 25–30. Springfield, VA: Society for Imaging Science and Technology, 2006.

Marshall, Catherine C., Frank McCown, and Michael L. Nelson. "Evaluating Personal Archiving Strategies for Internet-Based Information." In *Archiving 2007: Final Program and Proceedings, May 21–24, 2007, Arlington, Virginia,* 151–56. Springfield, VA: Society for Imaging Science and Technology, 2007.

Masanès, Julien. *Web Archiving.* New York: Springer, 2006.

Mayer-Schönberger, Viktor. *Delete: The Virtue of Forgetting in the Digital Age.* Princeton, NJ: Princeton University Press, 2009.

McCown, Frank, Catherine C. Marshall, and Michael L. Nelson. "Why Websites Are Lost (and How They're Sometimes Found)." *Communications of the ACM* 52, no. 11 (2009): 141–45.

McDonald, John. "Information Management in the Government of Canada: A Situation Analysis." Ottawa: National Archives of Canada, 2000.

McDonald, John. "Towards Automated Record Keeping, Interfaces for the Capture of Records of Business Processes." *Archives and Museum Informatics* 11 (1997): 277–85.

McDonald, John. "The Wild Frontier Ten Years On." In *Managing Electronic Records*, edited by Julie McLeod and Catherine Hare, 1–17. London, UK: Facet Publishing, 2005.

McIntosh, Robert. "The Great War, Archives, and Modern Memory." *Archivaria* 46 (1998): 1–31.

McKay, Eleanor. "Random Sampling Techniques: A Method of Reducing Large, Homogeneous Series in Congressional Papers." *American Archivist* 41, no. 3 (1978): 281–89.

McKechnie, Lynne, Lynda Baker, Martha Greenwood, and Heidi Julien. "Research Method Trends in Human Information Literature." *New Review of Information Behavior Research* 3 (2002): 113–26.

McKemmish, Sue. "Are Records Ever Actual?" In *The Records Continuum: Ian Maclean and Australian Archives First Fifty Years*, edited by Sue McKemmish and Michael Piggott, 187–203. Clayton: Ancora Press, 1994.

McKemmish, Sue. "Evidence of Me . . . " *Archives and Manuscripts* 24, no. 1 (1996): 28–45.

McKemmish, Sue. "Introducing Archives and Archival Programs." In *Keeping Archives*, edited by Judith Ellis, 1–24. Port Melbourne, Australia: Thorpe, 1993.

McKemmish, Sue. "Placing Records Continuum Theory and Practice." *Archival Science* 1, no. 4 (2001): 333–59.

McKemmish, Sue. "Traces: Document, Record, Archive, Archives." In *Archives: Recordkeeping in Society*, edited by Sue McKemmish, Michael Piggott, Barbara Reed, and Frank Upward, 1–20. Wagga Wagga, N.S.W.: Centre for Information Studies, Charles Sturt University, 2005.

McKemmish, Sue, Shannon Faulkhead, Livia Iacovino, and Kirsten Thorpe. "Australian Indigenous Knowledge and the Archives: Embracing Multiple Ways of Knowing and Keeping." *Archives and Manuscripts* 38, no. 1 (2010): 27–50.

McKemmish, Sue, Michael Piggott, and Barbara Reed. "Archives." In *Archives: Recordkeeping in Society*, edited by Sue McKemmish, Michael

Piggott, Barbara Reed, and Frank Upward, 159–96. Wagga Wagga, N.S.W.: Centre for Information Studies, Charles Sturt University, 2005.

McKemmish, Sue, Michael Piggott, Barbara Reed, and Frank Upward, eds. *Archives: Recordkeeping in Society*. Topics in Australasian Library and Information Studies, vol. 24. Wagga Wagga, N.S.W.: Centre for Information Studies, Charles Sturt University, 2005.

McKemmish, Sue, and Frank Upward. "The Archival Document: A Submission to the Inquiry into Australia as an Information Society." *Archives and Manuscripts* 19, no. 1 (1991): 17–32.

McLeod, Julie, and Catherine Hare, eds. *Managing Electronic Records*. London: Facet Publishing, 2005.

McRanor, Shauna. "Maintaining the Reliability of Aboriginal Oral Records and Their Material Manifestations: Implications for Archival Practice." *Archivaria* 43 (1997): 64–88.

Mears, Gillian. *The Grass Sister*. Sydney, Australia: Knopf, 1995.

Menne-Haritz, Angelika. "Access—the Reformulation of an Archival Paradigm." *Archival Science* 1, no. 1 (2001): 57–82.

Messina, Chris. "Where Data Goes When It Dies and Other Musings." *FactoryCity*, February 6, 2009. http://factoryjoe.com/blog/2009/02/06/where-does-data-go-when-it-dies/.

Metadata Working Group. Guidelines for Handling Image Metadata. February 2009. http://www.metadataworkinggroup.org/pdf/mwg_guidance.pdf.

Millar, Laura. "The Death of the Fonds and the Resurrection of Provenance: Archival Context in Space and Time." *Archivaria* 53 (2002): 1–15.

Miller, Andrew D., and W. Keith Edwards. "Give and Take: A Study of Consumer Photo-Sharing Culture and Practice." In *Proceedings of the SIGCHI Conference on Human Factors in Computing Systems*, 347–56. New York: ACM Press, 2007.

Miller, Frederic. "Use, Appraisal and Research: A Case Study of Social History." *American Archivist* 49, no. 4 (1986): 371–92.

Miller, Rich. "Who Has the Most Web Servers?" *Data Center Knowledge*. May 14, 2009. http://www.datacenterknowledge.com/archives/2009/05/14/whos-got-the-most-web-servers/.

Mishne, Gilad, and Natalie Glance. "Leave a Reply: An Analysis of Weblog Comments." Paper presented at the 3rd Annual Workshop on the Weblogging Ecosystem: Aggregation, Analysis and Dynamics, Edinburgh, UK, May 23, 2006.

Mitchell, Grant Alan. *Approaching Electronic Records Management in the Insurance Corporation of British Columbia: A Case Study in Organizational Dynamics and Archival Initiative.* Chicago: Society of American Archivists, 1997.

Mitra, Siddharth. "Characterising Online Video Sharing and Its Dynamics." Master's thesis, Indian Institute of Technology, 2009.

"Model Requirements for the Management of Electronic Records: Update and Extension." MoReq2 Specification. Hampshire, United Kingdom: Serco Consulting, 2008.

Montaña, John C. "Who Owns Business Data on Personally Owned Computers?" *Information Management Journal* 39, no. 3 (2005): 36–40, 42.

Morozov, Evgeny. "Speak, Memory: Can Digital Storage Remember for You?" *Boston Review* (May/June 2010). http://bostonreview.net/BR35.3/morozov.php.

Morris, Meredith Ringel. "A Survey of Collaborative Web Search Practices." In *The 26th Annual CHI Conference on Human Factors in Computing Systems: Conference Proceedings*, edited by Margaret Burnett, Maria Francesca Costabile, Tiziana Catarci, Boris de Ruyter, Desney Tan, Mary Czerwinski, and Arnie Lund, 1657–60. New York: Association for Computing Machinery, 2008.

Muller, Samuel, Johan Adriaan Feith, and R. Fruin. *Manual for the Arrangement and Description of Archives: Drawn up by Direction of the Netherlands Association of Archivists.* Translated by Arthur H. Leavitt. Chicago: Society of American Archivists, 2003.

Murray, Susan. "Digital Images, Photo-Sharing, and Our Shifting Notions of Everyday Aesthetics." *Journal of Visual Culture* 7, no. 2 (2008): 147–63.

Myllymaki, Jussi. "Effective Web Data Extraction with Standard XML Technologies." *Computer Networks* 39 (2002): 635–44.

Nardi, Bonnie A., and Deborah Barreau. "'Finding and Reminding' Revisited: Appropriate Metaphors for File Organization at the Desktop." *SIGCHI Bulletin* 29, no. 1 (1997): 76–78.

Nardi, Bonnie A., Diane J. Schiano, and Michelle Gumbrecht. "Blogging as Social Activity, or, Would You Let 900 Million People Read Your Diary?" In *CSCW 2004: Computer Supported Cooperative Work: Conference Proceedings, November 6–10, 2004, Chicago*, 222–31. New York: Association for Computing Machinery, 2004.

Naugler, Harold. *The Archival Appraisal of Machine-Readable Records: A RAMP Study with Guidelines*. Paris: General Information Programme and United Nations Educational Scientific and Cultural Organization, 1984.

Neal, Diane R. "News Photography Image Retrieval Practices: Locus of Control in Two Contexts." PhD dissertation, University of North Texas, 2006.

Nelson Mandela Foundation. *A Prisoner in the Garden: Opening Nelson Mandela's Prison Archive*. London: Viking, 2005.

Nesmith, Tom. "Archives from the Bottom Up: Social History and Archival Scholarship." *Archivaria* 14 (1982): 5–26.

Nesmith, Tom. "Still Fuzzy, but More Accurate: Some Thoughts on the 'Ghosts' of Archival Theory." *Archivaria* 47 (1999): 136–50.

Nielsen, Jakob. "Participation Inequality: Encouraging More Users to Contribute." *Alertbox*, October 9, 2006. http://www.useit.com/alertbox/participation_inequality.html.

Nightingale, Virginia. "The Cameraphone and Online Image Sharing." *Continuum: Journal of Media and Cultural Studies* 21, no. 2 (2007): 289–301.

Noble, Greg. "Accumulating Being." *International Journal of Cultural Studies* 7, no. 2 (2004): 233–56.

Norrie, Moira C. "PIM Meets Web 2.0." In *Conceptual Modeling: ER 2008: 27th International Conference on Conceptual Modeling, Barcelona, Spain, October 20–24, 2008: Proceedings*, edited by Qing Li, Stefano Spaccapietra, Eric Yu, and Antoni Olivé, 15–25. Berlin: Springer, 2008.

Norris, Thomas D. *Prison Inmate Records in New York State: The Challenge of Modern Government Case Records*. Chicago: Society of American Archivists, 1996.

Ntoulas, Alexandros, Petros Zerfos, and Junghoo Cho. "Downloading Textual Hidden Web Content through Keyword Queries." In *Proceedings of the 5th ACM/IEEE Joint Conference on Digital Libraries: Denver, Colorado USA, June 7–11, 2005: Digital Libraries, Cyberinfrastructure for Research and Education*, 100–9. New York: ACM Press, 2005.

O'Hara, Kieron, Richard Morris, Nigel Shadbolt, Graham J. Hitch, Wendy Hall, and Neil Beagrie. "Memories for Life: A Review of the Science and Technology." *Journal of the Royal Society Interface* 3, no. 8 (2006): 351–65.

Oravec, Jo Ann. "Constructive Approaches to Internet Recreation in the Workplace." *Communications of the ACM* 45, no. 1 (2002): 60–63.

O'Reilly, Tim. "What Is Web 2.0: Design Patterns and Business Models for the Next Generation of Software." *Communications and Strategies* 65 (2007): 17–37.

Orlikowski, Wanda J. "Learning from Notes: Organizational Issues in Groupware Implementation." In *CSCW '92: Sharing Perspectives: Proceedings of the Conference on Computer-Supported Cooperative Work, October 31 to November 4, 1992, Toronto, Canada*, edited by Jon Turner and Robert Kraut, 362–69. New York: Association for Computing Machinery, 1992.

O'Sullivan, Catherine. "Diaries, On-line Diaries, and the Future Loss to Archives; or Blogs, and the Blogging Bloggers who Blog Them." *American Archivist* 68, no. 1 (2005): 53–73.

Packard, Vance. "Don't Tell It to the Computer." *New York Times Magazine*, January 8, 1967, 44.

Palen, Leysia, and Paul Dourish. "Unpacking 'Privacy' for a Networked World." In *CHI 2003: New Horizons: Conference Proceedings, Conference on Human Factors in Computing Systems*, edited by Gilbert Cockton and Panu Korhonen, 129–36. New York: Association for Computing Machinery, 2003.

Palfrey, John, and Urs Gasser. *Born Digital: Understanding the First Generation of Digital Natives*. New York: Basic Books, 2008.

Palmer, Olga P. "The History of European Archival Literature." *American Archivist* 2, no. 2 (1939): 69–84.

Pant, Gautam, and Padmini Srinivasan. "Learning to Crawl: Comparing Classification Schemes." *ACM Transactions on Information Systems* 23, no. 4 (2005): 430–62.

Pant, Gautam, Kostas Tsioutsiouliklis, Judy Johnson, and C. Lee Giles. "Panorama: Extending Digital Libraries with Topical Crawlers." In *JCDL 2004: Proceedings of the Fourth ACM/IEEE Joint Conference on Digital Libraries: Global Reach and Diverse Impact: Tucson, Arizona, June 7-11, 2004*, edited by Hsinchun Chen, Michael Christel, and Ee-Peng Lim, 142–50. New York: ACM Press, 2004.

Papadakis, Maria C. "The Application and Implications of Information Technologies in the Home: Where Are the Data and What Do They Say?" Arlington, VA: National Science Foundation, Division of Science Resources Studies, 2001.

Paquet, Lucie. "Appraisal, Acquisition and Control of Personal Electronic Records: From Myth to Reality." *Archives and Manuscripts* 28, no. 2 (2000): 71–91.

Paradigm project. *Workbook on Digital Private Papers*. 2007. http://www.paradigm.ac.uk/workbook/.

Paulus, Michael J., Jr. "Blogging for the Record: A Study of Blogging from an Archival Point of View." *Journal of Archival Organization* 4, no. 3/4 (2006): 31–41.

Pearce-Moses, Richard. *A Glossary of Archival and Records Terminology*. Chicago: Society of American Archivists, 2005.

Pearce-Moses, Richard. "Janus in Cyberspace." *American Archivist* 70, no. 1 (2007): 13–22.

Pearce-Moses, Richard, and Susan E. Davis, eds. *New Skills for a Digital Era*. Chicago: Society of American Archivists, 2008.

Peisu, Xiang, Tian Ke, and Huang Qinzhen. "A Framework of Deep Web Crawler." In *2008 Proceedings of the 27th Chinese Control Conference: Kunming, China, 16-18 July 2008*, edited by Dai-Zhan Cheng and Min Wu, 582-86. Piscataway, NJ: IEEE Service Center, 2008.

Peters, Catherine Stollar. "When Not All Papers are Paper: A Case Study in Digital Archivy." *Provenance* 24 (2006): 23–35.

Phillips, Faye. "Sampling and Electronic Records." In *Congressional Papers Management: Collecting, Appraising, Arranging, and Describing Documentation of United States Senators, Representatives, Related Individuals and Organizations*, 163–81. Jefferson, NC: McFarland, 1996.

Piggott, Michael, and Sue McKemmish. "Recordkeeping, Reconciliation and Political Reality." In *Past Caring? What Does Society Expect of Archivists? Proceedings of the Australian Society of Archivists Conference, Sydney, August 13–17, 2002,* edited by Susan Lloyd. Canberra: ASA, 2002.

Pollak, Bernhard, and Wolfgang Gatterbauer. "Creating Permanent Test Collections of Web Pages for Information Extraction Research." In *Proceedings of SOFSEM 2007: Theory and Practice of Computer Science, Volume II, ICS AS CR, Prague, 2007,* 103–15. Prague: Institute of Computer Sciences, 2007.

Posner, Ernst. "Max Lehmann and the Genesis of the Principle of Provenance." In *Archives and the Public Interest: Selected Essays by Ernst Posner,* edited by Ken Munden, 36–44. Chicago: Society of American Archivists, 2006.

Poster, Mark. *The Mode of Information: Poststructuralism and Social Context.* Chicago: University of Chicago Press, 1990.

Powell, Rene, and Bernadette Kennedy. *Rene Baker: File #28 /ED.* Fremantle: Arts Centre Press, 2005.

Pratt, Wanda, Kenton Unruh, Andrea Civan, and Meredith M. Skeels. "Personal Health Information Management." *Communications of the ACM* 49, no. 1 (2006): 51–55.

Prost, Antoine, and Gerard Vincent, eds. *A History of Private Life.* Riddles of Identity in Modern Times, vol. 5. Cambridge, MA: Belknap Press of Harvard University Press, 1991.

Rafferty, Pauline, and Rob Hidderley. "Flickr and Democratic Indexing: Dialogic Approaches to Indexing." *Aslib Proceedings* 59, no. 4/5 (2007): 397–410.

Raghavan, Sriram, and Hector Garcia-Molina. "Crawling the Hidden Web." In *Proceedings of 27th International Conference on Very Large Data Bases, September 11–14, 2001, Roma, Italy,* edited by Peter M. G. Apers, Paolo Atzeni, Stefano Ceri, Stefano Paraboschi, Kotagiri Ramamohanarao, and Richard T. Snodgrass, 129–38. Orlando, FL: Morgan Kaufmann, 2001.

Rainie, Lee. "Tagging." Washington, DC: Pew Internet and American Life Project, 2007.

Ramasubramanian, Venugopalan, Thomas L. Rodeheffer, Douglas B. Terry, Meg Walraed-Sullivan, Ted Wobber, Catherine C. Marshall, and Amin

Vahdat. "Cimbiosys: A Platform for Content-based Partial Replication." Paper presented at the 6th USENIX Symposium on Networked Systems Design and Implementation, Boston MA, April 22–24, 2009.

Rapport, Leonard. "No Grandfather Clause: Reappraising Accessioned Records." *American Archivist* 44 (1981): 143–50.

Ravasio, Pamela, Sissel Guttormsen Schär, and Helmut Krueger. "In Pursuit of Desktop Evolution: User Problems and Practices with Modern Desktop Systems." *ACM Transactions on Computer-Human Interaction* 11, no. 2 (2004): 156–80.

Razum, Matthias, Frank Schwichtenberg, Steffen Wagner, and Michael Hoppe. "eSciDoc Infrastructure: A Fedora-Based E-Research Framework." In *Research and Advanced Technology for Digital Libraries: 13th European Conference. ECDL 2009, Corfu, Greece, September 27–October 2, 2009, Proceedings*, edited by Maristella Agosti, José Borbinha, Sarantos Kapidakis, Christos Papatheodorou, and Giannis Tsakonas, 227–38. Berlin: Springer, 2009.

Redmiles, David, Hiroko Wilensky, Kristie Kosaka, and Rogerio de Paula. "What Ideal End Users Teach Us About Collaborative Software." In *Proceedings of the 2005 International ACM SIGGROUP Conference on Supporting Group Work*, 260–63. New York: Association for Computing Machinery, 2005.

Reed, Barbara, and David Roberts, eds. *Keeping Data: Papers from a Workshop on Appraising Computer-Based Records*. Dickson, ACT, Australia: Australian Council of Archives and Australian Society of Archivists, 1991.

Reed, Barbara, and Frank Upward. *The APB Bank: Managing Electronic Records as an Authoritative Resource*. Chicago: Society of American Archivists, 1997.

Reference Model for an Open Archival Information System (OAIS). ISO 14721. Washington, DC: Consultative Committee for Space Data Systems, 2002.

Reilly, Bernard, Carolyn Palaima, Kent Norsworthy, Leslie Myrick, Gretchen Tuchel, and James Simon. "Political Communications Web Archiving: Addressing Typology and Timing for Selection, Preservation and Access." Paper presented at the Third ECDL Workshop on Web Archives, Trondheim, Norway, August 21, 2003.

Rhodes, Bradley J. "Margin Notes: Building a Contextually Aware Associative Memory." In *IUI 2000: 2000 International Conference on Intelligent User Interfaces, New Orleans, Louisiana, January 9–12, 2000*, edited by Henry Lieberman, 219–24. New York: Association for Computing Machinery, 2000.

Rhodes, Bradley, and Thad Starner. "The Remembrance Agent: A Continuously Running Automated Information Retrieval System." In *PAAM 96: Proceedings of the First International Conference on the Practical Application of Intelligent Agents and Multi-Agent Technology, 22nd–24th April 1996, Westminster Central Hall, London, UK*, 487–95. Blackpool, UK: Practical Application Company, 1996.

Riedlmayer, Andras. "Killing the Memory: The Targeting of Libraries and Archives in Bosnia-Herzegovina." *Newsletter of the Middle East Librarians Association* 61 (1994).

Robinson, Catherine. "Records Control and Disposal Using Functional Analysis." *Archives and Manuscripts* 25, no. 2 (1997): 288–303.

Rodden, Kerry, and Kenneth R. Wood. "How Do People Manage Their Digital Photographs?" In *CHI 2003: New Horizons: Conference Proceedings, Conference on Human Factors in Computing Systems*, edited by Panu Korhonen, Gilbert Cockton, Thomas Erickson, and Victoria Bellotti, 409–16. New York: Association for Computing Machinery, 2003.

Rose, Gillian. "Family Photographs and Domestic Spacings: A Case Study." *Transactions of the Institute of British Geographers* 28, no. 1 (2003): 5–18.

Rosen, Jeffrey. *The Unwanted Gaze: The Destruction of Privacy in America.* 1st ed. New York: Random House, 2000.

Rosenblum, Barbara. *Photographers at Work: A Sociology of Photographic Styles.* New York: Holmes and Meier, 1978.

Rosenzweig, Roy. "Scarcity or Abundance? Preserving the Past in a Digital Era." *American Historical Review* 108, no. 3 (2003): 735–62.

Ross, Fiona, Sue McKemmish, and Shannon Faulkhead. "Indigenous Knowledge and the Archives: Designing Trusted Archival Systems for Koorie Communities." *Archives and Manuscripts* 34, no. 2 (2006): 112–51.

Ross, Seamus. "The Expanding World of Electronic Information and the Past's Future." In *History and Electronic Artefacts*, edited by Edward Higgs, 5–27. Oxford, England: Clarendon Press, 1998.

Ross, Seamus, and Ann Gow. *Digital Archaeology: Rescuing Neglected and Damaged Data Resources*. London: British Library, 1999.

Rothenberg, Jeff. "Ensuring the Longevity of Digital Documents." *Scientific American* 272, no. 1 (1995): 42–47.

Runde, Jochen, Matthew Jones, Kamal Munir, and Lynne Nikolychuk. "On Technological Objects and the Adoption of Technological Product Innovations: Rules, Routines and the Transition from Analogue Photography to Digital Imaging." *Cambridge Journal of Economics* 33, no. 1 (2008): 1–24.

Russell, Lynette. "Indigenous Researchers and Archives: Mutual Obligations and Binding Trust." *Archives and Manuscripts* 34, no. 1 (2006): 32–43.

Saffady, William. *Managing Electronic Records*. 3rd ed. Prairie Village, KS: ARMA International, 2002.

Salganik, Matthew J., Peter Sheridan Dodds, and Duncan J. Watts. "Experimental Study of Inequality and Unpredictability in an Artificial Cultural Market." *Science* 311 (2006): 854–56.

Samuels, Helen Willa. "Who Controls the Past: Documentation Strategies Used to Select What Is Preserved." *American Archivist* 49 (1986): 109–24.

Sauermann, Leo, Gunnar Aastrand Grimnes, Malte Kiesel, Christiaan Fluit, Heiko Maus, Dominik Heim, Danish Nadeem, Benjamin Horak, and Andreas Dengel. "Semantic Desktop 2.0: The Gnowsis Experience." In *The Semantic Web: ISWC 2006: 5th International Semantic Web Conference, ISWC 2006, Athens, GA, USA, November 5–9, 2006: Proceedings*, edited by Isabel F. Cruz, Stefan Decker, Dean Allemang, Chris Preist, Daniel Schwabe, Peter Mika, Michael Uschold, and Lora Aroyo, 887–900. Berlin: Springer, 2006.

Schaeffer, Roy C. "Transcendent Concepts: Power, Appraisal, and the Archivist as 'Social Outcast.'" *Archivaria* 55, no. 4 (1992): 608–19.

Scheinfeldt, Tom. "Sunset for Ideology, Sunrise for Methodology?" *Found History* (blog). March 18, 2008. http://www.foundhistory.org/2008/03/13/sunset-for-ideology-sunrise-for-methodology/.

Schellenberg, T. R. "The Appraisal of Modern Public Records." In *A Modern Archives Reader: Basic Readings on Archival Theory and Practice*, edited by Maygene F. Daniels and Timothy Walch, 57–70. Washington, DC: National Archives and Records Service, 1984.

Schroeder, Stan. "HOW TO: Take Your Data Back from Google's Claws." *Mashable*. February 2, 2009. http://mashable.com/2009/02/02/google-backup/.

Schurer, Kevin. "Survey on the Relationship between Public Administration and Archive Services concerning Electronic Records Management in the EU Member States." Paper presented at the DLM-Forum on Electronic Records of the European Communities, Brussels, Belgium, October 18–19, 1999.

Schwartz, Dona B. "Doing the Ethnography of Visual Communication: The Rhetoric of Fine Art Photography." *Research on Language and Social Interaction* 21 (1987): 229–50.

Schwartz, Dona B., and Michael Scott Griffin. "Amateur Photography: The Organizational Maintenance of an Aesthetic Code." In *Natural Audiences: Qualitative Research of Media Uses and Effects*, edited by T. Lindlof, 198–224. Norwood, NJ: Ablex, 1987.

Schwartz, Joan M. "'We Make Our Tools and Our Tools Make Us': Lessons from Photographs for the Practice, Politics, and Poetics of Diplomatics." *Archivaria* 40 (1995): 40–74.

Schwartz, Joan M., and Terry Cook. "Archives, Records, and Power: The Making of Modern Memory." *Archival Science* 2, no. 1-2 (2002): 1–19.

Scott, Jason. "Datapocalypso!" *ASCII*. January 5, 2009. http://ascii.textfiles.com/archives/1649.

Scott, Jason. "Eviction, or the Coming Datapocalypse." *ASCII*. December 21, 2008. http://ascii.textfiles.com/archives/1617.

Scott, Peter J. "The Record Group Concept: A Case for Abandonment." *American Archivist* 29, no. 4 (1966): 493–504.

Scott, Peter J., and Gail Finlay. "Archives and Administrative Change: Some Methods and Approaches (Part I)." *Archives and Manuscripts* 7, no. 3 (1978): 115–27.

Seabrook, John. "Home on the Net." *New Yorker*, October 16, 1995, 66-76.

Sellen, Abigail J., and Richard Harper. *The Myth of the Paperless Office*. Cambridge, MA: MIT Press, 2002.

Sen, Shilad, Shyong K. Lam, Al Mamunur Rashid, Dan Cosley, Dan Frankowski, Jeremy Osterhouse, F. Maxwell Harper, and John Riedl. "tagging, communities, vocabulary, evolution." In *Proceedings of the 2006 20th Anniversary Conference on Computer Supported Cooperative Work*, 181–90. New York: Association for Computing Machinery, 2006.

Shamos, Michael. "Privacy and Public Records." In *Personal Information Management*, edited by William P. Jones and Jaime Teevan, 261–68. Seattle: University of Washington Press, 2007.

Shankar, Kalpana. "Order from Chaos: The Poetics and Pragmatics of Scientific Recordkeeping." *Journal of the American Society for Information Science and Technology* 58, no. 10 (2007): 1457–66.

Shipman, Frank M., III, and Catherine C. Marshall. "Formality Considered Harmful: Experiences, Emerging Themes, and Directions on the Use of Formal Representations in Interactive Systems." *Computer Supported Cooperative Work* 8, no. 4 (1999): 333–52.

Shirky, Clay. "Power Laws, Weblogs and Inequality." In *Extreme Democracy*, edited by Jon Lebkowsky and Mitch Ratcliffe, 46–52. Lulu, 2005.

Shove, Elizabeth, and Mika Pantzar. "Recruitment and Reproduction: The Careers and Carriers of Digital Photography and Floorball." *Human Affairs* 17, no. 2 (2007): 154–67.

Simonite, Tom. "How Do You Value a Historical Email?" *New Scientist*, February 13, 2009. http://www.newscientist.com/article/dn16589-how-do-you-value-a-historical-email.html.

Skrenta, Rich. "The Incremental Web." *Topix.net Weblog*. February 12, 2005. http://blog.topix.com/archives/000066.html.

Slater, Don. "Consuming Kodak." In *Family Snaps: The Meaning of Domestic Photography*, edited by Jo Spence and Patricia Holland, 49–59. London: Virago, 1991.

Smith, Abby. "Authenticity and Affect: When is a Watch not a Watch?" *Library Trends* 52 (Summer 2003): 172–82.

Smith, Robert Ellis. *Ben Franklin's Web Site: Privacy and Curiosity from Plymouth Rock to the Internet*. Providence, RI: Privacy Journal, 2000.

Society of American Archivists. *Describing Archives: A Content Standard.* Chicago: Society of American Archivists, 2004.

Solove, Daniel J. *The Digital Person: Technology and Privacy in the Information Age.* Ex Machina: Law, Technology and Society. New York: New York University Press, 2004.

Solove, Daniel J. *The Future of Reputation: Gossip, Rumor, and Privacy on the Internet.* New Haven, CT: Yale University Press, 2007.

Soper, Mary Ellen. "Characteristics and Use of Personal Collections." *Library Quarterly* 46, no. 4 (1976): 397–415.

Sprehe, J. Timothy, and Charles R. McClure. "Lifting the Burden." *Information Management Journal* 39, no. 4 (2005): 47–52.

Sproull, Lee S. "Computers in U.S. Households since 1977." In *A Nation Transformed by Information: How Information Has Shaped the United States from Colonial Times to the Present*, edited by Alfred D. Chandler and James W. Cortada, 257–80. New York: Oxford University Press, 2000.

Spurgin, Kristina. "The Sense-Making Approach and the Study of Personal Information Management." Paper presented at Personal Information Management—A SIGIR 2006 Workshop, Seattle, Washington, August 10–11, 2006.

SRA International. "Report on Current Recordkeeping Practices within the Federal Government." Arlington, VA: National Archives and Records Administration, 2001.

Srinivasan, Ramesh, Robin Boast, Jonathan Furner, and Katherine M. Becvar. "Digital Museums and Diverse Cultural Knowledges: Moving Past the Traditional Catalog." *Information Society* 25, no. 4 (2009): 265–78.

Stebbins, Robert A. *After Work: The Search for an Optimal Leisure Lifestyle.* Calgary: Detselig Enterprises, 1998.

Stebbins, Robert A. "Serious Leisure: A Conceptual Statement." *Pacific Sociological Review* 25, no. 2 (1982): 251–72.

Stebbins, Robert A. *Serious Leisure: A Perspective for Our Time.* New Brunswick, NJ: Transaction Publishers, 2007.

Steck, Larry, and Francis Blouin. "Hannah Lay and Company: Sampling the Records of a Century of Lumbering in Michigan." *American Archivist* 39, no. 1 (1976): 15–23.

Stephens, David O., and Roderick C. Wallace. *Electronic Records Retention: An Introduction.* Prairie Village, KS: ARMA International, 1997.

Stephens, David O., and Roderick C. Wallace. *Electronic Records Retention: New Strategies for Data Life Cycle Management.* Prairie Village, KS: ARMA International, 2003.

Stoler, Ann Laura. "Colonial Archives and the Arts of Governance: On the Content in the Form." In *Refiguring the Archive*, edited by Carolyn Hamilton, Verne Harris, Jane Taylor, Michele Pickover, Graeme Reid, and Razia Saleh, 83–101. Dordrecht, Netherlands: Kluwer Academic Publishers, 2002.

Stollar, Catherine, and Thomas Kiehne. "Guarding the Guards: Archiving the Electronic Records of Hypertext Author Michael Joyce." Paper presented at New Skills for a Digital Era, Washington, DC, May 31– June 2, 2006.

Stratford, Michael. "Judge Dismisses Alum's Libel Suit against University." *Cornell Daily Sun,* June 15, 2008.

Strodl, Stephan, Florian Motlik, Kevin Stadler, and Andreas Rauber. "Personal & SOHO Archiving." In *Proceedings of the 8th ACM/IEEE-CS Joint Conference on Digital Libraries,* 115–23. New York: ACM Press, 2008.

Stutzman, Frederic, and Terrell Russell. "ClaimID: A System for Personal Identity Management." In *Opening Information Horizons: 6th ACM/ IEEE-CS Joint Conference on Digital Libraries: June 11–15, 2006, Chapel Hill, NC, USA: JCDL 2006,* 367. New York: ACM Press, 2006.

Suchman, Lucille Alice. *Plans and Situated Actions: The Problem of Human-Machine Communication.* Cambridge: Cambridge University Press, 1987.

Suderman, Jim. "Defining Electronic Series: A Study." *Archivaria* 53 (2002): 31–46.

Summers, Anne, and Jeremy Leighton John. "The W.D. Hamilton Archive at the British Library." *Ethology, Ecology and Evolution* 13, no. 4 (2001): 373–84.

Swan, Laurel, Alex S. Taylor, Shahram Izadi, and Richard Harper. "Containing Family Clutter." In *Home Informatics and Telematics: ICT for the Next Billion*, edited by A. Venkatesh, T. Gonsalves, A. Monk, and K. Buckner, 171–84. Boston, MA: Springer, 2007.

Sweeney, Shelley. "The Ambiguous Origins of the Archival Principle of 'Provenance.'" *Libraries and the Cultural Record* 43, no. 2 (2008): 193–213.

Swift, Graham. *Ever After.* London: Picador, 1992.

Swift, Graham. *Waterland.* London: Picador, 1983.

Szary, Richard V. "Encoded Archival Context (EAC) and Archival Description: Rationale and Background." *Journal of Archival Organization* 3, no. 2/3 (2006): 217–27.

Tan, Desney, Emma Berry, Mary Czerwinski, Gordon Bell, Jim Gemmell, Steve Hodges, Narinder Kapur, Brian Meyers, Nuria Oliver, George Robertson, and Ken Wood. "Save Everything: Supporting Human Memory with a Personal Digital Lifetime Store." In *Personal Information Management*, edited by William P. Jones and Jaime Teevan, 90–107. Seattle: University of Washington Press, 2007.

Tancer, Bill. *Click: What Millions of People Are Doing Online and Why It Matters.* New York: Hyperion, 2008.

Taylor, Diane. *The Archive and the Repertoire: Performing Cultural Memory in the Americas,* Durham, NC: Duke University Press, 2003.

Taylor, Hugh A. "The Collective Memory: Archives and Libraries as Heritage." *Archivaria* 15 (1982-83): 118–30.

Teevan, Jaime, Christine Alvarado, Mark S. Ackerman, and David R. Karger. "The Perfect Search Engine Is Not Enough: A Study of Orienteering Behavior in Directed Search." In *CHI 2004: Connect: Conference Proceedings: April 24–29, 2004, Vienna, Austria: Conference on Human Factors in Computing Systems*, edited by Elizabeth Dykstra-Erickson and Manfred Tscheligi, 415–22. New York: Association for Computing Machinery, 2004.

Teper, Jennifer Hain. "Newspaper Photo Morgues: A Survey of Institutional Holdings and Practices." *Library Collections, Acquisitions, and Technical Services* 28, no. 1 (2004): 106–25.

Thelwall, Mike, and David Stuart. "Web Crawling Ethics Revisited: Cost, Privacy and Denial of Service." *Journal of the American Society for Information Science and Technology* 57, no. 13 (2006): 1771–79.

Thomas, Angela. "Blurring and Breaking Through the Boundaries of Narrative, Literacy, and Identity in Adolescent Fan Fiction." In *A New Literacies Sampler*, edited by Michele Knobel and Colin Lankshear, 137–65. New York: Peter Lang, 2007.

Thomas, Susan, and Janette Martin. "Using the Papers of Contemporary British Politicians as a Testbed for the Preservation of Digital Personal Archives." *Journal of the Society of Archivists* 27, no. 1 (2006): 29–56.

Tibbo, Helen R. "Archival Perspectives on the Emerging Digital Library." *Communications of the ACM* 44, no. 5 (2001): 69–70.

Tibbo, Helen R., Angela Bardeen, and Terrell Russell. "Capturing the Minds of Carolina." Paper presented at the Second IS&T Archiving Conference, Washington, DC, April 26–29, 2005.

Tibbo, Helen R., Chirstopher A. Lee, Gary Marchionini, and Dawne Howard. "VidArch: Preserving Meaning of Digital Video over Time through Creating and Capture of Contextual Documentation." In *Archiving 2006: Final Program and Proceedings, May 23–26, 2006, Ottawa, Canada*, edited by Stephen Chapman and Scott A. Stovall, 210–15. Springfield, VA: Society for Imaging Science and Technology, 2006.

Torrey, Cristen, David McDonald, Bill Schilit, and Sara Bly. "How-To Pages: Informal Systems of Expertise Sharing." In *ESCSW 2007: Proceedings of the Tenth European Conference on Computer Supported Cooperative Work*, edited by Liam Bannon, Ina Wagner, Carl Gutwin, Richard Harper, and Kjeld Schmidt, 391–410. London: Springer, 2007.

Tough, Alistair G., and Michael Moss, eds. *Record Keeping in a Hybrid Environment: Managing the Creation, Use, Preservation and Disposal of Unique Information Objects in Context*. Chandos Information Professional Series. Oxford: Chandos, 2006.

Trace, Ciaran B. "Resistance and the Underlife: Informal Written Literacies and Their Relationship to Human Information Behavior." *Journal of the American Society for Information Science and Technology* 59, no. 10 (2008): 1540–54.

Turkle, Sherry. "Cyberspace and Identity." *Contemporary Sociology* 28, no. 6 (November 1999): 643–48.

Turkle, Sherry. *Life on the Screen: Identity in the Age of the Internet.* New York: Touchstone Books, 1997.

Tynan, Dan. "The 25 Worst Tech Products of All Time." *PCWorld,* May 26, 2006. http://www.pcworld.com/article/125772/the_25_worst_tech_products_of_all_time.html.

Underwood, William E., and Sandra L. Laib. "PERPOS: An Electronic Records Repository and Archival Processing System." Paper presented at the International Symposium on Digital Curation (DigCCurr 2007), Chapel Hill, NC, April 18–20, 2007.

Underwood, William, Marlit Hayslett, Sheila Isbell, Sandra Laib, Scott Sherrill, and Matthew Underwood. "Advanced Decision Support for Archival Processing of Presidential Electronic Records: Final Scientific and Technical Report." Georgia Tech Research Institute. Technical Report ITTL/CSITD 09-05. October 2009.

Unruh, David R. "The Nature of Social Worlds." *Pacific Sociological Review* 23, no. 3 (1980): 271–96.

Upward, Frank. "The Records Continuum." In *Archives: Recordkeeping in Society,* edited by Sue McKemmish, Michael Piggott, Barbara Reed, and Frank Upward, 197–222. Wagga Wagga, N.S.W.: Centre for Information Studies, Charles Sturt University, 2005.

Upward, Frank. "Structuring the Records Continuum, Part One: Post-custodial Principles and Properties." *Archives and Manuscripts* 24, no. 2 (1996): 268–85.

Upward, Frank. "Structuring the Records Continuum, Part Two: Structuration Theory and Recordkeeping." *Archives and Manuscripts* 25, no. 1 (1997): 10–35.

Upward, Frank, and Sue McKemmish. "In Search of the Lost Tiger, by Way of Sainte-Beuve: Re-Constructing the Possibilities in 'Evidence of Me . . . '" *Archives and Manuscripts* 29, no. 1 (2001): 22–42.

Upward, Frank, and Sue McKemmish. "Somewhere Beyond Custody." *Archives and Manuscripts* 22, no.1 (1994): 136–49.

Urban, Richard. "Second Life, Serious Leisure, and LIS." *Bulletin of the American Society for Information Science and Technology* (2007): 38–40.

Vanderbilt, Tom. "Data Center Overload." *New York Times,* June 14, 2009, MM30.

Van Dijck, José. "From Shoebox to Performative Agent: The Computer as Personal Memory Machine." *New Media and Society* 7, no. 3 (2005): 311–32.

Van House, Nancy A. "Flickr and Public Image-Sharing: Distant Closeness and Photo Exhibition." In *CHI '07 Extended Abstracts on Human Factors in Computing Systems*, 2717–22. New York: ACM Press, 2007.

Van Wingen, Melinda, and Abigail Bass. "Reappraising Archival Practice in Light of the New Social History." *Library Hi Tech* 26, no. 4 (2008): 575–85.

Viégas, Fernanda B. "Bloggers' Expectations of Privacy and Accountability: An Initial Survey." *Journal of Computer-Mediated Communication* 10, no. 3 (2005). http://jcmc.indiana.edu/vol10/issue3/viegas.html.

von Suchodoletz, Dirk and Jeffrey van der Hoeven, "Emulation: From Digital Artefact to Remotely Rendered Environments." *International Journal of Digital Curation* 3, no. 4 (2009): 146–55.

Vroegindeweij, Sander. "My Pictures: Informal Image Collections." Hewlett-Packard Technical Report HPL-2002-72R1. Palo Alto, CA: Hewlett-Packard Labs, 2002.

Wallace, David A. "Custodial Theory and Practice in the Electronic Environment." *SASA Newsletter* (January–March 2002).

Ward, W. Peter. "Family Papers and the New Social History." *Archivaria* 14 (1982): 63–73.

Weinberger, David. *Everything is Miscellaneous: The Power of the New Digital Disorder.* New York: Times Books, 2007.

Weinberger, David. *Small Pieces Loosely Joined: A Unified Theory of the Web.* Cambridge, MA: Perseus, 2002.

Whalen, Tara, Elaine Toms, and James Blustein. "File Sharing and Group Information Management." Paper presented at Personal Information Management: PIM 2008, Florence, Italy, April 5–6, 2008.

White, Edmund. *The Burning Library: Writings on Art, Politics and Sexuality 1969-1993.* London: Picador, 1995.

White, Kelvin L. "*Mestizaje* and Remembering in Afro-Mexican Communities of the Costa Chica: Implications for Archival Education in Mexico." *Archival Science* 9, no. 1-2 (2009).

White, Kelvin, and Anne Gilliland. "Promoting Reflexivity and Inclusivity in Archival Education, Research and Practice." *Library Quarterly* 80, no. 3 (2010): 231–48.

Whittaker, Steve, and Candace Sidner. "Email Overload: Exploring Personal Information Management of Email." In *Human Factors in Computing Systems: Common Ground: CHI 96 Conference Proceedings*, edited by Michael J. Tauber, 276–83. New York: Association for Computing Machinery, 1996.

Whittaker, Steve, Loren Terveen, Will Hill, and Lynn Cherny. "The Dynamics of Mass Interaction." In *CSCW '98: Proceedings: ACM 1998 Conference on Computer Supported Cooperative Work, Seattle, Washington, November 14–18, 1998,* 257–64. New York: Association for Computing Machinery, 1998.

Wilde, Oscar, and Richard Allen Cave. *The Importance of Being Earnest and Other Plays.* Penguin Classics. London: Penguin Books, 2000.

Williams, Pete, Katrina Dean, Ian Rowlands, and Jeremy Leighton John. "Digital Lives: Report of Interviews with the Creators of Personal Digital Collections." *Ariadne* 55 (2008). http://www.ariadne.ac.uk/issue55/williams-et-al/.

Williams, Peter, Jeremy Leighton John, and Ian Rowland. "The Personal Curation of Digital Objects: A Lifecycle Approach." *Aslib Proceedings* 61, no. 4 (2009): 340–63.

Williams, Robert F., and Lori J. Ashley. "Electronic Records Management Survey: A Renewed Call for Action." Chicago: Cohasset Associates, 2007.

Wilson, William Jerome. "Analysis of Government Records an Emerging Profession." *Library Quarterly* 16, no. 1 (1946): 1–19.

Wingen, Melinda Van, and Abigail Bass. "Reappraising Archival Practice in Light of the New Social History." *Library Hi Tech* 26, no. 4 (2008): 575–85.

Winograd, Terry, and Fernando Flores. *Understanding Computers and Cognition: A New Foundation for Design.* Norwood, NJ: Ablex, 1986.

Woodyard, Deborah. "Data Recovery and Providing Access to Digital Manuscripts." Paper presented at the Information Online 2001 Conference, Sydney, Australia, January 16–18, 2001.

Yakel, Elizabeth. "Seeking Information, Seeking Connections, Seeking Meaning: Genealogists and Family Historians." *Information Research* 10, no. 1 (2004). http://informationr.net/ir/10-1/paper205.html.

Yakel, Elizabeth. "The Social Construction of Accountability: Radiologists and Their Record-Keeping Practices." *Information Society* 17, no. 4 (2001): 233–45.

Yates, JoAnne. *Control through Communication.* Baltimore, MD: Johns Hopkins University Press, 1989.

Yoder, Daniel G. "A Model for Commodity Intensive Serious Leisure." *Journal of Leisure Research* 29, no. 4 (1997): 407–29.

Yorke, Stephen, ed. *Playing for Keeps: The Proceedings of an Electronic Records Management Conference Hosted by the Australian Archives.* Canberra: Australian Archives, 1994.

Zook, Genevieve. "Technology and the Generation Gap." Law and Technology Resources for Legal Professionals, August 2007.

Zuckerman, Ethan. "Meet the Bridgebloggers." *Public Choice* 134 (2008): 47–65.

Contributors

Robert Capra is a Post-Doctoral Fellow and adjunct faculty member in the School of Information and Library Science at the University of North Carolina at Chapel Hill. His research interests include human-computer interaction, personal information management, and digital information seeking behaviors, tools, and interfaces. He holds a PhD in computer science from Virginia Tech and MS and BS degrees in computer science from Washington University in St. Louis. At Virginia Tech, he was part of the Center for Human-Computer Interaction where he investigated multiplatform interfaces, information re-finding, and digital library interfaces. Prior to Virginia Tech, he worked in corporate research and development, spending five years in the Speech and Language Technologies group at SBC Communications, focusing on voice user interfaces, speech recognition, and natural language processing.

Adrian Cunningham has worked at the National Archives of Australia since 1998; he is currently Director of Strategic Relations and Personal Records. Adrian was the Secretary of the International Council on Archives (ICA) Committee on Descriptive Standards (2002–2004), and is the Treasurer of the ICA Pacific Regional Branch, the convenor of the Australian Society of Archivists Descriptive Standards Committee, the Chair of the AGLS Metadata Working Group, and a member of Standards Australia's Committee IT/21, Records Management. Adrian previously worked at the Office for Government Information Technology and as a Private Records Archivist/Librarian at the National Library of Australia, the Pacific Manuscripts Bureau, and the State Library of New South Wales. Adrian was the President of the Australian Society of Archivists from 1998 to 2000, and was named a Fellow of that Society in 2007.

Thomas Hyry is the Director of Library Special Collections at the University of California, Los Angeles. From 2006 to 2010, Hyry was Head of the Manuscript Unit in the Beinecke Rare Book and Manuscript Library at Yale University. Prior to that, he spent nine years in Yale University Library's Manuscripts and Archives Department, where he began as an entry-level archivist and finished as the Head of arrangement and description. Hyry earned a master's degree in information and library studies from the University of Michigan and a bachelor's degree in history from Carleton College.

Leslie Johnston is the Manager of Technical Architecture Initiatives for the National Digital Information Infrastructure and Preservation Program at the Library of Congress. She was previously Digital Media Project Coordinator at the Library of Congress. Prior to that, she served as Database Specialist at the Getty Research Institute, Documentation Coordinator for the Historic New Orleans Collection, Academic Technology Specialist for Art and the Cantor Arts Center at the Stanford University Libraries, Head of Instructional Technology and Library Systems at the Harvard Design School, and Head of Digital Access Services at the University of Virginia Library. She founded the online journal *eSpectra*, edited the print journal *Spectra,* and served on the board of the Museum Computer Network. She holds a BA in anthropology and an MA in archaeology from University of California, Los Angeles.

Christopher A. (Cal) Lee is an Associate Professor at the School of Information and Library Science at the University of North Carolina at Chapel Hill. He teaches courses on archival administration; records management; digital curation; understanding information technology for managing digital collections; and the construction of policies and rules for digital repositories. He is one of the lead organizers and instructors for the DigCCurr Professional Institute, which is a week-long continuing education workshop on digital curation, and teaches professional workshops on the application of digital forensics methods and principles to digital acquisitions. His primary area of research is the long-term curation of digital collections. He is particularly interested in the professionalization of this work and the diffusion of existing tools and methods (e.g., digital forensics, web archiving, automated implementation of policies) into professional practice.

Sue McKemmish holds the Chair of Archival Systems at Monash University, and is Director of the Centre for Organisational and Social Informatics. She is engaged in major research projects relating to recordkeeping metadata, information portals, Indigenous archives, and the nexus between memories, communities, and technologies. She directs the postgraduate teaching programs in archives and records at Monash University, and has published extensively on recordkeeping in society, records continuum theory, recordkeeping metadata, and archival systems.

Catherine Marshall is a Principal Researcher at Microsoft Research's Silicon Valley laboratory after a six-year stint in Microsoft's product divisions. Her research interests include personal information management, the preservation of and long-term access to personal and scholarly digital belongings, and interaction with digital media. She was a member of the research staff at Xerox PARC and is an affiliate of the Center for the Study of Digital Libraries at Texas A&M University. Marshall has delivered keynote addresses at numerous international venues. She recently completed a book called *Reading and Writing the Electronic Book,* and has published more than eighty peer-reviewed papers. She also has been awarded nine patents, and has nine other patents pending.

Rachel Onuf teaches Preservation Management for Simmons College Graduate School of Library and Information Science, and works as a consultant for a range of collecting repositories. Much of this work involves preservation planning and collection assessment, and is grounded in her experience in various research libraries, including the Historical Society of Pennsylvania. She earned her MILS with a concentration in archives from the University of Michigan, and an MA from the University of Virginia, with a focus on the nineteenth-century South. She lives in western Massachusetts, where she also works with cows and teenagers on a school farm.

Kristina M. Spurgin is a Doctoral Candidate at the School of Information and Library Science, University of North Carolina at Chapel Hill. Her college photography professor said she could likely make a career out of photography, but would have to shoot a lot of chicken feed bags to make a living. She has never done professional photography. She studies how people make sense of personal information management, catalogs electronic resources, and teaches.

Susan Thomas is Digital Archivist at the Bodleian Library at the University of Oxford, where she is responsible for developing the library's capacity to curate, preserve, and provide access to born-digital archives. She is also an Honorary Lecturer at the University of Dundee's Centre for Archive and Information Studies, where she teaches the management and preservation of digital records for the MLitt and MSc programs. Thomas holds a BA in English language and literature from the University of Manchester and an MA in archives and records management from the University of Liverpool.

Index

The letters f or t following a page number indicate a figure or table.